ANTHROPOLOGY
OF THE CITY

An Introduction to Urban Anthropology

EDWIN EAMES
Baruch College—CUNY

JUDITH GRANICH GOODE
Temple University

PRENTICE-HALL, INC., ENGLEWOOD CLIFFS, NEW JERSEY 07632

Library of Congress Cataloging in Publication Data

EAMES, EDWIN.
    Anthropology of the city.

    (Prentice-Hall series in anthropology)
    Bibliography: p.
    Includes indexes.
    1. Urban anthropology.   I. Goode, Judith Granich,
joint author.   II. Title.
GN395.E25   301.36   76-57696
ISBN   0-13-038414-3

Prentice-Hall Series in Anthropology
David M. Schneider, Editor

Printed in the United States of America

10   9   8   7   6   5   4   3   2   1

PRENTICE-HALL INTERNATIONAL, INC., *London*
PRENTICE-HALL OF AUSTRALIA PTY. LIMITED, *Sydney*
PRENTICE-HALL OF CANADA, LTD., *Toronto*
PRENTICE-HALL OF INDIA PRIVATE LIMITED, *New Delhi*
PRENTICE-HALL OF JAPAN, INC., *Tokyo*
PRENTICE-HALL OF SOUTHEAST ASIA PTE. LTD., *Singapore*
WHITEHALL BOOKS LIMITED, *Wellington, New Zealand*

Contents

To our students, past and present,
who served as a sounding board for many of our ideas—
And to future students who, we hope, will use these ideas.

Acknowledgments

This volume owes much to many individuals. Although they are too numerous to single out, there are several groups and individuals whose contributions were particularly noteworthy.

Several of our colleagues in the Department of Sociology and Anthropology at Baruch College (City University of New York) and the Department of Anthropology at Temple University have made substantive contributions and been a source of encouragement. In particular, we would like to thank Norman S. Storer, Eugene Cohen, Henry Selby, and William Schwab. Through our teaching and collaborating with colleagues in the Urban Studies Program in the College of Liberal Arts at Temple University, an excitement about interdisciplinary urban studies was generated. These colleagues also provided many points of view and information reflected in this volume.

Baidya Nath Varma was particularly important in the development of this volume, since he presided over the Columbia University seminar on "Content and Methods of the Social Sciences," at which some of the ideas embodied in this text were discussed. This seminar presentation was later incorporated as a chapter in a volume he edited entitled *The New Social Sciences* (Westport, Connecticut: Greenwood Press, 1976).

Throughout this volume we have frequently incorporated primary data collected in two urban projects. The Italian-American food project in Philadelphia owes much of its success to Janet Theophano and Karen Curtis, whose imaginative and perceptive field research was outstanding. David Feingold and Karen Kerner of ISHI (Institute for the Study of Human Issues) were largely responsible for the formulation and development of that project. The Punjabi migrant research in Wolverhampton, England is heavily indebted to Howard Robboy.

We are most grateful for helpful comments on earlier versions of this manuscript from David M. Schneider, Bette Denich, Aidan Southall, Richard Fox, William Shack, and John Friedl.

Several students in particular have contributed significantly to the completion of this volume. These include: Don Burkins, Ceal Holzman, and Arthur Murphy. Secretarial services were provided by Virginia Lotz, Eledia Velez, Debbie Ciraolo, and Helen Wellington. The actual preparation of the manuscript owes much to the skill, patience, and unstinting efforts of Avrama Gingold.

Finally, the writing of any book has a traumatic impact on the daily activities of the authors and their families. Both the Eames family (Phyllis, Mona, Arthur, David, and Lori) and the Goode family (Paul, Larry, Andy, and Josh) were good sports and very helpful at various stages in the project.

Part One

WHAT IS URBAN ANTHROPOLOGY?

Anyone who has been aware of recent trends in anthropology must be struck by the movement of the field toward the study of life in cities. The popular image of the anthropologist clothed in khaki shorts and pith helmet, carrying a massive notebook, and interrogating natives as they pursue their tribal rituals is obviously in image that is no longer accurate. This change was underlined in a recent *Time* magazine article:

> When two well-dressed strangers turned up at a sleek apartment building on Chicago's Gold Coast, the doorman called the cops. The men explained they were anthropologists from the University of Chicago, anxious to study rich families. "The policeman couldn't believe it," said one of the men. "He looked first for my Encyclopedia Britannica, then for my vacuum cleaner and then asked what was the gimmick."

1

The gimmick is that anthropologists, after decades of following Margaret Mead to Samoa and Bronislaw Malinowski to the Trobriand Islands, have staked out new territory—the nonexotic cities and rural byways of the U.S. Indeed, scores of sessions at last month's American Anthropological Association's annual meeting in Mexico City were devoted to the problems and rewards of studying U.S. subcultures. These may range from Greek-Americans and company towns to female athletes and Appalachian snake cultists.[1]

A recent article in *The New York Times*, "Anthropology Now Looks to the Cities for Field Trips," was written by John F. Szwed, director of the Center for Urban Ethnography at the University of Pennsylvania, who stated:

Cultural anthropologists, or ethnographers, have traditionally studied exotic and isolated peoples. Taking up residence in an American Indian reservation or a village in India or Africa, they have pursued research that remains for the most part marginal to the everyday concerns of Americans. Although most anthropologists still follow this course, in the last few years an increasing number have turned to exploring the urban United States.

It's now not unusual to hear of anthropological studies of urban religious movements, the culture of drug addiction, the education of bilingual children, food and health practices of Italian-Americans, even the operations of a state Insurance Commission. And if all indications are correct, many younger anthropologists will be doing similar research in the future.[2]

Although both of these statements concern anthropology in American cities, the trend toward studying cities in other parts of the world is equally significant and, in many cases, has a longer history. This trend is the basis of the development of a new subfield called urban anthropology.

In the following two chapters, we shall discuss the development of urban anthropology as related to the history of anthropology in general. We shall also concern ourselves with the interface between urban anthropology and urban studies, especially in defining the nature of the "urban." In addition, we shall concentrate on those elements of the anthropological approach that add to our understanding of urban life.

[1] *Time* (New York), December 23, 1974, p. 54.
[2] Szwed, John, "Anthropology Now Looks to the Cities for Field Trips," *New York Times*, February 22, 1976, p. 14.

1

The Development
of Anthropology

CONCEPTUAL BASIS

Although the major thrust of this volume is in the direction of establishing the basic characteristics of the newly emergent subfield of urban anthropology, it is appropriate to place this development within the larger context of the history of anthropology. For many who have had little experience with professional anthropology, the popular image of the field is that it deals exclusively with exotic people and exotic customs. Actually, this view of traditionally based anthropology is not far removed from the truth. Anthropology did have its origins in the study of so-called "primitives," "savages," or "pagans," who were contacted as European nations expanded their colonial empires.

The origins of modern anthropological thought are usually attributed to major British, American, German, and French scholars of the nineteenth century. Among these, two significant figures were Edward B. Tylor in England and Lewis H. Morgan in the United States. Tylor contributed the first significant definition of the core concept of culture.[1] His work is still cited by most anthropologists as a major thrust in the direction of modern, scientific cultural anthropology. In addition, he held the first professorship in anthropology in England at Oxford University. Although Morgan did not involve himself in the development of anthropology as a recognized academic discipline in the United States, he pioneered the study of kinship, which has been maintained as a central area of anthropological research from that time to the present.[2] Both Tylor and Morgan were committed to a theoretical position referred to as *unilineal evolution,* an interpretation of the entire cultural history of mankind as a progressive development from more primitive or savage forms to civilized practices.

You may ask: why did anthropology (in the modern sense) emerge at this time? One answer is that the expansion of the West through exploration, discovery, and colonization into many other areas of the world resulted in contacts with people who had developed lifeways very different from those of Euro-American culture. A logical extension of this contact was curiosity about the variety of human lifeways and the related questions of why and how they had developed.

The nineteenth-century evolutionists directly confronted these questions and attempted to answer them. Although contemporary anthropologists have discarded many of the assumptions of unilineal evolution —such as the implications of European superiority, necessary stages of development, and inevitable progress—there are aspects of these earliest endeavors that shaped the field.

One of these was the emphasis upon the *comparative* approach. However, the purpose of comparison has taken on a different meaning in modern anthropology. For the nineteenth-century anthropologist, the study of exotic people was used to provide a picture of what we were like in the past; for the modern anthropologist, comparison is used to show the diversity of human lifeways and to define those aspects of human behavior that are shared or universal. The study of other people provides a better perspective from which to view our own way of life. Thus, for many an anthropologist, the ideal is to work with some newly discovered or unstudied group to determine patterns of behavior that, implicitly, can be used as a comparison with present day behavior and values. Unfortunately for most practicing anthropologists, there remain few "undiscovered" people today.

[1] Edward Tylor, *Primitive Culture* (New York: Harper and Row, 1958) (original 1871).
[2] Lewis Morgan, *Systems of Consanguinity and Affinity of the Human Family* (Washington, D.C.: Smithsonian Institution, 1870).

One of the most basic criticisms of the efforts of the nineteenth-century anthropologists is that their descriptions of primitive societies were not based upon direct contact with the non-western people discussed. These anthropologists are frequently referred to in derogatory terms as "armchair" anthropologists. Their primary sources of data were accounts of curious customs written by others—missionaries, traders, explorers, and colonial administrators. One of the most significant shifts in the twentieth century is the all-pervasive emphasis upon *fieldwork*. Boas in America, Malinowski and Radcliffe-Brown in England, all stressed the importance of doing fieldwork.

Emerging from this was the development of techniques to "do fieldwork," the most significant of which is referred to as *participant observation*. The underlying assumption of participant observation is that if you live with, participate in, and observe a people and their behavior, you gain a basic understanding of their way of life. We should note that this technique developed within the context of studying simply organized small groups of people. In this situation, an anthropologist spending a year of two living with a group of people could get to know most of them and could, in fact, see unfolding before his eyes the basic fabric of their culture. Under these conditions, the anthropologist could see the interdependence of the many aspects of life. Such a *holistic* view (total perspective) was lacking in the accounts of nineteenth-century armchair anthropologists, who tended to describe particular customs without reference to their context. The descriptive studies based upon fieldwork and participant observation are the ethnographies that form the core of the data anthropologists have collected and analyzed. One of the most significant contributions of the *urban* anthropologist has been to take these techniques into the city.

As anthropologists did more and more of these ethnographic studies, the potential for comparison expanded. In other social science disciplines, when the term comparative is used, it frequently has a more limited meaning than it does in anthropology, as, for example, most comparative government courses in political science focus upon other nation-states in Europe and North America. Recently, historians have added some greater breadth to this notion by including in their "comparative" repertory several of the non-western literate civilizations. However, when anthropologists are "comparative," they encompass the total expanse of human experience.

Most anthropologists would define their field as the study of man. However, even from this brief review of the development of the discipline, it is obvious that primary emphasis was placed upon the study of non-western people, with very little emphasis placed upon systematic study of complex Euro-American society. Only recently have anthropologists broadened their spectrum to include "us" as well as "them."

As anthropologists moved to the study of "us," they finally became truly comprehensive in their use of the comparative approach. By using a broader frame of reference, they were able to view complex modern phnomena within a much broader perspective than their sister social sciences.

Another related consequence of the anthropologist's use of field-work is *cultural relativism*. As anthropologists studied other people and tried to interpret their way of life to their audience, they began to recognize and subsequently emphasize the point that there are no valid ways of judging cultures as to superiority or inferiority, progressiveness or backwardness. Thus, Trobriand Island lifeways or Eskimo lifeways are as valid as those of the British or American observers. Each culture must be understood in its own terms.

A dilemma is apparent between cultural relativism and the basic goal of anthropology, which is to develop generalizations about human nature and the human condition. If anthropologists are culturally relative and emphasize the uniqueness of each culture, if they explicitly state that each lifeway can only be understood in its own terms, then how can they generate "laws" built upon comparison? The answer to this dilemma, as to so many others, is that you do not carry cultural relativity to its logical extreme. If you did, there would be no science of anthropology. Some radical relativists wish to describe other cultures solely from the native's point of view, using only native language categories, cognitive structures, and symbolic meanings. Descriptive ethnographies could still be written from this approach, but generalizations about mankind would be impossible.

In spite of the limits of cultural relativism, when anthropologists study a complex society, one of the most important contributions they make is the retention of a relativistic bias and the avoidance of judgmental or ethnocentric views of the groups they are studying. This basic point must be underscored and would, we believe, become obvious to anyone comparing accounts of the same groups (ethnic minorities, deviants, drug addicts, drag queens) written by anthropologists with similar accounts written by most sociologists, economists, or political scientists.

The Sociopolitical Basis

It should be noted that all of the nineteenth-century anthropology pioneers were representative of Euro-American nation-states that had previously passed through a stage of expansion based upon economic, political, and military domination of other regions of the world. Only recently have anthropologists, in examining their own relationship to politically dominant nation-states, taken notice of the close relationship between anthropology and the colonial expansion of those nations that produced the leaders of the field.[3]

Even in the first decades of the twentieth century, anthropological fieldwork was conducted among colonized peoples who were administratively incorporated into national empires. Malinowski did his work among the Trobriand Islanders, who were under the political domination of Australia, and Radcliffe-Brown did his work among the Andaman Islanders, who were controlled by the British as part of their India domain. Followers of these British anthropologists worked primarily in African areas dominated by the British. While many of their research efforts were directed toward answering questions about the human condition, it became increasingly difficult to disassociate the basic research from research to further administrative efficiency and control. Thus, the study of native African land tenure systems or leadership patterns might be of intrinsic value and concern, but the results of such research could be (and were) used to maintain control over native populations. Similarly in the United States, much of the research effort stimulated by Boas centered upon the American Indian population dominated by the United States government.

Like many other social sciences, anthropology was greatly influenced by World War II. The war, which directly involved the majority of mankind, generated a great variety of anthropological activities which, under other historical circumstances, might not have developel as quickly or in quite the same direction. One particular strand in the war effort directly involved anthropologists in efforts to understand "enemy" cultures in order to suggest techniques to hasten the victory of the Allied Forces. As an example of this we have the work of Ruth Benedict, whose "culture at a distance" studies were extremely significant and resulted in the publication of *The Chrysanthemum and the Sword*, a classic study of the Japanese.[4] Another group of anthropologists studied American food habits with the goal of introducing changes in the American dietary patterns in order to utilize items in great supply in the midst of a wartime food shortage.[5] A third effort utilized the talents of anthropologists

[3] Diane Lewis, "Anthropology and Colonialism," *Current Anthropology*, 14 (1973), 581-602.
[4] Ruth Benedict, *The Chrysanthemum and the Sword: Patterns of Japanese Culture* (Boston: Houghton Mifflin Co., 1946).
[5] Margaret Mead, "Changing Food Habits in the Post-War Period," in *Nutrition for Young and Old*, Legislative Document #76, New York State Joint Legislative Committee on Nutrition, 1946, pp. 60-64; "Significant Aspects of Regional Food Patterns," in *Conference on Food Acceptance Research*, Committee on Food Resources, War Department, Office of Quartermaster General, Washington, D.C., 1946, pp. 64-67.

in the administration and study of Japanese War Relocation centers in the United States.[6]

A major consequence of these endeavors in anthropology was the growth of a subfield presently referred to as Applied Anthropology. Although many earlier anthropological studies had policy implications for the control of subject peoples, these goals were not part of the anthropological intent. In the projects described above, however, the anthropologist was studying a particular population or problem with the explicit goal of developing policies, and thus the work had practical implications for solving problems.

Another effect of the war on the development of anthropology was the attempt to create a corps of language and area experts. Initially, training programs were concerned with Asia and the Pacific Ocean area, but later they were expanded to cover most of the developing world. The United States government, which sponsored language training schools, was at first concerned with the problem of post-war occupation and United States' responsibility for the administration of conquered areas. A major result of these programs was the development of a cadre of area experts, many of whom, in the post-war period, moved into academic disciplines such as political science, economics, and anthropology. The federal government continued its interest in language and area experts through support of academic programs, including the funding of programs through the vehicle of the National Defense Education Act. The continuing sponsorship of such academic efforts can be seen as one of the "weapons" in the Cold War and the subsequent concern with emerging nations, or the Third World.

When the Cold War became "Hot" (as in Korea and Vietnam), greater financial commitment to these activities was apparent. In a few cases, a direct effort was made by the United States government to use anthropology in the pursuit of war goals. One of the most blatant examples of this was the establishment of an Institute at Michigan State University, which, using the label of anthropology falsely as a cover, was concerned with the training of undercover agents for counter-insurgency efforts. This case, when it became public, infuriated the anthropological community in particular and the academic community in general. In addition to the immediate result of forcing a disassociation of the Institute and the University, it stimulated a reassessment of the relationship between academics and government-sponsored research. Other scandals, such as Project Camelot in Chile and some questionable counterinsurgency projects in Thailand, reinforced this concern.

[6] Alexander Leighton, *The Governing of Men: General Principles and Recommendations Based on Experience at a Japanese Relocation Camp* (Princeton: Princeton University Press, 1945).

The foregoing discussion documents the contention that the growth of anthropology is related to the larger sociopolitical system that stimulated it. For some years now, the American Anthropological Association, which is the official organization of the discipline in the United States, has been wrestling with the problem of developing a code of ethics to serve as a guide for future research. These ethical issues are central to the subfield of urban anthropology.

THE STUDY OF COMPLEX SOCIETY

While World War II and its aftermath stimulated certain changes in anthropological emphasis, other events had occurred even before the war that led to a changing constituency for the researcher. Many anthropologists were no longer doing fieldwork in isolated tribal societies, but were going to agriculturally based communities. The war itself gave greater impetus to such village studies in peasant societies.

Peasant Societies

The shift in the research focus of anthropology to developing nation-states entailed work in political systems of a different level of complexity from primitive and/or tribal societies. However, many of the village studies of the 1940s and 1950s did not recognize the fact that, in a complex system, one is dealing with a community of people that is not autonomous but is part of a larger economic, political, and cultural system. These early village studies often treated the village as an isolated unit to be studied without looking at the outside forces that impinged heavily upon the community. It was only later, when the ties between the village and the larger social context in which it was embedded were recognized, that the concept of a peasant society as a type of social system was defined and refined.

Peasant societies are characterized by a higher rate of per capita productivity than tribal societies because they have developed techniques for controlling water, soil nutrients, and soil quality. Moreover, the complex system of social differentiation in such societies necessitates integrative centralized economic and political institutions. Greater productivity releases part of the population from food-producing activities and permits full-time occupational specialization to develop. Closely related to this is the development of true *social classes*—hereditary groups with differential access to wealth, prestige, and power. Cities often develop as central points for administering large scale marketing, taxing, and other functions. Writing develops as a means of record keeping. However, most of the population remains a peasantry distributed in agricultural villages.

Once the peasant society was defined, the anthropologist had to recognize the impact of cities within such a society. From this it was a logical and predictable move to studies of people in cities and thus to urban anthropology.

Redfield: Folk, Peasant and City

The conceptual underpinnings of the study of complex societies developed under the guidance of Robert Redfield. Redfield's vision of anthropology has been validated; many studies of peasant society and the city are extensions of issues he raised.

Initially, even Redfield did not recognize the difference between folk and peasant societies; he lumped them together conceptually. Most of the previous fieldwork in American anthropology used the American Indian as the basic field subject, primarily because of geographic proximity, freedom of movement within the United States, accessibility, and minimal budgetary requirements. There was also a strong belief in the necessity of studying these tribal groups and their lifeways before they disappeared. Gradually through the 1920s, 1930s, and 1940s, the peoples of Mexico and Guatemala were included as American Indians—which in fact they historically were—sharing language families and culture traits. However, these people were not tribal societies, as were their North American counterparts, but were, in fact, components of complex states that had existed since before the Spanish conquest. Nevertheless, many anthropologists did their first fieldwork in these areas and treated the villages as if they were tribal units.

Redfield's most significant fieldwork was conducted in four communities located on the Yucatan peninsula of Mexico in the 1930s.[7] These four units of study were selected on the basis of several criteria: size, homogeneity and distance from major urban influences. It should be noted that even the smallest and most isolated of the four communities was part of a larger sociopolitical and economic market system that had impinged directly upon its life since before the Spanish Conquest. However, Redfield did not at first recognize this fact, and this error interfered with his initial theoretical formulations. This lack of perception of the larger nexus of the village was also apparent in his earlier study of the village of Tepoztlan, Mexico, where his description of village life was biased by a view of the community as an isolated folk community.[8]

[7] Robert Redfield, The Folk Culture of Yucatan (Chicago: University of Chicago Press, 1941).
[8] Robert Redfield, Tepoztlan, A Mexican Village (Chicago: University of Chicago Press, 1930).

This bias was exposed in Oscar Lewis's restudy of the same community.[9]

In 1947, Redfield wrote an article entitled "The Folk Society," which has been reproduced in many anthologies and stimulated a great deal of research (as well as criticism) in the ensuing two decades. The major goal of the article was to define the simple "folk" society. In developing attributes of this ideal type, Redfield added such criteria as sacred versus secular and stability versus rapid rates of change to those of size, homogeneity, and distance from urban influences previously used in his Yucatan study. Although primary emphasis was given to a description of the folk society, the implicit assumption was that the urban type has diametrically opposed attributes. Thus, if folk society is homogeneous and sacred, urban society is heterogeneous and secular. A major source of confusion lay in the use of the word *society* as opposed to *community*. Folk and urban were not total social systems, but merely community types. There is no such thing as an urban society, but urban communities can be component parts of either peasant or industrial societies. Redfield really was contrasting at two levels. On the one hand he was comparing tribal, peasant village and urban *communities,* while on the other hand he was comparing traditional and modern *societies.*[10]

Redfield's attempt to distinguish analytically between the two types of societies contained within it a bias toward the folk, or traditional, type. In many ways members of the folk society appear to be good and pure and to have spontaneous, satisfying social interactions. To a very large extent, Redfield was influenced by his sociologist colleagues at the University of Chicago, who initiated the emphasis upon study of urban phenomena in the United States. While many members of this group, like Park, Burgess, Wirth and others, were emphasizing alleged pathological aspects of modern urban life, Redfield idealized many aspects of folk lifestyles.

Redfield refined his analytic framework during the course of the next two decades. He shifted his research efforts to the study of ongoing peasant societies in Central America and, through his students, to India. He conceded that a simple dichotomy between folk and urban was an oversimplification of the real variation in social systems. He then moved toward defining peasant societies where the village community is a unit within a larger system. Once Redfield recognized that the peasant society was a distinctive type of social system and that the

---

[9] Oscar Lewis, *Life in a Mexican Village: Tepoztlan Restudied* (Urbana: University of Illinois Press, 1951).

[10] Robert Redfield, "The Folk Society," *American Journal of Sociology,* 41 (1947), 293-308.

peasant village was not autonomous (that is, not a society), he began to develop concepts to deal with this type of social system.[11]

The term *little community* was coined by Redfield for peasant villages and was used by his students. Thus, a volume containing studies of villages in India by anthropologists was subtitled "Extensions of the Little Community," and editor Marriott's introductory essay emphasized the extent to which an Indian village is *not* a self-contained social unit.[12]

The ramifications of Redfield's little community concept are numerous. It is obvious that a village community that is part of a bounded political state is under the domination of centralized political authority. In addition, the village community is usually linked economically to outside forces, in that it produces for and consumes from a system-wide market.

Centralized agencies are typically located in non-village types of communities, namely towns and cities. In addition, towns and cities are recognized as the major sources of what Redfield referred to as the Great Tradition (as opposed to the Little Traditions, which are the belief systems of the local villages). Thus, classical and orthodox forms of dance, music, and drama are found in urban centers, while folk expressions of these activities are found in villages. Such folk traditions show variability from region to region, but generally cities are centers for formal, orthodox religious ideology and for the literate and articulate purveyors of the centralized, unifying, statewide belief system.

Later still Redfield, in conjunction with Singer, began to emphasize the cultural roles of cities in the larger sociocultural system.[13] In his development of the distinction between the Great and Little Traditions, the urban Great Tradition is given primary importance. It interacts with and is stimulated by the Little Traditions of the villages, but the city dominates its hinterland and is seen as a major source of change. Although we never find a characterization of the city as positive in bias toward urban life as the folk notion was toward rural folklife, it is obvious that in his theoretical development, Redfield was shifting toward recognition of the city as a positive force in the maintenance of civilization and in cultural development.

The impact of Redfield's work on the development of the anthropology of complex societies was extremely significant. The elements of

[11] Robert Redfield, *Peasant Society and Culture* (Chicago: University of Chicago Press, 1956).

[12] McKim Marriott, *Village India: Studies in the Little Community*, American Anthropological Association Memoir, 1955.

[13] Robert Redfield and Milton Singer, "The Cultural Role of Cities," *Economic Development and Culture Change*, 3 (1954), 53-73.

his conceptual framework that are particularly relevant to urban anthropology will be described in greater detail in Chapter 3.

THE EMERGENCE OF URBAN ANTHROPOLOGY

Aside from the work of Redfield, there are several other examples of an early interest in the city that emerged well before the subfield of urban anthropology was recognized. These are the work of archaeologists on the origins of the city, the work of anthropologists on traditional preindustrial cities, the early community studies in the United States, and the movement of area specialists (Latin Americanists and Africanists) into urban-oriented work. All of these elements contributed to urban anthropology, but they were so unrelated to each other that it is only in retrospect that they can be viewed as strands in the development of the field, which did not formally emerge until the late 1960s.

Community Studies

One early attempt in anthropology to study life in the modern United States developed in the 1930s. The resulting literature bridged the fields of sociology and anthropology. This type of research is usually called community studies, since it attempts to understand a single local community using a combination of research strategies, including participant observation as well as more extensive survey techniques.

The major figure associated with this area of research is W. Lloyd Warner, who was trained initially as an anthropologist. After a three-year field trip to study the Murngin, an Australian tribe, Warner decided to transpose the emerging intensive anthropological research technique to the study of an American town. The result of this research was several volumes referred to as the *Yankee City* series, which described the community in detail and focused on such special areas as lifestyle differences between classes and effects of a strike.[14]

Warner viewed himself as a social anthropologist. Although Warner influenced Arensberg and Kimball, who studied Irish communities, most of his students studied communities within the United States. Most of these studies were holistic, that is, they attempted to describe the lifeways of an *entire* community. It should be emphasized that Warner and his followers recognized the limitations of these tools and suggested

---

[14] W. Lloyd Warner, *Yankee City* (New Haven: Yale University Press, 1963). Abridged version of volumes published between 1947-1959; study begun in 1930.

that these techniques could be used only in small communities (less than 20,000). Thus the urban centers they studied obviously were towns rather than cities.

One individual heavily influenced by Warner was William Foote Whyte. In his volume *Street Corner Society*, Whyte followed Warner's methodological lead, but transposed it to a neighborhood in a large urban center. A sociologist, Herbert Gans, later restudied the same community. His volume, *The Urban Villagers*, is a follow-up of Whyte's initial work and focuses upon the degree to which this ethnically homogeneous population has retained non-urban patterns of social organization and interaction. Gans also studied suburban communities and emphasized the differences and similarities between urban and suburban lifestyles.[15]

Whyte and Gans are considered sociologists by appointment and training, but they used the intensive, descriptive, ethnographic techniques pioneered by Warner in the study of modern American communities. The return of anthropologists to this approach was signaled when anthropologist Arthur Vidich collaborated with sociologist Joseph Bensman in the study of a community in the state of New York. The resulting *Small Town in Mass Society* specifically used techniques and orientations developed in anthropology. This study did not look at the town as an isolated unit, but focused upon its relationship to wider regional and national contexts.[16] Thus, at the same time that peasant communities were being viewed in relation to their larger contexts, a similar shift was taking place in American community studies.

As might be expected, the community study approach developed in the United States by Warner and later modified and expanded by sociologists and social anthropologists was eventually used in the study of urban centers in the developing world. Andrew Whiteford's comparative study of Querétaro, Mexico and Popayán, Colombia derives its impetus from Warner's approach.[17] Some recent urban anthropology research in urban neighborhoods in the United States can be viewed as lineal descendants of the Warner-Whyte-Gans approach, for example, Liebow's *Tally's Corner*.[18]

---

[15] William Foote Whyte, *Street Corner Society: The Social Structure of an Italian Slum* (Chicago: University of Chicago Press, 1955), originally published in 1943; Herbert Gans ,*The Urban Villagers* (New York: The Free Press, 1962); Herbert Gans, *The Levittowners* (New York: Pantheon, 1967).

[16] Arthur Vidich and Joseph Bensman, *Small Town in Mass Society* (Princeton: Princeton University Press, 1958).

[17] Andrew Whiteford, *Two Cities in Latin America* (Garden City: Doubleday and Co., Inc., 1964).

[18] Elliot Liebow, *Tally's Corner* (Boston: Little, Brown and Co., 1967).

Archeology

One group whose concern with the urban is early and continuous consists of the archaeologists who deal with early civilizations in the socioeconomic (and not merely aesthetic) sense. In excavating the urban centers of no longer extant peasant social systems, they saw the shift from small scale settlement patterns to large urban sites as one of the major changes in man's history. V. Gordon Childe referred to this as the "urban revolution" and related it to certain shifts in economic productivity. Childe's emphasis on the urban settlement was a continuation of the archaeologist's concern with the roots of contemporary civilization.

The archaeologist's contribution to urban anthropology was twofold. On the one hand it developed a long-term historical view of the urban process that focused upon the various conditions under which cities came into being. This aspect of the archaeological approach is exemplified in an early volume entitled *Courses Toward Urban Life*, edited by Robert Braidwood.[19] In addition, archaeology, by its very nature, must focus upon those aspects of life that produce concrete material artifacts. In this more narrow view of urban settlements, primary emphasis is given to physical factors such as architectural types, size of dwellings, street plans, and core versus peripheral patterns.

The Traditional City

Some anthropologists arrived at an urban orientation through the study of traditional cities in peasant societies. Among those we would cite the work of Miner in Timbuctoo and Schwab in Oshogbo.[20] These anthropologists were examining the characteristics of the traditional city using ethnographic techniques and providing a view of such communities other than that provided by archaeologists. Sjoberg, in his classic work *The Preindustrial City*, used primarily documentary history rather than ethnographic field techniques.[21] All these studies were attempts to get at the basic essence of the cross-cultural urban phenomenon. By studying traditional cities in various parts of the world, it was assumed

[19] Braidwood, Robert, *Courses Toward Urban Life*, Viking Fund Publications in Anthropology, 32 (New York: Wenner-Gren Foundation, 1962).
[20] Horace Miner, *The Primitive City of Timbuctoo* (Princeton: University of Princeton Press, 1953); William Schwab, "Oshogbo—An Urban Community," in H. Kuper (ed.), *Urbanization and Migration in West Africa* (Berkeley: University of California Press, 1965), pp. 85-109.
[21] Gideon Sjoberg, *The Preindustrial City* (New York: The Free Press, 1960).

that we would be able to place our own urban lives within a broader framework.

Area Studies

A large number of American anthropologists studied Mexican and other Latin American villages originally as an extension of interest in American Indians and later as the result of interest in peasant societies. For them, when modernization and massive rural-urban migration occurred, the impact of these forces on village communities could not be ignored. Some Latin Americanists began to discuss the urban phenomenon and its place in the human experience. Ralph Beals' article "Urbanism, Urbanization and Acculturation," in which he tried to differentiate among the three, stands out as one of the earliest evidences of an anthropologist's concern with the impact of cities on his traditional constituents.[22] Oscar Lewis also became one of the first "urban anthropologists" as he followed some of his villagers into Mexico City.[23] For Beals the city does not continue as a major focus, but for Lewis it does.

It is interesting to note that Beals' article (originally a presidential address before the American Anthropological Association) urged the study of cities and complex society in order to move away from a heavy overemphasis on psychology in American anthropology. Now, more than twenty years later, the concern is with maintaining a separation from sociology, the very discipline Beals had urged moving toward.

While American anthropologists were lured into cities of Latin America as a response to movements of the peasant population, a parallel phenomenon was taking place in British anthropology, centered primarily on cities in Africa. Classic British social anthropology emphasized the study of traditional and static aspects of tribal life. However, after World War II many British anthropologists became interested in social change. One major volume published in the early 1960s (based on research in the 1950s) was called *Social Change in Africa*.[24] Many of the articles in this volume dealt with an important aspect of the change being studied in Africa, which was the movement of tribal people into urban centers. As in Latin America, a similar concern with the migrant

[22] Ralph Beals, "Urbanism, Urbanization and Acculturation," *American Anthropologist*, 53 (1951), 1-10.
[23] Oscar Lewis, "Urbanization without Breakdown: A Case Study," *The Scientific Monthly*, 75, 1952.
[24] Aidan Southall (ed.), *Social Change in Africa* (London: Oxford University Press, 1961).

in the city was dominant. This early interest led to a later need to characterize what the urban was in an attempt to differentiate the urban social system and urbanism from the tribal social system.

RECOGNITION OF THE SUBFIELD
OF URBAN ANTHROPOLOGY

Despite all this interest in cities and urban life, actual recognition of urban anthropology took a long time. A major factor that delayed such recognition in the United States was overconcern with maintaining the uniqueness of anthropology and clearly distinguishing it from other social science disciplines, particularly sociology.

Students inevitably ask, "How does urban anthropology differ from sociology?" A partial answer to this question can be derived from our prior discussion of the essential concepts and methods of anthropology. However, there are other social scientists who have adopted several or all of these elements. The question is not crucial if the goal of urban anthropology is to understand cities and urban life. If concepts, methods, and constituencies are borrowed or shared with other disciplines, this is not threatening. There will be an overlap in those segments of all social science disciplines focused on the city. The mature development of anthropology as well as urban anthropology demands that we not waste so much energy on concern over our domain or turf. There are some real differences in the perspective of the anthropologist and in the nature of his or her research. We shall discuss these unique contributions of anthropology to urban studies at the end of Chapter 2. However, the boundaries between disciplines investigating the city are blurred, and we should not expect to find a precise division of labor.

It is worth noting in this context that when Vidich, who was trained in anthropology, collaborated upon the previously mentioned study of a small town in New York State, his identity as an anthropologist became ambiguous. When one of the authors of this text worked with a literate middle class group in Latin America, she was told by one of her colleagues that she was a sociologist, since her target population was neither illiterate nor barefoot, as were anthropologists' traditional informants. She had never taken a course in sociology.

Since a major emphasis in cultural anthropology is fieldwork in an alien culture, such fieldwork is significant in establishing the status of the professional practitioner. Fieldwork in cities was considered less legitimate, but in non-western cities, legitimacy was not as seriously questioned. The most legitimate and valid anthropology was done in non-western tribes or peasant villages. Non-western cities were considered less legitimate research sites, but the study of American cities continued to be considered tainted and impure until the 1960s.

These issues are more characteristic of American cultural anthropology than British social anthropology. Following the lead of Radcliffe-Brown, their work was considered comparative sociology and their identity concerns were not as significant. The transition from work in tribal groups to work in urban settings, even London, was easier. Nevertheless, in the last decade urban anthropology has been recognized as a valid specialty in American anthropology. We will now examine some of the reasons for this.

It is difficult to separate formal recognition of urban anthropology from a general trend in the academic world toward the study of urban phenomena. The emergence of interdisciplinary urban studies programs is noteworthy. In some places, urban studies programs have been, in effect, a simple experiment with the interdisciplinary extension of urban sociology, political science, history, or geography. In other places, urban studies has been the pooling of resources of several social sciences in conjunction with urban policy and planning. In still other programs, there has been an attempt to create a new discipline of urban studies with its own concepts and methods. In the last two instances, the work of urban anthropology has often been an integral part of the developing program.

Another contributory factor to the emergence of urban anthropology has been the relative decline of funding for the costly overseas fieldwork characteristic of traditional anthropology. Many public and private funding agencies have either cut back on funding or have shifted their major focus to the support of research that has relevance to domestic policy issues. Thus, some anthropologists must study in the United States because they are not sufficiently funded for overseas work, or because they have been specifically supported for work in the United States. Most of this research takes place in cities.

It would seem too simplistic to suggest that there is a linear cause-and-effect relationship between the availability of funds and the research direction of anthropology. Much of this change reflects a real concern with the problems of contemporary society, both within the United States and elsewhere. To a certain extent, this shift is the result of an increasing consciousness among anthropologists of the political implications of the work they do and their consequent responsibility to their informants. Some anthropologists have felt that the time has come for them to turn their attention to studies in their own urban areas that will eventually lead to programs to improve existing conditions.

Some general indications of the emergence of the field of urban anthropology can be seen in the growing literature specifically labelled as such. Since 1968, six edited collections of articles dealing explicitly with urban anthropology have appeared.[25] In addition, the publication of monographs based upon urban ethnography has increased. Another related phenomenon has been the greater attention given to urban anthropology by national and regional meetings, special conferences, and support agencies such as the Center for Urban Ethnography at the University of Pennsylvania. Several journals have had special issues on urban topics, and in 1972 a journal called *Urban Anthropology* initiated publication.

THE DOMAIN OF URBAN ANTHROPOLOGY

If one looks at the disparate literature called urban anthropology, it becomes apparent that a tremendous range of data, foci, and methods are included under this semantically diffuse label. When we examine this variety, there appear to be three different types of studies from which the field has taken its direction. These are:

1. Studies of peasant migrants to the city
2. Problem-centered studies.
3. Traditional ethnographic studies using the city as a laboratory.

Peasants in Cities

Within the larger framework of urban anthropology, a group of studies that is a direct outgrowth of traditional anthropology focuses upon rural-urban migration and the initial adaptation of rural peasants to the urban environment. At first, such research was an extension of village studies, which found that there was considerable movement of segments of population between village and city. After a while, the focus shifted directly to peasants in cities, without the research strategy of following the peasant from village to city, or examining the effect of migration from the village or tribal perspective. These studies emphasize the reasons for migration, patterns of migration, and the *initial*

[25] Elizabeth Eddy (ed.), *Urban Anthropology: Research Perspectives and Strategies* (Athens: University of Georgia Press, 1968); William Mangin (ed.), *Peasants in Cities: Readings in the Anthropology of Urbanization* (Boston: Houghton Mifflin Co., 1970); T. Weaver and D. White (eds.), *The Anthropology of Urban Environments*, The Society for Applied Anthropology Monographs, 11 (1972); Aidan Southall (ed.), *Urban Anthropology: Cross-Cultural Studies of Urbanization* (New York: Oxford University Press, 1973); George Foster and Robert Kemper (eds.), *Anthropologists in Cities* (Boston: Little, Brown and Company, 1974); John Friedl and Noel Chrisman (eds.), *City Ways: A Selective Reader in Urban Anthropology* (New York: Thomas Y. Crowell Co., 1975).

adaptation in the new urban context. Studies of initial adaptation have been done in most major world areas and form an important segment of the "peasants in cities" literature.

The basic assumption is that the city is essentially a new social environment for the newcomer. In addition to being confronted with unfamiliar people and places, newcomers are faced with new situations, new institutions, and new behavioral codes. They must find jobs and housing in a social setting that differs significantly from what they have known. Both the job pool and the techniques of recruitment and placement are unfamiliar. Types of housing as well as the housing market are also strange. Migrants must also develop new habits of handling money, which was probably not used as frequently in the rural areas; they must reorient their daily schedules and change their attitudes toward time to fit the urban rhythm; they must develop new social behavior to relate themselves to the formal legal, medical, judicial, and educational institutions of the city.

Adaptation studies include:

1. those that look at strategies that involve the mobilization of social ties primarily through the extension of kinship, fictive kinship (persons not related by blood or marriage who are given kin titles), tribal, regional, and friendship bonds
2. those that describe the transposition of organizational and structural models from the original community to the city
3. those that describe the problems of developing new identities and solidarity groups in the heterogeneous urban milieu

Peasant adaptation may also be viewed in a context larger than the city. Few peasant migrants completely sever their ties with their rural locale. Relationships with people and property left behind may be maintained by visiting, exchanges of money and gifts, and exchanges of child-rearing services. Visiting may be casual or related to vacations, religious ceremonies, family crises, and life cycle events. In addition to such contacts, land and other property retained in the rural area tie the migrant to the village. The relationships of the city to its hinterland based upon these patterns of exchange and interaction act as a source of change for both village and city. Anthropologists who focus primarily upon the peasant in the city provide insight into this process. In addition, those urban anthropologists who are interested in more traditional issues of culture change and economic development also see these ties as major forces.

Criticisms of Peasant Adaptation Studies. The "peasants in cities" genre contains much potential for comparative analysis. Many methodological strategies have been designed to compare different groups in relation to adaptation. Contrasts have been made between migrants in different cities, as well as between experiences of various regional and tribal groups in the same city, and between those who move short distances and those who move far. The phenomena of circular migration (repeated movement between rural and urban areas) and step or stage migration (movement in sequence from small to increasingly larger settlements) have also been dealt with comparatively.

In most of these studies there seems to be an emphasis on the persistence and/or modification of tradition. This is to counteract the negative view of the city as disorganizing, detribalizing, and deculturating so prevalent in problem-centered urban studies. This view is also partly the result of the anthropologist's familiarity with the migrants' traditional setting—his "rural ethnocentrism." It also follows from the anthropologist's belief in the impact of early training and in the permanence of cultural absorption. Perhaps we have gone too far in this direction and should begin looking more at flexibility and change.

An additional criticism of studies of peasants in the cities is that concentration upon the recent arrivals causes many aspects of the long term urban situation and the extant urban structure to be ignored. We have noted some of the historical reasons for this emphasis, but a fully developed urban anthropology would have to expand its scope to reveal greater understanding of ongoing urban life. Two categories of studies that do shift the focus away from the newly arrived are those we will label the *problem-centered* and the *analytical* approaches.

Problem-Centered Approach

In contrast to the "peasants in cities" literature, which derives *directly* from the long term interest of anthropology in peasant villages, the problem-centered approach, which is primarily characteristic of the urban anthropologist working in the United States, has no real traditional base in cultural anthropology. Growing recognition within anthropology of the various ways in which anthropologists or their data have been used by politically dominant groups and western colonial forces led to some of the studies we are calling problem-centered. Others stem from the development of Applied Anthropology. In many ways, the problem-oriented urban anthropologist follows an earlier tradition in urban sociology that emphasized the study of social deviants and minority groups. In anthropological studies, however, the approach usually emphasizes the role that the dominant classes and ecological factors play in the generation of problems. As an example of the problem focus in urban anthropology, we cite the following definition of this subfield: "The study of complex societies in terms of ethnic minorities, urban deterioration, and popular discontent." [26]

Within the group of urban anthropologists who are problem oriented, the range of positions on the policy implications of the research is broad. At one extreme, there are those who study "oppressed peoples" and attempt to help them develop tactics and strategies to radically modify the system. At the other end, there are those who study the same groups and attempt to work within established institutional frameworks to ameliorate the situation. Both positions are, in this sense, concerned with the action or policy implications of their research. These anthropologists feel a responsibility to their informants and assume the role of advocates for the people being studied. By contrast, some research on minority groups, deviants, and low income populations tries only to explain the existence of such groups; whatever policy implications exist are implicit.

Perhaps the largest component of problem-oriented studies is the literature on poverty. Within the last decade, many studies have been conducted that attempt to clarify and correct descriptions of the behavior and values of the poor developed in social science. The anthropological concern with poverty began with the writings of Oscar Lewis. His formulation of the "culture of poverty" concept generated considerable controversy and a massive literature. [27] It also stimulated urban ethnographic research, initiated by a desire to refute or modify the concept.

Although the literature on poverty is usually associated with college courses and readings labelled as urban anthropology, it is motivated by reasons other than an interest in the city, and often contains data and discussions that are not even urban-based. Neither the causes nor the manifestations of poverty are limited to the city. Throughout this literature, a concern with the general policy implications of research has been demonstrated. Since the development of the poverty literature provides so many examples of the methodological and conceptual issues of urban anthropology, we shall discuss this in greater detail in Chapter 8.

Research on minority groups, particularly in the cities of the United States, has been a core of urban anthropology. Many sessions at recent meetings of the Society for Applied Anthropology have been devoted to minority problems. Afro-Americans, Chicanos, Puerto Ricans, and Native Americans have recently been studied, often but not exclusively, in an urban context.

Within the framework of American urban anthropology, considerable attention has been paid to the study of specific urban institutions

[26] Gerald Berreman et al., *Anthropology Today* (Del Mar, California: CRM Books, 1971), p. 551.
[27] Oscar Lewis, "The Culture of Poverty," *Scientific American*, 215 (1966).

and their difficulties in delivering services. Such institutions as schools, hospitals, rehabilitation centers, and prisons are seen to be failing in their main objectives. They are primarily studied from an applied anthropological or policy perspective that asks the question: How can they be improved? The emphasis is on the malfunctions of these institutions. Explanations of these malfunctions are often couched in terms of intercultural misunderstandings or ineffective communication; corrective policies are explicitly recommended or implied.

American urban anthropology includes studies of a variety of deviant groups—people whose occupations or lifestyles are antisocial or illicit, at least by dominant class standards. In the anthropological studies, less stress is placed on the dysfunctional characteristics of these groups (for the larger society), and correspondingly more attention is paid to the internal structure, normative patterns, and cognitive worlds of these groups. Thus, addicts, skid row residents, prostitutes, transvestites, and transsexuals are viewed as subcultures. Some of these studies are attempts to illuminate the real, rather than the alleged, lifestyles of these groups. Some point out how mainstream groups contribute to the problems. Still other studies focus specifically on policies that would improve the position of the group. Any policy implications in these studies are aimed at changing the attitude of the dominant groups, rather than manipulating the subjects themselves. Actual suggestions for changes in law enforcement towards these groups have been included in several studies.[28]

Criticisms of the Problem Approach. Many of the researchers who have concentrated on lower and underclass groups have been criticized for their narrow view. It has been suggested that, for a more realistic view of the causes of urban problems, more emphasis be placed upon studies of the dominant segments who control the strategic resources and major institutions of society, such as the job market, educational and medical establishments. Thus the study of an oppressed group that locates the generation of the problem in the dominant class, but does not study the dominant group in detail, still leaves basic questions unanswered. For example, a study of minority/police relations that focuses on ethnography in the minority group without studying the peer milieu of police work may produce suggestions that are unrealistic.

Another criticism of problem-centered research is that, by narrowly

[28] The works of James Spradley on skid row residents and those of Jennifer James on prostitutes are generally acknowledged to have had input into local law enforcement policies. James Spradley, *You Owe Yourslf a Drunk* (Boston: Little, Brown and Company, 1970); Jennifer James, "On the Block," *Urban Anthropology*, 1 (1972), 125-40; and Jennifer James, "Sweet Cream Ladies," *Western Canadian Journal of Anthropology*, 3 (1973), 102-18.

focusing on certain phenomena, it bypasses the larger issue of the totality of urban life. Urban sociology has recently been much criticized for its belief that cities are the locus for all social problems. This problem of an anti-urban bias will be discussed in the next chapter.

Some of the reasons that anthropologists have confined their attention to the groups at the lowest rungs of the social ladder are that these groups are more accessible and vulnerable to the intrusive techniques of ethnographic study. There is a new trend to study groups other than the underclasses. It was illustrated at recent meetings of the American Anthropological Association and in several published studies.

Some of the difficulties anthropologists face when they try to use ethnographic techniques in the study of elites in the United States can be seen in the attempt of Laura Nader to have graduate students study a major law firm in Washington, D.C., using ethnographic techniques of face-to-face interaction and observation of everyday activity. The researchers were dismissed very quickly because of their obvious lack of sophistication about the operation of the institution they were studying.[29] Despite the difficulty faced by anthropologists when they attempt to study elites in their "natural settings," the endeavor must be continued.

The Traditional Analytic Approach

There is a third approach to urban anthropology that is more concerned with concepts and theory than with policy. It is more interested in extant urban structure than migrant adaptation. These studies, like those in the "peasants in cities" genre, are an outgrowth of traditional anthropological concerns. However, whereas the "peasants in cities" genre results from the movement of the anthropologist's traditional constituency to the city, the traditional approach results from the transportation of the long-term theoretical problems of the discipline to the city. The traditional questions about social structure and social process, or culture and cognition, are asked in urban settings as more and more of the world's population is found in cities.

There is some overlap between the "peasants in the city" genre and what we are calling the traditional approach. However, the former is characterized primarily by concern with urbanization, strategies of adaptation, and social change. The traditional approach is oriented more to general anthropological theory—kinship theory, socialization theory, or the community study method.

Many anthropologists do not give up their traditional concern with

[29] Laura Nader, "Up the Anthropologist—Perspectives Gained from Studying Up," in Dell Hymes (ed.), *Reinventing Anthropology* (New York: Random House, 1974), pp. 284-311. (Originally published in 1969.)

kinship as they move into cities. While many urban kinship studies relate to peasant adaptation, some focus on the role of kinship in permanent urban social structure. Anthropologists have pointed to the various ways in which kinship relationships are structured in an urban setting. One of the major innovations in the analysis of urban social relationships is the development of the social network concept. These person-centered sets of key social linkages are *chosen* by individuals, and thus differ from kinship ties, which are ascribed. Both kin groups and networks are primary social units and have a great impact on social norms and behavior. In many ways they are interrelated because an individual will select some kin for his network.

Other social groups in the urban setting have also been studied by anthropologists in an attempt to understand social process. Just as the interest in kinship follows from traditional anthropological concerns, so does the selection of ethnic groups as a unit of study, for it is assumed that each group is a "little culture." Anthropoligists define the group as a closed corporate unit, recruited by birth and shaped by enculturation. This definition allows them to use the traditional concept of culture and ethnographic techniques and feel that they are still performing as anthropologists. At a recent meeting of the American Anthropological Association, 20 percent (largest category) of the papers defined as "urban" dealt with ethnic groups.

Another non-kin group frequently studied is the neighborhood. This is because of the traditional reliance in anthropology on spatially bounded residential groups, even though place of residence may not be as as significant in the lives of urban people. The slum, or residential community of low-income residents, has been the most typical unit represented in urban anthropology monographs.

Another segment of traditional anthropology in the city is represented by studies that ask questions related to persistent issues in the anthropology of politics, economics, and religion. Urban anthropologists have studied leadership patterns and power relationships in urban neighborhoods, unemployment and marginal occupations, the retention of folk medicine and curers, and the maintenance of myths, folklore, and ritual.

Criticisms of the Traditional Approach. A major criticism of the traditional approach in the city is the lack of attention given to the holistic perspective developed in the study of small-scale societies. It is very difficult to focus on traditional questions and study the way of life in the "city-as-a-whole" in the same way that the traditional anthropologist studied a whole way of life in the tribe. In trying to study kinship, one cannot study the whole city. In trying to study ethnic subcultures as isolated "little cultures," or in studying neighborhoods as isolated "villages," one is missing the holistic perspective—the concern with the interrelationship of parts, the interwoven pattern of the total city.

The Importance of Urban Anthropology Despite The Lack of Clearcut Definition

One of the basic problems in defining any newly emergent subfield is the establishment of boundaries to distinguish it from others that already exist. Therefore, it should come as no surprise that other anthropologists will delineate the area of study in a different way, and that still others would suggest that a distinctive and new label is unnecessary and counter-productive, since many of the research questions could be subsumed under an already existing rubric.

If we look at the three types of studies in urban anthropology, it is apparent that each of them overlaps significantly with other areas of anthropology. Thus, the "peasants in cities" literature could be considered a part of the continuing interest of anthropology in social change or culture change, or more specifically related to the process of modernization often studied by the economic anthropologist. We have already shown that some of the early African studies of urbanism appeared in volumes concerned with general social change and not the city per se.

More recently, two volumes that deal with migration have appeared as a result of the 1974 International Congress of Anthropological and Ethnographical Science. One volume is entitled *Migration and Urbanization* while the other is called *Migration and Development*. The articles in both volumes could easily be interchanged without significantly affecting the meaning of the titles.[30] The very close relationship between problem-centered urban anthropology and applied anthropology has also been mentioned. Finally, traditional anthropological research in the city rather than in the tribe or peasant village can be viewed as simply part of general cultural anthropology and its institutional subspecialties: kinship, politics, economics, and religion.

Some additional problems of differentiation and overlap also exist between urban anthropology on the one hand and medical and educational anthropology on the other. Although these two new subfields focus on specific institutional complexes, they have developed largely in the urban setting and are as recent as urban anthropology. Thus, many studies in these two fields could be considered urban anthropology as well as the anthropological study of particular areas.

[30] Brian duToit and Helen Safa (eds.), *Migration and Urbanization* (The Hague: Mouton Publishers, 1976); Helen Safa and Brian duToit (eds.), *Migration and Development* (The Hague: Mouton Publishers, 1976).

The three categories of urban anthropology research (peasants in cities, problem-centered, and traditional) emerged as three almost entirely unrelated developments. Researchers working in one type ignored work in the others. Even within the "peasants in cities" genre, those who work in African cities were isolated from the Latin Americanists. This can be seen in the lack of references to each other.

We have been using these categories because they are helpful to describe and explain the growth of a wide-ranging disparate literature called urban anthropology. However, there is no logical basis for these categories and they serve no useful purpose as a framework for a viable anthropology of cities. Thus we will use them no further, but attempt to develop a more logical framework in the ensuing chapters.

As the result of the lack of a clearcut definition of the subfield of urban anthropology, some anthropologists reject the validity of a separate label entirely. Thus Moss says: ". . . if urban anthropology *is* different from all other anthropology, then it might as well be poor sociology." [31] He goes on to say that while he has taught "Urban Anthropology," he insists that what he really does is anthropology in an urban setting. He says, facetiously, that the label "Urban Anthropologist" is as necessary as that of "Peasant Anthropologist" or "Religious Anthropologist."

On the other hand, Leeds reacts negatively to the urban anthropology label for entirely different reasons. He states:

I consider such a field a spurious and retrograde one in that it tends to make an excuse for maintaining a subject matter within a discipline which cannot and should not handle it. [32]

He asks for more communication between the entire range of social science approaches, suggesting transdisciplinary approaches to urban problems, over and above interdisciplinary ones.

We would agree with Gulick, who argues strongly against a narrow focus or premature closure of the field. [33]

Much of the controversy concerning urban anthropology as a discrete area of study focuses upon the lack of clear understanding of what urban means or what are the major research questions of urban studies. This issue of defining the concept of urban and the field of urban studies will be discussed in Chapter 2.

Despite semantic confusion and lack of unified direction, many anthropologists call themselves urban anthropologists, many courses so

[31] Leonard Moss, "Review of T. Weaver and D. White (eds.), *Anthropology in Urban Environments*," in *Urban Anthropology Newsletter*, 2 (1973), pp. 39-40.
[32] Comment by Anthony Leeds in the first *Urban Anthropology Newsletter*, 1 (1972), p. 4.
[33] Comment by John Gulick in the first *Urban Anthropology Newsletter*, 1 (1972), p. 4.

labeled are taught, and many positions for urban anthropologists are advertised. In part, this is a result of identifying with the new discipline of urban studies, which is experiencing growth. It is also related to the lack of funds for research in tribal societies, as well as the refocusing on American society and its problems. These trends are also reflected in the job market, where employment opportunities for urban anthropologists appear to be greater than for those in many other subfields.

SUMMARY

Urban anthropology, as a clearly recognized subfield within anthropology, emerged in the middle of the sixties and is presently one of the most rapidly growing areas within the discipline. To understand why it has emerged and the direction it has taken, one must look at the history of the larger discipline, its conceptual basis, and the major strands that have had a direct impact on urban anthropology.

As a scientific discipline, cultural anthropology had its roots in the nineteenth century. The expansion of Western European nation-states as colonial powers led to contact with previously remote tribal groups. The exposure of Europeans and Americans to "strange" and "primitive" customs and institutions stimulated the development of the discipline. Much of the early efforts were based upon notions of cultural evolution that placed European customs and institutions at the apex of development as the most civilized or progressive. Despite these shortcomings, a group of specialists did emerge who were concerned with the study of tribal societies. They were comparing those societies to one another and to western society. Thus, the comparative approach was a vital element of early cultural anthropology.

In the early decades of the twentieth century, many of the basic attributes of contemporary anthropology emerged. A shift took place to the use of the comparative approach, field work was established as the basis of data collection, analysis of total sociocultural systems came to the fore, and cultural relativism became part of the cultural anthropologist's intellectual baggage.

To a certain extent, British and American anthropology took different paths. The British defined their endeavor as comparative sociology, while the Americans defined their field as the study of culture. As a result, many of the boundary-maintenance problems of American anthropology (particularly in relation to sociology) have not been important to the British.

Much of the recent growth in anthropology was a result of World War II (1941-45). The United States government utilized anthropologists in understanding the enemy (particularly the Japanese), in administering war relocation camps for Japanese-Americans, and in attempting to change American behavioral patterns to conform to the war effort. In addition, the federal government developed programs for the training of area specialists, some of whom subsequently became anthropologists. Governmental interest in anthropology has continued from that time, and is particularly apparent at times of outright conflict involving American troops.

Urban anthropology has had its own distinctive development within this larger context. The work of Robert Redfield is particularly significant. His studies of Mexican village life shifted the attention of anthropologists from tribal society to peasant society. An important component of peasant societies to emerge in Redfield's work was the significance of cities in these societies. At about the same time (1930s and 1940s), the anthropologist W. Lloyd Warner began his studies of smaller urban communities in the United States. Both of these men had an important impact on the growth and development of urban anthropology through their own work and through the stimulation they provided their students.

In the varied literature referred to as urban anthropology, there are several clusters of studies. One such cluster is labelled "peasants in the city." As a result of massive urban migration throughout the world, many people formerly studied by anthropologists moved to cities, and the anthropologists moved with them. Most of the studies that resulted emphasized the strategies used by migrants to adapt to city life.

Another cluster of urban anthropological studies focuses upon the "problems" of urban life, such as poverty, deviance, minority-majority group relations, and institutional failures (education, health services, law enforcement). Many of these studies are concerned with developing policies to solve or ameliorate the problem. It should be noted that British urban anthropology has not been particularly concerned with urban problems.

A third cluster of studies, primarily pursued in traditional non-western cities, attempts to look at the total entity of a particular city. Other anthropologists have taken the traditional areas of anthropological research (kinship, religion, socialization) and transposed them to an urban setting.

Obviously these varieties of urban anthropological literature present a rather bewildering image of the subfield. Some anthropologists doubt its legitimacy and suggest that we discard it entirely. Others suggest that it is like an infant: the basic features are there, but what it will look like as a mature adult is difficult to predict. All we can do is wait and see.

2

The Meaning of Urban
in Urban Studies and
Urban Anthropology

In the previous chapter we described some of the basic concerns and approaches of cultural anthropology and documented the historical development of the subfield of urban anthropology. Since the use of the concept *urban* is central to this endeavor, it would appear to be essential at this point to indicate the variety of ways in which urban anthropologists and others have used the term. After discussing this variation in usage, we devote some time to the various definitions and meanings of the term *urban* itself.

The word urban is used in three distinct ways in the label *urban anthropology*, frequently without an explicit recognition of the differences. This serves merely to muddy the waters where clarity is essential. One vital distinction appears to be between those to whom urban means *the locus or setting within which the study is pursued* (anthropology *in* the city), and those to whom the *urban itself is the prime focus of study* (anthropolgy *of* the city). Another difference is between the use of urban to refer to the study in or of *towns and cities*, that is, a particular type of settlement, as opposed to the much more diffuse meaning of the study of modern urban industrial social systems. In the latter case, the word urban is not really relevant, because a particular kind of settlement is not involved. Thus, urban anthropology is used loosely to mean 1) the study of contemporary, complex society, 2) anthropology *in* the city and 3) anthropology *of* the city.

ANTHROPOLOGY IN THE CITY

Anthropology in the city is the study of various aspects of life in which the city is merely the location or context of the activity, but is not, in itself, the focus of research. Obviously, the urban context has decided consequences for the particular aspect of life being studied, but it receives only minor attention as a factor influencing the aspect of life being studied or as an entity being influenced by the aspect of life.

Most of the literature labelled urban anthropology has been anthropology *in* the city. If we review the categories we used in Chapter 1, we can see the validity of this statement. Many of the peasants in cities studies can be viewed as focusing on the problems of newcomers shifting from one community to another. Only if the unique physical, demographic, and ecological characteristics of the city receive primary emphasis, or if the effects of migrants on the city as an entity are explored, can these studies be viewed as anthropology *of* the city.

A similar statement can be made about the problem-centered approach. Poverty and racism are problems of the larger society rather than the urban settlement. They become urban issues only if their relationship to urban social structure is addressed. Analytically oriented studies were defined in Chapter 1 as those focused on the traditional theoretical concerns of anthropology brought into the urban setting; therefore, they are largely anthropology *in* the city. Studies of kinship are more concerned with kinship theory than with urban theory.

Perhaps the best example of anthropology *in* the city is that body of literature that emphasizes the cognitive categories of groups and quasi-groups in the city. In these studies one is given the insider's view of the social milieu in which his life is played out.[1] Spradley calls this

---

[1] For example, see James Spradley, "Adaptive Strategies of Urban Nomads: The Ethnoscience of Tramp Cultures," in T. Weaver and D. White (eds.), *The Anthropology of Urban Environments*, Society for Applied Anthropology Monographs, 1972, pp. 21-38; and Jennifer James, "Sweet Cream Ladies: An Introduction to Prostitute Taxonomy," *Western Canadian Journal of Anthropology*, 3 (1972), 102-118.

type of study urban anthropology because cultural pluralism and complexity are inherent in city life. However, the unique features of urban life affect the groups being studied and the effects of these groups on the city appear to be a minor part of these studies. These are truly instances where the city serves merely as a laboratory for the observation of human behavior. This laboratory is not viewed as inherently different from others, but is increasingly characteristic of where people live at the present time. This kind of urban anthropology is an extension of the traditional study of people in their infinite variety.

URBAN INDUSTRIAL SOCIETY

To many, the term *urban anthropology* is interchangeable with *the anthropology of complex society* or *contemporary society*. Labeling the study of modern social systems as urban anthropology is a continuing source of confusion. It is generally recognized that the Industrial Revolution had a significant impact upon most areas of life in those societies where production is dominated by industrial techniques and organization. Aspects of life such as communication, transportation, diffusion of literacy, and medical practices have been revolutionized by changes in technology.

Perhaps the most significant change has taken place in relation to the *monetization* (use of money in almost all transactions) of all aspects of life and the growing emphasis upon commercialization. The sugar cane producer in Puerto Rico, the coffee grower in Colombia, the cotton grower in Egypt—all have become part of a cash economy and are affected by the world-wide market system. They are part of the modernization process, although they remain basically rural in residence and remain in agricultural occupations. The study of the impact of this socioeconomic process is a very important part of modern anthropology, but it is not coincident with anthropology *in* cities or anthropology *of* cities. In many ways this is the least precise use of the urban anthropology label.

The study of a particular settlement pattern (the city) is not identical to the study of urban industrial social systems. But as the city or metropolitan region becomes the dominant locus of settlement for this type of society, the distinction becomes less important; however, the distinction must be maintained as long as urban centers retain their unique characteristics.

The confusion between *urban anthropology* on the one hand and the study of *complex society* (or urban industrial society) on the other hand, is endemic in the field. Urban anthropology is logically a subspecialty of the study of complex society. If focuses intensively on the city as an institution within larger national and international social systems. Some ask if it is a necessary subspecialty or whether it is too narrowly defined. The major justification of the specialization in urban anthropology is the existence of the growing field of urban studies specializing in the city as an institution. In order for anthropology to communicate with and contribute to urban studies, a specialized urban anthropology within the larger study of complex societies is essential.

ANTHROPOLOGY OF CITIES

Since the anthropology *of* cities is the only aspect of urban anthropology that emphasizes the urban *context* as a major variable influencing life, it would seem to us that this area of research activity is central to urban anthropology and the development of new research strategies. In addition, it is that part of urban anthropology that is directly linked to urban studies.

For those concerned with anthropology *of* the city, a series of questions about the nature of cities themselves needs to be asked. What is unique about the city in contrast to other settlements? In what ways does the city as an institution influence behavior and beliefs? How does the relationship between groups and quasigroups in the city influence the urban center? To what extent can we develop a typology of cities in order to determine those characteristics that account for differentiation?

Goals of Urban Anthropology

Arensberg defines the goal of the subfield as the comparative study of cities in order to portray the range of variation of the urban center as an institution. Gulick remarks that only those studies that contribute to our understanding of the complex urban environment are urban anthropology. British urban anthropologists, emphasizing the uniqueness of urban social institutions, have also called for a primary focus on the urban. Leeds and Fox are even more emphatic in stating that the urban must be the primary focus of study in a meaningful urban anthropology.[2]

[2] Conrad Arensberg, "The Urban in Crosscultural Perspective," in E. Eddy (ed.), *Urban Anthropology* (Athens, Georgia: University of Georgia Press, 1968); John Gulick, "The Outlook, Research Strategies, and Relevance of Urban Anthropology: A Commentary," in E. Eddy (ed.), *Urban Anthropology*, pp. 93-98; J. Clyde Mitchell, "Theoretical Orientations in African Urban Studies," in M. Banton (ed.), *The Social Anthropology of Complex Societies* (New York: Frederick A. Praeger, Publishers, 1966), pp. 37-68; A. Leeds, "The Anthropology of Cities: Some Methodological Issues," in E. Eddy (ed.), *Urban Anthropology*, pp. 31-47; and Richard Fox, "Rationale and Romance in Urban Anthropology," *Urban Anthropology*, 1 (1972), 205-33.

Those who concentrate upon the study of the city itself as the *focus* of study have developed several basic approaches. One such approach is to accept certain distinctive attributes of urban settlement as given—scale, density of population, social, cultural, and economic heterogeneity, spatial segregation—and then study the impact of these characteristics upon other aspects of life, such as social relationships, cohesion, social interaction, social mobility, and adaptation. In other words, the predefined nature of the urban is assumed and is not itself under investigation.

Mitchell, in his classic article, "Theoretical Orientations in African Urban Studies," outlines what he considers to be the significant aspects of the urban: density of settlement, mobility, heterogeneity, demographic disproportion (in terms of sex and age), economic differentiation, and the constraints imposed by municipal administrations. He then urges the study of the effect of these features.[3] An example of a study specifically focusing on responses to density and crowding can be found in Anderson's work on Chinese responses to crowded housing situations.[4]

Another approach is to use the method of controlled comparison, in which behavior and structure in cities and rural areas are systematically compared and contrasted in order to isolate distinctively urban characteristics and effects. Even in this approach, however, some a priori notions of what makes a city different must be assumed before the comparison can be made.[5]

Still another approach in which the city is a central focus views the urban centers as dependent variables. Thus the city is seen to be the result of particular historical or contemporary economic, social, political, and cultural forces that form a unique urban context. Within this approach, there are several trends. The first is a search for the characteristics of a highly abstract universal concept of The City. When Arensberg suggested that a basic goal of urban anthropology is the comparative study of the city to obtain a range of variability and establish typologies of the urban, he exemplified this direction of interest. A number of anthropologists have blamed the failure to empirically develop such an understanding of the nature of the urban on the fact that the range of urban centers studied in depth has been limited almost exclusively to

[3] Mitchell, "Theoretical Orientations."
[4] E. N. Anderson, Jr., "Some Chinese Methods of Dealing with Crowding," *Urban Anthropology*, 1 (1972), 141-50.
[5] Examples of this type of work are: Ronald Provencher, "Comparisons of Social Interaction Styles: Urban and Rural Malay Culture," in T. Weaver and D. White (eds.), *The Anthropology of Urban Environments*, pp. 69-76; E. A. Hammel, "The Family Cycle in a Coastal Peruvian Slum and Village," *American Anthropologist*, 63 (1961), 346-54; and W. Mangin, "Similarities and Differences Between Two Types of Peruvian Communities," in W. Mangin (ed.), *Peasants in Cities* (Boston: Houghton Mifflin, 1970), pp. 20-29.

Western cities. Thus they do not accept a priori assumptions about the nature of cities used in the above approaches. What they want is a much more comparative approach than has been evident up to the present time.

Others feel that to understand The City as an abstract universal institution is not a useful goal. They would prefer to focus on cities in different culture areas of the world, stressing the differences in cultural traditions, resources, and historical processes. By thoroughly investigating small groups of cities closely related in time, space, and culture, they hope to ultimately understand the city in general.

A further development of this line of thought is the suggestion that, even within a single cultural setting or nation-state, urban centers have important differences that influence the behavior of their inhabitants. The nature of a particular city, rather than The City as a universal institution, or cities typed according to region, is the concern of this research. The particular city is viewed as a product of interactions between its component parts and/or interaction with external forces.

Leeds compares the Brazilian cities of Rio de Janeiro and Sao Paulo on the effects of differences in economic and administrative functions on the general contours of the city; these, in turn, affect the "man in the street" by making the labor force and local neighborhoods different. Rollwagen shows how demographic variables such as rate of growth, percentage of immigrants, and regional location produce differences in Mexican cities. Price compares the history, geography, and political/economic ties of two Mexican border towns (Tijuana and Tecate) in order to explain differences in their ways of life. A slightly different approach is taken by Nagata, who sees the historical development (particularly in relation to colonial rule) as a major factor influencing the nature of ethnic groups in two Malaysian cities. Fox and Estellie Smith have each compared aspects of two American cities and explained the differences in terms of each city's history.[6]

THE "URBAN" IN SOCIAL SCIENCE

A basic problem in the use of the word *urban* in social science is the lack of a clearcut and generally accepted definition. As we have just indicated, many of those engaged in the anthropology *of* cities see this definition as the end goal of research, not the beginning point.

[6] Leeds, "The Anthropology of Cities"; Jack Rollwagen, "A Comparative Framework for the Investigation of the City-as-Context: A Discussion of the Mexican Case," *Urban Anthropology*, 1 (1972), 68-86; John Price, *Tijuana: Urbanization in a Border Culture* (Notre Dame: University of Notre Dame Press, 1973); Judith Nagata, "A Tale of Two Cities: Life in Two Malaysian Towns," *Urban Anthropology*, 3 (1974), 1-26; Fox, "Rationale and Romance"; and M. Estellie Smith, "A Tale of Two Cities: The Reality of Historical Differences," *Urban Anthropology*, 4 (1975), 61-72.

Problems of Definition

The twentieth century has seen a frustrating attempt at defining the urban. It is even a difficult task for the archeologist dealing with the dawn of cities, as typified by a meeting on early urbanism described by Ruth Tringham:

> One result of the meeting expressed in the papers presented here, was that it became clearly impossible to agree on a definition of "urban." In the same way it was impossible to trace the early stages in the "urbanizing process," i.e. to define the point at which a non-urban settlement became urban.[7]

Definition by Form and Function

One method of distinguishing between the various definitions of the urban that have been offered is to classify them as to *form* and *function*. The category based upon form would include all those definitions that emphasize the internal structure of the urban center, such as population characteristics (size, density, heterogeneity) and/or geographic settlement patterns (distribution of activities and residences, variations in land use, and architectural forms). As opposed to these definitions, the category based upon function would include the particular roles urban centers perform (economic, political, symbolic), identified according to internal characteristics and the dynamic interaction between the urban center and its immediate hinterland or larger political/economic matrix.

Probably the best known attempt at definining the urban, as well as the lifestyle associated with it, in terms of form is presented by Louis Wirth in "Urbanism as a Way of Life." This article, which first appeared in 1938, defined the urban in terms of its internal demographic characteristics rather than its functions. Wirth says:

> . . . for sociological purposes, a city may be defined as a relatively large, dense and permanent settlement of socially heterogeneous individuals.[8]

Although there were many criticisms of this article during succeeding decades, most were related to Wirth's discussion of urban life rather

[7] Ruth Tringham, "Introduction," in Ruth Tringham (ed.), *Urban Settlements* (Andover, Mass.: Warner Module, 1973), pp. 1-2.
[8] Louis Wirth, "Urbanism as a Way of Life," *American Journal of Sociology*, 44 (1938), 1-24.

than to his definition of the city. The internal characteristics that were central to Wirth's definition are still subscribed to by many social scientists. Mitchell's inventory of the demographic prerequisites of the city is similar to Wirth's definition.[9]

The classic work of the German geographer Christaller on central place theory is an example of the functional approach.[10] Christaller views urban centers in terms of their function as economic central places serving their surrounding areas. Most geographers as well as many economists and political scientists have continued to use the concept of the city as a center of both economic and political dominance as a defining characteristic of the urban. Although this view developed as a way to *explain* the existence of cities, many social scientists explicitly or implicitly define the essence of "urbanness" in these terms.

An example of this type is Miner, who defines cities as "centers of dominance." To Miner, the role of the city as a power phenomenon is its essential quality. Logic ". . . draws political and economic power together in the city. . ." This view is echoed by Wheatley, when he refers to cities as "nodes of this order of dominance" that have "progressively extended the scope and autonomy of their institutional spheres." He points out that such "clusters of institutions" take a great variety of forms, and that morphology (structure) is so variable that it is "virtually useless for classification or analytical . . . purposes. Any regularities in the 'urban' . . . will be manifested in shared functions and in trends in systemic change rather than in form." Uzzell and Provencher also look at cities in this way, as efficient points for the exchange of goods, services, and ideas.[11]

From our perspective, the functions of urban centers in economic, political, and cultural dominance are primary characteristics of the city. Its form is the result of function. Different functions and a different hierarchy of functions lead to different forms.

A major concern of those analyzing contemporary urban forms or cities is the question of the *viability* of forms that currently exist. Based upon the conceptual framework developed here, we suggest that this issue can be clarified only if the relation between function and form is made explicit. Thus, the functions that gave rise to cities in the first

[9] Mitchell, "Theoretical Orientations."
[10] Walter Christaller, *Die Zentralen Orte in Süddeutschland* (Jena, Germany: Gustav Fischer Verlag, 1933), translated by C. W. Baskin and published by Prentice-Hall in 1966.
[11] Horace Miner, "Introduction," in H. Miner (ed.), *The City in Modern Africa* (New York: Frederick A. Praeger, Publishers, 1967), pp. 5-10; P. Wheatley, "The Concept of Urbanism," in Ruth Tringham (ed.), *Urban Settlements*, R-12, pp. 1-37; J. Douglas Uzzell and R. Provencher, *Urban Anthropology* (Dubuque, Iowa: Wm. C. Brown, 1976).

instance and to cities as they now exist have not changed. However, technology has led to a difference between the internal characteristics of preindustrial cities, early industrial cities, and contemporary cities. Today, technological change is occurring at such a rapid rate that the necessity of *central places* to perform such functions may no longer exist. Our cities, as forms, may be artifacts of historical development, and may very well disappear. Specifically, revolutionary changes in transportation and communication allow the dispersal of economic and political functions and activities well beyond the limits of urban places as demographically, spatially, and architecturally defined.

From the perspective developed in this volume, the functional aspects of the urban area are of greater significance than the formal ones. In the next chapter, we shall develop the theme of the functions, or roles, of cities in considerable detail. At this point, we must recognize that many of the social consequences of urban settlements are directly derived from their formal attributes, and therefore form must be considered.

General Contours of the Urban Form

Those who define cities in terms of form appear to use three main attributes: size, morphology, and social complexity. Most census definitions of urban as opposed to rural places are based upon simple population size. Thus, when Kingsley Davis writes about the urbanization of the world's population, he uses cities of a certain size (100,000 or more) as a basic indicator of this process, reflecting the belief that size alone can be diagnostic.[12] The United Nations has encouraged the international intellectual community to use a standardized measure of 20,000 to distinguish between rural and urban places. A basic reason for the widespread use of size as *the* defining characteristic of the urban is that it is the easiest, most available criterion that can be used.

Many recognize that size alone does not define a city. In fact, some census definitions concentrate on function rather than form. In these cases, small population centers that are neither dense nor socially complex are classified as urban because they serve as police or court headquarters (India) or county seats (Latin America), all defined as *urban* functions. Size and function are by no means independent of each other. Although size is related to the number of functions a city performs or the hierarchical rank of its functions, these are not related in a simple or direct way.

For demographers, size is not only a convenient defining attribute of the urban, it is the essence of the city, producing all significant urban

12 Kingsley Davis, "The Urbanization of the Human Population," *Scientific American*, 1965, pp. 41-53.

consequences. In contrast, many anthropologists look at other aspects of form as the essential ones. For some it is the particular morphology that defines the city. This is particularly so for the archeologist, whose primary source of data is the physical remains of urban life. On the other hand, cultural anthropologists focus primarily upon the social complexity and cultural heterogeneity of urban areas as the definitive characteristic.

To illustrate some of the emphases and relationships between formal criteria, we shall discuss them in several contexts that retain the historical and cross-cultural emphases:

1. the distinction between the pre-urban and the urban
2. the distinction between cities and rural areas in preindustrial state systems
3. the distinction between cities and non-cities in urban industrial society.

Urban versus Pre-urban

While we defer a discussion of the origins of the city to the next chapter, we would like here to pinpoint those aspects of cities that are regarded as unique to urban communities and are not characteristic of settlements in social systems without cities. Many of these characteristics occur singly in pre-urban (tribal) systems, but not in sufficient combination to make them cities. For example, while monumental temple architecture occurs in pre-urban societies (for example the Chibcha and Tairona cultures of Colombia), these sites do not have a sufficient number of other characteristics.

Certain specialized architectural forms relating to urban function and to large size and density occur only in the city and are neither necessary or possible elsewhere. Different land use patterns produce functional zones based upon the specialization of economic activity. For example, markets are found in specially designated spatial areas. In pre-urban societies, mercantile activities are frequently dispersed throughout the residential and public space of the village. In cities, government and judicial functions take place in specialized palace zones, while in simple communities, judicial events occur in multi-purpose public zones. The central area of the city is the most elaborated zone, with a concentration of population, buildings, and activities.

Even archeologists dealing with the origin of cities have difficulty defining the critical attributes of morphology. Sanders and Price insist that true cities must have a well-defined core focus and a recognizable boundary (not necessarily a wall) that separates the community from its surrounding area.[13] Thus they exclude some Mayan temple centers from their definition because the focus is not well-defined, there is continuous, even density throughout the area, and the unit lacks a significant boundary. Other archeologists disagree with these specific criteria.

Social Complexity and Cultural Heterogeneity

A distinctive attribute of urban settlement is its social complexity. Pre-urban social systems are characterized by little or no full-time occupational specialization. Almost everyone is a full-time food producer. Cities contain a large *number* of permanent resident non-food producers and a wide *variety* of types of occupational specialization. As Trigger has pointed out, however, many cities still contain large numbers of full-time farmers. Sometimes these comprise a majority of the population, so that a particular proportion of non-food producers cannot be specified as a defining attribute.[14]

An interesting case in point that illustrates some of the difficulties in defining the urban is that of the Yoruba, a West African group. For about two decades, anthropologists have argued this issue. As Lloyd points out:

> Two criteria are most commonly used to define an urban area. First, the size of the settlement, whether one takes census definitions of 2,000 or 5,000 or a more realistic figure of 20,000 . . . it is clear that many Yoruba settlements will fall within the category. If, on the other hand, one defines an urban settlement as one with less than half of its adult male working population engaged in farming, one excludes most, if not all, Yoruba towns.[15]

It is unfortunate that so much of the discussion of Yoruba towns has emphasized formal criteria, such as size and occupational specialization, rather than functional criteria. The market and trade functions of the towns were fundamental and would lead to easy acceptance of them as urban centers when this functional feature is combined with their size and density. There is, as Lloyd points out, considerable specialization within argricultural production. Many diverse items enter the

[13] William Sanders and Barbara Price, *Mesoamerica* (New York: Random House, 1968).
[14] Bruce Trigger, "Determinants of Urban Growth in Preindustrial Societies," in P. J. Ucko, R. Tringham, and G. Dimbley (eds.), *Man, Settlement and Urbanism* (London: Duckworth, 1972), pp. 575-96.
[15] P. C. Lloyd, "The Yoruba: An Urban People?" in A. Southall (ed.), *Urban Anthropology* (London: Oxford University Press, 1973), pp. 107-24.

town market systems, either directly or indirectly, from rural markets to urban wholesale markets. Much of the trade activity is in the hands of women, so that males are overrepresented in agriculture. In addition, there is some craft specialization in the towns, particularly in textiles and metal work, although Lloyd points out that the technological level is quite simple.

Since occupational groups develop differences in daily activity and differences in lifestyle, considerable cultural diversity results directly from the division of labor. Another source of cultural heterogeneity is that the city, unlike the community in pre-urban systems, is both the beginning and the end point in the continuous movement of large numbers of people. In pre-urban systems, the only types of mobility were the patterned nomadism of small bands related to hunting and gathering, or the creation of new communities through a fissioning or budding-off process. These movements rarely led to the permanent co-residence of culturally diverse populations. In drawing from a vast hinterland characterized by regional diversity in modes of dress, food, and language, all cities contain groups from different cultures of origin.

The city must, in some way, accommodate these diverse elements and integrate them into a viable functioning entity. In contrast, most pre-urban communities have relatively little need for such accommodation. While diverse ethnic or cultural groups occasionally live in contiguous areas, it is only in the commonly shared regions that such accommodation exists. Sometimes the groups may amalgamate for limited war or trade purposes, but full-scale accommodation based upon daily, permanent interaction is not that significant. In other areas, two groups may be in contact, but one is politically and/or economically dominant, and the process of accommodation has been worked out through dominance/subordination.

The Preindustrial City
in Traditional Agrarian Societies

One of the ways to approach the problem of definition is to look historically at the city as opposed to the village in preindustrial systems. In using the concept of the preindustrial social system (in contrast to the modern), we are comparing two highly abstract polar opposite ideals. The validity of this simple dichotomy has been challenged by many. However, we will use these types as a framework to pinpoint some of the essential characteristics of urban centers.

In preindustrial or agrarian societies, the city stands out as a unique *form* of settlement. Cities are frequently bounded (walled) units; when one reaches the outskirts of the urban settlement, a sharp contrast in house type, density, and other physical attributes can be observed. Multi-storied buildings, a continuous use of available land for building, a pattern of segregated land use functions, with the center of the settlement usually the locus of major economic, political, and religious activities, and monumental architecture are distinguishing characteristics of the city.

If one can derive a "pure" model of the traditional city, it had three major *functions:* political/administrative, economic, and cultural/symbolic. All three of these functions drew upon and served a diverse and large hinterland. In any large-scale peasant society, significant regional differences based on ecological and historical conditions exist. In the peasant village there was homogeneity in language, dress, housing, and ritual, but when diverse regions fed into the city, the migrants were brought into sustained contact with people with significant cultural differences. In the city, these various culturally distinct groups had to develop techniques to maintain some degree of relationship with each other as well as with the political elites who governed.

The functions of the city also created the division of labor that led to the proliferation of non-agricultural occupational groups such as the ruling elite, the bureaucratic clerks who carried out the instructions of the elite, the mercantile population who coordinated economic exchanges, and the specialized artisans who manufactured and sold goods. In addition to these, there were also farmers, generalized laborers, and underclass elements (beggars, street entertainers, thieves, prostitutes). While some occupational specialization occurred in the village, it was rarely of a full-time nature nor at a significant level.

One of the consequences of social complexity and cultural pluralism in urban areas is the greater choice or freedom accorded the individual in the selection of appropriate roles and behavior. The city was more open in its social system than the village. However, the preindustrial city was still a relatively closed system, when compared to its modern counterpart. Most statuses, particularly economic, community, and ethnic identities, were passed down from generation to generation, even in the city, and people were organized into localized corporate groups that maintained strong social control and discouraged interaction with others. Newcomers were often forced to enter marginal or illicit groups. Occupational groups were often *endogamous* (married only within their own group), based on common ethnic origins, and located in a single neighborhood in the city. This led to relatively isolated enclaves with overlapping sets of social ties, such as work relationships, neighbor relationships and kin relationships. There was little social mobility.

Changing Contours
in Urban-Industrial Societies

The urban characteristics of the city in traditional peasant societies seem to be clear and unquestionable by contrast to their rural hinterlands. However, when we shift to the city in urban-industrial societies, the attributes of the city are by no means as clearly distinct from the non-city.

By an urban-industrial society we mean one in which the residential locus of the majority of the population is in cities or in metropolitan areas that have cities as cores. Such a society is based upon an economic system characterized by industrial production. The boundaries between the city and its hinterland are not readily observable, either in the physical sense (density changes, house types, architecture) or the social sense (economic and cultural heterogeneity). With the exception of certain isolated areas, many of the characteristics noted above—unique location of manufacturing and non-farming activities, cultural pluralism—are found *throughout* the entire system and not merely within the urban settlement.

The difficulty of distinguishing between urban and rural areas is apparent in the shifting definition of these areas in the United States. With the post-World War II expansion of suburban or outer ring developments, the definition of major urban centers as a census category was shifted from the city to the metropolitan area, or *SMSA* (*Standard Metropolitan Statistical Area*). This definition (which includes all cities of 50,000 or more plus any adjoining counties functionally related to the city) has in turn been supplanted by the more recent concept of the *megalopolis*—a linkage of such areas. For the eastern seaboard of the United States, the concept of the megalopolis includes the entire region from Boston in the north to Washington, D.C. and its environs in the south. A parallel phenomenon is found on the West Coast running continuously from San Francisco to San Diego. In these areas, we find no breaks in the pattern of high density, urban housing, cultural pluralism, monumental architecture, and predominantly non-agricultural activities. What appears to be happening in the United States and other areas of the world is an extension of presumably urban characteristics to most of the land areas and populations in these systems.

While urban functions and form coexisted in preindustrial cities, some of the functions and many of the formal attributes resulting from them no longer coexist today, because modern technology allows functions to be performed without the same consequences in form. What has happened in the United States recently is that these central place functions and their morphological and demographic attributes have become increasingly dispersed and are found outside the traditional political and architectural units called *the city*. Thus, manufacturing, retailing, banking, and insurance enterprises have come to be located outside the city, with the accompanying urban social complexity. The variety of role relationships now occurs away from cities, but the physical characteristics of the area have not shifted to the same degree although, presumably, these characteristics too will follow and be modified by changing technology.

The classic distinction between the urban and the rural in traditional agrarian societies—contrasting the heterogeneity of the former with the homogeneity of the latter—begins to lose its relevance in an urban industrial society. Many of the traditional functions associated with the city are no longer localized within the physical urban settlement, and consequently, the occupational and cultural heterogeneity they produced are no longer solely a phenomenon of the urban center. Suburban areas and other regions not necessarily contiguous with the city sometimes show as great a division of labor and ethnic heterogeneity as the city itself.

THE NATURE OF URBAN CENTERS AS OPPOSED TO THE BEHAVIORAL CONSEQUENCES OF URBAN CENTERS

One notion of the urban that is confusing in both popular imagery and social science usage is the distinction between an *urban center* and an *urban way of life*. In contrast to using urban to refer to a type of community, many use the word to refer to lifestyles considered unique to towns and cities. In doing this they implicitly confuse urban form and function with their behavioral consequences. Some particular areas of behavior that have been viewed as different in urban settings are: styles of social interaction, patterns of group affiliation, individual aspirations, lifestyles, and values. In addition, many aspects of social organization—particularly the nature of domestic units, family, and kinship, the nature of religious beliefs, and political participation—are often used as if they were definitional attributes of urban centers, rather than consequences of urban function and form.

It is absolutely essential in the ensuing discussion to keep the notion of urban settlements as defined by form and function separate from the alleged behavioral consequences of such settlement; that is, the urban center is distinct from the urban lifestyle or value system.

Some anthropologists have attempted to suggest some of the consequences of urban life, as, for example, Harris and Reina. Harris refers to an urban ethos as distinct from a rural one, and Reina describes what he considers to be a distinct urban world view.[16]

We have just distinguished between the function and form of urban centers and the consequent sociocultural concomitants. We shall refer to the former as *the urban*, the nature of which is the primary question in urban studies. The sociocultural consequences of the urban will be referred to as *urbanism*, following Wirth's classic use of urbanism to refer to a way of life. Wheatley reverses our usage in "The Concept of Urbanism," when he refers to "urbanism" as the nature of cities and uses "urban" to characterize a "distinctive manner of life." [17] However, the more widespread impact of the Wirth definition is the basic reason to use the terms the way we propose.

A third term frequently found in the urban literature is *urbanization*. This term will be used here to refer to a *process* that social systems undergo resulting in an increase in both the number of urban centers and the size of urban centers, through shifts in the locus of economic activities, political power, and population concentration.

Unfortunately, these distinctions between *urbanization, urbanism,* and the *urban* have not characterized the social science literature. For example, Beals, in 1951, used the term urbanization as a form of acculturation in which the population develops urban ways of life.[18] In the framework suggested above, this would be considered the spread or diffusion of urbanism, rather than urbanization (the spread of the urban). He further confounded the basic issue by using urbanism to describe the nature of urban forms, as Redfield had done. In our scheme, this would be the urban. When Kingsley Davis wrote his classic article on the "Urbanization of the World's Population," he used the term to refer to an attribute of a social system, but limited it to a demographic shift in population with no attention to functional attributes.[19] Obviously, writers who suggest that a rather widespread contemporary social process is the "urbanization" of rural areas (meaning the spread of urban lifestyles or urbanism to the countryside) are not using the term as we define it.

[16] Marvin Harris, *Town and Country in Brazil* (New York: Columbia University Press, 1956); and Ruben Reina, "The Urban World View of a Tropical Forest Community in the Absence of a City: Peten, Guatemala," *Human Organization*, 23 (1964), 265-77.
[17] Wheatley, "The Concept of Urbanism."
[18] Ralph Beals, "Urbanism, Urbanization and Acculturation," *American Anthropologist*, 53 (1951), 1-10.
[19] Davis, "The Urbanization of the World's Population."

The Confusion of Urban Consequences with Industrial Consequences

Archeologists concerned with the emergence of urban centers have sometimes confused attributes of state-organized social systems with the unique attributes of the cities located in these systems. Thus, Childe's famous ten criteria for defining the *Urban Revolution* really apply to defining the civilized state and not the city.[20]

The same problem is true of many recent attempts at defining cities, which confuse attributes of industrial states with attributes of urban settlements. This confusion is reflected in the confusion between urban anthropology and the anthropology of urban industrial society.

Since the time of Wirth's derivation of the urban way of life as the result of the characteristics of urban settlements (1938), there have been repeated attempts to define urban values, urban aspirations, urban social structure, and urban lifestyles. However, since most of these attempts, including Wirth's, have been based upon the knowledge of *modern* urban centers, they consistently confused the effect of industrial production and modern life with the effect of the nature of the city. Harris' description of the urban ethos mentioned above is an example of this confusion.[21]

Consequences of the Industrial Revolution

Many writers have attempted to draw out of the historical record those essential currents in the industrialization and modernization processes that transformed the nature of human existence and established the general nature of contemporary life. Among these we should note Durkheim, Weber, Polanyi, Parsons and Moore.[22]

There are certain aspects of a "modern" social system that are generally considered definitive. Among these we would include:

1. changes in technology that affect the production and distribution of goods, services, and ideas

[20] V. Gordon Childe, "The Urban Revolution," *Town Planning Review*, 21 (1950), 3-17.
[21] Harris, *Town and Country.*
[22] This theme is exemplified by Durkheim's distinction between mechanical and organic solidarity; Emile Durkheim, *The Division of Labor in Society*, trans. by G. Simpson (New York: The Macmillan Company, 1933). Weber focuses on this distinction in *The Protestant Ethic and the Spirit of Capitalism* (London: Allen and Unwin, 1930). Parson's pattern variables are focused on this distinction; *The Social System* (Glencoe, Ill.: The Free Press, 1951), as is K. Polanyi's *The Great Transformation* (Boston: Beacon Press, 1944), and the work of Wilbert Moore, *The Impact of Industry* (Englewood Cliffs, N.J.: Prentice-Hall, Inc., 1965).

2. a new value emphasis upon a person's ability to control the natural and social environment
3. a shift toward secularism
4. a belief in an open social system

The Industrial Revolution is one of those major events in human history that have had a marked impact upon all aspects of human culture. This series of events is primarily related to the mastery of new sources of non-human energy and the development of new modes of production that utilize these energy sources. This ultimately affects human ability to produce goods and services. The development of large-scale production units located in specific geographic sites was interrelated with the development of new modes of transportation and communication. Thus, the earliest development of steam engines was followed by the adaptation of this machine to both production and transport facilities. Within the developing factory system, hierarchies emerged to coordinate and control the larger process. Jobs became minutely specialized. Individuals lost their work autonomy in the larger unit. Work places and homes became separate in space. Mass merchandising and the complexity of commercial exchange, banking, and finance were linked to mass production. The use of money as a generalized medium of exchange for all economic, political, and social goods emerged. The telegraph, telephone, and new postal systems resulted from the process and generated a communication revolution in their own right.

Another important element in the modernization process is related to one's view of one's self, one's society, one's nature and the emphasis upon one's ability to control the environment and one's own destiny. There is a marked shift from a value system that stresses otherworldliness to one that stresses secularism, or a concern with this life. As Weber pointed out in his *Protestant Ethic and the Rise of Capitalism*, there was a shift toward an ethic stressing individual autonomy, achievement, and success.[23] Historically these shifts in belief occurred before the Industrial Revolution and contributed to industrialization, which in turn reinforced them. Today they are considered important in the belief system of modern society.

An additional core element of this value system is an open social system in which mobility from place to place and status to status occurs. Social and geographic mobility become essential in the allocation of manpower to create efficient modes of production. Individuals are viewed as separate and autonomous actors, as opposed to previous views,

[23] Weber, *The Protestant Ethic.*

which saw them as embedded in social groups and communities. The social mobility of individuals is emphasized, and one's position is viewed as a consequence of one's own actions, as contrasted with earlier dependence upon one's ascribed fate.

The *urban revolution,* or the emergence of urban centers, predated the development of modern industrial processes by several milennia. Therefore, many of the characteristics of what is referred to as *modernism* are unique to the modern era and not essential to urban centers or urban lifeways, although they are often discussed as if they were. On the other hand, some elements are essential to urban centers as well. Where the two processes coexist, they naturally reinforce one another and exacerbate the differences between life in modern urban centers and in other social contexts (non-urban modern or preindustrial urban).

Obviously money was an important medium of exchange in preindustrial urban places, since the very nature of an urban center required economic exchange between specialized economic sectors, which were usually based upon the use of some form of money. However, they were not quite as money-oriented and the use of money was not as pervasive as it is in modern cities and modern societies.

Insofar as cities always received population from outside their boundaries and had to incorporate them into the urban occupational structure, the city was often the *only* significant locus of geographic and social mobility, but mobility was still very limited.

Many social scientists consider *bureaucracy* to be a fundamental element in the modernization process. However, bureaucratic modes of organization (large in scale and hierarchical in structure) have been characteristic of most urban centers and thus predate the modern era. However, these were limited to administrative functions. Modern bureaucracies are further expanded, reinforced, and extended to the production and mercantile units in the modern industrial era.

The spatial separation of domestic units from arenas for economic, political, and social activity requires a greater consciousness of the allocation of time. Although work and residence were not as separated in space in preindustrial cities, they were to some degree, and people had to travel for market exchange, recreation, dealings with the political bureaucracy, and religious ceremonies. Dependence upon measured time would be more significant in the city than in the village, but not as significant as in urban industrial society.

Although industrial production and modern life are related to the entire concept of the urban, there are certain spheres in which the first two must be separated from the urban. Obviously, the process of urbanization is related to industrial growth. In addition, certain trends of urbanism are reinforced by the newer productive systems. Finally, the form and even the function of urban centers may be radically transformed by industrial production. Despite all this, it is still essential that we recognize that industrial production is not synonymous with urban existence.

Urbanization versus Industrial Capitalism

In many contemporary discussions of the "problems of our cities," there is considerable confusion between factors related to the urban center and those related to the nature of the productive process (that is, capitalist, industrial). This confusion leads to a situation where many of our economic and technological problems are included in discussions of "the urban crisis." [24]

Although cities have always been defined in terms of their economic functions, the nature of capitalist-industrial production subordinates the city to regional, national, and international economic forces such as multinational corporations, which are highly centralized and bureaucratized. The labor market is an integral part of such a macrostructural system. The boom and bust cycles of such systems and their consequences are influenced by factors beyond the control of the locality. As an example poverty, often assumed to be an urban problem, is primarily a result of the economic system and not the city. (See Chapter 8.) The acceleration of material consumption patterns, often referred to as "urban" lifestyles, are more related to the mass merchandising and stimulation of market demands characteristic of capitalistic industry than to residence in the city.

There has recently emerged a vast literature dealing with alienation and urban life. Although the Marxist orientation toward alienation clearly relates it to the industrial productive process, many today call it urban-related. In part, this confusion results from the assumption that the proliferation of role relationships and relationships with strangers brought about the breakdown in primary groups and produced alienation. As opposed to this view, we would suggest that alienation is more closely related to the subordination of the individual to political and economic forces beyond his control and certainly beyond his locality.

Smog and air pollution caused by factories and automobiles, pollution of bodies of water caused by industrial wastes, potential destruction of the ozone layer by jet exhausts and aerosol spray cans—all have as their source the technological innovations of the industrial revolution. Of

[24] Edward Banfield, *The Unheavenly City* (Boston: Little, Brown and Company, 1970).

course, these elements are combined, reinforced, and exacerbated by the population density found in urban centers, but they are not essentially "urban" problems. For example, automobiles in rural areas pollute the atmosphere to the same degree. However, the cumulative effect of the number of cars in an urban area produces a much more dangerous level. Noise also pollutes the environment. Much of what is classified as urban noise can be viewed as primarily machine-related rather than city-related. Even in outdoor recreation areas far from urban centers, the noise created by outboard motors, trail bikes, snowmobiles, power saws, and lawn mowers can be extremely disturbing and, in some cases, harmful.

Once we have clarified the distinction between modernization and urbanization, then much of what is considered to be the diffusion of urban lifestyles to the hinterland can more adequately be seen as the diffusion of modern ideas and values transmitted through industrial communications technology. It is often more appropriate to talk about the modernization of rural areas than about the spread of urbanism to the countryside. Furthermore, we must distinguish between a society that is becoming modernized (mass production, mass communication, monetization, bureaucratization) and one that is becoming urbanized (increasing urban form and function) since the two processes are not the same.

Some anthropologists also talk about the peasantization or "ruralization" of cities.[25] Once again, this is an illogical notion, unless people from the rural hinterland are recapitulating rural settlement patterns and agrarian activities in the city. Those who use this phrase for cities in developing areas suggest that high rates of migration lead to cities containing a majority of residents who were born and socialized in the countryside. It is then assumed that they perpetuate rural patterns and thus "de-urbanize" the city. Certainly when former peasants are located in ethnic and regional enclaves, some of the preexisting patterns of behavior and social relationships can be maintained, and certain marginal occupations in the city can relate to the economy in the same way as peasant agriculture.[26] However, those aspects of life closely related to the nature of urban centers do change. In addition, most migrants do not settle in enclaves and are integrated into heterogeneous settlement areas. As an example of this, we might note Mangin's analysis of squatter set-

[25] Many writings on squatter settlements deal with their residents as peasants. Such communities comprise large proportions of the urban population. Michael Whiteford calls the settlement he worked in "rurban" in its characteristics; "Neighbors at a Distance," in W. Cornelius and F. Trueblood (eds.), *Urbanization in Latin America*, vol. 4, 1974. Suzuki describes a group of Turkish migrants as almost totally maintaining rural lifeways; "Encounters with Istanbul: Urban Peasants and Village Peasants," *International Journal of Comparative Sociology*, 8 (1976), 208-15.
[26] T. G. McGee, "Peasants in the Cities: A Paradox, A Paradox, A Most Ingenious Paradox," *Human Organization*, 32 (1973), 135-42.

tlements in Lima, Peru.[27] Before the studies done by Mangin and his colleagues, it was assumed that squatter settlements were manifestations of communal rural lifestyles in the city. However, he clearly shows that these settlements are the result of urban residence and their organization follows urban, not rural, models. Leeds further elaborates this point.[28] If it can, in fact, be demonstrated that rural migrants do bring certain aspects of behavior and values to the city and maintain them there, then it would be more appropriate to refer to this as the *traditionalization* of the city as a parallel to the notion of the *modernization* of the rural area.

OTHER SOURCES OF CONFUSION

In the preceeding discussion, we attempted to discuss and clarify some of the confusions based upon an improper use of the concept *urban* and the lack of distinction between certain aspects of urbanization and modernization. However, there are some additional sources of confusion in the diverse usage of the term urban to which the reader must be sensitized.

Dichotomous versus Continuous Variables

Some social scientists have given up the attempt to define and distinguish between rural and urban. Instead, they have chosen attributes that measure *relative degrees of urbanness* rather than establish an absolute dichotomy. They feel that settlements can be relatively more or less urban than one another, and that the scientific goals of explaining cities and city life can best be served by emphasizing the continuous rather than the discrete nature of urban characteristics. In this approach, urban form—size, density, and morphology—predominates. However, some functional schemes describe continua based on the increase in number or level of functions.

The City Core versus the Urban

There is a tendency in popular belief to confuse the large-scale metropolis, or city, with the entire range of settlement types called urban. As long as this confusion remains, many studies will be disregarded be-

---

[27] William Mangin, "Latin American Squatter Settlements: A Problem and a Solution," *Latin American Research Review*, 2 (1967), 65-98.
[28] Anthony Leeds and Elizabeth Leeds, "Brazil and the Myth of Urban Rurality," in Arthur Fields (ed.), *City and Country in the Third World* (Cambridge: Schenkman Publishing Company, 1970), pp. 229-72.

cause their focus is a town (the smallest urban settlement) or a suburb in a metropolitan area, rather than the center of the large metropolis itself. Skyscrapers, cement, and inner city slums are the typical images evoked by the word urban, but these are relevant images for only a small part of the urban environment. There is a hierarchy of urban places, from town to provincial capital to metropolis, and *all* such settlements are urban.

Studies done by anthropologists in places like Washington, D.C., Seattle, Lagos, Sao Paulo, and Bangkok are considered to be the core of urban anthropology. However, studies conducted in smaller, less well-known urban centers like Gwelo, Southern Rhodesia, Popayán, Colombia, and the community studies done by Warner and his followers should also be recognized as part of the field.

The extension of the modern city beyond its politically defined geographic perimeter should refocus our attention on settlements that do not have the characteristics frequently associated with the urban core. Gans, in an article critical of Wirth, suggests that "suburbanism" is a way of life that shares many of the characteristics of Wirth's notion of urbanism.[29] This should not be surprising, since suburbs are functionally *part* of urban centers and *not* their non-urban hinterlands. The encroachment of the form and function of the urban center in the outlying areas is responsible for this effect. Such notions as the metropolitan community and the Standard Metropolitan Statistical Area are further steps in the recognition of the urban nature of suburbs, outer rings, and other such categories.

The Political City versus the Ecological City

The legal boundaries of cities as political administrative entities are frequently artifacts of historic forces that may no longer be significant. Today such boundaries may be artificial, arbitrary breaks in a continuous settlement pattern of a functioning social and economic unit, thus making legally defined city boundaries irrelevant for some research questions.

The study of migration is an example of a research focus that would be too narrowly defined if politically delineated urban centers, rather than their functioning metropolitan areas, were used. Since much of the migration of middle class Americans is from suburb to suburb or city to suburb, the unit to be considered in migration studies would have to be the total metropolitan context. In developing nations, rural migrants often live in settlements outside the historically derived boundaries of

[29] Herbert Gans, "Suburbanism and Urbanism as Ways of Life: A Reevaluation of Definitions," in A. Rose (ed.), *Human Behavior and Social Processes* (Boston: Houghton Mifflin Co., 1962).

the city and yet can be considered to have functionally moved *into* these urban centers in every sense but the political definition of their place of residence.

Basic Ethnocentrism of Urban Definitions

One of the basic errors that has consistently permeated social science literature dealing with the city is the Western ethnocentrism of many concepts dealing with the urban. The results of this bias are twofold. The first is the lack of a universal, culture-free definition of urban centers. The second is the imposition of an underlying anti-urban bias.

Due to the lack of comparative studies, both historical and contemporary, the social science of the urban accepts the contemporary Western city as the prototype and the modern industrial city as a norm. As we have noted, the contemporary Western city is embedded in a society based upon both industrial production and unique Western values. Even Weber made this error, in a sense, when he tried to compare the Western city to the Eastern city and overlooked the effects of the Industrial Revolution. As one commentator pointed out, Weber was really talking about *preindustrial* or *ancient* cities in contrast to *industrial* cities, and not *East* versus *West*.[30]

In addition, some anthropologists, particularly those working in India, have suggested that the similarities in structure and culture between rural and urban areas outweigh the differences between them, thus suggesting that the rural-urban dichotomy itself may be a Western concept, or only valid in the West.[31] Hauser has pointed out that the definition of the urban developed by the Chicago School (Wirth's urbanism and Redfield's folk-urban continuum), expresses a strong Western ethnocentrism.[32]

One technique for overcoming this bias is to follow the suggestion made by Mangin that a definition of cities be derived by asking urban social actors in various cities of the world what their perceptions of the city are.[33] It is doubtful that such a hodgepodge of ethnographically derived views would be very useful. However, this approach does point

[30] Vatro Murvar, "Some Tentative Modifications of Weber's Typology: Occidental versus Oriental City," *Social Forces*, 44 (1966), 381-89.
[31] D. F. Pocock, "Sociologies: Urban and Rural," *Contributions to Indian Sociology*, 4 (1960), 63-81; O. Lynch, "Rural Cities in India: Continuities and Discontinuities," in P. Mason (ed.), *India and Ceylon: Unity and Diversity* (London: Oxford University Press, 1967), pp. 142-58.
[32] Philip Hauser, "Application of the Ideal-Type Constructs to the Metropolis in the Economically Less Advanced Areas," in S. Fava (ed.), *Urbanism in World Perspective* (New York: Thomas Y. Crowell Co., 1968), pp. 93-97.
[33] Wm. Mangin, "Introduction," in Wm. Mangin (ed.), *Peasants in Cities*; and John Gulick, "The Outlook, Research Strategies and Relevance of Urban Anthropology."

out the difference between an insider's view and an outsider's view. Most definitions of urban centers have been developed by social scientists who are "insiders" in their relation to Western cities but "outsiders" in their relation to others. Attention to insiders' views of the nature of cities from residents of Lagos, Nigeria and Bangkok, Thailand might provide some insights, even if they did not serve to develop a universal definition. Thus, it remains for the social scientist to develop such a definition, based, hopefully, upon a comparative perspective and some measure of objectivity.

The second aspect of the ethnocentrism of much social science writing on urban life is the underlying anti-urban bias, or negative image of the city in the West. The converse of this view is the romanticized picture of rural, agrarian life rooted in the writings of Rousseau, Toennies, early Redfield, and others. In general, there seemed to be a vision of a Golden Age, when people were happy, genuine, and spontaneous but this was destroyed by the city, which is unnatural, artificial, and inherently evil. The writings of Judaeo-Christian biblical texts support this view as well. Many of the early members of what is referred to as the Chicago School saw the city as unnatural and artificial. Urban centers were viewed as a source of all kinds of social and personality disorganization and deviant behavior. Many of their studies focused upon rooming house residents, taxi dance hall girls, and relationships that were shallow, transient, and manipulative. Wirth's description of urbanism as a way of life incorporated these biases by deemphasizing primary relationships and groups (based on mutual trust and affect) and emphasizing instrumental, segmented ties.

A recent manifestation of this anti-urban bias can be seen in Banfield's *The Unheavenly City*.[34] Almost every problem of modern life, from unemployment and poverty to the failures of mass education and transportation, is laid at the door of the city.

There is no question that the city is a man-made environment, but to view it as an unnatural environment is inappropriate. There is no question that the city is a unique social environment, but to view it as pathological is unacceptable.

The suggestion that the urban center is unnatural and artificial is based upon an implicit assumption that certain community forms are natural and genuine. With the variety of communities that have developed in different social systems throughout the world, conclusions about the naturalness or genuineness of any particular pattern are impossible. A basic characteristic of human beings in all situations is that they de-

[34] Banfield, *The Unheavenly City*.

velop cultural responses to their settings. Culture, by its very definition, is learned and not natural, inborn, or innate.

We might note that the city was not viewed as negatively in other times and places as it is in present-day Western industrial societies. During the Middle Ages, cities were associated with choice and freedom. Serfs who escaped to the city and could remain there for a certain period of time were legally freed. During the Enlightenment, cities were centers of culture and knowledge. However, the coalescence of industrialization and urban growth during the Industrial Revolution led to the view of urban life as dehumanizing. This is reflected in romantic English literature in the poetry of Wordsworth and Blake.

The dual association of the city with social disorder and artificiality has permeated the popular as well as the academic view of city life. Thus when a news magazine, radio, or television news department produces an urban affairs segment, this usually means the reporting of crime, poverty, low-income housing and assorted miseries. The view of the city as unnatural can be demonstrated by a recent TV advertisement for Boy Scouting depicting a forlorn boy wandering through the city. The message states that this boy lives in a shoddy, non-genuine world: "His stars are neon lights. Instead of grass, he has cement." Boys are urged to join the Boy Scouts and engage in camping to spend time in the countryside, get away from the urban scene. Thus they will become more human.

Views of the city and city life have varied from the extremes of total denial of benefits to those which see the city as a source of all benefits. In different eras and for different segments of the population, attitudes toward the city have changed. Within a given society, certain aspects of city life have been viewed positively, while others have been viewed negatively.

For some segments of the upper middle class in America, especially those in occupations for which intellectual activities are important, the attractions of the urban have drawn many back to the old core cities. These attractions include cultural elements (art, music, museums, theater) as well as nearness to place of work. For some, the stimulation of the diversity of choice is an additional attraction. These people are rejuvenating formerly deteriorating urban cores. Their pro-urban bias often leads to negative stereotypes about suburban life.

An interesting example of a subculture with a strong allegiance to the city core is the artist community in New York City. Over the last two decades, many professional artists have moved into a downtown section known as Soho. As Drechsler points out, the physical amenities (abandoned factories and lofts) are particularly adaptable to artists' use, particularly those who work on large-scale productions. Many of the buildings are readily converted into combined studios and living quarters. The artists have organized into a community action group that successfully convinced the planning commission to establish this section of the city for the exclusive use of artists. Not only does the area provide a good physical environment, but the geographic segregation has enabled artists to develop closely knit social networks, which provide professional stimulation, exchange of innovations, and sociability. The commercial art world has responded to this movement by establishing galleries in the area.[35]

Another group that has continued its allegiance to the city is the working class. Although many working class suburbs have developed, large segments of the working class remain in the city. As Gans has pointed out, the attractions for this group include the geographic proximity of old social ties (friends and relatives, the peer group), access to major institutions (churches and parochial schools), availability of work, and a traditional allegiance to a particular area.[36]

A Case Study of Confusion

A recently published Sunday newspaper feature on a study ranking American cities on the basis of "quality of life" indices was titled "There Are No Good U.S. Cities, Only Less Bad." [37] We have selected this article and the responses to it as an illustration of many of the points we have been making in this section. We shall be quoting from two responses: one in the same paper the following week and one in *Philadelphia Magazine* later.[38] Since the original article was nationally syndicated, it probably received similar treatment elsewhere.

The title selected for the article and the subsequent discussion all point to a basic anti-urban bias. It is interesting to note that when the author discusses city features he assumes *everyone* would favor, the first to be mentioned is plentiful parklands. As one of the critics points out, many of the "good" criteria of cities cited are basically non-urban. Suggesting that lower density is a measure of the "goodness" of cities takes the essence of urbanness—from which much of the unique potential of

[35] Richard Drechsler, "Composition and Function of Artistic Social Circles: The Informal Network of Communication Among Artists In New York" (Honor Essay 26, Baruch College, April 15, 1975).

[36] Herbert Gans, *The Urban Villagers* (New York: Free Press, 1962).

[37] Arthur M. Louis, "There Are No Good U.S. Cities, Only Less Bad," *The Philadelphia Inquirer*, Sunday, December 22, 1974, pp. 1F and 4F.

[38] Thomas Hine, "On the Whole, I'd Rather Be in Good Old Philadelphia," *The Philadelphia Inquirer*, Sunday, January 5, 1975, p. 1F; and "Editorial," *Philadelphia Magazine*, February 1975, p. 1.

urban life derives—and defines it as bad. As one critic says, "High densities of peer playmates might seem more important to young children than a high density of *trees!*" In the article, the best city becomes the "least" city-like, because of an implicit belief that cities are inherently unfit for human habitation.

The second problem is that politically defined cities are used as the units to be evaluated, rather than the real functioning unit—the metropolitan area. Some cities that have recently incorporated surrounding suburbs (for example, Tulsa) are those whose legal boundaries do tend to coincide with ecological boundaries; these are "less bad" because the newly incorporated areas rank high in non-citylike criteria. Thus, urban units that have retained archaic political boundaries rank lower because essentially different kinds of units are being compared. The critic suggests that the metropolitan regions of older units would have ranked higher than the Tulsas and San Josés if like units were compared. In fact, the city ranked worst (Newark, New Jersey) is not really a functioning autonomous unit at all; it is a specialized depressed area within the New York metropolitan area and should have been considered as such.

Still another response to this article defends cities in general. In this case, the critic falls into the basic dilemma we mentioned before: he confuses the central core with the city in its entirety. All of the positive features of cities this critic lists are characteristic only of city cores. While it is true that certain core segments of many older urban centers are becoming symbolically and physically rejuvenated, there is some question about using such small rejuvenated areas to typify the general nature of cities.

URBAN ANTHROPOLOGY AND URBAN STUDIES

We have previously noted the growth in programs of urban studies. To a very large extent, this is a result of the increasing proportion of population coming into cities in the developing areas of the world. In the developed world, urban growth is manifested in the extension of urban physical and social features beyond the city to the metropolitan area.

For social scientists, urban studies provides one of the most exciting grounds for a true interdisciplinary approach to society and behavior. For many years, lip service has been paid to the notion of interdisciplinary research efforts; however, this goal has not been realized. In urban studies, interdisciplinary research and explanation would seem to be a natural outcome. The urban geographer, historian, sociologist, political scientist, or economist, as well as the anthropologist can learn from one another and work towards systematic analysis of urban life. Each of these several fields has developed its own theories, viewpoints, emphases, methodologies, and techniques for data collection. By fusing these various approaches, we can begin to develop a truly integrated approach to the study of the city as an independent force.

Several alternative approaches leading to the goal of an interdisciplinary understanding of the city can be suggested. Some of these alternatives are directly related to *research*, while others focus primarily on *training* individuals who will have an interdisciplinary perspective. However, the dichotomy between teaching and research is more a matter of emphasis than mutual exclusiveness. An underlying assumption in higher education is that teaching and research are mutually reinforcing and lead to the acquisition of greater insights into the phenomenon being studied.

One research approach brings together a group (team) to develop the total research design. Disciplines included might be history, geography, psychology, economics, political science, sociology, and anthropology. Theoretical issues derived from all of these disciplines would be incorporated into a single integrated research design that focuses upon the urban scene. In addition, each of these disciplines has data collection techniques that would be integrated into the design. Although the units of analysis of these various disciplines have been traditionally distinct, the integration of these units would lead to a much larger frame of reference.

An Example of Interdisciplinary Research

Perhaps the best way of illustrating this approach is to use an example of ongoing research in which one of the authors has been involved. It will be apparent that, although the research had the potential of drawing upon various social science disciplines, in reality, only two disciplines were actively involved.

The focus of the research was an assessment of the techniques and degree to which identity, cohesiveness, and boundaries are affected by different features of the urban environment. This research focus was of potential interest to the historian, geographer, political scientist, sociologist, and anthropologist. The group selected for study were Italian-Americans in a particular geographic section of the city of Philadelphia. The design of the research involved geographers and anthropologists. The geographers were primarily concerned with how space, proximity, and intra-community movement patterns contributed to neighborhood boundaries. The anthropologists looked primarily at the effect of common cultural beliefs and kinship relationships on ethnic boundaries.

It seems obvious that historians who might have been involved in the planning of research would have focused upon the historic records of the community—newspapers, parish records, real estate transactions, and wills—as basic sources of information about the past. Their particular time perspective could have broadened the research to include a longer range view of changes in the nature of identity and boundary maintenance. Political scientists, with their particular focus upon power relationships, government, voting, and community organization, would have made other valuable contributions to the larger research effort.

In the actual research design, an area of mutual interest to the anthropologists and geographers involved was singled out; this was the area of foodways. The geographers contributed to the research design and techniques (surveys, scheduled interviews) by focusing their attention on the circulation of people and foodstuffs in the neighborhood, that is, the location of stores and restaurants and the shopping and eating out patterns of the population. The anthropologists looked at how ethnic cultural beliefs affected the selection of food for dietary patterns and how kinship affected eating patterns. Historians could have provided information about patterns in an earlier period of the century and provided comparative historical information from sources describing similar patterns in Italy, showing the persistence of particular food patterns. Economists could have shown how market forces, changes in food production, and wholesaling and retailing practices affected the actual food available. In other words, they could have provided tools to analyze the regional network of food production and distribution that sets the limits of what is available in the local area.

In the actual study, the data collected related to the interests of both the anthropologists and geographers. Research interests were jointly developed, and instruments and fieldwork were integrated. The same could have been true if more disciplines were involved. (In this case, with three anthropologists and two geographers, each with varied interests, the research actually did reflect five different perspectives.) [39] This team approach is in direct contrast to the approach to be discussed in the next section.

Other Interdisciplinary Approaches

A second approach to a general social science research strategy dealing with urban life is one in which each of the separate disciplines is represented by one or more people who pursue a specific research

---

[39] The Italian-American Food Project (Judith Goode et al.) has been concerned with the relationship between locality, ethnicity, class, and dietary patterns. It has been supported by a grant of NSF (National Science Foundation) institutional funds from Temple University and a Faculty Research Grant-in-Aid from Temple University.

focus related to their particular discipline. At some point, the results of the various research endeavors are brought together and related to each other.

An example of this approach can be seen in the case of the planning of Ciudad Guayana in Venezuela. The government planning agency (CVP) was in charge of the project of urbanizing an underpopulated region of the country. They contracted with the Joint Center for Urban Studies of Harvard-MIT to conduct interdisciplinary research that would feed back to the planning effort. It was the responsibility of the planning corporation, rather than the scholars, to integrate the research data. Economists and regional scientists focused primarily on the general economic structure of the community and region. Sociologists studied upper-level executives and decision makers of the corporate structures. An anthropologist, Lisa Peattie, did a two-year ethnography of a squatter settlement (as a resident participant observer). In addition to a specialized publication reporting the separate findings of each study, a general volume was produced that contained data and conclusions from all the projects.[40]

In many ways, this model of an interdisciplinary social science approach, in which a central body determined a very general research interest and then subsidized a variety of different projects, is the usual one found today. For example, when UNESCO, the Ford Foundation, the Institute of Race Relations in England, or the Research Programmes Committee in India, delineate a particular research problem, these bodies usually subsidize tangentially related research in different fields that is not centrally coordinated.

A third approach we may see more of in the future is one in which an individual trained in a variety of disciplines develops an integrated research project. We note this as a possible trend for the future because integrated social science research and teaching programs in urban studies are a recent development, and the full impact of these programs is yet to be felt. Even in such programs, however, the individual student usually concentrates upon one academic discipline, rather than receiving equal training in many fields.

Urban Studies Training

This last approach shifts our attention from urban studies research to urban studies training. Here again, several directions have emerged. One direction focuses primarily upon team teaching in which the various disciplines participate jointly in courses. Within team teaching, alterna-

[40] See Lloyd Rodwin et al., *Planning Urban Growth and Regional Development: The Experience of the Guayana Program of Venezuela* (Cambridge: M.I.T. Press, 1969). For more on the anthropologist's contribution, see Lisa Peattie, *The View from the Barrio* (Ann Arbor: University of Michigan Press, 1968).

tive modes have developed. One mode brings together various social scientists, who discuss common issues in urban studies from their particular disciplinary perspective; this may be done either collectively or in a series of individual presentations. Another mode is for each social scientist to discuss only the particular aspects of urban life his or her discipline has traditionally studied. Thus, the political scientist could discuss local community power structure, the geographer could talk about land use, and so forth.

Some urban studies programs are little more than loosely federated groups of courses that are traditionally offered in different departments. The student puts the courses together with the aid of an advisor. In this approach, it is the responsibility of the student, not the teacher, to integrate the disparate material. Other programs start their students in urban studies in an integrated core curriculum. Students take traditional courses in various departments and then come together in a capstone integration at the upper level. This last seems to be the most common mode, and can be used for both undergraduate and graduate curricula.

The student produced by most of these programs is probably more suited to an applied career in an urban agency than to a research career, for which firm grounding in a particular discipline is preferred. While such programs acquaint students with different research strategies, they are not sufficiently intensive to prepare for a professional research career.

For instance, programs developed at Baruch College and Temple University were geared to train individuals to move into positions in urban planning, urban government, and urban institutions, which did not require intensive knowledge of a single field. Such training should enable individuals to assess the validity of research being done in a variety of disciplines and allow them to evaluate and utilize those aspects of urban research relevant to their role. Thus, those who are responsible for making decisions about the future of a city can deal more meaningfully with knowledge derived from several social science disciplines.

Too often, those trained in a particular social science see their discipline as an entity whose logically determined boundaries are important to preserve. Frequently, when practitioners of one discipline read the work of practitioners of another who appear to have invaded their territory, they feel threatened. However, an objective review of the growth of the social sciences would suggest that these boundaries are a result of historical accident and are often purely arbitrary. Any attempt to maintain them is bound to fail. With the recognition that the "urban" is not the exclusive domain of any single discipline, a more relaxed position can be taken by various social scientists.

Although we do not have many examples yet of scholars emerging from training programs that emphasize interdisciplinary research strategies and foci, we can cite two examples of anthropologists who felt that, in order to come to grips with the phenomena they were studying (cities in the United States and cities in Brazil), it was necessary to expand their own competence beyond the limits of anthropology. Thus Fox does his own historical research, which was considered to be essential in the understanding of the differences between two cities in the United States, and Leeds does his own economic analyses, using existing data to better understand the differences between two Brazilian cities.[41]

The significance of this trend toward an integrated social science approach can hardly be overstated. A real interdisciplinary approach is not simply additive, where the historian contributes A, the economist B, and the result is A + B. . . . What we have here is parallel to what Gestalt psychologists mean when they say the whole is greater than the sum of its parts. Thus, there could emerge a level of explanation well beyond any in the social sciences today.

Anthropological Input to Urban Studies

What can anthropologists contribute to urban studies? Based upon our previous discussion, some answers come to mind. In Chapter 1, the following trends were noted: cross-cultural comparison, cultural relativism, ethnographic fieldwork, and holism.

Through a traditional emphasis on the cross-cultural approach, the urban anthropologist insists that we look at urban phenomena in all times and places. Any models or explanations of the urban must not be narrowly based upon Western experience or the modern era. Related to this is the thrust against ethnocentric thinking—judgmental views of different behavior, ideas or structures. From this perspective, New York, Calcutta, Bogota, Timbuctoo—all must be recognized as part of their cultural contexts and deemed equally relevant to any explanation of the nature of the city. In addition, the variable meanings and evaluations of the urban experience must be included to avoid overemphasizing the anti-urban bias of the western industrial world.

Ethnography

Another significant contribution of urban anthropology to urban studies relates to the way sociocultural units are studied. Most urban anthropologists still concentrate on the in-depth descriptive study of

---

[41] Fox, "Rationale and Romance," and Leeds, "The Anthropology of Cities."

small units within a larger context. Through participant observation and intimate face-to-face experience, they derive descriptions of everyday routine, the patterned regularity of people's behavior in real situations. They also tend to use native views of experience, underlying meaning, values, and cognitive categories. Thus, the data they collect can serve as the basis for deriving generalizations about how and why people behave as they do, how groups are created and maintained, and how the interactions among such groups affects and is affected by cities.

Gulick has stated that the anthropologist is a "visualizer" and a "participator."

> The anthropologist likes to gather his material so that he can portray the reality which he has experienced and studied. . . . Anthropologists are often irritated by sociological findings not so much because they are "quantified" but because they are abstracted so far from the behavioral context and from situations that can be visualized.[42]

In attempting to describe other ways of life, the fieldworker in many situations discovered a discrepancy between what people said should occur and what actually did occur. This is now considered to be the difference between *real culture* and *ideal culture*. The only way of determining the degree to which rules and norms that are adhered to verbally are valid behaviorally is through the direct observation of such behavior. It should be apparent that the distinction between ideal and real is as relevant, if not more so, in the study of complex urban settlements as it is in tribal or village settings.

The Time Perspective

Another consequence of the fieldwork background is concern with the continuity of behavior over time. In order to describe the patterned regularity of cultural behavior, the anthropologist had to spend a relatively long period of time in close-knit interaction with informants in the culture. For example, if anthropologists wanted to describe a marriage ceremony or an initiation ceremony, they realized that the observation of only one event would not give them the typical attributes or contours—what is truly patterned and repetitive.

This long-term perspective in anthropological studies also led to the recognition that typical activities (subsistence and ceremonial) varied with the annual cycle. For agricultural and horticultural garden-

[42] John Gulick, "Urban Anthropology: Its Present and Future," *Transactions of the New York Academy of Science*, 25 (1963), 454-55.

ing societies, the various activities related to preparation of fields, planting, weeding, and harvesting are usually related to seasonal changes in climate, which occur regularly during the year. For herders, the same relationship exists. Hunting and gathering peoples are similarly influenced by climatic changes, particularly in those climates characterized by alternating cycles of wet and dry. For most anthropological studies, therefore, a minimum fieldwork period of fifteen months was considered essential, and a longer period was desirable. Although this time emphasis might not be considered essential in urban anthropology studies, there is a tendency to carry the time commitment over to such studies to observe recurring events that provide a better grasp of the complexity of patterned behavior in various situations, as well as a better view of continuity and change than studies done at a single point in time.

In an industrial urban situation, there appear to be time cycles that should be considered in a study of a neighborhood, ethnic group, occupation, association, or any other micro-unit usually studied. Thus, there is a daily cycle alternating work, domestic, and leisure activities. In addition, there is a weekly cycle with particular days set aside for different activities, and a seasonal cycle, which includes holidays, festivals and vacations that recur on a regular basis. Such variations can only be seen in a study that has a long time perspective to obtain the full range of behavior.

The food and nutrition study previously noted can be used to illustrate this particular approach. This study, designed to look at the maintenance of ethnic group boundaries, recognized that a typical nutritional questionnaire that asked people to recall the meals they ate on a particular day would lose the range of variation over time that the anthropologist usually sees. In view of this, a variety of participant observation and intensive interviewing techniques were used to develop a picture of the pattern of behavior. Based upon these data, the following temporal patterns emerged:

1. There is a weekly pattern in which certain foods are eaten on specific days of the week.
2. The time of the major meal shifts from working days to leisure days.
3. On particular ceremonial occasions (holidays, weddings, etc.) foods specific to that occasion are eaten that are seldom eaten at other times.

All of these variations are part of a temporal pattern of food consumption that must be recognized in order to develop generalizations about this group's foodways.

Another carryover of the traditional concern with continuous, processual flows of time is the emphasis upon the life cycle of the individual. Even though the anthropological fieldworker spent a year or so collecting data, he or she could not observe directly the changes that occurred during an individual's lifetime from infancy to childhood, on to adulthood and old age. Since the anthropologist realized that these changes in status were fundamental to an understanding of the full range of human activities, two basic approaches were used to obtain information about them. In one approach, the anthropologist in the field would study groups of infants, children, adults, and the aged in an attempt to derive a picture of the development cycle and changes in status. In the second approach, he or she worked with adults and collected their life histories—recollections of their own development and the changes that occurred in their status over time.

Once again, these traditional approaches have been maintained in urban anthropology and give us a broader view of the flow of cultural behavior. A logical development has been the description and analysis of family life in terms of domestic cycles that parallel life cycle phases, as opposed to analysis of family structure at a single point in time. The same is true for careers: one's occupational category at a given point in time is not as significant for understanding a person's norms and lifestyle as the career cycle.

The Search for Informal Structure

Urban anthropology has maintained an interest in describing not only the formal, institutionalized aspects of a social system, but also the contours and structure that exist underneath the explicit formal organization. Once again, this concern is related to the study of traditional and primitive societies, where formal markets and formal governments did not exist.

In early anthropological studies of primitive peoples, a general assumption was made about the lack of such formal structures as legal court systems and government. However, it was apparent that some people had more power and influence than others, and that some sort of patterned regularity existed in the way decisions were made and social control was maintained, even without formal office. Often, control was maintained through domestic, kin, and friendship structures. These elements are viewed as informal structures because there are no explicit titles of office, rules for succession to office, or insignia.

As the anthropologist moved into the study of complex societies where such formal structures as legal systems and articulated levels of government do exist, he retained the interest in the substructural, underlying importance of such informal ties (domestic, kin, and friendship) in the operation of society.

In an important statement, Eric Wolf notes,

> . . . the formal framework of economic and political power exists alongside or intermingled with various other kinds of informal structure which are interstitial, supplementary, parallel to it. . . . The anthropologist has a professional license to study such interstitial, supplementary and parallel structures in complex society and to expose their relation to the major strategic, overarching institutions.[43]

In most economic studies, the measured items usually used by the economist derive from the formal money economy—that is, they are located in the production and exchange system, which is large-scale, monetized, and recorded in statistics such as the Gross National Product. However, there are some aspects of production and exchange that never enter this system. Exchanges between relatives and friends of goods and services (for example, baby sitting cooperatives), production of goods by a household for its own consumption (baking, sewing), the informal sale of secondhand goods (garage sales) are all aspects of life that are revealed by ethnographic techniques but are usually beyond the scope or concern of economists.

If so many examples can be drawn from our modern, formal system, many others exist in the developing world. In these systems, large segments of the urban labor force are employed in work outside the formal economic system: street vendors, scavengers, ragpickers, porters, watchmen, beggars, messengers, and others abound in the urban setting. Their productivity is unmeasured by formal techniques. They can only be studied ethnographically so as to understand their relationship to the economic system.

Holism

In the study of primitive societies, the relationships between various aspects of political, economic, and social life are so tightly interwoven that the anthropologist has to be explicitly concerned with them. In fact, when anthropologists talk about a *holistic* approach, they mean that the fabric of primitive life is so closely woven that it is impossible to describe political activities without also describing domestic groups, kinship groups, religious beliefs, and magical beliefs. A holistic perspec-

[43] Eric Wolf, "Kinship, Friendship and Patron-Client Relations in Complex Societies," in M. Banton (eds.), *The Social Anthropology of Complex Societies* (London: Tavistock Publishers, Ltd., 1966), p. 2.

tive emphasizes the way parts fit together in a system as a whole. One of the characteristics of urban life, and more particularly life in urban industrial societies, is the segregation of these institutional components: family, government, economy, and so forth. However, urban anthropologists, with their traditional conceptual tools, still look for the relationship between these supposedly separate areas of life. The continuation of the anthropologists' concern with holism in the urban context causes them to lock any unit studied in the city into a larger contextual framework to see how domestic units, neighborhoods, or ethnic groups fit together within the larger system of the whole city.

By contrast, a political scientist, even if he uses participant observation, might observe a group involved in a decision-making process in governmental activities and describe both the formal and informal aspects of the situation. However, he would rarely bring in such factors extrinsic to political institutions as the influence on the individual of family structure, friendship patterns, and other institutions.

When anthropologists did traditional fieldwork, they collected data on the full range of human activities: political, economic, religious, social. Over the years, subspecializations within cultural anthropology focused upon these delineated areas; thus, the subspecializations of psychological anthropology, economic anthropology, political anthropology have shown considerable growth in the last two decades. To a certain extent, anthropology, with its holistic tradition, might serve as a model for the development of an integrated social science approach to the study of urban life.

We can view urban anthropology as the most recent developing subfield within anthropology, one which has as its cognate field urban studies. Since traditional anthropology has been concerned with small systems (tribal and peasant peoples), it may lack much of the conceptual and theoretical sophistication developed by other social sciences, which have always dealt with complex society. This obviously is a weakness. However, we believe this is more than compensated for by the transposition of many of the traditional concepts and frames of reference lacking in the other social sciences. These can readily be used in the study of urban life to add considerable depth and humanism to this particular area of study.

SUMMARY

This chapter dealt with the difficulties in defining *the urban* and suggested a three-part conceptual vocabulary distinguishing between the urban, urbanism, and urbanization. Approaches to the city based on form and function were discussed, with the recognition of the greater significance of the functional approach. The particular attributes of the anthropological approach that can be used in the study of cities were enumerated and will serve as a basis for later discussion. Finally, the relationship of an emergent field of urban anthropology to interdisciplinary urban programs has been clarified. The succeeding chapter will discuss the functions of the city in terms of the historical and cross-cultural comparisons characteristic of all anthropology that are lacking in many discussions of the nature of the city.

The term urban has been a source of confusion in urban anthropology as well as in the other social science disciplines. We have traced three types of endeavor within urban anthropology, which we have labeled as anthropology in the city, anthropology of the city, and the anthropology of urban industrial (complex, modern) society. The first uses the city as the setting within which the research is pursued, but does not see the city (or the urban) as a fundamental variable. The third variety is a system-wide endeavor that looks at the complex forms of modern life, not specifically the urban aspects. The second variety, which we consider to be the core of urban anthropology, sees the urban as a fundamental aspect of the research design.

In attempting to distinguish between urban, urbanism, and urbanization, we have suggested the following:

1. *Urban* or *the urban* will be viewed as both a form of settlement and a set of specific functions. Thus, there are two aspects of the urban—*form* and *function*. Formal attributes include demographic characteristics, architectural forms, and settlement zones. Functional attributes include economic, political, educational, and recreational activity.

2. *Urbanism* is defined as those characteristics, social and cultural, that are a result of the urban. Thus, we have Wirth's definition of urbanism as a *way of life* that results from the urban.

3. *Urbanization* is defined as the *process* by which a society becomes more urban. This can be the result of population shift from non-urban to urban areas or the spread of urban forms and functions to previously non-urban areas.

Certain formal and functional features of the urban and urbanism can be revealed by comparing urban and pre-urban (tribal) settlement and by comparing the traditional city in peasant societies with its surrounding hinterland. Urban centers are places of high population and population density. They have a large range of occupational specializations, with a relatively small proportion of the total labor force involved in agricultural production. In functional terms, urban centers are sources of political, social, and economic dominance over their hinterlands. The degree to which urban settlements must have clearly defined boundaries, elaborate cores or central places, and massive architecture is still being debated by archeologists and historians. Some of the urban characteristics are social and cultural heterogeneity, which allow greater occupational and personal choice and freedom.

The distinction between the urban and non-urban is much more difficult to determine and maintain in modern, complex societies. In such societies, the diffusion of urban forms and functions, as well as of urbanism, to non-urban settlements is marked. This is clearly recognized in the change of terminology from cities or urban centers to the concept of a metropolitan area or megalopolis in contemporary society.

Another source of confusion in dealing wtih contemporary urban phenomena in complex societies is the difficulty in distinguishing those aspects of modern life that are the direct result of the urban from those that are the result of the industrial productive process. Many of what are called "urban problems" are more the result of the industrial process than the urban. Obviously, it is difficult to disassociate these two phenomena, which are both ubiquitous at the present time, but every effort should be made to do so where possible.

Despite the difficulties of definition, there is an obvious movement toward a generalized focus upon the urban in all of the social science disciplines. This trend has led to the development of a field called urban studies. In the future development of urban studies, urban anthropology has a potentially useful role to play. The traditional goals and techniques of the cultural anthropologist remain central in urban anthropology. The type of studies pursued by urban anthropologists can make urban studies a more vital area of academic activity.

Part Two

CITIES IN PERSPECTIVE

It should be apparent that urban anthropology, as a segment of the larger anthropological endeavor, is a loosely amalgamated area of study that, in one way or another, attempts to describe and explain the urban scene. Thus far, we have emphasized the general framework of anthropology, the growth of urban anthropology, and some of the major issues that have emerged in urban studies up to this time.

Within that category of urban anthropological studies called the anthropology *of* cities, two approaches have come to the fore. One suggests that, since the basic strength of anthropology is in the ability to do ethnographic fieldwork in small social units, the urban anthropologist should provide an essentially ethnographic and phenomenological view of the urban natives' world. The opposing view stresses the holism of anthropology and urges the need to focus on the whole city and its relationship to the larger system in which it is embedded.

The fact that cultural anthropology always viewed cultures in relation to their ecological systems and looked at whole communities as systems is offered as an argument against ethnographic study of micro-units in the city. We believe that the dichotomy between holistic studies and micro-unit studies is a false one; both strategies can be legitimate, even in the same research problem. In Part Two we shall focus on the holistic view of cities in relation to their contexts, and attempt to illustrate what an urban anthropology of macro-units adds to the goal of understanding urban life.

When anthropologists discuss the role of cities, they focus primarily upon the relationship of urban centers to the larger social system. Some general questions that are asked are:

1. How did cities and hierarchies of urban communities emerge historically as a product of political, economic, and cultural forces?
2. What are the economic, political, and symbolic relationships between the urban center and its immediate hinterland, that is, what are the various functions that cities perform for the systems in which they are located, and what type of feedback occurs between the system and the urban settlement?
3. How can a typology of urban places be developed, that is, how is the variation among cities a product of interactions with the larger system, and how can we explain these differences?
4. What are the differences between modern industrial cities and traditional preindustrial cities?

3

The Role of Cities

The discussion that follows will cover these topics: the anthropological/ archeological perspective on the origin of the first cities as part of developing cultural systems; the functions or roles cities perform; the attempts by the anthropologists to study the dynamic relationships between cities and their larger contexts; and the effects of these relationships on the nature of cities (the urban and urbanism).

ORIGINS OF THE CITY

The historical emergence of cities is recognized as a fundamental change in human existence that had far-reaching effects upon all aspects of life. For much of our knowledge about this development and its impact, we must turn to the work of archeologists. Excavations in many parts of the old and new world have documented the emergence of the city as a new form of settlement.

The emergence of cities is invariably linked to changes in the modes of food production. In an economy that focuses on the subsistence techniques of hunting and gathering, nomadism is usually characteristic, since the dispersion of "wild" food requires movement over large areas according to the seasonal cycle. Large, dense, nucleated settlements would have been unsuited to such food searches and could not have been developed or sustained.

When human beings developed techniques for cultivating the land, the scene was set for the emergence of cities. However, in terms of time span, there was a gap of several thousand years between the rise of agricultural food production and the first cities. In general terms, the food-producing revolution in which cultivation of plants was developed took place approximately 12,000 years ago, while true urban centers first emerged about 5,000 years ago.

In the Old World (Eurasia), there were three separate zones in which the first cities appeared; in all cases, these were located in flood river basins. The three sites were the Tigris-Euphrates valley (Mesopotamia), the Indus River valley (India), and the Huang-Ho basin (China). Later cities emerged in river basins in Europe, Southeast Asia, and West Africa. One significant factor all these basins had in common was the constant seasonal flooding which deposited rich alluvial soils, thus permitting continuous cultivation of grain crops on a large scale.

In the New World (North and South America), a parallel, independent emergence of urban centers has been traced. Cities in the New World were found in Meso-America (largely in Mexico and Guatemala) and the Andean region. Here maize agriculture was the basis for development.

Civilizations, States, and Cities

Anthropologists have debated at great length the relationship between *cities* and *civilization*. Civilizations are complex, state-organized, market-integrated sociocultural systems, while cities are an important type of settlement within them. In effect, both of these phenomena are dependent upon a similar set of circumstances, but they are not equivalent terms. Civilization may exist without cities, but cities do not develop until after the rise of civilization.

This process also relates to the emergence of *state* political systems. In his earlier writing, Childe saw the urban revolution, that is, the emergence of the archeologically observable city as diagnostic of the

existence of the state.[1] In his view, the city was a prere
state. At present, the issue relates more to the emergence
the city as merely a frequent but not necessary type of set'
in the state.

Although cities are not necessary to the existence of the state, they
are efficient central places from which to administer a complex system.
Cities are characterized by economies of scale. Political and economic
functions and the institutions of the state tend to aggregate in one location to increase their access to labor and markets. Thus cities become
centers for the exchange of goods, services, labor, and ideas. The need to
defend such significant locations tends to further *nucleate* (centralize)
the city.

However, in order for there to be cities, the right kind of ecological
setting must exist in which a high rate of land productivity permits agricultural areas to be densely populated in order to amass a food supply
for the even denser, nucleated settlements of urban non-food producers.

THE ECOLOGICAL PERSPECTIVE

Cultural ecology is a perspective that has gained considerable following in contemporary anthropology and has consequently had an impact upon urban anthropology. By *cultural ecology* we mean the focus
on the complex interplay between the human organism, culture, and
natural resources. In this interplay, each element—resource distribution,
culture, production, demographics—in turn affects all other components
in the ecosystem. Change is built into the system. Most explanations for
the evolution of society, the move from tribal to state systems, and the
emergence of the city are based upon an ecological perspective.

In the early study of the rise of complex society and urban centers,
the emphasis was placed upon technological innovation and increased
productivity as prime forces. However, it has been recognized more recently that increased production and surplus food alone could not create
complex stratified state systems. Changes in social organization—particularly in the acquisition of coercive power by certain groups—were necessary to create the occupational specialization, structured inequality, and
state control that evolved. Thus, both the evolution of technological control and political centralization are essential to the process.

The emergence of states was preceded by a quantitative and qualitative change in resource utilization and the productive capacity of land

[1] V. Gordon Childe, "The Urban Revolution," *Town Planning Review*, 21 (1950),
3-17.

through intensive agriculture. Techniques that increased the control of soil fertility (terracing, fertilizing, plowing), water (irrigation, paddy rice), and seed improvements resulted in increased productivity. Advances in food production led to an increase in the multiplicity of parts. This involved both territorially dispersed settlements and interdependent, specialized non-agricultural occupational groups. The proliferation of these occupational and territorial components led to centralized bureaucracies to coordinate the system. Thus, administrative bureaucracies, statewide ideologies, and market systems developed and were controlled by an elite with coercive power. Certain circumstances, such as the need to centrally control river flooding (Old World) or to coordinate essential interregional trade (New World), contributed to the rise of centralized power.

Such a logical, deductive description of the development of the state takes on real meaning when we look at actual archeological evidence in particular ecological zones. We can see then how population pressure affects productive innovation and how the relative storability of food affects growth. For example, the cereals of the Old World and maize in the New World are capable of long storage without spoilage or loss of nutrients. This greatly extended the possibility of system growth. However, in some ecological zones of the Andean civilization, it was too high and cold to grow storable grains. The development of techniques to freeze the white potato of that area enabled the area to remain an integral part of the Inca state.

Variations in resource distribution and cultural practices of resource utilization led to variations in both population distribution and political centralization. Adams, looking at the emergence of three distinct city-states in Mesopotamia (one in the north and two in the south), described variations in the process where one area developed slowly over a period of a thousand years, another showed a sudden spurt, and the third, a spiral development cycle.[2]

An example of a state system that did not have cities is the early Maya civilization. In the Maya system of cultivation, *swidden agriculture* (slash and burn) was the usual technique employed. In this process, natural vegetation was cleared annually by slashing and burning. This is not a form of intensive agriculture, since no intensive control of water or soil nutrients occurs. The only fertilization is the minimal amount derived from the burnt remains of cut vegetation. Consequently, soil nutrients are exhausted after several years and agricultural sites are

[2] Robert M. Adams, "Patterns of Urbanization in Early Southern Mesopotamia," in Ruth Tringham (ed.), *Urban Settlements: The Process of Urbanization in Archaeological Settlements* (Andover, Massachusetts: Warner Modular Publications, Inc., 1973), R16, pp. 1-15.

shifted. Recent ecological analysis of this cultivation process indicates that the subsistence yield for the amount of labor invested (man-hours) is relatively high. However, large areas of land must be available for the constant shifting of sites in order to let land lie fallow and recoup nutrients. As population density increases, land resources become strained. Thus, the population is widely dispersed and cannot generate or transport goods to serve dense central urban places. Nevertheless, the Maya system was state organized. Occupational specialization and a dispersed coercive elite were maintained, as well as the ceremonial trappings of a theocracy whose ritual centers were densely inhabited only at certain times of the year.

Related Developments in the Advance of Cities

A related issue is the degree to which writing is a necessary characteristic of states and/or cities. Childe first made this assertion, and Sjoberg's emphasis upon literacy as a characteristic of urban places has led to much dispute and confusion.[3] Writing, like cities, adds to the efficiency of states, but there is no necessary relationship between writing and urban life.

The existence of writing had two fundamental functions. First, literacy, or some functional equivalent, was necessary for the record keeping demanded where taxes were collected, exchanges made, goods redistributed, and deferred payments allowed. For these, some notational form indicating amount and time was needed. The *quipus* of the non-literate Inca state (a system of notation based on knotted strings) is an example of a functional alternative to the record-keeping function of writing.

The second function of writing was to transmit, through time and space, the centralized ideological underpinnings of the large, complex state. When the area encompassed was extensive and contained heterogeneous groups, a basic technique for integrating the various segments of society was the development of an ideology, or Great Tradition, that could be commonly adhered to by the various segments. This was comprised of laws governing secular relationships and sacred scriptures governing supernatural relationships. These were codified and promulgated by legal and religious specialists and disseminated by the church and/or state.

Incipient states or proto-states that never became full, complex

---

[3] Childe, "The Urban Revolution"; Gideon Sjoberg, *The Preindustrial City* (New York: The Free Press, 1960).

societies can be found in many times and places. They never develop centralized coercive political systems or occupational specialization, although they involve multiple, dispersed communities linked by kings or chiefs with important ceremonial and ritual power as well as certain legal and economic rights that produce limited control over a dispersed population. Often these ritually potent symbolic leaders work the fields during most of the year. Thus, the position of chief is not a full-time occupational role. In these systems there are localities—usually the residence of the king or chief—that serve as centers for ritual and ceremony. These sites draw large populations for annual ritual occasions but are not permanent urban centers. Examples of these proto-states are the Swazi kingdom in Africa, the Chibcha Chiefdom in pre-hispanic Colombia, and the kingdoms of Hawaii.

The emergence of heavily symbolic power leads to true states (with centralized coercive authority) and cities in the demographic sense (large, nucleated, densely populated centers with a large proportion of non-agriculturalists) *only* if ecological conditions permit such a settlement. The proto-states listed above never developed further because of ecological limitations. However, many states with urban centers had phases in their archeological past that were proto-states or symbolic kingdoms with ritual centers. These centers subsequently developed into true cities.

Many early true urban centers were in a tenuous balance with their surrounding ecological areas and many were abandoned after a short existence. Evidence has indicated that, in most cases, ecological forces were responsible. For example, Harrapan cities in India are now thought to have been abandoned as a result of changes in the water table, and early Mesoamerican cities are thought to have declined as a result of ecological imbalance.

THE FUNCTIONAL ROLES OF CITIES

Apparently, urban form (density of habitation and monumental architecture) is intimately related to the economic and political roles the settlement plays within the larger system. In this section we shall discuss the functional roles of cities and broaden our perspective beyond the political and economic roles. For much of this discussion, data derived from historical and geographic sources as well as anthropology will be used.

The historian's view of the city is often rather narrowly focused upon the Western city. In dealing with preindustrial cities—following the work of Pirenne,[4] and some of the responses to his work—historians viewed the cathedral city of medieval times as the preindustrial proto-type. In doing so, they missed the full significance of the variety of these forms, which provides greater insight into the impact of earlier forms of urban life throughout the world. While a few historians specialize in Islamic, Asian, and Latin American cities, this ecumenical view is not characteristic of the discipline. Both authors of this text have worked with urban historians who use only Greco-Roman and medieval models.

This criticism of historians cannot be made of urban geographers. They recognized the diversity of internal structure and external rela-tionships of cities everywhere and pioneered analytical techniques that view these cities as linked in systems to one another and to the hinter-lands surrounding them.

One of the characteristics of the literature is the tendency to dis-tinguish between the preindustrial and industrial city. While this ideal typology, like all ideal types, does distort reality, the impact of the In-dustrial Revolution on cities cannot be ignored. This distinction is so pervasive in the literature on cities that we shall use it as a basis of our discussion.

In this discussion, we shall focus our attention upon the variety of roles or functions of urban centers throughout the world. The simplest format is to subdivide the types of functions into three groups: eco-nomic, political-military, and cultural. However, it must be noted that any city that has emerged or been created for one dominant function will quickly draw to itself ancillary functions (due to economies of scale). At any point in time, originally dominant functions may be re-placed by new ones. Thus any static typology based upon the dominant function or functional mix of a particular city distorts the reality of change and growth.

Another intriguing issue directly related to function is the degree to which a particular urban function or functional mix will affect the entire ambiance and contour of city life, including the very form of settlement. Cities are not isolated geographic units. They are linked in dynamic interaction with a hierarchy of contexts, from the local hinter-land to regional, national, and even international fields.

The smallest unit in the hierarchical system of urban contexts is the contiguous geographic region in the immediate hinterland. Some cities primarily service and relate to their environs. Their population is largely drawn from the immediate areas, and their economic, political, and cultural functions extend to this locality. Particular functions of the

[4] Henri Pirenne, *Medieval Cities* (Princeton: Princeton University Press, 1925).

unit may vary in the extent of their zone of influence. Thus, a localized economic function may coexist with a political function performed for a more widespread area.

The next level of context is a larger region, which consists of many cities and their hinterlands. It should be noted that the city is embedded in a network of relations with other cities, forming a macro-region in which the cities are hierarchic and specialized. These networks cover large geographic areas within a single nation, such as the southeast, midwest, or northeastern coastal corridor in the United States.

The next level is the nation-state itself, a system that exerts considerable political and economic force on the city. The broadest contexts are those outside of the nation. Cities are influenced by an exert their own influence upon the community of nations at the level of regional subsets of nations. The European Common Market and the Latin American "little common market" are formal examples of contemporary regional subsets. The British Commonwealth was an older example, one based not on geographic regionalization as much as on political ties. The ultimate context is the totality of the international system, even in its present tenuous state.

Zones of influence are not static; over time, certain zones may extend while others contract. The city affects its context and is affected by it in return. The relationship is dynamic and characterized by feedback. Thus by examining the dynamic interplay between urban function and external context, we can discern the difference between cities and their resultant effects upon behavior and lifestyle.

Economic Roles

A distinction must be made between the functions a city performs for its internal population and those it performs for the external spheres. Obviously the existence of a large dense settlement creates a need for special economic and political control activities to serve the local population. However, the *raison d'être* for the city relates to its functions for the external context. Geographers distinguish between these two levels by calling the larger contextual role of the city its *basic* activity and its role for the local population its *non-basic* activity. Although geographers developed this distinction for economic roles, we shall extend the usage to other roles as well.

A major role of cities concerns economic production and distribution. From archeological evidence as well as evidence from historical preindustrial cities, urban centers were the loci of large-scale mercantile and artisanal activities. The objects produced by craftsmen and the mercantile transactions there had many possible market destinations:

the local urban population (non-basic), the immediate surrounding hinterland, and the state or even international system beyond. Within this larger social system, some cities could be viewed as having *specialized* economic roles vis-a-vis the higher level systems.

All preindustrial cities are centers of some marketing. Agricultural products from the hinterland come into the city, where they are redistributed for the subsistence of the urban population via the locally oriented market. Similarly, products of urban manufacture are aggregated by merchants and eventually reach the hinterland. Thus, the exchange within the city's context is handled by market specialists whose storehouses, transaction activities, and even residences are largely urban. It must be noted that localized rural markets are also involved in the beginning or end of the exchange, but that large scale storage facilities and record keeping are an urban phenomenon. Trigger notes:

> Long-distance trade was centered in the towns rather than [the] rural sites because the former were also centres of production, because of the scale economies that were gained through centralization and because of the greater security and protection that urban centers offered.[5]

Trigger further noted that some specialization of production is characteristic of non-urbanized zones of complex societies (military production attached to outposts and mills and foundries attached to agricultural estates).[6] However, the development of multiple, interlocking, productive specialization is directly related to the growth of urban centers.

Most of the artisanal manufacture in the city is for consumption within the city. A large number of textile manufacturers and processors (tailors, seamstresses), potters, furniture manufacturers, and metallurgists produce luxury items for the consumption of the elite and middle segments. Most peasant households manufacture their own basic consumer goods (food, clothing, housing, tools, furniture, and utensils) but there are always some goods (ceremonial paraphenalia, prestige and decorative objects) manufactured in the city for a rural market.

Since these localized production and exchange activities are universal to all preindustrial cities, what differentiates them in terms of economic role is their relationship to other cities and to the state. One such distinction can be made between trade and manufacture. River and ocean port cities act as major entry points for goods produced beyond

---

[5] B. Trigger, "Determinants of Urban Growth in Preindustrial Societies," in P. J. Ucko, Ruth Tringham, and G. Dimbley (eds.), *Man, Settlement and Urbanism* (London: Duckworth, 1972), p. 585.
[6] Ibid., pp. 577-78.

the surrounding region and often from other state systems. Such port cities have functioned as entry points for international goods from the very beginnings of the urban revolution (for example, ports in Harrapa). Other specialized trading cities exist in land-locked systems at geographically strategic locations, where they serve as points for collecting and distributing goods as well as serving their own population and region. Such settlements are exemplified by the "caravan" cities of the vast Middle Eastern land routes. According to Trigger:

> The cities of the Levant appear to have flourished as trading centers, first between Mesapotamia and Egypt and later between the Mediterranean and regions further East. In addition to being collecting centres for the incense trade, the cities that developed in the first millennium B.C. in South Arabia were entrepôts in vast networks of trade that embraced India, East Africa and the Mediterranean.[7]

Cities that specialized in trade developed specialized occupations related to trade. In addition to hierarchies of wholesalers and retailers, there were, "men who transport goods and craftsmen who construct and maintain the means of transportation. In the thirteenth century, the population of Cairo was reported to have included the crews of 36,000 Nile boats and 30,000 renters of mules and donkeys."[8] Obviously, the function of the city affected its composition and the styles of life of its residents.

Another form of specialized economic role occurs in centers known for the artisan manufacture of particular items. These craft goods are dispersed throughout the entire state and often enter international trade. India as a state system before the British colonial phase affords some excellent examples of such specialized craft functions. The city of Madras was known for its cotton textiles, Benares (Varanasi) for its silks, and Srinigar (Kashmir) for its papier maché objects. It should be noted that these were all primarily prestige items produced for an elite market throughout India.

The distinction between production for local markets and for larger markets can be demonstrated by the case of medieval Fez. As Trigger notes:

> In medieval Fez, for example, over 20,000 persons were employed in weaving but much of the cloth produced was either used locally or sold in the surrounding countryside. On the other hand, a limited amount of very expensive cloth and most of the production of the

[7] Ibid., p. 586.
[8] Ibid., p. 585.

city's famous tanning and leather goods industries were exported all over the Arab world.[9]

The economic changes that accompanied the industrial process resulted in a variety of urban centers that had new economic roles. The most obvious example is the emergence of a city that is the base of large-scale industry. The first type of manufacturing to be seriously affected by the Industrial Revolution was textile production. Thus, the city of Manchester, England can be considered to be the prototype of an early industrial city based on textiles. Since the textile industry was based upon machine production of large quanties of standardized goods, it required the development of heavy industry to produce the machinery and the basic materials for machinery. Thus, industrial functions themselves differentiated into a variety of types—large versus small, primary versus secondary, odious (in terms of noise, odor, pollution) versus nonodious. In England, the emergence of Birmingham as a steel-producing center was an obvious response to this requirement. The economic functions and the characteristics of such cities were different in kind from those of the preindustrial city and different also from one another. Capital goods produced in Birmingham or Pittsburgh were distributed throughout the entire network of cities that emerged as manufacturers of consumer goods for more local markets.

An ancillary phenomenon was the growth of transport and commercial centers to distribute goods. It can be argued that many preindustrial cities—particularly port cities and inland trade cities—had performed transportation and distribution functions; port cities and inland trade cities have existed for a long time. However, new types of production and marketing on the one hand led to the increase in sheer numbers of new urban centers. On the other hand, new modes of transport (such as railroads) led to new types of commercial cities (such as Topeka, Kansas). These cities were certainly different in many ways from the traditional port and trade cities.

Political Roles

All cities serve some political role in the control and administration of their own population and often of their immediate hinterland. In addition to serving as controlling bodies or markets for locally produced agricultural products, city governments were usually empowered to administer and tax their surrounding areas.

One of the most intriguing political questions is the relationship

[9] Ibid., p. 585.

between the city and the state in which it is embedded. In some cases, the urban settlement and its state political system are one and the same. These cases are referred to as city-states and occur in early phases of complex societies. Wheatley considers them to be insignificant phases in the growth of empires.[10] More commonly, the city is embedded in a state system that is widespread territorially and contains a hierarchy of settlement types.

In such systems, some cities could be characterized as specializing in political activity as a basic activity. This is particularly the case where a city has been established by a ruling dynasty as either its primary seat of power and embodiment of the state or as a provincial or satellite seat, which has power over a limited province and which is part of a larger dynastic order. Often a ruler would select a site and establish himself there. Frequently such palace or court cities were established at whim and could be abandoned at will. However, once established, they tended to draw to themselves additional economic, defense, and cultural functions that reinforced their stability. Examples of these are Agra, Bangkok and Rangoon.

It should be noted that the establishment of a palace, fortress, or castle in and of itself did not mean the establishment of a city. It is only when such sites drew to themselves additional functions and population that they could be considered a real city. For a ruler, such governing cities were not only the center of coercive power but also the symbolic representation of his reign. Thus rulers would frequently lavish great resources in building their own residences and in the maintenance of the entire urban center. As Trigger indicates:

> Babylon grew to be the largest city in Mesopotamia after it was selected to be the capital by the second ruler of the Hammurabi dynasty. When the city of Fez, which had hitherto been a centre of craft production, was designated as the capital of the Marinide empire in the thirteenth century, its rulers left the old city largely intact but founded a smaller new district about 750 yards to the east of it. This new city, later called Fez Jedid (New Fez), contained the palace of the sovereign, the residences of principal court dignitaries and two quarters occupied by foreign troops loyal to the king, as well as eventually the Jewish ghetto, which was under royal protection. While the Old City was governed by functionaries appointed by the king, who acted in consultation with leaders nominated by the notables of the community, Fez Jedid was under

---

[10] Paul Wheatley, "The Concept of Urbanism," in Ruth Tringham (ed.), *Urban Settlements: The Process of Urbanization in Archeological Settlements* (Andover, Massachusetts: Warner Modular Publications, Inc., 1973), R12, pp. 1-37.

direct royal rule. When the king was away fighting or touring the provinces, the official city was largely abandoned.

While cities may grow to exceptional size as the actual centre or as symbols of political power, the withdrawal of such support can very quickly undermine their ability to support the population they have acquired. Assur was abandoned with the fall of the Assyrian Empire, and following the disintegration of Roman power in the West in the fifth century A.D., Rome declined, to become a small town. Even more dramatic fates may befall capitals in states which remain large and prosperous. The ancient Egyptian city of Akhetaton was founded, overtly for religious reasons, as a new court centre. Within a few years its houses, palaces and temples sprawled along eight miles of river front and the city functioned as the administrative centre of the Egyptian empire. Yet, following the rejection of its founder's religious innovations, the court left the city, and only a few decades after the city had begun the site was once again uninhabited. Likewise, the vast city of Samarra was founded in A.D. 836 by the Caliph Mu'tasim on a site removed from the major trade routes of the Near East but also remote from the political turmoil of the previous capital of Baghdad. Despite the compulsory settlement of thousands of merchants and artisans in the new city, it endured for less than fifty years before another political shift led to its abandonment.[11]

In the maintenance of political authority, it was frequently essential to establish defensible and fortified sites to provide stability and coercive force. Walled cities, with parapets manned by defenders and gates to control the flow of population, were built in many parts of the world. Frequently such cities were located in topographically defensible places such as hills or river bends.

In the building of empires, cities that function as launching points for colonial settlement or for the military control of indigenous populations are often found. They are usually located on the defensible periphery of a ruler's domain. They serve as outposts to defend the ruler's territory against outside competition or native revolt, and for the expansion of colonial settlement and rule. The cities of Roman colonies and the Spanish settlements in the New World are classic examples. As Trigger indicates, "Many famous Arab cities, such as Basra, Kufa, Yustat and Kairouan began as military camps which the Arab armies founded on the edge of the desert and from which they dominated conquered territory." [12] Although legally defined as cities from their beginnings, such settlements do not begin as full-blown cities in terms of size and com-

---

[11] Trigger, "Determinants of Urban Growth," p. 588.
[12] Ibid., p. 590.

plexity; however, if they survive, they grow and take on the full form and functional variety of major urban centers. Cologne, Germany is an example of a military outpost of the Roman empire which developed into a city and has survived over centuries.

In large-scale postindustrial states, cities have been created for purposes that parallel those in earlier state-organized societies. Most states are subdivided into regional entities for administrative purposes, and such territorial units have designated political seats, which frequently draw to themselves economic and cultural functions providing the basis for urban growth.

In addition, the center of national power is located in a particular city, which then symbolically represents the state. In some cases, again paralleling the preindustrial empires, these centers may be created at the whim of the national ruling elite. In the United States, Washington, D. C. was created to symbolize the emergent nation-state and has been politically separated from all other units in the national system. Brasilia was created to symbolically move power inland away from the old Brazilian seats of dominance. New Delhi in India and Islamabad in Pakistan were similarly created *de novo* to symbolize new political bodies.

Students of urban life representing a variety of disciplines have concentrated their attention upon changing economic and political functions of the city. Geographers and historians in particular have cast most of their analyses in terms of changing relationships between the city and its larger contexts in political and economic terms. As an example of this sort of analysis, Murphey's contrast between Western European and Chinese cities suggests that the dynamic impact of Western cities on their larger nation-states is a result of their unique economic role. In China, the economic functions of cities were minor, and the city was primarily a headquarters for the ruling bureaucratic elite. Chinese cities resisted economic change. Murphey suggests that the Western notion, which emphasizes the role of the city in economic development and modernization, must be questioned on the basis of a comparative perspective.[13]

CULTURAL ROLES

Since the cultural role of cities has been of primary interest to the urban anthropologist, we shall now discuss this in considerable depth.

[13] Rhodes Murphey, "The City as a Center of Change: West Europe and China" in P. C. Wagner and M. M. Mikesell (eds.), *Readings in Cultural Geography* (Chicago: University of Chicago Press, 1962), pp. 330-41.

This discussion will develop three themes: cultural integration, the maintenance and transmission of traditional ideology, and ideological change.

Integration

During the course of human history, wherever cities are found, they tend to be centers not only for political and economic activities but also for a variety of activities, both sacred and secular, which serve to ideologically unify large regions or states. By housing the symbols of identity and by being the site for ritual and ceremonial activities that bring together large numbers of socially differentiated population segments, the city serves as a culturally integrating mechanism. The cultural role of the city can be seen as both *maintaining* the cultural system through transmission (formal education and communication), as well as providing the basic sources of *change* in ideology.

We have previously noted that the city must be viewed within larger geographic contexts. The same applies to any analysis of the cultural role of cities. When we discuss the subcategories of sacred and secular cultural roles, it is absolutely essential that we recognize the embeddedness of the city in larger regional and national systems.

It is in the area of the cultural roles of cities that the anthropologist can make the greatest contribution. From its inception, urban anthropology has considered the city as a cultural force to be a central theme in the emerging discipline. Redfield and Singer developed this theme in an early article entitled "The Cultural Role of Cities" [14] (1954), which will be discussed subsequently. A different approach was suggested by Moore, who, following Steward, viewed the city as a particular level of sociocultural integration.[15]

Sacred Activities. Cities in preindustrial times were usually the centers of formal sacred knowledge and ceremonies. The large architectural forms and aesthetic symbols found in European cathedral cities and Mayan and Asian temple cities are a physical representation of the significance of the sacred in the total life of the society. For many societies, the city was the place where this world (the mundane) and the other world (the sacred and supernatural) actually met and coalesced. The medieval European cathedral, the center of cities of that time, symbolized a reaching upward to God, and attempts were made to build

[14] Robert Redfield and Milton Singer, "The Cultural Role of Cities," *Economic Development and Culture Change,* 3 (1954), 53-73.
[15] Kenneth Moore, "The City as Context: Context as Process," *Urban Anthropology,* 4 (1975), 17-25.

them as high as possible, given the limited architectural technology of the time.

Heine-Geldern indicates that in Southeast Asian states, the city was also seen as the sacred center where the entrance to the other world was effected.[16] Von Grunebaum also indicates the sacred symbolic centrality of the city in Islamic cosmology.[17] Rowe states, ". . . the Indian city has provided a symbolic representation of the social order, both in its spatial arrangements and in its social structure." [18] In the establishment of Indian cities, there had to be religious sanctions. Each city had to have a Sanskritized deity. The founder had to inject his caste deity into the central core of deities. Thus the city played a role in the development of a cosmology, and the cosmology in turn sanctioned the city. Furthermore, in Hindu beliefs, rivers are the most sacred places, and since cities are often located on rivers, they become significant cosmological points.

Ceremonial and ritual activities, which were central to the function of the church, frequently acted to integrate and solidify the entire population of the city and the region. Usually these ceremonies used a technique of processions, in which large numbers of people marched through the city carrying or pulling representations of deities and performing music and dances. The Juggernaut ceremony in Madura, the Holy Week processions of medieval Europe, and Carnival in Brazil are some examples. These ceremonies were highly organized, with people from different neighborhood, occupational, or ethnic groups having different roles (dance groups, provision of supplies), but with everyone working together toward a single goal. People from the provincial hinterland came in for the ceremonies too, often as spectators but often also as participants.

Not only did those from the surrounding region use the sacred institutions of the city during these large-scale cyclical events, but they also frequently required personal ceremonial services. For instance, Hindu cremation grounds were located in cities (near rivers); at the death of a family member, the body was accompanied to the crematory grounds, where funeral rituals were held. In instances of baptism and wedding law involving conflict or legality, a high level religious practitioner (a member of the urban hierarchy) was consulted.

Some urban centers perform specialized religious functions for the total system that parallel specialized economic and political functions

---

[16] Robert Heine-Geldern, *Conceptions of State and Kingship in Southeast Asia* (Ithaca, New York: Southeast Asia Program, Cornell University, 1956).
[17] G. E. von Grunebaum, "Islam," *American Anthropologist*, Memoir 81, 1955.
[18] William Rowe, "Caste, Kinship and Association in Urban India," in Aidan Southall (ed.), *Urban Anthropology* (London: Oxford University Press, 1973), p. 212.

in that they serve not merely the local population or region. Once every twelve years, the city of Allahabad in northern India is the site of a special religious festival called the Kumbh Mela. This event lasts for three months, during which a pilgrim population of three to four million may come into the city on particularly auspicious days. Some estimates suggest that thirty or forty million people from all over India visit the city at some point during the cycle. In the modern world, with the growth of international religions such as Islam and Christianity, certain sacred cities, such as Mecca, Rome, and Jerusalem, come to be viewed as the embodiment of the world religion.

Secular Activities. Frequently we find the identity of a region symbolically embedded in the city. An obvious example of this occurs when the name given to the city and to the larger region is the same.

In the modern city, new types of ceremonial events, usually secular in nature, perform much the same integrative function as sacred rites did in the past. The Macy's parade in New York, Mummers' parade in Philadelphia, Cherry Blossom Festival in Washington, Mardi Gras in New Orleans, Stampede in Calgary, and celebrations related to political independence all over the world are all examples. Often they are residues of traditional religious ceremonies, or they commemorate recent historical events, or celebrate local culture. Not only are the events themselves integrative, but the organizations created to plan and prepare them are also integrative. For instance, dance groups for the Carnival in Rio and musical groups for the Mummers parade meet throughout the year and cross-cut class and ethnic lines to work toward common goals. These two examples are well known because they, in fact, draw from national and even international audiences, but every city has its local and less-known version.

The integrative function of ceremonial events and public performances involving mass participation has been recognized by municipal leaders, who now seek to create these events to draw people to the city and reinforce their identity with it. New York City's utilization of Central Park for concerts, plays, and celebrations is an example of this attempt to establish a place of common identity. Although the following discussion draws heavily on the examples of New York and Philadelphia, readers are encouraged to use the framework and apply examples from their own experience.

Philadelphia recently experimented with "spontaneous happenings." First Head House Square, a focal area of the old city, became an outdoor food and craft market in the summers. Later Super Sundays were initiated, and people gathered in a central location to buy and sell food and craft items. Finally, Olde City Sunday was held. The entire colonial historical area was blocked off for the performance of plays, fife and drum corps, and other activities. Such an unanticipated number of people turned out that special mass transit schedules were overwhelmed and food purveyors ran out of food in the first hour. The media deemed the event a total success in terms of people reestablishing identity with the city. The media quoted people as saying, "It makes me feel good to be a Philadelphian," "Philadelphia is really alive," "I haven't seen this many people having a good time in years." Many stated that they were from outer ring suburbs and had not been in the city center for years.

Another important type of secular activity that takes place in the city and draws people from the surrounding region is the athletic contest or sporting event. Roman gladiatorial performances in huge stadiums and the large ball courts found in ancient Mexican and Peruvian cities give testimony to the importance of these athletic contests. Intercity rivalries only underscored the function of these activities in integrating populations and developing pride and solidarity.

In the past, public punishment of law violators also drew mass audiences from the region and could be classified as spectator events. Public executions were frequently viewed by large crowds.

In the modern city, we see a further development of professional sports and stadium complexes. Major modern cities are frequently associated with professional events. In the United States, baseball, football, basketball, hockey, and other increasingly numerous mass spectator sports are organized on the basis of urban franchises, and teams become identified with particular cities and regions. The building of arenas for such events requires major investments on the part of cities, often comparable to the medieval cathedrals as municipal projects. In other parts of the world, soccer is the sport that develops this kind of institutional complex and support.

Besides the economic and political importance of sports to cities, the importance of teams for regional identity and pride cannot be underestimated. As many have suggested, the winning of the Stanley Cup by the Philadelphia Flyers did more to develop a commitment to the city and region than all the organized attempts by local mercantile/political organizations in previous decades. Bumper stickers, team jackets, shirts, hats, and other insignia proliferate as symbolic representations of this commitment. Similarly, negative images follow poor performances. The focus on local sporting events as major items of conversation and social activity in all cities is significant. Rallies, parades, urban riots in reaction to winning, and mass airport greetings become significant events both for individuals and for the urban center as a whole.

In a study done by an undergraduate class that focused upon suburban youngsters and their knowledge of and interaction with the city, it was observed that most of their contact with the city was based on sports. In the modern world, with its occupational and cultural heterogeneity, sports events become one of the few common foci capable of capturing the attention of almost everyone and intensely involving their emotions and loyalties. By contrast with such mass phenomena as rock festivals, sporting events draw all age, class, and ethnic groups.

The fact that major teams, performers, or stadium complexes are associated with a particular city serves to make people in the surrounding region identify favorably with the urban center, which is otherwise ignored because of the anti-urban bias. Frequently, the stadium itself becomes a new architectural form and stimulates urban revitalization. The stadium can become the symbol of the city, as in the case of Houston's Astrodome. When St. Louis underwent successful and massive urban renewal on its riverfront, the two major new constructions were the Gateway Arch and the stadium.

Politicians capitalize on this integrative force, as did John Lindsay when he used the Mets' unexpected pennant victory in 1969 to emphasize the health and vigor of New York City to overcome his negatively perceived performance record.

Other forms of leisure-time activity and entertainment are also basic integrative mechanisms for cities and their larger contexts. The existence of a potential mass audience leads to the existence of specialized entertainment facilities: permanent theaters and arenas for drama, dance, concerts, puppet shows, jugglers, performing animals and others.

In addition, the city draws people to it by purveying illicit forms of recreation. As an occupation limited to the city, prostitution has existed well before the Industrial Revolution. Most preindustrial cities had segregated quarters for such activities. This area is still referred to as the "red light district." Other activities, such as gambling and drinking alcoholic beverages, that may be considered illegal or immoral are often found in segregated urban areas where patrons can come and go anonymously. The size of the city provides opportunities for lotteries and gambling on a large enough scale to produce the kind of extremely attractive jackpots not possible elsewhere.

Some cities specialize in leisure-time recreation as their *basic* activity. This role increases in importance in the postindustrial period. Such large-scale centers as Miami, Florida; Atlantic City, New Jersey; and Las Vegas, Nevada; are almost entirely dependent on the economics of purveying good times. This type of city depends upon industrial modes of transportation capable of moving large numbers of people. It also depends upon industrial occupations that dole out leisure and vacation times at regular and predictable intervals. A good example of this is the situation that currently prevails in England. In cities like

Coventry, Birmingham, and Manchester, which are major industrial centers, the work force is given a set two week annual holiday. The time period is staggered from region to region so that the entire industrial work force does not descend upon resorts like Blackpool at the same time. Accordingly, some cities close all their industry during the last two weeks in July, others the first two weeks in August, and still others the remaining two weeks. Cities like Blackpool and Brighton are supported almost completely by revenue earned during this time.

A few examples of such cities can be found in the preindustrial world. For example, Roman elites would travel to certain cities for their seashores or bath facilities. Several English seacoast resorts, like those mentioned above, began as recreation areas for Roman soldiers along Hadrian's Wall. In India, the elite would move to higher altitude cities during the heat of summer. In all cases, such leisure cities bring together geographically or socially differentiated segments of the population of the total system.

The City as a Center of
Cultural Continuity and Transmission

Besides housing the symbols and events that serve to integrate the system culturally, the city also houses the institutions that maintain and transmit the previously developed cultural system or world view. In his writing about peasant societies as opposed to folk society, Redfield introduced the notion of the Great Tradition and the Little Tradition.[19] The Little Traditions are the cultures of the dispersed peasant villagers, while the Great Tradition is the formal, orthodox view of the literate elite, predominantly located in urban centers. The Great Tradition is a formulation of the more formal, codified, explicit, and consciously transmitted culture. In some ways, this formulation can be viewed as analogous to the distinction made in modern society between "mass culture" and "high culture."

In the preindustrial city, cathedrals and temples drew to themselves the literate creators and transmitters of the sacred tradition, which contained the underpinnings of world view and values. Urban-based religious activities were the source of much of the creative production in the classical arts: drama, music, dance, art, and literature. Church or temple music frequently set the standards for all musical production.

Almost all formal education was directed by elites for their own

[19] Robert Redfield, *Peasant Society and Culture* (Chicago: University of Chicago Press, 1956).

children. As the purveyors of formal tradition, elites had to acquire literacy and have higher levels of learning. Advanced forms of education were almost always located in the city. Elites often resided in the city or had a dual residence pattern, which kept them dispersed on rural estates some of the time but together in cities for the rest. Thus elites could maintain contact with each other, their children could marry each other, and they could maintain their special lifestyles. Rural-based elites sent their children to the central place, where they could learn (as well as meet, court, and form ties).

The schools for the Inca in Cuzco are an example. Not only were provincial Inca brought in to acquire common world views, but the old princes of captured states were brought to Cuzco to be indoctrinated in the Inca world view. Not only was the official world view transmitted, but also the specific culture of the ruling class. In feudal Europe, children of minor nobles were sent to schools attached to the households of major nobles for their education, which included learning the art of combat, the code of honor, and social etiquette. Such training instilled allegiance to a cultural tradition.

Elite education served to link together the entire social system, because the common core of beliefs and world views filtered through the entire system from the elite in their roles of priest, administrator, and landlord. The transmission of the Great Tradition was vital to the preindustrial system, and the city was the locus for the maintenance and transmission of this world view.

In modern times, the city continues its function as the locus of "high" culture. Museums, symphonies, art galleries, zoological and botanical parks, publishing houses, theaters, and universities are still located primarily in cities. Such institutions draw people from the hinterland as well as from the city population. Thus the city could still be considered the locus for institutions that preserve, maintain, and disseminate the formal high culture of the society.

One of the significant changes that has occurred in recent times is the development of mass education and literacy. This has led to the development of a large audience that can purchase the output of cultural production. Newspapers, magazines, and certain books have large circulation. The new electronic communication media generated by the postindustrial era (television, recordings, radio, film) also produce cultural art forms for mass consumption.

The domination of a unified culture by religious institutions and elite segments has been replaced more recently by secular mass communication. Usually the core of particular communication industries is located in urban areas. Nashville functions as the country music center and Hollywood as the film-TV center, although their products are disseminated nationally. The location of particular media in particular cities has influenced the nature of these cities and their lifestyle.

Price notes for the American Indian that the extensive publication network of magazines and newspapers are urban based, even though their readership is the population with the least urban residence in the United States.[20]

The city has a somewhat different relationship to mass culture. Mass communication media—television, radio, magazines, newspapers—originate in urban locales. As a result of this, much of the news reported deals with urban events and activities. While early television in the United States often romanticized rural and small town life, a recent article demonstrates that there has now been a shift toward emphasizing urban life.[21] Cultural themes for the mass national system have become more urban. Media cities specialize in mass culture as a basic activity, that is, their cultural role transcends their specific region. They reach the population of the whole national system and reflect a national or sometimes international cosmopolitanism.

The City as Generator of Ideological Change

We have been discussing the role of cities in the maintenance and transmission of culture and the integration of the regional and state system. However, the city also plays a cultural role in regard to change. An understanding of this role has been the goal of those interested in cities since the 1960s.[22] The analytical framework of the discussion that follows owes much to the early formulations of Redfield and Singer.[23] Redfield's early formulation of the folk society concept set the stage for much of his later theoretical work. Redfield was always concerned with the world views of societies—their notions of the cosmos and morality.

Throughout much of the writing in the later part of his career and in his work with Singer, Redfield was concerned with the way the Little Tradition (local peasant view) interacts with the Great Tradition

---

[20] John Price, "U.S. and Canadian Indian Urban Ethnic Institutions," *Urban Anthropology,* 4 (1975), 35-52.
[21] Stephanie Harrington, "Life in the Imaginary City," *Harper's,* 251 (1975), pp. 39-40.
[22] Sylvia Thrupp, "The Creativity of Cities," and John Friedmann, "Cities in Social Transformation," *Comparative Studies in Society and History,* 4 (1961), pp. 53-64 and 86-103.
[23] Redfield and Singer, "The Cultural Role of Cities."

(formal orthodox culture) and becomes amalgamated with formal orthodox belief.

Redfield and Singer suggest that the city is the center of change and that this susceptibility to change is reflected in two types of cities—*orthogenetic* and *heterogenetic*. Recognizing the classic distinction between preindustrial and postindustrial cities, they classify all postindustrial cities as heterogenetic.

The orthogenetic city is one which is a center of native bureaucratic functions. Its population is relatively homogeneous in culture of origin. The cultural role of such an urban center is to maintain and continually reintegrate the Great Tradition by injecting elements of Little Tradition through interaction of the city and peasantry. Redfield and Singer state that this type of city is basically conservative, although some change does take place as city and countryside interact with each other. They suggest that there is continuity between aspects of the Great Tradition at various points in time, and it is the city that maintains and insures this continuity. Examples of this type are Benares in India and Peking (Peiping) in China.

While all orthogenetic cities are preindustrial, heterogenetic cities include one type of preindustrial city and two postindustrial types. In all cases, heterogenetic cities include people of different cultures of origin as well as influences from outside the local social system. In some cases, these outside influences are from beyond the political boundaries of the state itself; in other cases, they are from beyond the immediate hinterland. The main function of such cities as a place for the exchange of goods and services requires standardized values. Trading activity involves items and individuals representing regions stretching long distances in both time and space. As a place where divergent cosmologies and lifestyles are juxtaposed, the city becomes a major source of new ideas.

If we refer back to the distinction previously made between Great and Little Traditions, a heterogenetic city of the preindustrial type is one in which a variety of Great Traditions interact with one another, producing amalgams and changes of a different level from that of the orthogenetic city.

Shifting our attention to the postindustrial heterogenetic city, we discover two types: the new administrative city and the financial city. Examples of the new administrative cities are Washington, Canberra, and New Delhi. These are centers established for the centralized bureaucratic activities that control the general population. They draw upon a diverse population, indigenous as well as foreign. Many colonial cities established during the period of Euro-American expansionist policy can be placed in this category as well. The financial cities are exemplified by New York, London, Shanghai, and Bombay. They are enmeshed in an international network of financial and mercantile activities, which bring to them foreign influences from all parts of the world.

Despite Redfield and Singer's emphasis upon the distinction between preindustrial and postindustrial cities, they are very weak in their coverage of heterogenetic postindustrial centers. For instance, they make no reference to centers that have primarily a manufacturing function, such as Detroit and Pittsburgh in the United States, Manchester in England, Milan in Italy, or even such preindustrial manufacturing centers as Ahmedabad (textiles) and Kanpur (leather), India. Their typology seems to be overrepresentative of preindustrial and non-manufacturing cities. Are these types of cities implied to be more significant for cultural change?

Following the position developed in the earlier article with Redfield, Singer analyzed the dynamic relationship between the Little and Great Traditions in the contemporary Indian city of Madras. He sees the Brahmanic elite in the city as the purveyors of the Great Tradition. Their constant exposure to elements of the Little Tradition enables them to select from these various sources to create an amalgam. Singer suggests that there is a multiplicity of Great Traditions as well as Little Traditions. Since the Great Tradition in Madras is not a single-stranded cultural set, the process of the amalgamation of Great Tradition and Little Tradition is a very complex one. Singer notes:

> The long-run result of this process has been consolidative and selective. Some elements of language, learning, and the arts, as well as of ritual custom, drop out . . . ; new ones are added. . . . Aspects of heterodox sectarian movements and of tribal and regional custom are assimilated to orthodoxy. Fragments of little tradition have been absorbed into the Great Tradition, and the culture of the villages and tribes has, in the long run, also been responsive to the authoritative teachings of literati.[24]

In all of Singer's discussion, the issue of change and the impact of the city on paths to salvation is kept in the forefront. Singer notes the emerging emphasis on bhakti, or devotion, (as a primary path to salvation) as an urban-based emphasis upon a path that had not been heavily emphasized in traditional Hinduism. The other two major paths, ritual observances and acquisition of sacred knowledge, are deemphasized. Sacred cultural performances in the city are shortened, regularly scheduled, held in public places, and are open to members of various

[24] Milton Singer, "The Great Tradition of Hinduism in the City of Madras," *Journal of American Folklore*, 71, 1958. Reprinted in Charles Leslie (ed.), *Anthropology of Folk Religion* (New York: Random House, 1960), p. 165.

castes and sects. Some of the traditional and hereditary leaders are re-placed by new professionals. In the realm of cultural performance, Singer notes the development of devotional song fests (bhajans), de-votional plays, devotional concerts, and even films. Thus, the modern mass media are contributing to the spread of the devotional movement.

In the earlier work of Redfield and Singer, the leaders are dif-ferentiated into literati and intellectuals. The literati are typically found in the orthogenetic city, while the intelligentsia are characteristic of the heterogenetic city. For Madras, Singer subdivides the literati into two categories: a traditional priestly group following the paths of ritual ob-servances and/or knowledge, and new literati following the path of devotion and developing a classical performance style in music and dance based on ancient but dormant forms. The intelligentsia are those leaders who concern themselves with secular themes (novelists, artists, film makers). Both new literati and the intelligentsia are overtly con-cerned with change and do not see their role as that of static maintainers of a rigid and historically derived tradition.

An interesting example of the use of traditional cultural per-formances for the purpose of culture change is found in Peacock's analysis of shadow plays in Indonesia. Here, the government of Indonesia made a conscious effort to stimulate the production of new shadow plays that focus upon aspects of modern life. Since the locus of these performances is primarily the urban area, the city may be seen as the place where traditionally integrative cultural performances are used to introduce elements of culture change to a mass population.[25]

In many ways, the dichotomy between orthogenetic and hetero-genetic cities is a distortion of reality. To a certain extent, Redfield and Singer recognize this and suggest that even in the orthogenetic city, there are sources of heterogeneity based primarily upon regional dif-ferences. Thus, a city like Benares depends not only upon its regional hinterland of Little Traditions, but upon other major regions of the state as well. In addition, even the heterogenetic city may have ortho-genetic characteristics; at different periods of time, the central emphases of the two types may shift, not necessarily in a unilinear direction.

Uzzell and Provencher point out that many cities in Asia and Africa that were heterogenetic (in that they were established by colonial powers) have been reclaimed by the native population and are being redefined as orthogenetic cities—symbolic centers of new nation-states.[26] This shift is often reinforced by monumental architecture, which is used

---

[25] James Peacock, *Rites of Modernization: Symbols and Social Aspects of Indonesian Proletarian Drama* (Chicago: University of Chicago Press, 1968).

[26] J. D. Uzzell and R. Provencher, *Urban Anthropology* (Dubuque, Iowa: Wm. C. Brown Company, Publishers, 1976).

to emphasize symbols of the new Great Tradition, or by converting symbols of prior colonial domination to symbols of national pride.

In a recent student project, individuals from different Third World cities were contacted and asked about those parts of their native cities that all visitors should be shown as important symbols. In most cases, the place mentioned is a fort, cathedral, temple, park, or other remnant of prior colonial rule. Instead of being destroyed, these monuments have been reinterpreted. For example, a resident of Bombay suggested that the "Gateway to India," an imperial monument built by the British, is something every visitor to Bombay should see.

In modern society, the impact of the city as a source of change for the entire social system is more difficult to isolate. This difficulty was not really addressed by Redfield and Singer, which indicates that, while their distinction of traditional orthogenetic and heterogenetic cities is valuable, their discussion of the industrial and postindustrial city does not provide insight about the role of the modern city in change. One reason for this may be that changing technology in communication makes real space and distance less important in the communication of ideas, with the consequence that the city as a geographic center becomes less significant.

In preindustrial and early industrial cities, the communication of ideas depended on spatial proximity and direct contact, so the city was an efficient central point for receiving, reworking, and diffusing ideas. However, radio, television and other electronic devices facilitate a different flow of information. Isolated individuals on the farm have rapid and direct access to new modes of thought and can contribute innovations directly themselves. However, technological capacity and access alone do not *cause* new directions in change, because differences in the social contexts of city and non-urban places still exist.

In the modern industrial state we face the difficulty of defining an urban center and have created such new concepts as Standard Metropolitan Statistical Area. Thus, any discussion of the city as generator of change must also deal with distinctions between urban, suburban, and urban-fringe segments.

In terms of change, contrasts are often drawn between city centers and suburbs. The former are frequently thought of as dynamic communities that are major sources of change, especially in the arts, lifestyles, and belief systems. Suburbs, on the other hand, are thought of as stultifying, conventional, and extremely homogeneous in lifestyle, belief, and values. Suburbs are thought of as inhibiting change and innovation.

This distinction between city and suburb is artificial. Many who work in center cities live in suburbs. Suburbs differ greatly from one another and are not always homogeneous internally. Lumping all such communities into a type with alleged stagnancy characteristics is a gross distortion of reality. As Gans has pointed out, suburbanism as a way of life is not different from Wirth's notion of urbanism.[27]

Since many large urban centers have extended spheres of influence, it can be suggested that the entire region in which the city is found will be influenced by the distinctive ambience (feeling, tone) of that particular urban center. However, there are probably significant segments of the population—particularly those in the outer rings—who are less influenced by the particular city than by the generalized national culture. For many of those in the outer ring, the core of the metropolitan region is irrelevant. Thus, an individual who moves from the outer rings of Dallas to the outer rings of Chicago may bring with him and continue to display a lifestyle not specifically related to Dallas or Chicago but similar in both places. He can also introduce changes without involving elements in the city core. We have recently seen the emergence of changes in lifestyle in urban outer rings that were not generated by the city cores: the rebirth of domestic do-it-yourself activities in bread-baking, needlepoint, crocheting, and similar crafts are examples of this trend that were transmitted by mobile families and later picked up by the mass media for specific target audiences. Swinging as a sexual style preference is thought to have been invented, transmitted, and maintained by personal networks and specialized journals, with little intervention from the institutions of the central urban core.

However, the city center still contains significant elements that contribute to change, such as high culture institutions, a large proportion of intellectuals, the physical presence of the media, and the diversity of alternative lifestyles. Urban social relationships create the possibility for the slow incubation and isolation of these lifestyles. A heightened protection of privacy allows for the developments of new alternatives in a milieu which facilitates the recruitment of converts, transmission of information, access to media dissemination, and mingling with those who specialize in intellectual activities. While many major ideological movements cannot be viewed as urban movements, since their spread throughout the system has been so rapid, they did first emerge and grow in urban centers. A study by Kandel and Pelto, which compares the development of the health food movement in a rural Connecticut college town and an urban center, points out how the nature of the urban

[27] Herbert Gans, "Urbanism and Suburbanism as Ways of Life: A Reevaluation of Definitions," in Arnold Rose (ed.), *Human Behavior and Social Processes* (Boston: Houghton Mifflin Co., 1962), pp. 625-48.

center contributes to the greater success of the movement.[28] Thus the city has maintained an important role in culture change in spite of the communication revolution.

URBAN TYPOLOGIES

In the previous discussion, we have been using the categories of preindustrial versus modern industrial types of cities. This is an example of one possible typology of cities: a typology based on the level of technological complexity of the larger social system in which the city is found. An extension of this basic typology would include a third category, namely, the city in a "developing" society or "transitional" society. Several anthropologists have recognized such a distinction for Third World cities, which are undergoing industrialization within the severe constraints of a world dominated economically and politically by the advanced industrial states.[29] Earlier, we discussed the oversimplification inherent in the preindustrial/industrial typology.

Another possible way of categorizing cities is to group them according to nearness of their social systems to each other in time and space (and presumably culture). Thus, starting with the separate origins of cities according to different regions and subregions of the world (Mesoamerica, South Asia, China, the Near East), one could trace the particular histories and contacts between cities in each region, classifying them by their location in space and time. Thus, traditional West African cities in the early twentieth century could be considered one type and could be contrasted to both their modern 1970s counterparts or to the European-imposed Central African cities. This kind of typology has been widespread in urban anthropology and has led to a parochialism that limits one to dealing with a single continent or region at a time.[30] This precludes the ability to see some obvious similarities and parallels between particular cities in different times and places.

Both of these typologies fall short because they deal with static, single characteristics, which by themselves cannot meaningfully predict differences in the forms of cities or in their ways of life. A third way of categorizing cities is one we shall discuss below. This typology, if developed, could include both the level of technological development

[28] Randy Kandel and Gretel Pelto, "Vegetarianism and Health Food Use Among Young Adults in Southern New England" (mimeo., n.d., 43 pp.).
[29] This is reflected in P. C. W. Gutkind's book, *Urban Anthropology: Perspectives on "Third World" Urbanization and Urbanism* (New York: Barnes and Noble Books, 1974).
[30] Judith Goode, "Progress and Parochialism in Urban Anthropology," *Reviews in Anthropology*, 2 (1975), 479-88.

and the location in time and space. However, it is more specific than the other modes.

We are proposing that cities be distinguished according to their functions, the magnitude of their relevant zones of influence, and the nature of the relationship between city and context. This enables us to deal with general evolutionary level and regional location, as well as with the particular historical processes of the individual city. The real core of this approach would be the nature of the interaction between the city (function) and its zone of influence (context).

THE DYNAMICS OF CONTEXTUAL RELATIONSHIPS

We have previously differentiated relevant contexts for cities in terms of their spheres or zones of influence—local, regional, national, and international. Cities interact with their hinterlands as well as compete with other cities in the system.

Most cities have a variety of economic, political, and cultural functions and subfunctions (for example, manufacturing could be divided into subspecialties, as in the case of Fez, where textiles were produced for local markets, while luxury items and leather were produced for the entire Middle East). These different functions or subfunctions each have different relevant contexts. Techniques for delineating relevant hinterlands for economic functions have been developed by geographers. This task is not simple, but devising ways of measuring political and cultural hinterlands is even more difficult.

In the growth of cities and, frequently, in their decline, their relevant contexts shift. This is readily seen in the economic sphere, where changing technology results in growth, decline, or relocation of economic activity. Major cities on the overland trade route in the Middle East were adversely affected by the development of all-water routes connecting Europe and Asia. River port cities in Colombia were adversely affected by the rise of commercial air freight. In both cases, the contexts of the cities shrank from large-scale regional size to local, contiguous areas. One of the consequences of serving an international economic market is that there is very little political control over that hinterland so that the city is vulnerable.

In the area of political relationships, changes in the relationship between city and state as a result of legislation, decree, or war will have an impact on the city. The city-state (or contiguous city and state) is unusual. The city is usually embedded in a larger state context. Frequently the distinction between city and state is difficult to see, because the state's machinery and ruling elite are located in the city. In a detailed discussion of city-state relationships, Fox shows how the city is subordinate to the state in centralized political systems where the location of central administrative offices in the city works to the detriment of a unified corporate city that can effectively challenge the authority of the state.[31] Much of the following discussion of preindustrial cities is based upon Fox's work.

There are certain common modes of organization found in cities in dominant states. The dominance of state authority is symbolized by palaces and castles. The state controls land use. Certain parts of the population are kept from developing class consciousness through residential segregation and through state control over appointments of local administrators. Whatever threats there are from merchants or the underclass are defused by the state through taxation, expropriation, and police control.

Historical changes in ecology, technology, or political events create a dynamic tension between city and state. In his analysis of Paris in the sixteenth and seventeenth centuries, Fox notes that the declining influence of a centralized authority (primarily because of internal religious warfare) led to greater autonomy in the city. However, with the end of war and the reestablishment of centralized authority, Paris once again became subordinate to the French king. The city's intermittent autonomy was reflected in the increased importance of the bureau de ville, which began to take over planning and municipal services. When the king reemerged, he took control of the bureau and appointed his own men.

A somewhat different pattern of state-city relationships prevails where there is fragmented or weak state authority over a relatively long period of time. Florence, Padua, and Tolouse in the twelfth century and Japanese port cities prior to the Tokugawa state developed loose, decentralized political systems during times when landed nobility were engaged in warfare. One effect of the independence of the city is manifested in the importance of achieved status as opposed to hereditary status. Wealth becomes the basis of social hierarchy, and wealth is more readily accessible. As the state loses its ability to reward and sustain the landed elite, and as warfare further fragments them, they move to the city and assimilate with wealthy money lenders and land speculators to form a new patrician class in which mercantile interests are dominant. In this mercantile city, the residents identify with the city strongly. Citizenship in the city, loyalty, and allegiance to it become more important. Smaller guilds that were isolated and controlled in state-dominated cities are systematically articulated and integrated in municipal government. Loy-

[31] Richard Fox, *Urban Anthropology: Cities in Their Cultural Settings* (Englewood Cliffs, New Jersey: Prentice-Hall, 1977).

alty and allegiance lead to investment in science, arts, and architecture: a cultural florescence. People bequeath wealth to the city, as opposed to the pattern of noble family inheritance. When the state reemerges, the city again becomes subordinate. In all of Fox's examples, this eventually happens.

An examination of dynamic tension between cities and states will help us understand and be able to predict the local urban structure and way of life. In colonial relationships, the city in the colonized area is economically and politically subordinate to the colonial power. In some cases, a city was created where none existed before, while in other cases, existing cities that had previously performed functions for other contexts became centers of administration and commerce. Thus their relevant contexts became international in scope, but their power relations diminished as they became economically and politically subordinate. This change in contexts affected the very form of the city; certain zones were set aside for foreign administrators and merchants. As Brush pointed out for the Indian city, this led to a dualistic form, where there was a "native" and a "colonial" segment of the city.[32]

In the contemporary postindustrial city, certain new relationships between political and economic institutions affect their roles as contexts for cities. The nature of industrial production requires a large, concentrated labor force. More significantly, industrial enterprises require accumulation of great wealth and bureaucratic mechanisms for controlling the production unit. In the past, bureaucracy (the hierarchical ordering of positions and authority) was characteristic of state organization but less important to productive units. After industrialization, corporations based upon bureaucratic models of control emerged. In the beginning, industrial enterprises tended to be localized and subordinate to the relevant governments. However, very shortly, business corporations expanded so that they were no longer contiguous with localities or even states. The expansion into control over raw materials, transportation, and distribution of products resulted in the creation of what are now called *the multinationals*—economic structures whose activities and personnel are not bounded by city or national lines.

In state-dominated preindustrial cities, the well-being of the city in terms of its defensive capabilities, architecture, and other forms of symbolic representation of state power was extremely important to the state. In effect, the prestige and power of the state were embodied in the opulence of the city as the site of state authority. In cities that developed during periods of weak state authority and were primarily commercial,

[32] John E. Brush, "Spatial Patterns of Populations in Indian Cities," *Geography Review*, 58 (1968), 362-91.

the well-being of the city was of great concern to the inhabitants, particularly the mercantile elite, who devoted time, energy, and wealth to
maintain the urban center.

In the colonial period, the city was also extremely important because it represented the wealth and power of the ruling nation. As the
entry point of the dominant state and the residence for colonial representatives, its well-being was paramount.

Contrast this with the modern city, where, for the first time, we find
powerful economic and political forces that are basically unconcerned
with the well-being of the city. Multi-national corporate structures, a
logical outgrowth of unfettered capitalism, have as organization goals
the viability and profit of the corporation.

In his history of Philadelphia, Sam Bass Warner suggests that, in
the colonial city, the aggregate private economic interests represented the
corporate or collective interests of the city itself.[33] At the present time,
however, this same city, Philadelphia, is embedded in a national and
international context, and it has been argued that the interests of the
population are no longer coincident with the common good of the city
as a unit. For instance, people's political allegiance is drawn to state and
national politics; their economic interests are tied to private corporations,
which are not local and are often multi-national. The goals of these non-
local systems are thus more salient than the goals of local controlling
forces—that is, the city government and/or merchants. The latter lose
constantly in their attempts to pursue local goals.

When we turn to the study of power relationships between city government and other governments, the American situation is unusual, because of the traditional balance of power between municipal, state, and
federal governments. The general term used for this system is *federalism*.
Other nation-states in the modern world have also used the federal model,
Switzerland, for example. In the historical development of political structure in the United States, major emphasis has been given to taxation and
governance at the national and state level, with minor significance given
to municipal or city government, which is often dependent for support
on outside forces. Most of the power of any political entity is based upon
its economic viability. The limits placed on municipal taxation by federal
and state governments have hampered their power and independence.
When the American city was a place of residence for the middle class
as well as other economic groups, its economic base was wider, and the
limited forms of taxation available could be used to develop economic
strength. Even then, however, state control frequently meant the distri-

[33] Sam B. Warner, *The Private City* (Philadelphia: University of Pennsylvania Press,
1968).

bution of political power and economic resources in a way that discriminated against the city. Control by state legislatures over apportionment frequently meant an underrepresentation of the city at the state level. As a result, state taxes drained money out of the city, returning only a small portion. In recent years, the shift of the middle class to areas outside the city has meant a further decline in the economic viability and consequent political independence of American cities.

The decline in political and economic autonomy of American cities is primarily a result of their inability to annex neighboring areas or establish regional forms of government in which the city proper would be the dominant force. Most social scientists recognize the need for metropolitan or regional governments to perform certain political functions. In the Philadelphia metropolitan area, for example, there are over three hundred local governments competing for taxes and providing municipal services in a fragmented, overlapping, inefficient manner. However, any attempts at regionalization have been thwarted by surrounding suburban areas.

In other metropolitan areas, some limited forms of regional cooperation have developed, particularly in transportation, but they have been limited in scope and power. Other types of cooperative units, especially educational, are strongly opposed. Exceptions to this include Dade County, Florida and Tulsa, Oklahoma. In other parts of the world, regional governments serve as functioning units in which the core city plays a dominant role. Examples are the Greater London Council, Tokyo, Bogotá, Cologne.

This generalized pattern of the American city and its larger economic and political contexts varies from city to city as a result of the particular history of relationships between the city and its economic and political hinterlands. Fox demonstrates this in his comparison of two American cities, which we shall discuss below.[34]

An area we know much less about is the cultural context. Cities may vary in their cultural hinterlands over time; centers of art, knowledge, and fashion may lose their dominant influence over a large geographic zone, while other centers may gain preeminence. Athens, which was an international center of learning at one period, has seen its intellectual spheres of influence change. Paris has also lost its cultural centrality for the Western world. Shifts in cultural hinterlands are tied ultimately to changes in the economic system or political events, unless they result from ideological movements that develop their own momentum (as in the case of the growth of sacred cities resulting from widespread religious movements).

[34] Richard Fox, "Rationale and Romance in Urban Anthropology," *Urban Anthropology,* 1 (1972), 205-33.

One phenomenon illustrating the creation of wide cultural spheres in the modern world is the selection of sites for Olympic Games and world expositions. In these cases, an international body selects a particular city for the impending event. The city thus designated goes through a rapid although short-term period of expansion of its culturally relevant hinterland. The selection of the city is related to economic and political factors and has an effect on economic growth. However, the ostensible function is cultural, in the sense of international symbolic integration, and the city draws to it tourists and spectators from an international zone. What makes these events particularly noteworthy is the fact that they are manipulated and artificial. They generally have a short-term effect on the city and its sphere of influence, except insofar as the construction of an infrastructure leads them to be used more frequently for such events.

Aside from shifts in the spheres of influence or geographic contexts of the city, there may also be shifts within the functional mix itself. Thus, a city that is primarily a political-administrative center may become primarily a mercantile center over time. Such shifts in the internal rank or mix of functions in the city influence its growth or decline, as well as its form and ambience. The introduction of new technology has frequently led to shifting functions, as have political events that change the ruling elements. Many administrative centers became centers of manufacture or commerce after the Industrial Revolution (as, for example, Latin American colonial cities that had served only political/religious functions in the past). Many economically dominant cities gained political functions when new rulers so decreed, as in the case of Fez.

DYNAMIC INTERACTION AND URBAN ANTHROPOLOGY

Changes in function and spheres of influence are parts of the dynamics of urban process that are of interest to the urban anthropologist because of the impact of these changes on the form of the city and the nature of life in it. When a city expands its zones of influence or changes its functions, this leads to changes in occupational structure and the mechanisms of the labor market that ultimately affect rates and distance of migration, cultural diversity, housing markets, land use, and internal structure. The particular mix of functions and the dynamic tension between the city and its relevant contexts also affects the nature of the sub-units or components of the city and their relationships to each other and this internal organization has a direct impact on lifestyles and behavior. Some recent anthropological studies allow us to trace these relationships in greater detail.

Price, in his study of Reno, Nevada, indicates the process by which

Reno emerged as a city specializing in a particular function.[35] He suggests that the political entity of the state of Nevada, through legislation, influenced the emergence of Reno as a major gambling and divorce center in the United States that draws to itself a nation-wide population. Thus, its interaction sphere extends well beyond the larger region of which it is a part. In this sense, Reno could be considered cosmopolitan in its diverse population. Its specific function also has a decided influence on the lifestyle of its permanent residential population. Price suggests that organized prostitution was intimately related to gambling and divorce activities, which affected the normative consensus of the general population. In spite of the primary relevance of Reno's specialized function for the national market, the region in which it is located also affects the city. This is demonstrated in the importance of the symbols and beliefs of cowboy culture to the urban residents. Reno thus has two culturally relevant external spheres: the region and the nation, the latter resulting from the city's unique function.

Price has also done work in Mexican border communities. He demonstrates that the very different ambience in the cities of Tijuana and Tecate can be attributed to their different functions. Tijuana's role as a tourist town leads to a local economy geared to outside consumers. The rate of growth has been great, and the state and national governments have responded with political and economic support. The city has lost much of its Mexican flavor. Tecate, on the other hand, has never become a tourist town. Price indicates that this was a conscious choice on the part of the inhabitants, who observed the transformation of Tijuana and found it unpleasant. Tecate is a city that still serves a localized hinterland. This is reflected in the form of the city, its way of life, and its traditional Mexican ambience.[36]

Leeds, in his article "The Anthropology of Cities: Some Methodological Issues," contrasts the Brazilian cities of Rio de Janeiro and São Paulo.[37] A major source of the difference between these two systems is their political and economic functions. Rio is characterized as an administrative city, the major focus of state and national governmental agencies; Leeds' analysis of its labor force statistics shows a high proportion of people gainfully employed in governmental and service occupations. São Paulo, on the other hand, is a major industrial center which Leeds again substantiated in the analysis of labor force statistics. This early and major

[35] John Price, "Reno, Nevada: The City as a Unit of Study," *Urban Anthropology*, 1 (1972), 14-28.
[36] John Price, "Tecate: An Industrial City on the Mexican Border," *Urban Anthropology*, 2 (1973), 35-47.
[37] Anthony Leeds, "The Anthropology of Cities: Some Methodological Issues," in Elizabeth Eddy (ed.), *Urban Anthropology* (Athens, Georgia: University of Georgia Press, 1968), pp. 31-47.

contribution of Leeds to the understanding of differences between cities focused primarily on the effect the different roles of Rio de Janeiro and São Paulo had upon the city in terms of cultural values.

Leeds explored how overt values concerning sexuality and sensuality were linked to different styles of elite prestige manifestation, which were ultimately linked to the function of the city. The position of Rio as a capital city produced an elite consisting of public officials, "whose symbols of office must constantly receive overt validation as part of the mechanism of maintaining power, influence and prestige." Such a need for display leads to physical arenas for such display and the resort town atmosphere and economy (beaches, vistas, carnival). In São Paulo, by contrast, the elite are financial and industrial executives, whose "basic operations, interests, knowledge . . . are enhanced by privacy." Thus, public arenas and public displays do not exist.

Leeds asks why there is such an intensive level of sensuality in Rio de Janeiro society. He concludes as follows:

> The answer to this specific question, I believe, lies in the role that the city of Rio de Janeiro . . . and by contrast, the role that the city of São Paulo . . . plays in the body politic as a whole.[38]

In a different article, Leeds focuses upon the spheres of influence of various urban centers.[39] This article emphasizes that the city cannot be understood as an isolated entity. Each city must be understood in terms of the larger region: the network of cities and the nation-state of which it is a part. He calls these supralocal forces.

A slightly different approach is taken by Fox in his comparison of two American cities.[40] A significant variable for him is the historical process of dynamic tension between each city and its respective economic and political hinterland that has influenced the present position of the two cities. These changing relationships are largely a function of changing roles in economic activity and political dominance. Both role and sphere of influence are interrelated and mutually reinforce one another.

In this comparison of Charleston, South Carolina and Newport, Rhode Island, Fox is concerned with the cities' relationship to the state and whether the state is centralized or not. In Newport, where the model of the New England town meeting was influential, the city remained independent of the state system. Furthermore, Newport was economically independent of its hinterland through its functional specialization as a

[38] Ibid., p. 37.
[39] Anthony Leeds, "Locality Power in Relation to Supralocal Power," in Aidan Southall (ed.), *Urban Anthropology* (New York: Oxford University Press, 1973), pp. 15-41.
[40] Fox, 1972, "Rationale and Romance."

leisure center for East Coast old money families. In contrast, Charleston was dominated by a state-centered authority since colonial times, and the plantation system made the city dependent on its hinterland and unable to develop autonomously. The consequences of these processes led to two quite different cities, in spite of their similarities in size and national context.

The segment of urban anthropology exemplified by these works is concerned with developing techniques to pinpoint essential *qualitative* differences between cities (as opposed to the quantitative techniques of geographers and economists). They do this by looking at functions and the dynamic interactions of cities with their economic, political, and cultural contexts. In most instances, they look at the consequences of function and external interaction for the *whole* city as a unit.

Such a view of urban anthropology would have it focus upon the study of cities as wholes rather than upon the smaller units within them. As we noted in Chapter 1, part of the general framework in cultural anthropology is this emphasis upon *holism*. The field researcher in a small and relatively isolated tribal unit could see the entire way of life of a people portrayed. Unfortunately, the cultural anthropologist has developed no real techniques for being able to study *cities* as wholes in the same way that he studied tribal cultures as a whole.

The one research technique emerging from anthropology is that of ethnography. When this technique is transposed to the city, obvious difficulties develop (see Chapter 7). Those who invoke the importance of holism often are forced to reject ethnographic research because it is impossible to do an ethnography of a whole city. However, the contributions of ethnography are very important to the understanding of urban organization and life, and are by no means incompatible with a holistic perspective. Thus ethnography must not be discarded in urban anthropology.

Working with subunits within the city that are amenable to ethnographic research can be holistic if one takes into account the contextual structures and institutions. In this perspective, the city can be viewed as the sum and result of its interacting components in their dynamic relationships with one another. In addition, the city as a whole is influenced by its context, and, to a certain extent, these external contexts impinge directly upon the micro-units themselves. Thus the ethnographic study of the micro-unit embedded in its whole-city and extra-city contexts can provide insights about the dynamics of both the city as an entity and about its relationships with extra-local forces.

Probably the best example of the way in which such ethnography can be useful in the understanding of larger contextual units can be found in the work of Leeds. In a variety of articles produced in the last decade, Leeds has consistently maintained the need to develop analytic models that bring together the directly observed behavior of people in the small-scale ethnographic situation with the larger contexts that both influence the small-scale unit and are affected by it.[41] His major effort has focused on favelas and other types of proletarian housing units in Brazil. He discusses the impact on the favela of whole city, regional, national, and international contextual variables, such as wage controls, taxation, and construction policies. At one point he discusses the number of levels of context within the metropolitan area of Rio de Janeiro itself:

. . . favela Babilônia, within the area called Lido, within the area called Copacabana, within the Regional Administration of Copacabana, within the area called the South Zone, within Rio de Janeiro City, within Greater Rio de Janeiro, and so on.[42]

Later, he adds:

Doing such research requires specification of those forms of national structures and institutions which are almost always, at best, treated peripherally in anthropological studies, though it is specifically the supralocal or national character of these entities that ties communities or localities into a single system.[43]

In other cases, he discusses the effects of the favela on the total city structure and process. In an interactive fashion, the favela responds to the outside by developing techniques to deal with supralocal forces. Its residents organize, hide insiders from the police, hide or distribute resources to avoid taxes, collectively tap into municipal service lines, and so forth. He points out the strengths of the local unit in meeting outside forces. Leeds ultimately combines ethnography in the locality with an analysis of context.

Press studies the effect of different local responses to such national policies as rent freezes and labor legislation in order to define Seville as a unique whole city.[44] The essential uniqueness of Seville is used as a backdrop for microethnographic analysis. In her comparison of Portuguese adaptation in two New England cities, M. Estellie Smith uses labor market differences, housing differences, and historical changes in

[41] Leeds, "The Anthropology of Cities" and "Locality Power"; "The Significant Variables in Determining the Characteristics of Squatter Settlements," *America Latina,* 12 (1969), 44-86.
[42] Leeds, "Locality Power," p. 24.
[43] Ibid., p. 36.
[44] Irwin Press, "The City as Context: Cultural, Historical, and Bureaucratic Determinants of Behavior in Seville," *Urban Anthropology,* 4 (1975), 27-34. This and the following articles appear in a special volume of *Urban Anthropology* titled *The City as Context: A Symposium.*

urban economic function as context variables to explain both the adaptation and organization of the two groups of Portuguese and the stereotypes held by the dominant classes, which in turn affect adjustment.[45] Rollwagen discusses the need to use such variables as "cause for existence" (function) and "historical development" (the process of dynamic interaction with contexts) to differentiate between whole cities as contexts before one examines any microethnographic question.[46] He too is interested in explaining the experience of ethnic groups in different cities.

The foregoing studies demonstrate that the ethnography of micro-units is not incompatible with a concern with *whole* cities. If used together, both perspectives provide the greatest amount of knowledge about the effects of larger forces on micro-units and the effects of micro-unit interaction processes on the city as a whole. The following chapters will discuss the transposition of the ethnographic method to the urban social system.

SUMMARY

A basic element in urban anthropology is the analysis of entire cities or city systems. For this analysis, archeological, historical, and contemporary studies are used as sources of data. This chapter centered upon the differing functions cities have performed during different periods of human history.

A basic issue for all urban anthropology, but which is central to archeology, is the origin of the city. Evidence available at the present time suggests that the origin of the city is relatively recent in human history, going back about five thousand years. It is apparent that a certain level of technology had to exist before the city as a settlement pattern could emerge. However, the mere existence of surplus agricultural production does not suffice as an explanation. Recent debate has focused upon the emergence of state political systems as a necessary condition for the rise of cities. A position linking the economic-ecological argument and the political control and centralization argument states that the integration of a highly sophisticated and complex economic system based upon a real division of labor required the introduction of centralized coercive authority. This then led to the rise of cities.

One of the results of the archeological evidence is the recognition of the variety of urban centers, their differential patterns of growth, and

[45] M. Estellie Smith, "A Tale of Two Cities: The Reality of Historical Differences," *Urban Anthropology*, 4 (1975), 61-72.
[46] Jack Rollwagen, "The City as Context: The Puerto Ricans of Rochester, New York," *Urban Anthropology*, 4 (1975), 53-60.

their differing functional and hierarchical systems from the very beginnings of urban existence. Thus, an in-depth historical perspective forces us to recognize that, from their very beginnings, urban centers have displayed great variability in form and function. Further archeological evidence may throw additional light on the complex interrelationship between economic and political factors in the early development of cities.

There are three major functions that cities perform for larger state and regional systems. These are economic, political, and cultural.

As economic centers, cities are loci of production and mercantile activities. All cities perform such functions for their internal and hinterland populations. In addition, some cities are specialized as market and production centers for a state-wide or even international economic system. Some of the major urban centers of antiquity performed these economic functions.

As political centers, or centers of centralized authority, cities have been extremely important. Historically, when powerful rulers emerged, they tended to locate their palaces in cities. Such cities became the symbolic representations of the authority of the ruler. Frequently these sites were established by a particular ruler, and their existence depended upon the maintenance of power by that ruler or dynasty. In the modern world, capital cities serving this same function have frequently been created where no urban settlement previously existed. In the Western colonial period, European powers created new cities in many parts of the world.

For the urban anthropologist, the cultural role of the city has been a major area of speculation and study. Here again the work of Redfield is significant. The cultural role of cities is viewed in three ways: integration, continuity, and change.

Cities have frequently been the source of integration of larger cultural regions. In addition to representing the political authority of the state or ruler, the city also represents the common ideology of a diverse and segmented population. Religious ceremonies, sports events, and festivals serve to bring together the city population and segments of the hinterland population. Cities serve to establish identity for regional populations.

In terms of cultural continuity and transmission, cities perform a major function. As Redfield and Singer suggest, the city is the place in which the Great Tradition emerges and is transmitted to other areas. Within the city we find representatives of the intellectual as well as political and economic elite. The major function of the intellectual elite is to transmit an ideology that buttresses the privileged status and resource access of the entire elite stratum.

In addition to maintaining tradition and transmitting it, cities are also centers of change. Much of the change that occurs in the Great Tradition and becomes the new orthodoxy takes place in the city. The city also serves as an incubator for radical changes in the sociocultural system. As a result of the social heterogeneity and domestic privacy characteristic of most cities, radical changes can develop and spread.

In modern societies, many of the functions of the city have declined and become dispersed; cities often become subordinate to the regions in which they are located or to the national system particularly in the United States. However, the cultural role of cities in modern states still remains a dominant one.

In contemporary studies of entire cities by anthropologists, overt recognition is given to the larger historical, political, regional, economic, and social contexts. The traditional ethnographic approach in anthropology can be maintained and can add to the understanding of urban life when such ethnography of small population units is linked to their larger contexts.

Part Three

URBAN
ETHNOGRAPHY

In Chapters 4 and 5 we shall discuss those studies that focus upon parts or components of the city in terms of the characteristics of the units discussed. In Chapter 4, the most primary or personal units will be treated: these are egocentric networks, ascriptive kinship units, and the domestic unit. In Chapter 5, we shall describe studies of the formally bounded, corporate units that are major components of the urban center. In Chapter 6, we shall look at both formal and informal institutions and at temporal or spatial situations that bring together different segments of the urban population forging integrative mechanisms that link elements of the city together.

In the three chapters, we shall be concerned with the relationship of particular studies to questions about the urban. What do we learn about urbanism (the effect of the city on the unit)? What do we learn about the social construction of the city and urban process?

Since much of anthropology is concerned with process and the dynamic interaction of units, another theme of the next three chapters is the degree to which the study focuses upon a *static* as opposed to a *dynamic* analysis. The previous chapters have developed the thesis that urban life is always in a process of change through the interaction of the component parts with one another and with their external contexts. The city—locked into a larger political, economic, and cultural context—is constantly being affected by outside forces. It is the nexus of the exchange of goods, services, people, and ideas. In turn, the city—as a major force in its own right—influences its many hinterlands, the state, and the larger cultural system. At the level of the whole city, social and cultural heterogeneity is both the source and result of constant change as groups within and outside interact.

4

Primary Units

Many of the early writings that attempted to establish the uniqueness of urbanism as a way of life intimate that city life is based upon shallow, impersonal ties between people. They imply that such ties lack emotional commitment and trust; they are instrumental and manipulative. An extension of this line of thinking can be seen in recent theories of mass society, with its attendant alienation and *anomie* (lack of purpose, ethical values).

This immediately raises the question: To what extent does urban ethnographic literature corroborate this view of urban social relationships? More specifically, what evidence have anthropologists accumulated about the maintenance of close, deep, personal ties between individuals?

Related to the foregoing is a concern with the persistence of kinship as an important basis for social ties in the city. Nineteenth-century social scientists recognized a dichotomy between simple and complex societies, wherein the former were based on *ascriptive* ties of kinship, while the latter were not. The pioneer anthropologist Lewis Henry Morgan is associated strongly with this idea,[1] as are Wirth and Redfield. Consequently, urban anthropologists have been concerned to investigate the degree to which ties based on ascriptive kinship are maintained and modified in the city.

One body of urban ethnographic literature deals with social networks. The social network as a concept and the techniques for studying this phenomenon were largely developed by a group of British anthropologists. In many ways, the concept parallels one developed earlier by Simmel, namely, the social circle.[2] In both cases, the context within which networks or circles are important is the complex modern society—particularly urban areas.

Underlying the network concept is the assumption that individuals in complex, urban social systems are faced with a large range of potential social relationships. Rather than acting largely as a member of ascribed kin groups, the individual *selects* from this potential range those with whom he or she will establish social ties. Such networks are *egocentric*—in the sense that a particular individual selects those with whom he will establish bonds of intimacy and mutual obligation. Thus, no two individuals will have exactly the same social network.

In many traditional and less complex social systems studied by anthropologists, egocentric social networks are not significant. Where one is born into an ongoing kinship unit (such as a lineage or a clan), the individual is expected to have the most significant social ties with fellow kinsmen. While voluntary social links do exist, anthropologists were so concerned with the more politically and economically important kin relationships that they never devoted much time to analyzing social networks.

In complex society, the element of choice and selection (as opposed to ascription) is basic to one's most important ties. This, however, should not be taken as an indication that kinship loses all significance in urban settings—a point we shall elaborate later in this chapter. The realities of urban life affect the bonds of kinship but do not destroy them.

SOCIAL NETWORKS AND DYADIC TIES

The social network concept in anthropology (as opposed to sociometry and social psychology) was largely an aspect of British social anthropology. In the American literature, a parallel interest in voluntary

[1] Lewis Henry Morgan, *Systems of Consanguinity and Affinity of the Human Family* (Washington, D.C.: Smithsonian Institution, 1870).
[2] Georg Simmel, *The Sociology of Georg Simmel,* ed. and trans. by Kurt H. Wolff (New York: The Free Press, 1950).

and potentially dissolvable *dyadic ties* (two-person relationships) was developed by Wolf and Foster largely in the context of Latin American peasant studies.[3] Dyadic ties between kinsmen, friends, and patrons with clients (those with resources and their supporters) were analyzed as to the processes of formation, content, and dissolution. Social networks and dyadic relationships are related to each other; in fact, in many descriptions of the manipulation of social networks, dyadic ties—or ties between ego and single members of his or her network—are often discussed one at a time. However, an individual's social network in its total configuration is more than simply the sum of all his dyadic ties.

Network Structure

Social networks have a variety of structural properties, which are each important in relation to their effect on the individual. Networks are frequently divided into segemnts based upon the closeness of an individual to members of his network. Most frequently a dichotomy is suggested between the effective segment and the extended segment. The *effective segment* of one's network consists of those others with whom there is closeness—as manifested by frequent interaction, trust, intimacy, and affect. The *extended segment* consists of those who are more distantly known. Because this dichotomy is an attempt to categorize a complete set of social relationships into two mutually exclusive subcategories, it is an oversimplification of reality. Boissevain has refined this dichotomy. He divides the effective segment into two parts—the inner core of ego's close ties as an intimate segment, and a less intimate portion. He further distinguishes between an extended segment of people who are known to ego and can be contacted, and a potential outer ring of contacts whom ego does not know but has the potential of knowing. In the outer ring are people in the effective segments of ego's own effective segment (friends of friends).[4]

It is very important to recognize that different social segments have different meanings and potentials for action. It might also be suggested that some of the earlier conclusions about the quality of urban life that emphasize shallowness and instrumentality fail to recognize segment differences and/or overemphasize the *extended* segment of individual networks.

[3] See Eric Wolf, "Kinship, Friendship, and Patron-Client Relations in Complex Societies," in M. Banton (ed.), *The Social Anthropology of Complex Societies* (London: Tavistock Publications, 1966), pp. 1-22, for a general overview; for the specific seminal ideas, see George M. Foster, "The Dyadic Contract: A Model for the Social Structure of a Mexican Peasant Village," *American Anthropologist*, 63 (1961), 1173-92.

[4] Jeremy Boissevain, "The Place of Non-Groups in the Social Sciences," *Man*, 3 (1968), 542-56.

Since choice and individual selection are fundamental attributes of social networks, the determination of which social contexts are to be used as sources for one's network is basic. There are a variety of sources available to the individual, which can be tapped to provide members for all network segments. Among these we would include kinsmen, neighbors, fellow workers, people from the same region or ethnic group, and former school or army mates.

To illustrate, let us focus on recent migrants to the city. Denich traces network development for rural-urban migrants in Yugoslavia. Before migrating, rural residents establish networks in the city that are an extension of their rural-based networks. The villager has had prior contacts with people from the city, whom he may incorporate into his network either prior to his leaving or immediately after his arrival. These are fellow villagers who have previously migrated and returned to the village to visit or for ritual occasions (weddings, funerals, christenings). When the migrant transfers to the city, he begins to recruit new elements into his network. These individuals are fellow workers, neighbors, and those who are met on a casual basis in marketing activities and in public eating places. In a table entitled "Sources of Urban Friendships," Denich notes for those in the city several years: 50 per cent of friends are workmates; an additional 21 per cent are neighbors; the remainder fall into categories such as fellow villagers, 10 per cent; kinsmen and schoolmates, 19 per cent.[5]

A network with ties recruited from one source will be different from a network recruited from many sources. The former will likely include many people who know each other. The latter will broaden one's access to a variety of urban social resources. The range of sources of recruitment used by the individual will have important implications for him or her.

Another important factor that differentiates types of networks is the actual activities and exchanges involved in the relationships between ego and members of the network. Network ties can involve mutual aid, exchange of goods and services, diffusion of ideas and information, as well as emotional support and sociability for its own sake. Some ties have very specific, narrow content, while others involve all content areas.

Roberts describes two kinds of friendship in two Guatemala City poor neighborhoods. In one type, individuals go to movies and sports events together and do each other short-term, small-scale favors. Other friendship ties based on long-time depth are valued more for their intrinsic sociability. These are ties of warmth, and aid is never requested.

---

[5] Bette S. Denich, "Migration and Network Manipulation in Yugoslavia," in R. Spencer (ed.), *Migration and Anthropology* (Seattle: University of Washington Press, 1970), pp. 133-48.

However, it is from these sources that massive and significant aid comes in major crisis situations.[6]

Finally, a structural property of social networks that has received considerable attention is the degree to which the members of ego's network (particularly the effective segment) are known to each other. Networks in which members are mutually known and socially relevant to each other are referred to as close-knit, dense, highly connected, or consistent. Networks in which members are not mutually known are referred to as loose-knit, dispersed, loosely meshed, or unconnected.

Network Process

The structural properties of networks have received considerable attention here because of their implications for an individual's social life and integration in the city context. In contrast to the stability of many of the ascriptively based social units found in traditional societies, social networks are constantly going through the dynamics of change. Ego may expand or contract his network; a shift in status or residence creates new source groups for recruitment and causes old ties to dissolve; members of the extended segment may be converted to the effective segment and vice versa. The content of ties may change; networks may become more dense or less dense.

An ethnographic approach, which emphasizes the actual relationships as seen by the ethnographer and which emphasizes the temporal processes involved in networks, can give us a more adequate view of the processes involved in network formation, change, and ruptures.

One of the most illuminating descriptions of such process can be found in Robert's work in Guatemala City, where he uses life history data to describe and classify the process of establishing and dissolving social ties. He discusses the implications of pre-urban activities and statuses, as well as types of residential and occupational mobility, for kinship, friendship, and general social relationships. He finds that his population, which is characterized by high rates of job instability and residential shifts, by and large have their closest ties with a selected few, recruited and maintained from very early work or army experiences. Kinship ties are continually losing importance; neighborhood and workplace gain importance for relatively new and shallower ties.[7]

Boswell describes the changing network of a male in Zambia as he goes through his education, acquires an occupation, marries, and becomes politically active. He looks at how changes affect network ties: which ties are affected, how the content of reciprocity is changed, how

[6] Bryan Roberts, *Organizing Strangers* (Austin: University of Texas Press, 1974).
[7] Roberts, *Organizing Strangers*.

significant are changes in domestic status, and what are the effects of the move to national independence.[8]

In analyzing network dynamics, anthropologists can focus on the processes of recruiting and cementing new ties. They can examine the degree to which ties must be continually validated by direct contact or the degree to which latent ties can be easily activated. They can study the process by which one converts an acquaintance into a friend, as well as other forms of conversion of content or segment. Finally, the process of rupturing ties can be examined.

Network Analysis

There are two major ways of collecting network data for network analysis. Anthropologists either have asked people about those with whom they have links and the nature of such links (through intensive interviewing), or they have collected data on actual activities and interaction. Bott, who used the former approach, estimated that she spent at least thirteen hours in intensive interviews with each of her informant families.[9] Epstein used actual case material developed through diary keeping to describe the network of an individual and analyzed all the contact activities and the nature of the ties involved.[10]

These anthropological techniques contrast with those of social psychologists and sociologists, who use either tightly controlled experimental conditions and/or very specific questionnaire data. In the following discussion, we shall use data collected ethnographically by anthropologists.

In the development of the social network concept, a basic dualism seems apparent. Some analysts view social networks as ends in themselves, that is, significant social units, while others view networks as means for extending social ties to achieve ends.

If the researcher asks, "Who would you contact to get the name of an abortionist?" he or she would get a series of instrumental links extending out from an individual's close personal friends to indirect contacts (the extended segment). On the other hand, if the researcher focuses on those with whom people socialize most and the content of that interaction, he or she would obtain information about the inner ring of close intimate ties (the effective segment). Since the ramifications of a network extend outward and include a potentially large number

[8] D. M. Boswell, "Independence, Ethnicity, and Elite Status" in A. Cohen, ed., *Urban Ethnicity* (London: Tavistock Publications, 1974), pp. 311-36.
[9] Elizabeth Bott, *Family and Social Network*, 2nd ed. (New York: The Free Press, 1971).
[10] A. L. Epstein, "The Network and Urban Social Organization," in J. C. Mitchell (ed.), *Social Networks in Urban Situations* (Manchester: Manchester University Press, 1969), pp. 77-116.

of individuals, the research strategies adopted focus on either the most significant primary ties or on a segment mobilized for particular ends.

When the social network is regarded as an end, two major analytic foci emerge: one emphasizes the affect, or emotion-laden quality, of this set of personal relationships, and views the unit in terms of sociability; the second views the network as a unit of norm socialization and social control.

For those who focus on the instrumental nature of networks, there are several foci. One is the transmission and exchange within the network of goods, services, and information. Another is the utilization of networks in adaptation to the urban setting, both short-term (rural-urban migrant adaptation) and long-term. Another strand of network analysis focuses upon specialists in network relationships (sometimes called brokers) and the relationship between their positions, their networks, and urban process. Finally, there is a concern with the networks of strategic and powerful individuals.

One recurring issue in this volume has been the need to refute the view of the urban setting as dehumanizing and depersonalizing. This is what Wirth referred to in discussing the breakdown of primary relationships in the city. In the network literature, this view is counteracted by shifting the focus from large-scale structural attributes of social relationships to smaller-scale relationships, dynamic in nature, which begins with the individual and flow from him.

In Bott's study of London families, whether describing networks that are dispersed or that are highly-connected, the given family is enmeshed in a complex set of intimate, trusting, personal social relationships that involve common interests, frequent common activities, and common feeling. Networks appear to be extremely important factors in sociability and leisure time activities (recreation, entertainment, vacations).[11]

Denich notes that the Yugoslavs distinguish friends from acquaintances and casual contacts. Friendship is set aside for a few special ties. Friendship is not lightly bestowed. Once friendship is bestowed, a set of mutual ties and obligations develop that are very strong and include such mutual aid activities as lending money and also significant sociability activities.[12]

Roberts too discusses different notions of friendship in Guatemala City. He emphasizes general Guatemalan distrust of intimate ties outside the family and its effect in restricting such intimate friendships. He also discusses the effect of the larger urban context (rapid, uncontrolled urban growth and competition for jobs and space) on friendship ties.

[11] Bott, *Family and Social Network.*
[12] Denich, "Migration and Network Manipulation."

In his study, friendship—as distinct from acquaintanceship—is reserved for sociability and activities that are intrinsically worthwhile, while casual ties are more instrumental.[13]

A recent attempt to measure degrees of commitment, caring, involvement, trust, and intimacy can be seen in the work of Brim. He has developed techniques for eliciting information about the dimensions of trust, concern and caring, value and interest similarity, and the enjoyment of interaction. He is interested in examining differences in close, personal network ties between different status categories.[14]

As we previously noted, there is a dynamic element in network formation, expansion, contraction, and dissolution. Thus, Liebow notes in *Tally's Corner* the ease with which *intimate* ties are established and discontinued. He relates this relative speed in the process to the circumstances of the men, such as geographic mobility and changes in marital or cohabitation status.[15] Gutkind too notes the ease of formation and rupture of close, intimate, interdependent ties between the long-term unemployed in two African cities, also related to these circumstances.[16] Both Gutkind and Liebow emphasize the brittle nature of social relationships for these populations. Ties are frequently broken as a result of conflict and mistrust rather than mobility. Both authors relate this to the basic insecurity and inability to predict the future, particularly in the economic sphere.

A very different segment of the African urban population was studied by Jacobson in Mbale, Uganda. The target population of the study was the emerging bureaucratic elites in the government. For these individuals, members of the social network were primarily recruited from among their co-workers. Since the work role entailed geographic mobility from one city to another at the whim of upper echelon decision-makers, the establishment of intimate, personal, mutual aid ties between co-workers meant that the individual would often encounter former friends from other locations or could be referred to friends of former friends. In addition, such network relationships could help the individual move up in the bureaucratic structure. On the other hand, the networks of the wives were spatially localized; their recruitment arena was limited to the immediate neighborhood. Jacobson also noted the tendency of his target population to develop instant friendships with friends of

---

[13] Roberts, *Organizing Strangers.*

[14] Joseph Brim, "Social Network Correlates of Avowed Happiness," (unpublished mimeo., Department of Anthropology, Rutgers University, n.d.).

[15] Elliot Liebow, *Tally's Corner* (Boston: Little, Brown and Company, 1967).

[16] P. C. W. Gutkind, "The Energy of Despair: Social Organization of the Unemployed in Two African Cities," *Civilisations*, 17 (1967), 186-211; and "The Poor in Urban Africa," in W. Bloomberg and H. J. Schmandt (eds.), *Power, Poverty and Urban Policy*, Urban Affairs Annual Review, vol. 2, 1970.

friends when they moved. In cases of location in cities where they had no latent friendship ties, they would be referred to friends of former friends and quickly develop the same kind of intimate, joking, trusting relationship. For Jacobson's informants, network ties were extremely important affectively. They involved almost all non-working time in a variety of leisure-time activities.[17]

Chanda, the Ndola resident whose network was analyzed by Epstein from a diary of activities, was an urban African whose career had been characterized by great mobility, both occupational and geographic. He had lived in many towns and worked at many jobs, and this was reflected in the large number of friends and leisure-time partners who were former co-workers or former neighbors.[18]

Based upon Jacobson's work, it can be suggested that those who are very mobile because of occupation or other status attributes but have relatively secure and upwardly mobile futures will be characterized by similar network processes, in which the phenomena of relatively quick tie-formation and easy reactivation of latent ties can be expected. Networks can be based upon expectations of continuity, rather than upon the actual maintenance of contact over long periods of time; that is, individuals can drop ties when they leave one area and reestablish them at some future time when they become situated near one another again.

Jacobson's work involves the issue of *latency*, the degree to which one can reactivate old ties after long periods of inactivity. Roberts' work emphasizes this same point. For one of his informants, Pepe, the launching of a new business led him to reactivate several old, latent ties, which immediately resumed their old footing. This point is often missed in sociological literature when it is assumed that feeling, trust, and intimacy are measured by frequent and current interaction.

Harries-Jones provides us with an example of a situation in which ties must be continually validated if one expects to reactivate them in the future. His Zambian urban migrants who expect to return to their home villages maintain ties with a special category of "home boys," who act as links between city residents and their rural location.[19]

Thus far we have been focusing upon the dynamics and processual development of networks. It should be obvious that various statuses and situations influence both the process of network formation and the structural properties of networks. Brim suggests that various statuses (sex, age, marital status) influence the shape of one's effective network,

[17] David Jacobson, *Itinerant Townsman* (Menlo Park, California: Cummings Publishing Company, 1973).
[18] Epstein, "The Network and Urban Social Organization."
[19] P. Harries-Jones, " 'Home-Boy' Ties and Political Organization in a Copperbelt Township," in J. C. Mitchell, *Social Networks*, 1969, pp. 297-347.

that is, the number of intimate ties, their content, and their affective nature. He then relates the nature of network ties to people's perceptions of their happiness or mental states.[20]

A somewhat different approach is taken by Parker and Kleiner, who see a connection between the properties of one's network and interpersonal dysfunction, or mental illness. They indicate that mental illness —which has typically been viewed as an individually induced, personality-related phenomenon—can be directly linked to the nature of the social network of an individual. They reject both individual personality characteristics and such categories as class and ethnicity as precise, predictive variables of mental illness. Basically, they suggest that individuals who have affectively involved, close-knit, mutually known social ties will be less prone to mental illness. Thus, the notion that cities or lower class status per se produce mental illness is not accurate.[21]

Norms

With the development of the network concept, new insight was gained into the phenomenon of norm transmission and social control in the urban setting. As Epstein notes, some concept was needed as the linking mechanism between the family or domestic group as agent of socialization and the larger social structure.[22] Some analysts have suggested that social networks are frequently used as basic reference groups. By this we mean that individuals evaluate themselves and their behavior in terms of the way in which the network perceives them.

Bott, in her classic work, views the network as the basic unit for the development and maintenance of norms that effectively regulate the behavior of the members of the network. Bott's study of twenty London families indicates the process by which the social network operates as a mechanism of social control. Gossip about other members of a network tells individuals not only what is expected of them, but also acts to control their behavior. Husbands and wives perceive their own behavior as conforming to the views of proper behavior held by friends, neighbors, co-workers, and relatives in their network.[23]

The members of Tally's friendship circle in *Tally's Corner* acquire their views of women, family life, fatherhood, child care, work, and

[20] Brim, "Social Networks."

[21] R. Kleiner and S. Parker, "Network Participation and Psychosocial Impairment in an Urban Environment," in H. Meadows and E. Mizruchi (eds.), *Urbanism, Urbanization and Change*, 2nd ed. (Reading Massachusetts: Addison-Wesley Publishing Co., 1975).

[22] Epstein, "The Network and Urban Social Organization."

[23] Bott, *Family and Social Network*.

leisure-time activities through the group. Networks are particularly important for the transmission of consumption styles and preferences.[24]

In her study of London families, Bott draws a distinction between highly connected networks and dispersed networks. A highly connected network is one in which the individual interacts frequently with the other members. A variety of activities are performed with other members of the network, involving a good deal of exchange of aid and support. The most significant element of a highly connected network, however, is that the individuals are members of each other's network—that is, they tend to be mutually known to each other. The individual whose effective network (more intimate ties) is characterized by these dense, overlapping ties derives clear-cut basic norms from it. This kind of network is almost a group, because of the ties between the individuals and their frequent collective activity.

A dispersed network seldom acts like a group. Most members of ego's network do not know each other. Very often they are recruited from disparate social fields. The individual receives many different sets of norms and values, and there is no consensus within the set of "significant others" about appropriate behavior, style preferences, and similar matters. However, the individual with a loose network *may* be plugged into a variety of urban subgroups and thus have wider access to resources.

Bott characterizes the networks of many of her informants as *intermediate* (composed of segments of both types). Moreover, she notes that those who were formerly members of highly connected networks find it difficult and frustrating when they move socially or geographically into occupations or neighborhoods where such networks are not customary. Conversely, those who have been socialized in the context of dispersed networks and who find themselves in occupations or neighborhoods where highly connected networks are customary find this transition equally difficult. In both cases, Bott suggests, some transitional type of network with some connected segments and some dispersed segments would be found.

What is interesting is that Bott finds that the type of network a family has is very important in determining family structure and conjugal roles. In fact, the type of network is more important than social class in this respect. Class itself does not directly affect family roles, and class does not affect the nature of the network in any simple way. Such variables as occupation (affecting the opportunity for non-localized ties), neighborhood homogeneity or heterogeneity (affecting the likelihood of localized networks), and the individual's geographic and social mobility affect the nature of the network in a complex fashion.

[24] Liebow, *Tally's Corner.*

Bott says:

> The economic and occupational system, the structure of formal institutions, the ecology of cities, and many other factors affect the connectedness of networks, and limit and shape the decisions that families make. Among others, factors associated with social class and neighborhood composition affect segregation of conjugal roles, not solely and not primarily through direct action on the internal structure of the family, but indirectly, through their effect on its network. Conceptually, the network stands between the family and the total social environment.[25]

Epstein and Kapferer examined the relationship between networks, norms, and gossip in separate studies in two South African urban settings. Epstein described the way in which a gossip "set" (network) operated in Ndola. Two gossip networks were activated by a case of adultery in which the offended party (male) thrashed the individual who was caught in the act and on subsequent meetings repeated the beating. The incident was reported to Epstein through his assistants, who each belonged to different networks. Much of the article focused upon these separate networks of gossipers. Interestingly, the norm maintenance aspect of the gossip did not stress the act of adultery, but was focused more upon a negative view of the offended party's behavior and his relationship with his wife. In part, this was the result of the types of networks investigated, since the individuals comprising these various gossip sets were of relatively high social status, and members were linked in some way with the individual who was caught in the act. He was of their status, in contrast to the offended party, who was of lower status. Much of the gossip focused upon the married couple, because a woman of higher status (based upon education, style of dress, familial and tribal background) had married a man of lower status, and it was this, rather than the adulterous act, that was wrong. One must then assume that the normative function of the gossip was not to castigate adultery, but to point out the difficulties attendant upon the marriage of people of very different statuses. As Epstein points out, he was unable to interview the offended party or to tap gossip sets that might have been more sympathetic to his position. Such networks might have been more concerned with reinforcing other types of norms, particularly norms against adultery and the misbehavior of wives while their husbands are absent on business trips.[26]

[25] Elizabeth Bott, "Urban Families: Conjugal Roles and Social Networks," in J. Friedl and N. Chrisman (eds.), *City Ways* (New York: Thomas Y. Crowell Company, 1975), p. 144.
[26] A. L. Epstein, "Gossip, Norms and Social Network," in J. C. Mitchell (ed.), *Social Networks*, pp. 117-27.

Kapferer discusses the way in which networks of co-workers in an African copper belt factory develop and transmit norms about work performance, and how they exert control over their own members. He analyzes the way social status and fears of witchcraft are used to force compliance with the network's standards of productivity.[27]

Another example of the effect of networks in social control can be seen in Hill's study of American Indians in Sioux City, Iowa. As Hill indicates, a young, unmarried Indian male frequently fills the role of "hell-raiser." His network is composed of his peers, whose behavior and attitudes reinforce his. He is expected to spend much of his time on street corners, prove his masculinity by fighting and seeking thrills, visit bars with his friends, pursue women, and not worry about stable employment or saving money. When he marries, he is expected to shift his role from that of "hell-raiser" to that of "family man." This does not occur immediately after marriage. The fundamental process involves shifting his network from peers to older kinsmen (either his own or those acquired through marriage). These new members of the network frown upon many of his former activities and force him to conform to the new pattern. From Hill's description, it is obvious that this is a painful experience and takes a considerable period of time. It can be observed and measured through the breaking of old network ties and recruitment of new ones.

One carry-over from former behavior is drinking, which is not totally frowned upon by the new network. However, he changes his drinking mates from peers to kinsmen. In addition, many of the behaviors formerly associated with drinking, such as fighting, pursuit of other women, and petty theft, are frowned upon. In addition, where the cost of drinking interferes with the economics of the household unit, such behavior is disapproved. In this example, it is not the nature or characteristics of the social network (highly connected versus dispersed), but the shift in its composition that produces changes in norms and social control.[28]

Roberts notes changes in network composition as one enters old age in Guatemala City. Because of the job market and rapid growth in Guatemala City, and because of the absence of social security mechanisms, the old are downwardly mobile, as well as restricted in their geographic mobility. Roberts finds this reflected in changes in their social relationships—particularly a contraction of ties, which then have an effect on norms and roles.[29]

[27] Bruce Kapferer, "Norms and the Manipulation of Relationships in a Work Context," in J. C. Mitchell (ed.), *Social Networks*, pp. 181-244.
[28] Thomas W. Hill, "From Hell-Raiser to Family Man," in J. Spradley and D. W. McCurdy (eds.), *Conformity and Conflict* (Boston: Little, Brown and Co., 1974), pp. 186-200.
[29] Roberts, *Organizing Strangers*.

Network Ties as Instrumental

Much of the work on networks has been oriented toward understanding the role of network manipulation in adaptation to urban life.
While studies of networks as affective units or normative units focus on
the effective segment, studies of the instrumental uses of network ties
examine both the effective and extended ties in the exchange of goods,
services, and information. In such cases, ties are frequently looked at as
social capital, which can be used in the same way as other resources. Ties
are seen as potential resources, but they also entail reciprocal obligations.
Thus they are, in a sense, speculative risks. The mobilization of such ties
is usually studied in relation to migrant adaptation, survival of extremely
insecure social groups, and occupational or political mobility.

One way of viewing the network instrumentally is to look at exchanges of goods and services between ego and network members. In
this kind of discussion, dyadic relationships are usually treated individually. Some basic distinctions must be made in regard to the content and
temporal duration of exchange and assistance. Some ties involve significant exchanges of resources—large amounts of money or domestic or
nursing aid in case of illness; others involve small-scale loans or favors.
Some involve long-term continuing aid—loan or investment in business;
others involve short-term assistance.

There are also many kinds of recurring exchanges of goods for
services based on people's different access to particular goods or skills.
As an example of this, we can cite Michael Whiteford's data on neighbors in Popayán, Colombia, who set up regular exchanges of cooked
food for firewood or water when one household has greater access or
cooking skill.[30]

Another distinction must be made between ties between social
equals (kin or friends), which involve exchange of like goods and services, and asymmetrical ties (patron-client ties), where individuals exchange different kinds of items. Often the superordinate individual
provides resources or political intervention, while the subordinate individual offers deference, esteem and menial services, such as running
errands.

Roberts points out that in Guatemala City, such ties are important
to those of higher status who want support at election time. The kinds
of goods and services clients can seek or hope for in return are specified
(not diffuse aid) and controlled (in terms of what is given and when)

[30] Michael Whiteford, "Neighbors at a Distance: Life in a Low-Income Barrio," in
W. Cornelius and F. Trueblood (eds.), *Latin American Urban Research,* 4 (1974),
157-82.

by the patron. Thus the relationships are not easy to manipulate for survival or mobility.[31]

Denich notes that in Yugoslavia, if those in the restricted category of friends (as opposed to acquaintances) move upward socially, this does not lead to the dissolution of friendship ties. One remains as intimate and friendly with those who achieve upward mobility; the relationship does not become like patron-client ties between people of different status. Here the higher status individual does not expect or receive deference in return for goods and services. Exchanges remain symmetrical, in spite of differences in status.[32]

Network exchanges are often centered on crisis or unexpected events. Sociological work in the United States has indicated that different kinds of ties (kin, friend, and neighbor) are used, depending on the amount of resource and time commitment. Illness requires both short-term assistance (nursing and sometimes domestic help) and often long-term aid, if one loses income or a job. Different kinds of ties would be mobilized in each case. Unanticipated events—like breakdowns in transportation, babysitting services, or unusual needs (transportation to the airport at a late hour)might each lead to mobilization of different kinds of ties. Extended ties or shallow ties may be used if time and amount is not significant, while the most effective ties are reserved for more significant situations.

Roberts notes that among the relatively poor in Guatemala City, kin and close friends are not asked for small favors. A conscious attempt is made to avoid making many small demands on them. Kin are treated with special respect and reserve, as if they are being saved as insurance for extreme cases of need or hardship. Friends are asked for advice, counsel, and special aid in situations not likely to be recurring. Those asked for small-scale, short-term help are likely to be neighbors or workmates who are not close friends. This differs from many other studies, in which kin are utilized in everyday regular recurring exchanges for suvival.[33]

For those living under conditions of great income insecurity and instability, regular exchanges seem to be common and are often described in the literature. Eames and Goode describe this phenomenon among the urban poor throughout the world. The ease with which crisis aid is requested and granted is also commented upon. Kin as well as friends are intensely involved.[34]

[31] Roberts, *Organizing Strangers.*
[32] Denich, "Migration and Network Manipulation."
[33] Roberts, *Organizing Strangers.*
[34] Edwin Eames and Judith Goode, *Urban Poverty in a Cross-Cultural Context* (New York: Free Press, 1973), Chapter 5.

Some of the most detailed descriptions of actual exchanges and processes of exchanges have been done by anthropologists studying economically marginal segments of the population. Lomnitz lists the following as among "the most important objects of exchange in the networks" in a shantytown in Mexico City:

> *Loans,* of money, food, blankets, tools, clothing and other goods.
> *Services,* including the lodging and care of visiting relatives, widows, orphans, old people; care and errand-running for such neighbors, and minding children for working mothers. Assistance among men includes help in home construction and in transporting materials. Children must lend a hand in carrying water and running errands.
> *Sharing of facilities,* such as a television set or a latrine (which the men may have built jointly).[35]

Stack describes the institutionalization of swapping and trading for survival in a Black community in the United States. Thus people trade "food stamps, rent money, a TV, hats, dice, a car, a nickel here, a cigarette there, food, milk, grits, and children." She says:

> Whether one's source of income is a welfare check or wages from labor, people in the Flats borrow and trade with others in order to obtain daily necessities. The most important form of distribution and exchange of the limited resources available to the poor . . . is by means of trading, or what people usually call "swapping". As people swap, the limited supply of finished material goods in the community is perpetually redistributed among networks of kinsmen and throughout the community.
> Trading in the Flats generally refers to any object or service offered with the intent of obligating. An object given or traded represents a possession, a pledge, a loan, a trust, a bank account— given on the condition that something will be returned . . .

Degrees of entanglement vary from intense daily or even hourly swapping on the part of cooperating households to occasional trades.[36]

Ashton describes the importance of friendship ties for one lower class group in a housing project in Colombia. He talks of how women depend on their friends (*amigas*) both in minor and major crisis events. Minor crises lead to food exchanges. "A number of street sellers have daily food exchange relationships and even lend children to one another for selling purposes." Major events, such as serious illness and abandon-

---

[35] L. Lomnitz, "The Social and Economic Organization of a Mexican Shantytown," in W. Cornelius and F. Trueblood (eds.), *Latin American Urban Research,* 4 (1974), p. 149.
[36] Carol Stack, *All Our Kin* (New York: Harper and Row, 1974), pp. 32-35.

ment, call forth financial aid and medicinal plants. *Amigas* are also likely to attend their friends in childbirth.[37]

It has been assumed that middle class networks are used predominantly for gaining access to mobility or obtaining short-term crisis aid, since grave risks are usually protected against by formal insurance and savings. This class was considered not to be characterized by regular exchanges of goods and services, since these are not necessary for survival. However, in view of what we know about exchanging child care services in the United States and the increase of women entering the labor force, this assumption about the middle class can no longer remain unverified by research.

In examining network exchanges, one must examine issues of reciprocity. Foster has suggested that such ties must be continuously validated by exchanges, but that they must never be fully balanced or reciprocal, since this would end the relationship. Rules about permissible time lags in reciprocity vary. When exchanges do not involve equivalent goods or services, measures of equivalent values become difficult.[38]

In A. L. Epstein's description of the activities of Chanda, there is a segment in which Chanda is invited by a friend to join him in drinking beer. Chanda initially demurs and finally admits that he has no money. His friend, who has been having an affair with a female kinsman of Chanda's, indicates that he will provide the money needed. Underlying this exchange is the assumption that Chanda will act on his behalf in the liaison in return.[39]

Since there are no agreed-upon equivalences in the exchange process (especially in a loose-knit network of people recruited from varied arenas with different norms and expectations), differing definitions and expectations of reciprocity may often lead to the rupturing of ties. Quarrels and disagreements about reciprocity are frequent.

One of the most significant areas of information for those in a complex, stratified urban situation is job market information. In much of the recent literature on migrants' adjustment in cities throughout the world, information concerning the job market is a vital concern. Migrants use their previous ties (kinsmen, fellow villagers, and tribesmen) to obtain such information and also activate and use the farthest-reaching, indirect ties for these pragmatic ends. Studies of instrumental manipulations of network ties show that very often the individual uses his effective network to reach referrals. Thus, his friend or kinsmen sends him to

---

[37] Guy Ashton, "The Differential Adaptation of Two Slum Subcultures to a Colombian Housing Project," *Urban Anthropology*, 1 (1972), p. 186.

[38] Foster, "The Dyadic Contract."

[39] A. L. Epstein, "The Network and Urban Social Organization," in J. C. Mitchell (ed.), *Social Networks*, pp. 77-116.

a third individual, who continues the process of referral to yet another level.

In an article reviewing the anthropological literature on migration, Nancy and Theodore Graves point out that almost all initial job and housing information is acquired through kin or friend contacts in the city.[40] Roberts points out that, while contacts based on old pre-urban ties become less significant with length of urban residence, only 13 percent of his migrant informants in Guatemala City had no such contacts when they came to the city. There is a difference between using kin and friends to get jobs and using them to get job information. Roberts points out that, while most people previously used kin directly as "sponsors" who spoke for them in getting jobs, since 1955 this has no longer been true. He points to increasing specialization in the labor market and increased attention to such formal attributes as education to account for this. No longer is reputation or recommendation sufficient. However, job information largely acquired through the network is still most important.[41]

In many urban contexts in the United States, Europe, and the developing world, employers implicitly recognize the existence and function of such networks and tell employees about open jobs and rely on their communication for recruitment. In the following two examples in advanced industrial systems, jobs were secured directly from network ties manipulated by employers.

Research that was conducted by Eames and Robboy on East Indians in a northern industrial English city covered the formal recruiting mechanisms of the factory. Interviews with the personnel managers indicated that, in the recruitment of new workers where Indians were already established, the personnel managers relied almost entirely on their existing workers to fill openings. In the interviewing situation, there was one instance in which an individual was applying for a job. The personnel officer asked her why she had come to this factory. When she indicated that a friend of hers who was already employed there suggested it, this was noted on her application. The personnel officer subsequently pulled the friend's file and told us that he would hire the applicant after an interview with the friend to make sure she had truly recommended her. Such recruitment through existing social networks, in addition to saving resources in advertisement and interviewing, also gives the employer an additional means of controlling the employee.[42]

[40] Nancy B. Graves and Theodore D. Graves, "Adaptive Strategies in Urban Migration," in B. J. Siegel (ed.), *Annual Review of Anthropology*, 1974, pp. 117-51.
[41] Roberts, *Organizing Strangers*.
[42] Research on Punjabi migrants in Wolverhampton, England was conducted during 1969 and 1970. Researchers were Edwin Eames and Howard Robboy. Research was supported by a study leave from Temple University and N.I.M.H. Grant Number DHEW-IRO3-MH 18799-01.

In the Beech Creek study of Kentucky migrants to northern Ohio industrial cities conducted by Schwarzweller and associates, the factory owners repeatedly said that the social control of behavior (through gossip and shame) that prevails when they recruit people from common networks is clearly viewed as advantageous.[43]

A very specific study of the use of social networks to obtain job information and jobs themselves is found in Denich's study of migrants in Yugoslavia. Denich notes that social networks are explicitly used by migrants in obtaining employment. In a table entitled *Sources of Help for Finding Jobs,* the most significant category was "friend or acquaintance in an influential position," followed immediately by "friend." Where an individual intervened on behalf of the migrant in obtaining employment, in more than half the cases, that individual was in one of these two categories. The remainder, less than half, were almost all kinsmen.[44]

In the Yugoslavian situation, the manipulation of network ties for an individual's self-interest is considered quite proper. One must have "connections" and use them in order to be successful in the urban situation. Instrumentality of relationships does not appear to jeopardize them in any way. The individual who refuses to help in situations where he can is generally designated as unkind or selfish. This pattern of relationships based upon what friends can do for you is characteristic of all Yugoslav society, not just the city, thus negating the notion that it is urbanism that fosters this. However, it is in the urban situation where the individual can use his ties in a variety of ways and a variety of situations. The individual who lacks connections will be at a distinct disadvantage in the urban arena.

In addition to the job market, Denich notes the use of ties in the acquisition of housing. Apartments have been built by the government but are in short supply. There is a waiting list for such housing. Simply placing one's name on a waiting list will usually be futile. Connections are used to move one's name higher on the list. Since apartments are scarce, many of the migrants eventually build their own houses. The building of a house requires a variety of government approvals (Denich notes that some fifty government permits may be involved), as well as the use of contractors. To expedite the house building, one must use one's connections again. It should be noticed once again that connections include kinsmen, friends, acquaintances, and casual contacts.

In Roberts' study of a shantytown in Guatemala City, he found that everyone in his sample of residents had been recruited to the newly forming community through a kinsman or a friend. In the migration literature,

---

[43] Harry K. Schwarzweller, James S. Brown, and J. J. Mangalam, *Mountain Families in Transition* (University Park, Pa.: Pennsylvania State University Press, 1971).
[44] Denich, "Migration and Network Manipulation."

information about the housing market in general is greatly affected by
network ties. Initial housing is usually arranged by prior contacts, and
subsequent housing is frequently the result of urban-based ties.

Acquiring information about where to shop or whose services to
hire is other area where the extended network becomes important. A
study of middle class lay referral networks for physicians noted that
effective ties were not as important as shallow, extended ties in getting
information about doctors. A major concern was that doctors be in the
local area; therefore neighbors, rather than close friends or kin, were
consulted. In an analysis of this data, Bazakas suggests that there were
two types of clients—the rationals and the traditionals. The rationals
assumed that they would not easily find good medical aid, and they
shopped around, using many different sources of doctors' names and
trying them out. Traditionals believed they should establish a close and
long-term tie with a practitioner, and they used fewer, better known,
and more trusted sources of referral.[45]

Another example of a group that uses network ties in the selection
of medical aid is the urban gypsy group in the United States. The services provided and the costs of care are carefully and continuously evaluated and information about practitioners is readily spread throughout
the network.[46] Graves and Graves indicate the importance of network
ties for various migrant groups in relation to health care in various urban
centers.[47]

Network Specialists

As we have just seen, urbanites develop networks to serve a multiplicity of functions. However, there are some urban actors who, for
a variety of reasons, become more significant or strategic in the urban
context in terms of *informal roles* in networks, rather than formal posts.
Therefore, the relationships they establish with others and the way they
operate are of central concern to urban analysts.

From the point of view of the individual, these specialists provide
access to whatever the particular goals may be: bargain purchases,
illegal services, legal intervention, job information. These are *connections*. From the point of view of the community, these individuals serve
an integrative function for the larger social system by providing junc-

[45] Mary Bazakas, "How to Find a Doctor: Network Ties and Lay Referrals" (unpublished Masters' thesis, Temple University, Department of Anthropology, 1977).
[46] J. C. Salloway, "Medical Care Utilization Among Urban Gypsies," *Urban Anthropology*, 2 (1973), 113-26.
[47] Graves and Graves, "Adaptive Strategies."

tures between networks. Their role in such intermeshing structures will be discussed in Chapter 6.

Specialists in network relationships can be classified as *influentials* or *brokers*. An influential is an individual who, by virtue of his position in some strategic institution in the social structure, can use the power of his position directly to help others. He is directly involved in the distribution of scarce resources. In the Yugoslav study cited above, these would be industrial managers and government bureaucrats.

A broker, on the other hand, is an individual who has access to influentials and uses this, rather than the direct power of his position, to help others. The broker's position as a mediator may derive from the nature of his or her own network, which may include influentials in either the effective or extended segment. This position may enable the broker to reciprocate favors for influentials, that is, influentials may frequently act as brokers in reciprocal trade-offs with other influentials. An example of this is provided by Denich when she describes a government bureaucrat who has found jobs for over one hundred fellow villagers by interceding with his bureaucrat colleagues.[48] In other words, brokers of this type have effective ties with high level people and extended ties with petitioners.

In many cases, influentials are utilized directly in obtaining employment, housing, and other scarce resources.

Rollwagen describes a case where members of a particular Mexican village obtained prominence in the popsicle industry in many Mexican cities. Some of their enterprises are small scale, while others are very large. Some of the villagers become entrepreneurs and serve as employers of large numbers of fellow villagers, who serve as street vendors. Almost everyone who leaves the village has a guaranteed job.[49] The contrast between this case and the Yugoslav case is obvious. Here the employer is clearly an influential, the very source of a job. In the Yugoslav case, the bureaucrat is a broker, one with access to influentials.

In India, there is a general notion that the Bombay milk industry is controlled by entrepreneurs from the state of Uttar Pradesh. Eames has noted this as an example of the use of influentials by migrants. One individual from a small village in that state had migrated some twenty years before and had established a successful milk business. His operation was located on the outskirts of the city, where he established a large scale operation that employed a large number of workers. Anybody from his village migrating to the city, whatever their caste, was

---

[48] Denich, "Migration and Network Manipulation."
[49] Jack Rollwagen, "Mediation and Rural-Urban Migration in Mexico: A Proposal and Case Study," in W. Cornelius and F. Trueblood (eds.), *Latin American Urban Research*, 4 (1974), 47-66.

guaranteed employment and housing by this entrepreneur. It was tacitly acknowledged that the jobs and housing were temporary, and the individual migrant would seek other situations in his spare time.[50]

Other types of brokers do not themselves have strategic positions or effective ties with those in strategic positions, but have access to them through extended ties. In one type of case frequently reported in the urban anthropological literature, the broker has a strong effective network segment made up of equals who seek access to goods, services, and information (often called a quasi-group or star network). The individual has extended ties with influentials.

Butterworth describes a case in Mexico City in which a broker is the center of a quasi-group of ex-fellow villagers. This group meets once a week at his house for drinking and sociability. This is a network as opposed to a group, because the tie between the broker and each individual is well defined, but there is no relationship between the other constituents. The broker has been able to provide jobs for most of his friends through his access to factory managers as foreman.[51]

In Harries-Jones' analysis of the political utilization of networks in Luanshya, he notes that one individual is the center of a network of individuals from Malawi and another individual is the center of a network of regular attendees at meetings of the dominant political party. Since the party now subsumes many of the functions of the dispersed offices of the former colonial government (housing, employment, and credit), both of these central network figures have access to and can manipulate their extended social ties in the political hierarchy. Thus they can serve as brokers to the members of their quasi-groups. Once again, their effective ties are with petitioners, but they have extended ties with influentials.[52]

Ablon describes the brokerage function of a few individuals in a Samoan community in a California city. She indicates that three Samoans, two men and a woman, "have together probably helped place more than 150 Samoans to whom they were related or who they knew would be good workers." These brokers do not work on behalf of everyone in the Samoan community. In selecting those whom they will sponsor, they take into account the closeness of the relationship and their assessment of the individual's character and willingness to perform well.[53]

[50] Edwin Eames, "Some Aspects of Rural Migration from a North Indian Village," *Eastern Anthropologist,* 7 (1953), 13-26.
[51] D. Butterworth, "A Study of the Urbanization Process Among Mixtec Migrants from Tilantongo in Mexico City," in W. Mangin (ed.), *Peasants in Cities* (Boston: Houghton Mifflin, 1970), pp. 98-113.
[52] Harries-Jones, " 'Home-Boy' Ties."
[53] Joan Ablon, "The Social Organization of an Urban Samoan Community," *Southwestern Journal of Anthropology,* 27 (1971), 92.

Still another type of broker is an individual who has a very large extended network, which enables him to manipulate weak ties with a variety of other intermediaries. His effective segment is inconsequential, but he is a potential connecting point for many shallow extended ties. He is important in information diffusion, and his position comes from a combination of cumulative statuses, personality, and skills in interaction. This type of individual is exemplified by Roberts' description of the networks of the small-scale self-employed entrepreneur in his sample in Guatemala City. Such individuals typically have few close kin and friends and little sociability. However, their social resources (contacts) are many, and they establish a large inventory of *latent* ties, which they activate resourcefully when needed. These individuals tend to be important mediators and contact points.[54]

Within the urban context, there are significant political, economic, and social institutions that are strategic forces on the urban scene. Wolf has suggested that anthropologists focus their research activities on power cliques and factions in the arena of strategic economic and political institutions.[55] Utilizing this same orientation, Leeds described the nature of cliques that dominate in Brazil.[56] Gonzalez studied the same kind of elite cliques in a city in the Dominican Republic.[57] In many ways, these studies parallel a form pioneered by Hunter in his study of community power structure.[58]

Many anthropologists have suggested that we could learn much by studying the nature of the networks of such specialists as brokers and influentials and the way in which they manipulate their social capital. Since the network of a broker or influential is a more significant social unit than most others, it provides insight into how the system works.

Issues in Network Studies

Once the study of social networks in urban settings becomes important, the issue of the relationship of such networks to other social categories (such as class and ethnicity) takes on a different perspective. Bott suggests in her study of conjugal roles in the family, that the type of network in which a family is embedded has greater explanatory value than class. In fact, networks do not co-vary with class. Whereas it is

54 Roberts, *Organizing Strangers.*
55 Wolf, "Kinship, Friendship and Patron-Client Relations."
56 A. Leeds, "Brazilian Careers and Social Structure: An Evolutionary Model and Case History," *American Anthropologist,* 66 (1964), 1321-47.
57 N. Gonzalez, "The City of Gentlemen: Santiago de los Caballeros," in Foster and Kemper (eds.), *Anthropologists in Cities,* pp. 19-40.
58 Floyd Hunter, *Community Power Structure* (Chapel Hill: University of North Carolina Press, 1953).

frequently assumed that the nature of the network will be a function of class, this is not necessarily the case.

In addition, an assumption is made that network members are primarily recruited from an ethnic group or that different ethnic or tribal groups will have different *kinds* of networks. Thus, we find much of the African literature focusing on ties between "home-boys" (fellow tribal members), as if these were always most significant.

One important conclusion to be drawn from the existing literature is that other specific variables seem more related to the nature of networks than such gross categories as class and ethnic group. Such variables are: degree of economic insecurity, occupation (nature of workplace and work), occupational mobility (rate of change), residential mobility, and changes in the life cycle.

Liebow and Gutkind have shown how economic insecurity affects network process; Bott, Jacobson, and A. L. Epstein have shown the effect of workplace and residential transiency on network ties; and Boswell, Roberts and Hill have illustrated how network changes occur with changes in the life cycle. Further investigation of these issues is needed.

KINSHIP

Social networks are an amalgam of personally selected kin, friends, and acquaintances. Kin are selected from all available relatives, while friends and acquaintances are recruited from neighbors, co-workers, schoolmates, and other social fields—past and present. In almost all studies of social networks, kinsmen form a significant segment of the individual's effective and extended ties. Following a traditional anthropological emphasis, many studies focus exclusively upon the kin segment or the relationships between kin in the city.

Kin-Mediated Migration

In most studies of migration, the influence of kinship ties is marked. Migration is obviously not a random movement of population. The center to which one moves is made attractive by a complex interlinking of social and economic factors. Kinsmen may serve as a source of information about employment opportunities, but in addition they serve as the initial mediators between the migrant and the urban world.

A common pattern in many parts of the world is that kinsmen offer immediate hospitality in the form of housing and food to their relatives who join them in the city. Kemper refers to this in his discussion of living "arrimado" (up close to) in Mexico City, an institutionalized way of denoting living with kinsmen or temporarily rent free.[59] In the previous discussion of networks and migration, we noticed a similar pattern involving fellow villagers and friends from the homeland. However, kinship linkages (when they are available) seem most significant in studies of migration.

A basic question is: To what extent are such ties maintained after the initial period of migration? An interesting study because of its time depth is that done by Stack, in which she examines the kinship network of a particular individual, Viola Jackson. The study, using life history data, spans a period of fifty years from 1916–1967. The geographic base of the group was rural Arkansas, and the areas to which they migrated were cities in the midwest in Michigan, Wisconsin, and Illinois. Stack notes that the migration of members of this kinship network was mediated through kinship ties. Usually a group of ten or more kinsmen lived in the same area of an urban center. The pattern of residence of this lower income Black quasi-group was characterized by instability. Individuals frequently moved within a single city, shifted from one city to another, and also moved back and forth between the city and their rural base. The information provided established that kinship ties were extremely strong and were maintained and even strengthened throughout this long period of time.[60]

Lomnitz studied a lower-class neighborhood in Mexico City and soon discovered that, for the migrants in that neighborhood (as opposed to Mexico City born), kin-based networks were the most significant social units. Almost all migration had been kin mediated, and kinsmen were expected to take up residence in close proximity to others. Where this was not initially possible, the migrant was expected to actively try to move nearer to his kin. If he did not try to do this, this was taken as negative behavior, and those who had preceded him would cut off ties. In some cases because of economic reasons or housing shortage, a family that could not obtain housing nearby would move in with a related family, although this often led to tensions and conflict. For these migrants, kinship was the basis of all effective ties—the basis of mutual aid, joint economic ventures, and sociability.[61]

Long-term maintenance of kinship ties was also noted by Simic for migrants to Belgrade, Yugoslavia. Its importance was demonstrated by the lament of a native-born urbanite, who saw himself as lacking

[59] Robert Kemper, "Family and Household Organization among Tzintzuntzan Migrants in Mexico City," in W. Cornelius and F. Trueblood (eds.), *Latin American Urban Research.*
[60] Carol Stack, "The Kindred of Viola Jackson," in N. Whitten and J. Szwed (eds.), *Afro-American Anthropology* (New York: The Free Press, 1970).
[61] Lomnitz, "The Social and Economic Organization of a Mexican Shantytown."

something by not being incorporated within such a tightly knit group as the kinship groups of the migrants. Simic suggests that ties are maintained because of the strong linkage between rural and urban areas.[62] This theme is also found throughout much African and Asian urban literature and will be discussed further in Chapter 6.

A similar pattern was found by Schwartzweller and his associates in their study of migration from a Kentucky mountain community to Cincinnati and other industrial Ohio cities. Migrants who were part of the same kin network in the village aided one another in employment and housing. The influence of the network on the behavior of its members in many areas of life was marked. Their role in establishment of norms and the maintenance of social control by gossip was strong.[63]

In a study of Chinese restaurant workers and entrepreneurs in London, Watson notes that all the members of the migratory pool can trace their relationship back to a common male founding ancestor. This patrilineal kinship unit serves as the basis of migration, and for those who do migrate, this kinship unit serves as the basis for sociability. The migrants cut themselves off from contact with alien segments of the population, thus reinforcing their ties to each other.[64]

In most of these examples, kinship ties are maintained long after the initial period of adaptation in the city and obviously help the migrant adapt to urban life. However, there are cases in which such ties are not maintained. Gutkind reports a rather intriguing shift among the long-term unemployed in Lagos, Nigeria and Kampala, Uganda. When these men initially migrate to the city, their social networks consist primarily of close kinsmen from the tribal area who have preceded them to the city. Such individuals are instrumental in providing housing, some support, and employment opportunities. As the new migrant encounters failure in the job market, he shifts his network and frequently his residence away from his more successful urban kinsmen. This appears to be a two-way process: the unemployed individual wants to leave and establish other ties, while the successful kinsman wants to disassociate himself from the demands of his unsuccessful relative. An important reason for this shift for the unemployed individuals is that they have already explored the aid and information available from their relative. Instead, they establish ties with other long-term unemployed with whom they can pool job information and their sporadic incomes to survive. An implied psychological con-

---

[62] Andrei Simic, "Kinship Reciprocity and Rural Urban Integration in Serbia," *Urban Anthropology*, 2 (1973), 205-13.

[63] Schwarzweller et al., *Mountain Families*.

[64] James Watson, "Restaurants and Remittances: Chinese Emigrant Workers in London," in G. Foster and R. Kemper (eds.), *Anthropologists in Cities* (Boston: Little, Brown and Co., 1974), pp. 201-22.

comitant of this shift is that it is less frustrating to have continuous daily contact with those in similar situations than with those who have not experienced lengthy unemployment.[65]

Some additional insights into this phenomenon can be obtained from Lewis' study of Puerto Rican migrants in New York City. Lewis describes several instances in which individuals who have recently migrated are welcomed into a kin-tied household unit but are expected to disassociate themselves physically after a certain length of time. If they do not conform to this pattern, then they will be gently, or not so gently, forced to leave.[66]

Mr. Lewis cites quarrels with relatives as a major reason for leaving, but often the quarrels have an underlying financial component. He finds an interesting correlation between the length of time spent living with a relative and the particular kin relationship. Generation level was also important.

> If the informant lived with a son or daughter, he was likely to remain for a considerable length of time. The average was over three years. If the informant lived with an older relative, usually an aunt or uncle, the mean length of residence fell to two years. However, if he moved in with a relative of his own generation—most often a sibling, and usually a sister rather than a brother—average length of time dropped to less than a year. Friction between siblings is more likely to develop than friction with a member of the older generation.[67]

In the Gutkind and Lewis studies, the rupturing of kin ties over time is frequently the result of financial conflict. Roberts finds that, over time, kinship ties for migrants to Guatemala City also become less important. Whereas initially, such ties are the focus of a network (if available), they become less significant as time in Guatemala City increases.[68]

One variable that seems to affect the maintenance of kin ties is the career patterns of migrants and their kin. (We shall discuss this point below in the discussion of kinship and class.) Another variable is the difference in emphasis placed upon kinship by various ethnic groups within the population. Where kinship is heavily emphasized in the culture of origin, the tendency to maintain kin relationships and to pool resources will mitigate against the breaking of such ties. Gutkind points out that the tendency to turn away unsuccessful relatives varies between

[65] Gutkind, "The Energy of Despair."

[66] Oscar Lewis, *Slum Culture: Backgrounds to La Vida* (New York: Random House, 1968).

[67] Ibid., p. 132.

[68] Roberts, *Organizing Strangers.*

different tribal groups in both the cities he studied.[69] In a similar fashion, Southall notes the difference between two tribal groups in the city of Kampala. For one group, the traditional emphasis upon kinship is maintained in the city, and members of this group form a kin-based enclave in the city and become significant individuals in the socialization and care of each other's children. In contrast, members of the other group are geographically dispersed in the city and do not form a kinship quasi-group. The differences relate not only to culture of origin but to the demographic proportion of each group and the distance from the homeland.[70]

Kinship Extensions

Many works that suggest that kinship ties are insignificant or break down under urban conditions have been challenged in the urban anthropological literature. Obviously, the entire kin group or set of kin ties cannot be recapitulated in the urban center; however, rather than destroy kin ties, this may lead to the recasting or reinterpreting of them. One of the major points of Lewis' early article "Urbanization Without Breakdown" was a direct challenge to the general assumption of weakened urban kin ties. He found that kin ties remained important and were strengthened under urban conditions where competition and conflict among kinsmen lessened and cooperation increased.[71]

Another frequent pattern is the development of close ties with formerly distant kinsmen in those societies where kinship is the basis of social life and where the full complement of a person's close kin ties are not available in the city. In fact, Graves and Graves suggest that in some cases, individuals prefer sponsoring relatives who are relatively distant. This enables the sponsor to apply sanctions to the behavior of an individual. It might not be as possible to control the behavior of a very close relative.[72]

An intriguing phenomenon that has been noted by many urban anthropologists is the degree to which non-kinsmen in many urban areas are amalgamated into one's network through the process of putative or fictive kinship. In classificatory kinship systems (where large numbers of individuals loosely connected to ego in a similar way are called by the same term) it becomes simple to extend kin terms to non-kinsmen in an urban setting.

[69] Gutkind, "The Energy of Despair."
[70] A. Southall, "Urban Migration and the Residence of Children in Kampala," in W. Mangin (ed.), *Peasants in Cities* (Boston: Houghton Mifflin, 1970), pp. 150-59.
[71] Oscar Lewis, "Urbanization Without Breakdown: A Case Study," *The Scientific Monthly*, vol. 75, 1952.
[72] Graves and Graves, "Adaptive Strategies in Urban Migration."

In the African literature, tribal models of kinship are frequently transposed to the urban center, and the new contacts are fictitiously placed within the kinship nexus. For example, Epstein's description of Chanda's activities over a two-day period indicates how he developed such relationships with a wide variety of individuals, not only from his own tribe, but others with similar linguistic and kinship systems. When Chanda is introduced to an individual not previously known, both men immediately explore all the potential ways of assigning a putative kin tie to each other and eventually are able to do so.[73]

Harries-Jones has indicated the degree to which putative or fictive kinsmen are amalgamated into one's personal network. The following is one example of this process derived from data collected in Luanshya:

> In the case of *bakumwesu* [home-boy] ties in urban neighborhoods, kin links may be fictionalized because they are mutually beneficial or because they establish one in a beneficial position. . . . Her ability to establish a . . . tie with Nalenga . . . greatly extended her range of social contacts within the neighborhood. [It] gave her a close relationship with a woman who was respected both for her sound advice on marital problems and her knowledge of African medicines.[74]

The relationship between NaDorothy and Nalenga was fictive kinship. Nalenga had many such ties with a wide variety of individuals within the neighborhood, which she constantly utilized. Thus, kinship terms like "mother," "daughter," "sister," "sister-in-law" were used for various neighbors who were not directly related to Nalenga. Vatuk also reports extensive use of fictive kin terms in an urban neighborhood in North India.[75]

A slightly different point, but one that still shows the impact of the urban on kinship, is the tendency of members of a tribal or regional group to extend kin terminology, and sometimes rights and obligations, to members of the entire group residing in the city. An example is found in Rowe's description of migrants from Uttar Pradesh to Bombay, India. All of these migrants tend to refer to one another in kinship terms, with the most loosely used term being *bhaya* (brother). The term is used so ubiquitously by these migrants that other groups in the city call the group *the Bhaya*.[76] Bruner notes the tendency of

[73] A. L. Epstein, "The Network and Urban Social Organization," in J. C. Mitchell (ed.), *Social Networks*, pp. 77-116.
[74] Harries-Jones, " 'Home-Boy' Ties," p. 320.
[75] S. Vatuk, "Reference, Address and Fictive Kinship in Urban North India," *Ethnology*, 8 (1969), 255-72.
[76] William Rowe, "Caste, Kinship and Association in Urban India," in A. Southall (ed.), *Urban Anthropology* (London: Oxford University Press, 1973), pp. 211-50.

all Toba Batak in Medan, Indonesia, to act toward each other in kin terms.[77]

In general, migrants from small communities with strong kin emphases know their local fellow-kinsmen. When such individuals move to urban centers, they frequently come into contact with members of their tribe whom they have not previously known. They then attempt to link these strangers (who are members of the same tribe) to themselves in a meaningful way through kinship.

Stack discusses the need to extend kin terms to important relationships in her discussion of the urban Black poor in a midwestern city. She says:

> The offering of kin terms to "those you count on" is a way people expand their personal networks. A friend who is classified as a kinsman is simultaneously given respect and responsibility.[78]

These shifts are important since kin ties are more enduring, and essential kin are recognized as having both duties toward and claims on an individual. Friendship, on the other hand, is seen as ephemeral.

In systems that do not rely heavily on classificatory kinship, other ways of creating quasi-kin relationships have developed: a classic example is ritual co-godparenthood found in Europe and Latin America. This refers to the relationship between parents and the godparents they choose for their children. There is some contradictory evidence regarding the significance of this institution in the urban setting. Lewis and Denich, in their respective studies of urban migrants in Mexico and Yugoslavia, suggest that the basis of selecting godparents shifts as individuals move.[79] In the rural areas, where emphasis is placed on reinforcing already close ties, relatives and friends are often chosen. In the urban area, however, the selection of godparents is seen as an opportunity to extend one's ties to those who can help one to adapt and to transform nebulous or extended ties to effective ones; therefore kin are not selected. Lomnitz indicates that for the low income population she studied, *compadrazo* (ritual co-godparenthood) is a critical institutionalized relationship used to reinforce and cement localized network ties essential to survival.[80] A very different view of godparenthood is found by Roberts in his study of migrants in Guatemala City. He finds

[77] Edward Bruner, "Kin and Non-Kin," in A. Southall (ed.), *Urban Anthropology*, pp. 373-92.
[78] Stack, *All Our Kin*, p. 58.
[79] Lewis, "Urbanization without Breakdown"; and Denich, "Migration and Network Manipulation."
[80] Lomnitz, "The Social and Economic Organization of a Mexican Shantytown."

that the institution becomes relatively unimportant in the urban center, and choices are made quite casually.[81]

Kinship and Class

Many studies of the maintenance of kin ties in cities have looked at the issue in the context of class. Kinship ties are generally analyzed in terms of visiting patterns and mutual aid (affective sociability and instrumental exchanges). It is frequently suggested that kinship is more important for both the stable working class and the unstable laboring class than it is for the middle class.

For Bott, kin-based relationships are a fundamental segment of most social networks; they are more important in the lower class London families, but are still significant in the middle class sample. Jacobson and Mayer, in comparing educated and lower class groups in Africa, point out the great importance of kinship to the latter and the lesser importance to the former.[82]

Young and Wilmott who focus exclusively on working class families in London, see kinship as one of the most important ingredients in all aspects of the lives of their population.[83] Gans notes the same for a similar population in Boston.[84] Marris, utilizing the work of Young and Wilmott, studied the similar importance of kinship ties in Lagos, Nigeria.[85] Peattie, Lomnitz, and Stack emphasize the heavy reliance on kin for those with great economic insecurity.[86] Less work has been done on middle class kinship, but Schneider's work in the United States and the work of Firth, Hubert, and Forge in London show that kinship is by no means insignificant for these groups.[87]

In most of these studies, class is viewed as a static element and is

[81] Roberts, *Organizing Strangers.*

[82] Jacobson, *Itinerant Townsmen;* and Philip Mayer, *Townsman or Tribesman: Conservatism and the Process of Urbanization in a South African City* (Capetown: Oxford University Press, 1961).

[83] M. Young and P. Wilmott, *Family and Class in a London Suburb* (Baltimore: Penguin Books, 1957).

[84] Gans, *Urban Villagers.*

[85] Peter Marris, *Family and Social Change in an African City* (London: Routledge and Kegan Paul, 1961); and "Methods and Motives," in Horace Miner (ed.), *The City in Modern Africa* (New York: Frederick A. Praeger, Inc., 1967).

[86] L. Peattie, *The View from the Barrio* (Ann Arbor: University of Michigan Press, 1968); Lomnitz, "The Social and Economic Organization of a Mexican Shantytown"; and Stack, *All Our Kin.*

[87] David Schneider and Raymond T. Smith, *Class Differences and Sex Roles in American Kinship and Family Structure* (Englewood Cliffs: Prentice-Hall, 1973); and Raymond Firth, J. Hubert and A. Forge, *Families and Their Relatives* (London: Routledge and Kegan Paul, 1969).

defined in very general terms. However, mobility and life cycle status, factors that influence relations to kinsmen, are not embedded in the static view of class.

An important current issue is the degree to which strong kinship obligations inhibit mobility. If the lower class is highly dependent on kin for sociability and mutual aid, then does pressure on kin to pool resources prevent individual mobility? Another way of putting this is: Is it necessary for those who are upwardly mobile to rupture ties and ignore kin if they are to succeed in establishing themselves?

The answer to these questions is not simply yes or no. In some cases, kinship and mobility seem unrelated. Roberts describes one case of a brother and sister whose class levels were quite different. The sibling relationship remained strong, with frequent visiting and contact. Moreover, the reciprocity did *not* change as a result of status differences. The brother (lower in class) never asked favors of his sister and tried in many ways to reciprocate on an equivalent basis for all goods and services.[88] In other cases, ties can be used to launch an upwardly mobile career. The strategic use of kinsmen and their resources can lead to upward mobility for all. When various individuals in a network of kinsmen are employed in different sectors of the economy, the interests of the group are protected against the negative impact of a downturn in any one sector. On the other hand, if one kinsman is supported judiciously in an expanding sector of the economy, he can move upward and use his position to aid other kin.

In spite of these possibilities, the literature generally emphasizes the limitations in mobility imposed by maintaining kin obligations. The study by Gutkind shows that relatively established migrants tend to break ties if their kin cannot become self-sufficient.[89] Marris also describes a tendency for successful urban residents to try to escape from their needy kin.[90]

On the other hand, in her study of a squatter settlement in Venezuela, Peattie shows that resource pooling by kin is a strong norm, and that in cases of windfalls and unexpected income, one is obligated to redistribute these within the group.[91] Lomnitz and Stack report similar situations of pressure against investing resources for individual mobility.[92] Although Roberts indicates that kinship ties are relatively weak in the Guatemala City communities he studied (in terms of frequency of visiting and small-scale mutual aid), kinsmen were thought of as

[88] B. Roberts, *Organizing Strangers.*
[89] Gutkind, "The Energy of Despair."
[90] Marris, *Family and Social Change.*
[91] Peattie, *The View from the Barrio.*
[92] Lomnitz, "The Social and Economic Organization of a Mexican Shantytown"; and Stack, *All Our Kin.*

insurance for really major needs, such as illness or total financial collapse.[93]

The issue of conflict between kinship obligations and its effect on individual mobility is still an open question. If the kinship group studied is in the lowest segment of the urban class system, then the pooling of resources becomes a matter of survival—and the recognition of total mutual dependence supports the norm of kin obligations. However, there are many cases where individuals acquire resources and successfully evade kin obligations. More research is needed to identify the particular variables that affect such choices.

A recent study of two segments of the American middle class shows significant differences in kin orientations between the two. Album, in her study of kin networks in Rockland County, New York, found very different kin networks among businessmen and professionals with the same level of income and housing. The middle class businessmen retained strong kinship ties, while the middle class professionals tended to have weak ties, both in visiting and mutual aid. Professionals tended to disassociate themselves from their kinsmen in favor of co-workers, neighbors, and friends. For the businessman, the mobilization of kinship ties was an economic asset in developing contacts. Not only could he draw upon kin for direct financial aid, but he could also utilize them for expanding a clientele. Many spoke of the advantages of borrowing money from kin over using banks. Interestingly enough, mobility was not a factor. Differences in class between informants and their kin were not significant in the maintenance or rupture of ties.[94]

Kinship and Proximity

For many in the lower social classes, frequent face-to-face visiting is an important ingredient in the maintenance of kinship ties. Obviously, close geographic proximity is an important ingredient in the maintenance of these visiting relationships. Lomnitz says that distance eventually leads to the severing of ties for lower class residents in Mexico City.[95] Marris indicates the same for Lagos, Nigeria.[96] Young and Wilmott suggest that, when a working class family moves away from Bethnal Green, there is a tendency to break their ties; however, these ties tend to be reestablished some time after the move.[97]

Great geographic distance, even for lower and working class

[93] Roberts, *Organizing Strangers.*
[94] Irene Album, "Extended Family Networks in a Suburban Community," (Honor Essay 25, Baruch College of City University of New York, April 14, 1975).
[95] Lomnitz, "The Social and Economic Organization of a Mexican Shantytown."
[96] Marris, *Family and Social Change.*
[97] Young and Wilmott, *Family and Class.*

groups, does not necessarily hamper daily or weekend visiting patterns particularly in cities with mass transit systems. Padilla tells of one Puerto Rican woman in the Bronx who visits her daughter in Brooklyn every day, even though the subway trip takes hours each way.[98] Album found that the working class families she studied in suburban Rockland County maintained visiting patterns almost every weekend, even when they were over forty miles apart.[99] The ability to do this depends upon money, time, and transportation systems. Thus transportation becomes an urban contextual variable that influences the maintenance of kinship ties.

Another urban contextual variable, the nature of the housing market, has a direct impact on the proximity of kinsmen. Assuming that proximity is desired, the availability of housing affects the ability of kin to live near each other. Lomnitz describes a population whose desire for proximity is great, but who are dependent on houses becoming available. She states that if a house is available and a kinsman does not take it, this is taken as a denial of kin ties, and the relationship is broken.

An extensive literature deals with the impact of new housing—often large public housing projects in urban centers—on lower class kin proximity. Forced relocation of lower class residents occurs in cases of urban renewal or peripheral housing estates built to accommodate expanding populations and leads to the disruption of existing kin networks.

Bryce-Laporte describes this for a case in San Juan, Puerto Rico where the government controlled access to public housing. Many of those forced into public housing were unhappy about the effect of such moves on their kin ties. In one case, there was an attempt to recreate a kin-based network focused on an elderly dominant female, in spite of geographic and legal difficulties.[100] Marris notes a different response. Initially those who moved into housing estates on the periphery of Lagos were unhappy about leaving their kin. Later they stated that such a move was good because it kept their more dependent kinsmen from frequently asking favors. Had they remained enmeshed in a network of ties, they would have depleted their resources.[101]

For the middle class, proximity does not seem important in the maintenance of kinship ties. Frequently, visiting is replaced by other contacts (letter writing, phone calls). Kinship ties also seem to focus on ceremonial occasions rather than daily contacts. Life cycle events,

[98] E. Padilla, *Up From Puerto Rico* (New York: Columbia University Press, 1958).
[99] Album, "Extended Family Networks."
[100] R. Bryce-Laporte, "Urban Relocation and Family Adaptation in Puerto Rico: A Case Study of Urban Ethnography," in W. Mangin (ed.), *Peasants in Cities*, pp. 98-113.
[101] Marris, *Family and Social Change*.

such as christenings, confirmations, marriages, and funerals, bring together the extended kin networks of an individual even when no daily, weekly, or monthly patterns of contact exist. Such events reestablish and reinforce ties. In addition, the gift-giving, cooking, entertaining, sewing and other functions have both symbolic and real impact. Such events can be viewed as a real economic contribution to the launching of a newborn member or a newborn domestic unit. In addition, they establish patterns of reciprocity for those participating.

Many mutual aid activities performed by proximate kinship groups for the lower segments are not necessary to the middle class, with its higher level of economic security, or are performed by formal insurance mechanisms. However, on the basis of studies that have been done, kinsmen will still be important to some middle class groups much of the time and to all of them in times of major events or crises.

Matrilaterality

Although the matrilateral hypothesis developed by William J. Goode is not based on physical proximity, it is ultimately related to it. Goode has suggested that there is a tendency in urban society, whatever the initial focus of the kinship system may be, to shift to a *matrilateral* focus—an emphasis on the mother's (wife's) relatives. The argument runs along the following lines: in most urban situations there is a geographic distance between work place and residence. Since it is usually the male who is the major income producer, his work activities take him away from the domestic unit for extended periods of time. Thus, the female, who remains within the domestic unit and is responsible for child care, becomes the controlling influence in the social relationships maintained by the domestic unit. The female is usually linked to her own kinsmen more affectively than to those in her husband's kinship unit and therefore tends to maintain close ties with her kinsmen rather than those of the male.

An example of matrilaterality is found in Bott's study. In one highly connected network, she notes that the kinsmen of both the husband and the wife reside in the same local area, making them equally accessible on a geographic basis. However, the wife visits her mother every day. In addition, her sisters are also frequent visitors, and collectively they visit the mother's mother. Bott notes that, in many ways, this segment of the kinship unit operates as a truly organized group, with mutual ties and collective activities.[102]

[102] Bott, *Family and Social Network.*

The matrilateral focus is also noted by Young and Wilmott and is further reinforced by a system of *ultimogeniture matrilocality*. By this we mean that when the youngest daughter in a household unit marries, there is a pattern in which her husband joins her in her parents' residence. This is related in part to the nature of the large-sized flats available in Bethnal Green and the general scarcity of housing. In addition, the area is a stable one with a strong feeling of local commitment, so the newly married male is quite willing to move in with his wife's family.[103]

Many studies of American postmarital residence and visiting have noted the tendency toward matrilaterality. Given equal access to both sets of relatives, the wife's relatives are preferred. However, others have found that matrilaterality is not a general characteristic but seems to be related to social class.[104]

The universality of this tendency toward matrilaterality in urban life and the causal links leading to the emergence of this pattern have been challenged by Vatuk in her study of an urban neighborhood in Allahabad, India. She discovered that in this *patrilineal* and *patrilocal* society (based on systems of tracing descent through the male line and residing with the husband's family after marriage), where husband's kin are present in the city, there is a tendency for ties with them to be stronger than those with wife's kin. If no such kinsmen are available, effective ties are maintained with wife's kin. Where both exist, more emphasis is placed on patrilateral than matrilateral ties, but both are included in the effective network. This represents a movement away from a single line emphasis to a bilateral one in order to maximize contact with kin in the city.[105]

A similar pattern was noted for Belgrade residents by Simic. Traditional Serbian kinship was patrilateral. In the city there was a noticeable shift toward a bilateral system; the net of kin ties was widened.[106]

Thus, it would seem that matrilaterality—like network structure and kin tie maintenance—is not related in a simple way to modern urban life. Class, occupation, career mobility, geographic mobility, and the nature of the traditional kinship system all operate to create differences. The maintenance and reinforcement of kin ties are adaptive strategies that are related to the socioeconomic situation of each family.

[103] Young and Wilmott, *Family and Class.*
[104] David Schneider, personal communication, 1976.
[105] Sylvia Vatuk, "Trends in North Indian Urban Kinship: The 'Matrilateral Assymetry' Hypothesis," *Southwestern Journal of Anthropology*, 27 (1971), 287-307; *Kinship and Urbanization* (Berkeley: University of California Press, 1972).
[106] Simic, "Kinship Reciprocity."

Domestic Units

Another primary social unit central to urban anthropology is the domestic group or family. A *domestic group* consists of individuals who pool economic resources and cooperate in the performance of domestic activities: shopping, cooking, eating, cleaning, laundry, and child care.

The issue of common residence is complex. Some co-residential units consist of non-relatives or boarders who, in fact, maintain separate budgets and perform domestic activities separately. On the other hand, some separate households cooperate so intensively in pooling resources and sharing domestic activities that these non-coresiding groups actually resemble a domestic unit.

One of the issues here concerns the effect of the city on domestic groups. A long-held belief is that the density and land use patterns of the city work toward an emphasis on smaller family units than in non-urban situations. Robert J. Smith finds this tendency in historical records of preindustrial Japan where nuclear families in the city were smaller than those in rural areas. On this basis, he develops a hypothesis about the effect of smaller families on capital accumulation and investment leading to industrial growth.[107]

Others indicate that there are many cities in which, under certain circumstances, large domestic groups (including a number of separate nuclear families tied to one another through kinship bonds) are quite common. In India, some of the largest joint families are found not in the villages, but in the urban centers. As Singer points out, this tendency to common residence is reinforced by the amalgamation of household members into large-scale family enterprise.[108] In a case study of a textile mill in Ahmedabad, Hutheesing describes how a widow founded a factory that initially employed the various members of a household unit. As the enterprise prospered, other employees were recruited, but the managerial level was still controlled by members of the co-residential household unit.[109]

Turning from the traditional Indian city to Indians who have migrated to an industrial British city, we find a continuing emphasis upon the maintenance of the joint family. In Wolverhampton, England, many

[107] Robert J. Smith, "Town and City in Pre-Modern Japan: Small Families, Small Households and Residential Instability," in A. Southall (ed.), *Urban Anthropology*, pp. 163-210.
[108] Milton Singer, "The Indian Joint Family in Modern Industry," in M. Singer and B. S. Cohen (eds.), *Structure and Change in Indian Society* (Chicago: Aldine Publishing Company, 1968).
[109] Otome Hutheesing, personal communication, 1976.

of the larger old residences have been purchased by Punjabi migrants; this housing is not desired by any other group. The households contain a variety of joint family structures based upon migratory patterns. Since it is unusual for an entire joint family to migrate, the units do not contain all the potential household members. However, it is not un-common to find two brothers with their wives and children, or an older husband and wife, their married sons and families, and their unmarried sons and daughters living in the same domestic group.

In these cases, both available housing and income permit the maintenance of the cultural ideal with its attendant economic coopera-tion. Kemper notes that the wealthier migrants from Tzintzuntzan in Mexico City recapitulate the rural patrilocal joint family phase when their children marry. In this case, they have the economic resources to acquire large homes.[110] Young and Wilmott also note the tendency for London East End families to incorporate their youngest daughter, her spouse, and children in one household. Here too, the nature of the hous-ing stock is a factor, since housing is scarce and houses are large.[111]

The joint family made up of more than one nuclear family is dif-ferent from the *truncated* family, in which individuals such as wife's mother, husband's brother, or husband's brother's child are part of the household. Studies all over the world show that such truncated families are important in the city. As Kemper points out, in the rural areas, such families are largely formed by widowhood and separation, which create homeless individuals. In the city, mobility creates such units, as migrants live with relatives and people send children to the city to live with relatives to better their life chances.[112] These patterns are found world-wide. While many such enlarged domestic groups are temporary, others exist for long periods of time, and co-residing relatives may be continu-ously replaced by a steady stream of kinsmen. These truncated structures and the true joint families negate the stereotype of the small urban family.

One of the most interesting kinds of domestic groups in the city is formed by nuclear families with low and unstable income, whether co-residential or not, who tend to act as a single economic unit and co-operate in domestic activities. We shall refer to these as *cooperative* domestic units. The nature of urban housing tends to mitigate against co-residence for these units. Lomnitz reports that in her study she found both co-residential and non-co-residential cooperative units. Since co-residence led to tension, overcrowding, and conflict, co-residential units were more short-lived than the others. Non-residential units always in-

[110] Kemper, "Family and Household Organization."
[111] Young and Wilmott, *Family and Class.*
[112] Kemper, "Family and Household Organization."

volve close proximity of residence (usually in the same building or block, but always in the same neighborhood). Lomnitz calls these "nuclear families in a compound-type arrangement" and finds them to be the dominant mode of household organization in the shantytown she studied. Such compounds are "groups of neighboring residential units which share a common outdoor area for washing, cooking, playing of children and so on." Each nuclear family is a separate economic unit, except for the frequent exchanges of money, goods and services.[113]

Kemper finds what he (and Leeds) call *extended family enclaves* very important among his population. These are kin-related families, often siblings, who reside in close proximity and share social and domestic activities. An example is given of two brothers who migrated and married in the city. Their shack became cramped. To add to this, their father came to join them after his wife died. When an apartment opened up across the street, one nuclear group moved there, but they still combined many social and domestic activities with the other family. The men spent most of their leisure time together, and the women shopped, cooked, laundered, and watched children together. Among the poorer of Kemper's sample, several nuclear families often lived co-residentially, "sharing cramped quarters to stretch insufficient incomes." He points out that this kind of joint family is a unique response to urban conditions, since in the village joint families existed only in response to the patrilocal residence rule.[114]

Some of the most interesting work on cooperative households is found in Stack's study of urban Black poor in a midwestern city. The basic social units in her study consist of individuals who are tied to one another through bonds of kinship. They live in close proximity, although not in the same dwelling unit, and act cooperatively in many social and economic activities. The basic kinship tie is between siblings, either brother and sister, or sister and sister. Because of the function of females in domestic activities, brother-brother units are not found. One specific example described by Stack is that of Viola Jackson's brother, who moved a block away from his sister. He and his two sons became part of her cooperative domestic group. They ate there, spent most of their time there, and contributed to the income of the Jackson family. She says:

> In the Flats the responsibility for providing food, care, clothing and shelter and for socializing children within domestic networks may be spread over several households. Which household a given individual belongs to is not a particularly meaningful question, as we have seen that daily domestic organization depends on several

113 Lomnitz, "The Social and Economic Organization of a Mexican Shantytown," p. 142.
114 Kemper, "Family and Household Organization."

things: where people sleep, where they eat, and where they offer their time and money.[115]

Eating together and contributing toward rent are the most significant ways of reckoning allegiance. As she later points out, ". . . domestic organization is diffused over many kin-based households which themselves have elastic boundaries." [116]

Stack describes three cooperating households in which the three female members pooled and shared many resources and activities. They pooled food stamps, shopped together, and shared the evening meal at one of two houses. The children frequently slept at each other's houses to fit in with the late evening visiting pattern of their mothers.

In recent research by one of the authors on household cooperation among Puerto Ricans in Philadelphia, the following case was found: A domestic unit consisting of a woman and her children and her divorced husband's brother functioned as a close-knit domestic group. The woman and her mother-in-law had sponsored the migration of her husband's younger brother. This obviously set up ties of mutual obligation between them. The male, who maintained a separate residence, was sporadically employed and received welfare payments and contributed regularly to the maintenance of the woman and her children. Although he slept in his own apartment, he usually spent at least half of the days in the week (depending on work schedule) in his sister-in-law's household. He ate most of his meals there, and often watched his nieces and nephews. He had free access to the house (his own key) and came and went as he pleased. (One common feature of such cooperative units is that people have free access to each other's homes and facilities. They often enter without knocking, and use kitchen, bathroom, and appliances without special permission.) When the woman attempted to establish a home-based food enterprise selling snacks in the street, the ties between the two units strengthened. Another indication of their cooperation was the purchase of a car by the brother-in-law for the purpose of taking his sister-in-law and her family for their frequent clinic visits.[117]

In general, the nature of urban housing stock and the nature of the traditional family pattern exert a strong influence on the nature of domestic units. However, data about cooperative domestic units demonstrate once again that neither urban housing structures nor other urban pressures prevent large-scale units from cooperating in domestic activi-

[115] Stack, *All Our Kin*, p. 90.
[116] Ibid., p. 93.
[117] The research on Puerto Rican domestic networks was carried out in 1972-4 by Goode with support from the Center for Urban Ethnography at the University of Pennsylvania (United States, Public Health Service, National Institute of Mental Health grant #MH17216).

ties. Moreover, the insecurity of the unstable low-skill labor market increases the size and cohesiveness of such units, even when such large units may not have been part of the traditional pattern.

SUMMARY

In the analysis of primary relationships, the emphasis has been upon those aspects of urban life that have a direct impact on the kind and content of those relationships. Networks, kin ties, and domestic groups are the important primary units in the urban center.

Within an urban context, the nature of the labor market (possibilities for job security and mobile careers) and the housing market have the most direct impact on these units. The nature of urban life, the nature of the city, and the nature of migratory patterns also have direct impact.

It is impossible to replicate within the city the full range of rural or tribal relationships. Therefore the migrant must select from the supply of potential relationships those who will become part of his or her meaningful world. Choice emerges, but within constraints imposed by the urban setting. Networks, kinship segments, and domestic groups are all found universally in urban centers and are, in fact, basic to urban social life. Their actual forms and emphases result from a complex interplay between cultural values and the forces of the particular urban center. It is certainly apparent that the city does not destroy such units, but frequently strengthens them in their modified forms.

A major consequence of urban ethnography has been to counteract those views of social scientists in the earlier part of the twentieth century that characterized urban life as depersonalizing and that emphasized the loss of close, deep, and affective social ties. From the studies done by urban ethnographers, it is apparent that meaningful social ties have been retained by those who live in cities.

One basic social unit described and analyzed by urban ethnographers is the social network. Such units can be viewed as the urban counterparts of the bounded corporate groups found in societies traditionally studied by cultural anthropologists. The social network is an egocentric unit of social actors selected by an individual to become part of his or her meaningful social world. Network members are frequently recruited from available kinsmen, neighbors, co-workers, and schoolmates, present and past. A major characteristic of such units is that their membership is based upon choice, rather than birth and ascription.

Analysts distinguish between the effective and the extended network. The former is characterized by closeness, affect, and maximal interaction. The latter contains individuals who are less well known, less intimate or less frequent partners. Such extended ties link the individual to other segments of the urban milieu and broaden his opportunity structure. Another distinction is made between networks that are primarily ends in and of themselves and those that are used for other purposes (instrumental). Social ties that are ends are either used for sociability or for norm reinforcement. Social ties that are instrumental may be used to obtain goods, services, or information; they may be used in a general way in urban adaptation; or they may be used to tap the networks of strategic individuals (brokers and influentials).

Once social networks are recognized as a viable element of contemporary urban life, several research questions emerge. How are such ties formed and terminated? How are particular individuals recruited into and terminated from a network? What is the relationship between network formation, dissolution, and social and geographic mobility?

Some studies indicate that those individuals who are characterized by geographic and social mobility, as well as those who face economic insecurity, develop particular techniques or patterns of network formation. Some studies have focused upon the role of gossip in social networks as a device for social control and norm transmission. Other studies have focused upon the exchanges that occur within a network; they view such units as sources of reciprocity in which one gains social capital.

An overlapping category of urban ethnographic study is urban kinship. It is recognized that kinsmen form a part of an individual's network, but kinsmen have frequently been treated as a separate primary social unit. The complete kinship system characteristic of many tribal groups cannot be maintained in the city. However, this does not mean that kinship loses its significance. Urban ethnographers have shown, in a variety of urban settings, that kinsmen do remain important. Where urban migration is a central concern of the research, the role of kinsmen is significant, at least initially. The time depth of such relationships is still at issue.

Domestic groups form the third primary unit discussed in the chapter. It has frequently been suggested that such units are smaller in size in urban areas than their counterparts in rural areas. Certainly the urban housing situation in most areas of the world fosters such smaller units. However, the data do not uniformly point in this direction. A more intriguing phenomenon noted in many urban ethnographies is the existence of cooperative domestic units, which are not co-residential, but do provide a great deal of interaction and mutual aid.

In this discussion of primary units, certain major issues emerge. What is the relationship between social class and these various units? Certain patterns of network formation, kinship relationships, and domestic units are apparent in studies of the more economically insecure segments of the urban population. To what extent are these patterns shared by other segments? Another basic questions concerns the effect of mobility patterns and life cycle stages on all of these units.

Obviously, more urban ethnography of primary units is needed to deal with these questions. And as we have noted, one of the biases of urban ethnography is its emphasis upon the lower income segments of the urban population. We know a great deal about this segment, but not enough about others.

5

Major Urban Components: Neighborhood, Ethnic Group, and Occupation

In the previous chapter, we focused upon the anthropological analysis of primary social units that are suited to the ethnographic method. We noted that such units are an extension of the traditional kinship orientation of anthropology, derived from the study of societies in which kinship was the primary organizing principle.

In this chapter, we shall focus upon three other organizing principles, which are the basic sources of social and cultural diversity in cities. These are groups based on common residential territory (*neighborhoods*), common culture of origin, (*ethnic groups*), and common role in the division of labor (*occupational status communities*).

GROUPS BASED ON COMMON RESIDENCE

In the first chapter, we discussed community studies as a major element in American sociology that was stimulated by an ethnographic approach. Some of the numerous studies in this area have been of entire urban communities, while others have focused on smaller units, namely, neighborhoods in a larger city. Some have used ethnographic fieldwork techniques extensively, while others have been based on surveys. In the ensuing discussion, however, we shall focus upon more recent studies, which are clearly ethnographic. Independent of the American community study approach, neighborhoods have been studied by anthropologists in a variety of urban settings throughout the world.

One striking feature of most urban ethnographic studies of neighborhoods is that they target areas of the city primarily inhabited by low income populations. Thus, studies of slums, squatter settlements, and public housing areas abound in the literature, but few studies of middle class or elite residential communities are found.

Another bias in the existing literature relates to the area of the world in which the research has been done. For instance, we find fewer neighborhood studies in the African urban literature, while the Latin American literature contains many examples of such studies.

The neighborhood studies vary greatly in terms of their research foci. Some studies select the neighborhood as a convenient ethnographic unit within which to study other problems (related to such matters as primary groups, ethnicity, class). Others are primarily concerned with the nature of the neighborhood itself. Some research, basically comparative in nature, attempts to develop typologies of neighborhoods and attempts to delineate critical indices that explain differences. Other studies look at communities through time as they go through a developmental cycle, seeking to account for differentiation or for neighborhood success or failure.

There is a distinction between the study primarily concerned with the neighborhood as a self-contained unit and the study concerned with the neighborhood within a larger relevant context (city, region, or nation). This latter approach is characteristic of more recent neighborhood studies.

A number of the earlier neighborhood studies were primarily concerned with refuting some common assumptions about the nature of urban life that could be traced to Wirth's analysis of urbanism as a way of life.[1] Perhaps the most explicit refutation of Wirth is found in Gans'

[1] Louis Wirth, "Urbanism as a Way of Life," *American Journal of Sociology*, 44 (1938), 1-24.

study of an Italian working class neighborhood in Boston.[2] The title of the volume, *The Urban Villagers,* indicates Gans' conclusion that many of the characteristics of village life—primary group relationships, intensive interaction, knowledge of one's neighborhood, lack of privacy, and *above all,* social cohesion—were maintained in an urban neighborhood.

Gans noted that the residents of the community came from various regions in Italy, and therefore the characteristics of their present life-styles were not a direct transplant of the traditional Italian culture of origin, but rather a working class subculture. Since Gans was primarily interested in describing the way of life in a homogeneous geographic community, his approach was static and did not pay much attention to the larger urban context or the interaction of heterogeneous components. Furthermore, as Granovetter noted, the study focused on several limited networks (which are by definition cohesive) rather than on the neighborhood as a whole.[3] This had the effect of overemphasizing solidarity and cohesion. Despite this limitation, Gans' ethnographic description is very complete. As an early study designed to challenge stereotypes of physically substandard urban neighborhoods as socially disintegrated, the study satisfies its major functions.

In the Latin American literature, a similar myth-breaking function was undertaken by Mangin in his ethnographic research in squatter settlements located in Lima, Peru.[4] Such communities are found in most regions of the world, and in some developing areas they contain a large proportion of the residents of particular cities. Squatter settlements are usually established on land owned publicly but which is not being used. They are characterized by self-constructed substandard housing, put up quickly by residents in establishing the neighborhood. They are assumed to contain the very poor, the recent rural migrant, the politically radical, and the criminal or anti-social element. Very frequently they are described as "cancers" on the urban scene.

In an article appearing in *Scientific American,* which had great impact in social science, Mangin specifically attacks many of these misconceptions about such communities. He indicates that the original settlers are not peasants who have just arrived. The degree of planning necessary for a successful invasion of urban land leads to a high degree of organiza-

[2] Herbert Gans, *The Urban Villagers* (New York: The Free Press, 1962). Gans' work can be seen as a continuation of the earlier work done by Whyte in the same community and falls into the more general category of early community studies stimulated by W. Lloyd Warner. See William F. Whyte, *Street Corner Society* (Chicago: University of Chicago Press, 1955 [first published in 1943]).
[3] Mark S. Granovetter, "The Strength of Weak Ties," *American Journal of Sociology,* 78 (1973), 1360-80.
[4] William Mangin, "Squatter Settlements," *Scientific American,* 217 (1967), 21-29; "Latin American Squatter Settlements: A Problem and a Solution," *Latin American Research Review,* 2 (1967), pp. 65-98.

tion. He specifically attacks the notion that such communities are characterized by high crime rates or other indices of social disorganization. Residents are not political revolutionaries, but tend to be conservative and view themselves as having a stake in the future. In some cases, individual squatters have eventually become real estate speculators and entrepreneurs by renting their facilities to others and expanding their neighborhood holdings. Finally, he notes that the residents of these communities represent a population that is very heterogeneous in class and occupation. Teachers, policemen, white collar workers, young professionals live here, as well as the sporadically unemployed.

Social Cohesion

The issue of the degree of social cohesion in urban neighborhoods, particularly lower or working class neighborhoods, has been a theme running through many urban ethnographic studies. However, the evidence relating to this issue (derived primarily from Latin America and North America) is inconclusive.

We have previously noted Gans' emphasis upon social cohesion in an Italian American neighborhood. A similar conclusion emerges from the work of Safa, who suggests that a San Juan, Puerto Rico shantytown is characterized by informal social cohesion and solidarity.[5] Her general thesis is that a capitalist society creates an isolated social stratum at the bottom (the poor). This group's isolated residential areas develop a level of solidarity that can be viewed as an adaptive response to their powerlessness.

Certainly the view suggested by Safa of a cohesive community in which members are all closely enmeshed through informal ties is quite different from the descriptions found in other accounts. Mithun has also noted the high degree of social cohesion based upon informal and formal social relations. In a study of a Black neighborhood in a northeastern city in the United States, Mithun notes several sources of solidarity and cooperation. Informal mutual aid is common among extended kinsmen, neighbors, and friends; formal associations include the church, social clubs, block associations, and associations related to the Model Cities program. Commitment to the neighborhood can be seen in efforts to upgrade it through mutual effort, and in some cases ties are continued even after families move to other areas of the city.[6]

[5] Helen Safa, "The Social Isolation of the Urban Poor: Life in a Puerto Rican Shanty Town," in Isaac Deutscher and E. Thompson (eds.), *Among the Poor* (New York: Basic Books, Inc., 1968).
[6] Jacqueline Mithun, "Cooperation and Solidarity as Survival Necessities in a Black Urban Community," *Urban Anthropology*, 2 (1973), 25-34.

Lomnitz notes that the shantytown she studied in Mexico City "is not organized around central institutions of any kind." She notes the importance of small networks of kin and friends as the basic social unit. "Other forms of organization at the community level are relatively rudimentary." There are several football teams and a medical center organized by middle class women. "Groups of neighbors may band together for specific issues." This has happened several times in relation to public water, oil spillages from a nearby refinery, and other significant problems.[7]

A central issue in Peattie's work in a squatter settlement in Venezuela is the question of the degree of social cohesion and organization within that neighborhood. She notes that formal organization is weak, and that informal social control mechanisms are minimal, but that cohesion tends to wax and wane. Increased cohesion results from crisis situations, such as the sewer controversy that occurred during her two-year residence in the neighborhood. The sewer incident concerned the attempt by a national planning body to introduce a sewage exit that would dump waste into the river adjacent to the community. This part of the river was used for bathing and laundry. The threat served to arouse residents' concern with collective community interests. Social cohesion increased and the efforts of the residents to divert the potential disaster escalated. However, because of the insensitivity of the planners and the difficulties in gaining access to them, a successful outcome would have been dubious without the intervention of the anthropologist. Peattie notes the existence of smaller informal networks and groups in the neighborhood that take on responsibility for limited activities, such as two men who built a playground. The question she raises in her work is whether an overall, permanent, organizational structure is necessary for the neighborhood to be healthy and viable. Her answer is that such formal organization is not essential.[8]

This issue of social cohesion and its relationship to the solution of particular problems is investigated by Jones.[9] He describes the attempts of a neighborhood-based organization to influence urban policy concerning the neighborhood. The government agency involved remained aloof from these pressures. Rather than viewing the action as a failure because of poor organization at the community level, he attributes it to external forces and power that were immune to local pressure.

[7] Larissa Lomnitz, "The Social and Economic Organization of a Mexican Shantytown," in Wayne Cornelius and F. Trueblood (eds.), Latin American Urban Research, 4 (Beverley Hills: Sage Publications, 1974), pp. 145, 146.
[8] Lisa Peattie, The View from the Barrio (Ann Arbor: University of Michigan Press, 1968).
[9] Delmos Jones, "Incipient Organization and Organizational Failures in an Urban Ghetto," Urban Anthropology, 1 (1972), 51-67.

An example of a neighborhood study that addresses itself to many of the issues raised in this discussion is Wiebe's analysis of the social life and order of an Indian slum.[10] Once again, we should note the emphasis upon the study of the "bottom," although Wiebe justifies this by suggesting that we can learn about the top by looking up from the bottom. Wiebe does *not* stress the community as a self-contained unit, but is explicitly concerned with the variety of ways in which the local community, Chennanagar, located in the city of Madras, is a part of that larger entity. He pursues this theme in every aspect of social life treated in the volume.

Chennanagar is an illegal community, and, paralleling the situation in Latin American cities, much of the effort of the slum population is directed toward legitimizing their claim to the land and the provision of municipal services, which are not only necessary for subsistence, but also serve as a semi-formal claim to legal recognition. The community is a bounded unit, named and recognized as an entity by both its residents and outsiders.

Another very significant indicator of the degree of cohesion of the community is the existence of a temple and the support of a priest who officiates at the temple. The building was constructed with common funds, and the priest is supported by common contributions.

In political terms, Chennanagar is highly organized. There are three political associations (*mamrams*) within the community, which are tied to municipal, state, and national political parties. There is intense interest in local elections, and a large segment of the eligible population votes. Because of its high level of organization, the community has been able to gain access to water and certain other municipal services. The people in the community recognize that their power is limited and can only be effective if collectivized, or, alternatively, based on an extremely personalized patron-client relationship. In all of these aspects of Chennanagar life, the relationship to the larger community is paramount.

Another major aspect of life that links the community to its larger context is that of economics. Most of the residents' jobs are outside the community or dependent on outside resources. Residents perform a variety of jobs at the lower-skill and lower-paid levels of the occupational spectrum. Some of these jobs (potter, barber, weaver, sweeper) are carry-overs of caste tradition, but the vast majority are not caste linked. As Wiebe points out, the difficulty is not in obtaining jobs, but in obtaining permanent jobs that provide a level of income sufficient for survival. As in many such communities, there is some mobility of residents, and

[10] Paul Wiebe, *Social Life in an Indian Slum* (Durham: Carolina Academia Press, 1975).

the community can point to several former members who have become politically and economically influential. Of course, there is an attempt to retain ties to these individuals as important patrons.

A very different view of neighborhood cohesion is found in Michael Whiteford's study of a squatter settlement in Popayán, Colombia. He notes an extreme lack of cohesion, cooperation, and mutual knowledge between the community residents.[11]

One of the major studies of a public housing settlement in the United States focused on the Pruitt-Igoe project in Saint Louis. Rainwater described this community in a number of publications, and some further analysis has been done by Yancey.[12] From all that has been written about this project and from its subsequent demise (the project was eventually closed), it can be concluded that it was a large-scale residential community that lacked almost all of the social attributes of community life. Most of the analysis dealt with why this spatially localized unit could never become a cohesive community. To a large extent, the researchers blamed the design of the man-made space. There was almost no public space in which residents could meet one another, interact, and develop long-term social relationships. There were no play areas for children, no open corridors where neighbors might meet, and one of the potential loci for female interaction—the laundry room—was perceived as a dangerous place. Children, frequently the source of adult links through their peer interactions, were not encouraged to play outside, since the building was oriented in such a way as to prevent parents from overseeing their activities from the house.

Internal Complexity

One of the most significant studies of the internal complexity of the neighborhood, which includes within it a dynamic as well as a systems approach, is that done by Suttles.[13]

In his approach to the study of neighborhoods, Suttles did basic ethnographic fieldwork and focused upon the residents' cognitive map of neighborhood space. Working from these insiders' views of the community and from outsiders' (administrative agencies) delineation of the community, he suggests a tripartite division of social segments: the face-

---

11 Michael Whiteford, "Neighbors at a Distance: Life in a Low-Income Barrio," in W. Cornelius and F. Trueblood (eds.), *Latin American Urban Research*, pp. 157-82.
12 Lee Rainwater, "Fear and the House-as-Haven in the Lower Class," *Journal of the American Institute of Planners*, vol. 32, 1966; William Yancey, "Architecture, Interaction and Social Controls: The Case of a Large-Scale Housing Project," *Environment and Behavior*, 3 (1971), 3-21. Both articles are reprinted in John Helmer and Neil Eddington (eds.), *Urbanman* (New York: The Free Press, 1973).
13 Gerald Suttles, *The Social Order of the Slum* (Chicago: University of Chicago Press, 1968); Gerald Suttles, *The Social Construction of Communities* (Chicago: The University of Chicago Press, 1972).

block, the defended community, and the community of limited liability. The *face block* is a primary unit in which the nature of social bonds and trust are close. The *defended community* is a unit of identity that protects itself from the outside by generating a reputation through myth and action or by actual security measures. In both of these communities, the stranger is easily identified. The *community of limited liability* is largely a product of boundaries drawn by outsiders such as planners, census-takers, and school boards.

In his analysis of the community of limited liability, Suttles focuses upon the interface between local territorial units and the larger context of the city. By looking at this relationship as well as the interaction between ethnic components, Suttles employs a systems approach that considers the nature of neighborhoods, how they are constructed, and how they affect the social construction of the city.

In the Addams area of Chicago, Suttles finds a defended community consisting of four ethnic segments. He describes the way in which these groups interact with one another and maintain their own territoriality. Each maintains different patterns for the use of neighborhood space. The ethnic groups themselves are segmented into age groups and lifestyle groups, each of which have different rules and standards for behavior. Teen-age gangs are particularly important in setting standards for neighborhood interaction. In spite of the fragmentation by age, ethnicity, and spatial usage, the neighborhood has developed a neighborhood-specific set of rules and public morality, which is integrative and emphasizes the neighborhood level of organization. The neighborhood is integrated by a principle of "ordered segmentation," in which the neighborhood level frequently becomes an inclusive, effective community, subsuming lower-level loyalty groupings.

Hannerz, in his study of a block in a Black community in Washington, D.C., notes that in spite of common ethnicity, there are several distinct lifestyles in this community, some based on age and others on life careers.[14]

Another neighborhood study, which would seem to have great potential for an understanding of the nature of community complexity as well as the relationship between the neighborhood and the larger urban setting, is that by the Valentines in New York City.[15] They explicitly developed a methodological approach that emphasizes the dynamic na-

---

[14] Ulf Hannerz, *Soulside* (New York: Columbia University Press, 1970).

[15] For some preliminary reports of fieldwork in a Black community, see Charles Valentine and Betty Valentine, "Making the Scene, Digging the Action, and Telling It Like It Is; Anthropologists at Work in a Dark Ghetto," in Norman Whitten and John Szwed (eds.), *Afro-American Anthropology* (New York: The Free Press, 1970); "Ethnography and Large-Scale Complex Sociocultural Systems," (mimeo), 1969; and the section on Blackton in G. Berreman et al., *Anthropology Today* (Del Mar, California: CRM Books, 1971).

ture of the neighborhood and its relationship to outside forces. They analyze the effect of jurisdictional boundaries drawn by outsiders on the cohesion and cognitive views of territory held by insiders. They also study some of the institutions with which members of the community have intensive and continuous contact. Their tentative conclusions indicate that, despite the proximity and outsiders' view of common ethnicity, there is great *variability* in people's relationships to each other, in familial backgrounds, in ethnic origin (West Indies, rural South, etc.), and in relation to outsiders. A major theme of the Valentines' work is that this community is primarily a result of imposed external economic and political forces. However, within this context, the Valentines demonstrate the creativity and adaptive manipulation of the population and suggest that they are not merely surviving, but are effectively reacting to outside forces, in spite of their inability to control them.

Differentiation

A somewhat different approach, which is comparative in nature, attempts to develop typologies of neighborhoods by delineating those factors that differentiate neighborhoods from one another.

One such approach is developed by Uzzell in his study of irregular communities in Lima, Peru.[16] Once again the approach is ethnographic and, in this case, explicitly comparative. In many ways, Uzzell is attacking the generally accepted notion that irregular communities are all similar and unchanging (have a stable population). The dynamic element used by Uzzell is based upon the life cycle of the community (in terms of physical characteristics, historical antecedents, geographic location, legal status, and social composition). The life cycle of the community is articulated with the life cycle of the individual residents. The important components of the latter are stages in the domestic cycle and the direction of the career cycle.

If we begin at a single point in time, an irregular community is characterized by a particular set of physical, historical, and locational characteristics, a legal status, and social composition. This set of characteristics will attract others to the community. As new members of the community enter, they and other inhabitants are changing their life cycles (household composition and careers) and their needs. They, in turn, modify the original characteristics of the community (physical and legal status), thus inducing some to leave and new members to enter. Temporary housing may give way to permanent housing, subject to greater

[16] J. Douglas Uzzell, "The Interaction of Population and Locality in the Development of Squatter Settlements in Lima," in W. Cornelius and F. Trueblood (eds.), *Latin American Urban Research*, pp. 113-34.

control by residents. There may be a shift from straw and scrap wood or metal to brick and cement block. Size and services may change. An illegal settlement may obtain government recognition, thus changing both legal status and the degree of government control of land use, quality, and taxation. These changes further influence the recruitment of new individuals and the exit of some old residents. In some cases, changes in the career patterns and domestic cycles may be a fundamental element of the turnover in population. It would be a rare case, indeed, to find an illegal community with temporary housing and no services retaining a population that is upwardly mobile.

The goal of this particular orientation to the study of neighborhoods is to develop a set of predictive criteria related to social composition, legal status, and historical antecedents, which ultimately change the nature of the neighborhood. By studying several neighborhoods, Uzzell is attempting to identify the range of potential predictive characteristics.

Uzzell's work is related to the very detailed, long-term ethnographic study done by Roberts, which compares two low income neighborhoods in Guatemala City.[17] Roberts emphasizes the problems in collective organization in this fast growing city because of diverse origins, differing careers, and mobility within the city of the low income population. Since there are few nonresidential bases of collective identity (ethnicity is not used to differentiate, nor do people have stable occupational status), the neighborhood becomes the major potential focus for cohesion and integration.

Roberts points out that formal organizations are pervasive in both communities: one a shantytown and the other a planned community. There are betterment associations, sporting clubs, mothers' clubs, consumers' and producers' cooperatives, mutual benefit associations, and church groups. However, they are not well attended nor long-lived. Roberts points out that these formal organizations do not promote neighborhood cohesion. They largely reflect cliques and segmented networks and are not truly inclusive or integrative. Moreover, they are more a response to external activities than to internal needs. Much of the organization is a result of attempts by outsiders to organize the community in order to advance their own interests or to minimize the perceived threat of previously unknown masses viewed as dangerous. Thus, in many ways, formal groups are *not* useful indicators of cohesion and organization by the urban poor.

In comparing the two communities, Roberts points out, as have others, that the shantytown in its early stages does tend to be more organized, because of the need to plan the formation of the community and

---

[17] Bryan Roberts, *Organizing Strangers* (Austin: University of Texas Press, 1973).

to negotiate with municipal agencies. While the other community has also experienced periods of greater organization in relation to issues that require interaction with the city, such intensification of organization is temporary and related to particular issues and events.

Roberts looks at some of the local variables that affect organization. The differences in legal status and process of formation between the shantytown and planned development have already been noted. Moreover, locational features are also significant. The shantytown's central location makes for easier movement and articulation with the city. The planned community is on the edge of the city, making it more inaccessible.

Roberts is pessimistic about the degree to which low income populations are effectively organized and able to participate in the urban social system. On the one hand, residence seems the only possible basis for organization, but on the other hand, transiency and unstable life careers negatively affect this process. Moreover, local organization is controlled by outsiders, who manipulate the process for their own ends. Organizations tend to be divisive, and factionalism is pervasive in local level politics.

Leeds' work (previously discussed in Chapter 3) attempts to delineate the differences between irregular settlements (Brazilian *favelas*) in Rio and São Paulo.[18] Pointing out the differences in the history of the two cities in terms of population, function in the national system, and occupational strucure, Leeds attempts to link these differences in the larger urban context to differences in the nature of the favela. He tries to develop this theme systematically by pointing out three levels of external variables that impinge on the nature of irregular communities in all of Latin America: city variables (like the ones mentioned above), regional variables, and national variables. His data are originally ethnographic, but he also uses non-ethnographic data sources to describe contexts.

In the same vein, David Epstein, in his study of squatter settlements in Brazilia (the new capital of Brazil), discusses the degree to which the favela movement in Brazilia is a result of national policy and macroeconomic forces, rather than local indigenous factors.[19]

[18] Anthony Leeds, "The Anthropology of Cities: Some Methodological Issues," in Elizabeth Eddy (ed.), *Urban Anthropology* (Athens: University of Georgia Press, 1968), pp. 31-47; "Locality Power in Relation to Supralocal Power," in A. Southall (ed.), *Urban Anthropology* (New York: Oxford University Press, 1973), pp. 15-41; and "The Significant Variables in Determining the Characteristics of Squatter Settlements," *America Latina*, 12 (1969), 44-86.

[19] David Epstein, "The Genesis and Functions of Squatter Settlements in Brazilia," in Thomas Weaver and Douglas White (eds.), *The Anthropology of Urban Environments*, Monograph 11, Society for Applied Anthropology, 1972, pp. 51-58.

Issues in the Neighborhood Approach

There are several major problems in the urban ethnography of neighborhoods. One we have already pointed out mistakes the study of a few localized networks for a neighborhood. Another problem is that of the representativeness of a particular neighborhood of all neighborhoods. Another set of problems emerges when the neighborhood is viewed as a bounded unit without explicit recognition of its relationships to the larger context. Most of the studies described above do not do this, but other studies do have this limitation.

Still another issue is raised when a particular research problem has nothing to do with the nature of the neighborhood, but the neighborhood is selected as a unit in which to do research. This frequently creates a narrow, localized view of the problem. An example of this latter difficulty can be found in the work of Michael Whiteford in Popayán, Colombia.[20] He chose, initially, to study a neighborhood and to spend his field time there. One of the major conclusions of Whiteford's work is that the residential community is *not* cohesive. He maintains that people do not know each other well and do not interact frequently or intimately with neighbors in the community. Whiteford also indicates that the community itself is isolated and not really integrated with the city of Popayán; he uses the term *rurban* to denote this rural fringe relationship. However, it is apparent from occasional references to work situations that members of this locality are, in fact, integrated into the larger urban context through work and patron-client ties, but these ties are not followed up by fieldwork outside the neighborhood.

There seems to be an underlying assumption in the work that integration follows a linear progression—one must have neighborhood cohesion at the lowest level, and then the neighborhood will be integrated into the larger setting. This is a very questionable assumption and probably would not be made by those working in middle class communities, where integration into the urban social structure is not based upon neighborhood. Much is made of the lack of concern and knowledge expressed by residents for others living there, but we are not given any insights into their network ties outside the community.

It is fairly obvious that one bias of urban anthropology already noted in relation to network analysis applies to neighborhood studies as well, namely, that the work done so far is oriented primarily toward lower classes. In spite of this, ethnographic data involving long-term contact with informants has provided us with insights into the realities

[20] Whiteford, "Neighbors at a Distance."

of neighborhood life. Earlier neighborhood studies were primarily concerned with refuting negative stereotypes of low income urban neighborhoods. As a result, the issue of neighborhood cohesion became central, and a number of individual case studies of solidarity in neighborhoods were done. When it was recognized that neighborhoods were not
homogeneous communities, then the issue of internal complexity was
addressed in several studies.

The sophistication emerging in urban anthropology can be seen in
the way longitudinal life history data and information about history,
political forces, demography, and other context variables are used in
creating dynamic models and explaining differences. The recognition of
diversity resulting from comparative studies has as its goal the development of typologies of neighborhoods based upon a wide range of variables.

Groups Based on Common Culture of Origin

Ethnic groups are those based upon a *common culture of origin*.
Since the city draws to it a population from diverse regions and/or
tribal-linguistic groups and even nation-states, the existence of such
ethnic groups in cities is a universal cross-cultural characteristic. Such
groups frequently emphasize common descent and blood relationships.
As a result, it is easy to develop strong sentiment and group commitment by alluding to this common ancestry and history. Frequently, social
scientists consider such identities to be the most fundamental for the
individual, that is, their basic social status. However, the subsequent discussion will indicate that such identities are not always basic and their
saliency for individuals must be validated empirically. Such groups may
maintain boundaries that segregate them from other groups and help
develop internal cohesion. A major concern in urban anthropology research is to understand the various conditions under which boundaries
are intensified or weakened, as well as the techniques ethnic groups use
to maintain their boundaries and the fluctuation of boundaries over time.

One of the difficulties with the urban anthropological literature
dealing with ethnic groups is that ethnicity is frequently viewed as both
a cultural and structural phenomenon—without adequately distinguishing
the two. By a *cultural* view, we mean that an ethnic group is defined
as maintaining a learned tradition of culture (food and dress, language,
family organization, and values), developed in the place of origin and
transposed almost intact to the city. Since the city relies on recruitment
from outside, those coming in will have been enculturated in a different

tradition. It has been noted by many that the majority of residents in most Third World cities are migrants. Thus, the city has significant cultural diversity, which can but does not always become a basis for organization.

The other aspect of ethnicity, the *structural*, deals with the formation of groups based upon a feeling of common heritage, which emerges within the urban setting. Actual commonality of culture traits may not be significant; common social identity and social cohesion may have little to do with common learned traditions.

The creation of ethnic groups is a complex process involving a multiplicity of relationships between the urban setting and the particular ethnic group. In the process of migration, members of the same village, extended kin group, or dialect group tend to become residentially clustered if possible, or at least to interact frequently if they are dispersed. As a particular group with a common culture of origin becomes recognized by others in the city, they are stereotyped by the others primarily on the basis of *assumed* common culture traits. It is this view by others —frequently associated with discrimination against the group or competition with other groups and/or forms of involuntary segregation— that gives the group itself a strong basis of organization and cohesion through time, in spite of a possible loss of common cultural traits. Some recent studies of the relationship between ethnic groups and political organization suggest that when such groups turn to political action, they can frequently mobilize the resources of their membership effectively This, in turn, adds strength to the group and helps maintain it through time. At other times, groups use their common identity to develop access to and control over particular economic niches.

Not only may we view the development of particular ethnic groups as partly a response to the urban setting—as opposed to a result of culture trait carry-overs—but in many cases we find *symbols* of identity to be newly created or else borrowed from one limited segment of several cultures of origin.

Some of these processes can be illustrated by symbols of Afro-American (Black) ethnicity. This group represents a very large and diverse population, both in the past and present. Recognizing this, there has been an attempt to develop unity in the population through collective symbols. These include the creation of a flag (a totally new item), the use of a language (Swahili, which is drawn from a minor segment of the African heritage), a hairstyle (which is of limited importance in traditional Africa), dress styles (which are predominantly West African in origin), and a food pattern (which is drawn from historical conditions in the American South).

Village, Caste and Religion

In the preceding discussion of ethnicity, we have primarily used national, regional, and tribal categories; however, there are other units of origin to which an individual might have a basic identity commitment and which will serve as the focus for intensive relationships.

Where relatively large numbers of individuals from a particular village are found in a city, the village of origin may be viewed as a basic source of ethnicity. A number of urban anthropologists working in southern Africa have focused upon the concept of "home-boy" or "home-fellow" as a very important native category for the designation of others in the urban setting and the incorporation of others within one's personal network. Interestingly, in Mexico City, while Butterworth found that village origin was very important for migrants from Tilantongo, Kemper found that village was very insignificant to those from Tzintzuntzan.[21]

In India caste as an ethnic-like unit is worth noting. Lynch's study of the Jatavs of Agra shows that they form a very strong bounded unit, culturally different from other groups, and with intensive interaction within the boundaries.[22] Berreman suggests that caste is an ethnic category used by urban Indians to catalogue those with whom they interact.[23] He notes the complex interplay between such factors as region of origin, mother language, religion, caste, and current occupation. In particular situations, these various statuses can be manipulated by the individual to his advantage.

Since caste groups are bounded, culturally distinct units within the village, they represent a segment of a village population. However, since caste segments in one village interact with like caste segments in neighboring villages (mostly in relation to marriage), they represent a regional subculture, which they transpose to the city as a basis for high levels of interaction and cohesion. Gould, Srinivas and others have noted the multiplicity of functions taken on by caste associations in the city.[24]

Another basis for cultural differentiation in the rural area, which is frequently carried into the urban areas as a basis for ethnic group

[21] D. S. Butterworth, "A Study of the Urbanization Process Among Mixtec Migrants from Tilantongo in Mexico City," in W. Mangin, 1970, *Peasants in Cities*, pp. 98-113; Robert Kemper, "Family and Household Organization Among Tzintzuntzan Migrants in Mexico City," in W. Cornelius and F. Trueblood (eds.), *Latin American Urban Research*, pp. 23-46.

[22] Owen Lynch, *The Politics of Untouchability* (New York: Columbia University Press, 1969).

[23] Gerald Berreman, "Social Categories and Social Interaction in Urban India," *American Anthropologist*, 74 (1972), 567-87.

[24] Harold Gould, "The Adaptive Functions of Caste in Contemporary Indian Society," *Asian Survey*, III (1963), 427-38; M. N. Srinivas, *Caste in Modern India and Other Essays* (Madras: Asia Publishing House, 1962).

formation, is religion. In Gulick's [25] description of Tripoli, Lebanon, it is the religious sect groups, rather than regional or linguistic groups, that form the basic, bounded cultural entities in the city.

The Effect of the Urban on Ethnicity

As we have noted throughout this entire volume, one of the generally agreed upon characteristics of urban centers is their cultural heterogeneity. Many anthropologists have suggested that ethnic group identity in the city is an overt attempt to respond to heterogeneity and bring order to urban complexity.

Gluckman pointed out rather early that tribalism in Africa is primarily a response to the urban situation rather than a characteristic of tribal life in the hinterland.[26] Where people live in a homogeneous tribal setting, their identity as members of a particular tribal group need not be great, and such groups are marked by cleavages based on kinship, politics, and other factors. In contrast to this situation, in the urban areas, where people live in a pluralistic setting with many tribal groups, a heightened sense of tribal identity comes to the fore.

One might argue that in many non-urban parts of the world, ethnic groups interact regularly. In fact, an earlier work on ethnicity in anthropology by Barth examined such non-urban situations.[27] They consisted of long-term, well-established relationships between culturally differentiated groups. There were usually no more than two or three groups involved. However, in the urban area, the number of groups is greater and their relative sizes change over time. Since no stable set of relationships exists in a setting where constant population shifts are inherently characteristic, urban ethnicity is different.

Mitchell, building upon Gluckman's work, suggests that tribalism is a consequence of the individual's need to make sense of the large, complex, and heterogeneous urban environment.[28] Where one is constantly confronted by unknown individuals or strangers, tribal identity can become a basic way of anchoring the relationship in terms of comprehensible models of social categories.

Berreman in his study of Dehra Dun, India, notes the same use of

---

[25] John Gulick, *Tripoli* (Cambridge: Harvard University Press, 1967).

[26] Max Gluckman, "Anthropological Problems Arising from the African Industrial Revolution," in Aidan Southall (ed.), *Social Change in Modern Africa* (London: Oxford University Press, 1961).

[27] Frederick Barth (ed.), *Ethnic Groups and Boundaries* (Boston: Little, Brown and Co., 1961).

[28] J. Clyde Mitchell, "Perceptions of Ethnicity and Ethnic Behavior: An Empirical Exploration," in A. Cohen (ed.), *Urban Ethnicity* (London: Tavistock Publishers, 1974), pp. 1-35.

social categories for identifying oneself to others.[29] However, the units used are not simply tribal, but are based upon such other ethnic attributes as region or state of origin, language, and religion.

One intriguing point that seems to emerge in some of the literature is that structural differences within tribal groups (lineages, political factions) sometimes disappear in most urban circumstances, and emphasis is placed on the *unity* of the group. There is a strengthening of in-group feeling. An example of this is found in Bruner's study of the Toba Batak in Medan, Indonesia, where differences in village, descent group, and other identities within the tribe are ignored in the distinction between *US* (Toba Batak) and *THEM* (strangers).[30] A more extreme case of this phenomenon is indicated by Paden, who points out that an urban ethnic group, the Bangala, in Kinshasa (Congo) have no ritual counterpart. The several tribes located in one hinterland region take on a single tribal identity in the city.[31]

The Effect of Particular Urban Contexts

Since most urban ethnographic studies of ethnic groups look at them within the context of particular urban centers, we can begin to see some general patterns evolve from specific case studies.

A fundamental issue in much of the literature dealing with urban ethnic groups is related to the dominance of particular groups within the urban setting. A group may be culturally, economically, or politically dominant, and the dominance may derive from a combination of demographic and historic processes and geographic location.

One variable related to the development of ethnicity, ethnic identification, and ethnic groups has been referred to as *critical mass*. This means that the actual number of individuals representing a social category may influence the development of ethnicity. A group that is too small to maintain a language or support special institutions will not retain significance. More comparative research must be done before we can identify strategic population levels. Many cases of early migration (for example, Indians in England) indicate that when there are small numbers

[29] Berreman, "Social Categories and Social Interaction in Urban India.

[30] Edward Bruner, "Urbanization and Ethnic Identity in North Sumatra," *American Anthropologist*, 63 (1961), 501-21; "Medan: The Role of Kinship in an Indonesian City," in Alexander Spoehr (ed.), *Pacific Port Towns and Cities* (Honolulu: Bishop Museum Press, 1963), pp. 1-12; "Kin and Non-Kin," in Aidan Southall (ed.), *Urban Anthropology* (New York: Oxford Press, 1973), pp. 373-92.

[31] N. Paden, "Urban Pluralism, Integration and Adaptation of Communal Identity in Kano, Nigeria," in R. Cohen and J. Middleton (ed.), *From Tribe to Nation in Africa*, 1970.

of migrants, there is no external stereotyping, avoidance of interaction, or perceived competition by the dominant class. As more migrants arrive, these processes begin. Thus, when Hodge studied the Navajo in Albuquerque, there were so few in the city that there was no collectivization or high degree of self-identification with tribe of origin.[32]

Comparing two cities in Malaysia on the nature of Malay ethnicity as a response to city context, Nagata suggests that certain historical factors determine distinct modes of Malay ethnicity in the two cities.[33] Kuala Lumpur is a colonial city founded by a dominant group, the Europeans, who encouraged Chinese entrepreneurial activities. The Chinese have thus had a position of economic dominance leading to significant political clout in the post-colonial period. Bandao, on the other hand, was created by a local ruler who remained independent of the European colonial empire; Chinese entrepreneurial activity was discouraged, and Malays retained political dominance.

In most African studies, the urban centers had been under colonial domination and were frequently differentiated in terms of European and native residential loci. The "locations" (areas set aside for native Africans) drew to them a diverse African population because of the labor needs of colonial enterprise. The dominant ethnic group were the British, French, Spanish, or Portuguese.

In the earlier studies done under colonial conditions, there was recognition of ethnicity, although the basic group cleavage was seen to be racial. The control of jobs, housing, and urban politics by the Europeans restricted ethnic group formation by creating a racial cleavage and conditions that fostered frequent circular migration and temporary residence in the city. In the post-colonial situation, a locally dominant ethnic group, which is the demographic majority, has political control over the city and acts as a cultural model for behavior within the city.

In Plotnicov's article, "Who Owns Jos?" the notion of "ownership" of the city in Nigeria is related to the historical association of a particular ethnic group to the geographic locus of the city.[34] This group is also demographically superior because of the closeness of their tribal base to the city. In many Nigerian cities, a dominant tribal group is overtly recognized as the cultural, political, and demographic power in the city, either because the tribe founded the city before the colonial period, or

[32] William H. Hodge, *The Albuquerque Navajos* (Tucson: University of Arizona Press, 1969).

[33] Judith Nagata, "A Tale of Two Cities: Life in Two Malaysian Towns," *Urban Anthropology*, 3 (1974), 1-26.

[34] Leonard Plotnicov, "Who Owns Jos?: Ethnic Ideology in Nigerian Politics," *Urban Anthropology*, 1 (1972), 1-13; for further information, see *Strangers in the City* (Pittsburgh: University of Pittsburgh Press, 1967).

because the tribe inhabited the region in which a colonially created city was located.

A number of studies of Kampala, Uganda identify the culturally and politically dominant position of the Ganda tribe, whose home base was the region in which the city was located by Europeans. They are numerically superior, and their cultural values are held as ideals and set the standard for life in the city. Gutkind suggests that their dominance makes the Ganda unique, with different mobility and associational patterns than the many other tribes in the city.[35] Parkin has compared the Ganda and Luo in Kampala and suggests that the differences in demographic and cultural dominance have a direct impact on their associations. Furthermore, when he contrasts the Luo in Nairobi to the Luo in Kampala, he also finds that their relative demographic and political positions affect their organization.[36]

In Shack's study of the Guraje in Addis Ababa, Ethiopia, the dominant ethnic group in the city are the Amhara.[37] This group traces its dominance back to the founder of the city (1890), who was the political leader of this tribe and pacified the countryside. The Amhara did not represent a numerical majority for some time. In 1952, a census showed that they were a majority, but Shack questions this figure, suggesting that many non-Amharans manipulate their ethnicity and label themselves as members of the dominant group. Shack notes that many other groups emulate the behavior and values of the Amhara as soon as they become economically able to do so.

Leaving the African scene, we can turn to the work of Bruner, who studied ethnicity in two cities in Indonesia: Medan and Bandung.[38] In Bandung, there is a dominant ethnic group (in terms of numerical strength, home base, and political control). In Medan there is no population majority or locally dominant culture. In the latter city, "ethnic cleavages are sharply defined, relations are tense, and each group tends to encapsulate itself."[39] In Bandung this is not true; the same groups intermarry more and there are greater cultural and attitudinal differences between age groups within ethnic groups than between ethnic groups.

[35] P. C. W. Gutkind, "African Urbanism, Mobility and the Social Network," *International Journal of Comparative Sociology*, 6 (1965), 48-60.
[36] D. Parkin, "Congregational and Interpersonal Ideologies in Political Ethnicity," in A. Cohen (ed.), *Urban Ethnicity*, pp. 119-58.
[37] W. A. Shack, "Urban Ethnicity and the Cultural Process of Urbanization in Ethiopia," in Aidan Southall (ed.), *Urban Anthropology* (London: Oxford University Press, 1973), pp. 251-86.
[38] Edward Bruner, "Urbanization and Ethnic Identity," "Medan," "Kin and Non-Kin"; "The Expression of Ethnicity in Indonesia," in Abner Cohen (ed.), *Urban Ethnicity*, pp. 251-80.
[39] Bruner, "The Expression of Ethnicity," p. 269.

Bruner has also examined the functions of Toba Batak associations in three Indonesian cities. In Djakarta (capital), the Toba Batak constitute a very small segment; they tend to participate in multi-ethnic associations that promote nationalism. In Bandung, the Toba Batak are a relatively small group; their associations are oriented to promoting their political interests in competition with another group. In Medan, close to their homeland, they comprise a large segment of the urban population and are organized into many small groups with mutual aid and ceremonial functions.[40]

An interesting extension of Bruner's work is his analysis of the nationally dominant group, the Javanese, and their response to life in a city where they are a minority. He finds that because of their national position, ethnicity plays a small role in the organization of their lives, and they are not concerned with their role in the city power structure. In many ways they are similar to White Anglo-Saxon Protestants (WASPs) in the United States.

Much of our information about the effects of particular urban contexts on ethnic groups is based upon comparative studies, in which the same ethnic group is examined within different urban centers. It is from such comparative research that the most illuminating insights develop.

Opportunity Structure and Economic Niches

The maintenance of ethnic ties is obviously related to economic opportunity, and the issue of dominance raised in the previous discussion carries over here. When a dominant group can restrict the opportunities available to minority groups, this will have an obvious impact upon their position within the urban economic and institutional structure. Even where there is no single dominant group, competition between ethnic groups still exists.

Group cohesion and economic success are frequently related. Where a group acquires monopolistic control over a particular economic niche or occupation, this will reinforce group ties in order to maintain the monopoly. In much the same sense, strong group ties will enhance the possibility of gaining monopolistic control.

Cohen, in his classic work on the Hausa in Ibadan, noted that they have been able to develop monopolistic control over the cattle and kola nut trade in the city. Cohen's major point is that Hausa ethnicity is a political response to the need to protect the economic interests of the group. It is a response to urban life, rather than a result of the strength of cultural values and cultural carry-overs. Economic success in the city

[40] Edward Bruner, "Batak Ethnic Association in Three Indonesian Cities," *Southwestern Journal of Anthropology*, 28 (1972), 207-29.

has strengthened Hausa ties. In contrast to other groups in Ibadan, they live in a residentially segregated enclave, have their own political organization, and minimize their interaction with outsiders; they are distinctive in dress and in many behavioral patterns that are carefully controlled by the group.

Cohen was one of the first to point out the significance of economic niche protection for the strengthening of ethnic ties. As a corollary, he has suggested that groups that do not have such niches are less likely to use ethnicity as a basis for organization.[41]

The poor of all ethnic groups will recognize common interests, as will the wealthy. On the other hand, Hannerz has suggested that even where great differences in wealth and status occur among members of a single ethnic group, they can still be cohesive based on ethnicity through techniques of vertical integration. He describes the use of patron-client ties between members of an internally stratified ethnic group as a means for maintaining cohesion and using ethnicity as a basis for political and economic activity.[42]

Grillo looks at this same process in Kampala. He finds that the lower class segment of the ethnic group have a vested interest in reinforcing ethnic solidarity and common sentiments with the upper levels of the group. Moreover, the upper segments who are economically and politically ambitious often find uses for the support, services, and clientage of the lower levels.[43]

Another example of ethnic control over a niche is found in Shack's study of the Guraje.[44] He notes that the politically and culturally dominant Amhara eschewed manual labor and mercantile activities as demeaning. This allowed the Guraje to take over many activities over which they developed monopolistic control. The internal marketing activities of the city were dominated by the Guraje, as were the shops, street hawking, and peddling to rural areas. On the other hand, the large-scale capitalization necessary for import-export trade was beyond their capacity and therefore remained in the hands of the Arabs.

A classic case of an ethnic group that has maintained tight boundaries over long periods of time is the Gypsies. They are found over widely dispersed areas of the world and recently have been drawn to major urban centers. Until recently they were not much studied by anthropologists because of their suspicion of all outsiders; however, now there is an ethnographic literature on them.

[41] Abner Cohen, *Custom and Politics in Urban Africa* (London: Routledge and Kegan Paul, 1969).

[42] Ulf Hannerz, "Ethnicity and Opportunity in Urban America," in Abner Cohen (ed.), *Urban Ethnicity,* pp. 37-76.

[43] B. D. Grillo, "Ethnic Identity and Social Stratification on a Kampala Housing Estate," in A. Cohen (ed.), *Urban Ethnicity,* pp. 159-86.

[44] Shack, "Urban Ethnicity."

In most areas, Gypsies occupied a particular niche in the economic structure that provided the means for maintaining closed boundaries and a strong, persistent cultural heritage, which includes language and dress. Frequently their economic activities have been clandestine or illegal—petty theft, confidence games, fortune telling. This legal marginality has led to strong boundary maintenance. Gypsies have been the object of derision, discrimination, and negative stereotyping by many other groups and in turn look down upon outsiders.

In her study of Samoans in California, Ablon finds that certain occupations drew most heavily from the population. For the men, shipping and shipyard work was primary, while the women were employed as aides in nursing homes. Samoans exerted influence on these occupational domains through informal control of job recruiting and informal organization on the job. However, they did not have administrative, or entrepreneurial control.[45] In most of the preceding examples of occupational monopolies, the ethnic groups did have entrepreneurial control.

A more general view of the relationship between ethnic groups and opportunity structure is found in the work of M. Estellie Smith.[46] In her study of the Portuguese community in two New England towns, she indicates that the greater economic opportunities available in one town resulted in considerably more economic success and mobility for the Portuguese resident. In the more successful community, ethnically based activities were more highly organized and there was considerably greater group cohesion. Although the Portuguese were a minority group in both situations, in the more open economic system, they had greater access to economic success and to a broader spectrum of levels of occupation, largely because of the economic growth of the town. The town's diversified economic structure made it more adaptive to changes in the economic system. The success of the town and resultant success of the Portuguese led to a positive stereotype of the group by the dominant class. This, in turn, reinforced their access to a broad spectrum of jobs.

Politics

Frequently the manipulation of political power within the city is enhanced by the ability to mobilize fellow ethnics, and correspondingly politics becomes a technique for reinforcing ethnic identity and solidarity. Many ethnic associations have as their goal the "advancement" of the position of the group within the city. In many cases, ethnic asso-

[45] Joan Ablon, "The Social Organization of an Urban Samoan Community," *Southwestern Journal of Anthropology*, 27 (1971), 75-96.
[46] M. Estellie Smith, "A Tale of Two Cities: The Realities of Historical Differences," *Urban Anthropology*, 4 (1975), 61-72.

ciations are organized to help in the collective upward mobility of the group.

Associations of lower caste groups in India attempt to raise their status in the system collectively by discarding elements that identify them as low ranked and emulating the activities of higher ranked groups. This process is buttressed by recreating a mythology that claims original high status. Lynch has shown that in addition to these strategies, the Jatavs of Agra have organized themselves into a potent political force that operates both in the city and state legislature to improve the group's position.[47]

The Hausa in Ibadan described by Cohen are also organized for participation in the urban political arena.[48] In this case, the group uses its strength to protect political and economic advantages already gained.

Much of the African literature emphasizes the role of tribal membership in the organization of political parties. Where many ethnic groups are found and none dominate, given parties may be supported by blocks of tribes, and each tribe thus tends to support one party.

In a discussion of political activities in Luanshya, Zambia, Harries-Jones has shown the significance of ethnic-tribal identity in the development and maintenance of political organizations.[49] He describes a group from Malawi who became part of a "section" (party) led by a Malawian. This segment of the population disassociated itself politically from other groups in the neighborhood, but in other activities, particularly drinking and leisure-time activities, they interacted freely with Bemba and others.

Grillo studied the political process in depth within the railway workers' unions in Kampala. He found that ethnic sentiments are frequently appealed to in the manipulation of the electoral process. However, ethnicity is not a dominant factor, because there are no mechanisms for sanctioning those who ignore ethnic appeals.[50]

The history of American urban politics shows the continuing influence of ethnic groups on the political process. When politicians talk about a "balanced" ticket in a city election, they are frequently talking about balanced ethnic representation. Historically, ward politics were organized along ethnic lines, frequently encouraged by outsiders who desired political supporters. Eventually insiders replaced outsiders in the control of ethnic block votes, and the structure has continued over time.

Glick has shown how the recent formation and cohesion of Haitians

[47] Lynch, *The Politics of Untouchability.*
[48] A. Cohen, *Custom and Politics.*
[49] P. Harries-Jones, " 'Home-Boy' Ties and Political Organization in a Copperbelt Township," in J. Clyde Mitchell (ed.), *Social Networks in Urban Situations* (Manchester: Manchester University Press, 1969).
[50] B. D. Grillo, "Ethnic Identity and Social Stratification."

as an ethnic group in New York was a direct response to political competition.[51] Non-Haitian politicians, who recognized the potential power base of the rapidly in-migrating Haitians, became involved in organizing the group as a political interest group. Using the institution of the church and the status of Haitian priests, they developed an effective political block for the mutual benefit of both groups.

Frequently ethnically based political organizations emerge that are initially concerned with using power to benefit the place of origin. Little has noted for West African tribal associations that much of the initial concern is with improving conditions in the hinterland.[52] Others who have criticized Little suggest that such associations are developed to manipulate the urban situation for the benefit of urban residents. These two functions are obviously not mutually exclusive; they may succeed one another or be continuous simultaneous goals. Doughty's description of regional associations in Lima, Peru emphasizes their concern with using power to achieve benefits for the regions of origin.[53] However, they are used to protect the urban interests of the group as well.

Although ethnicity may be used as the basis of political organization it is not always the case that groups based on culture of origin are unified politically. In many European cities (for example, Hamburg, Germany and Oslo, Norway), groups based on culture of origin are not relevant to the political process. In addition, many ethnic associations are organized for different political goals, or the process of organization may be different. Outsiders may play a role in some cases, while the process may begin within the group in others. To develop a fuller understanding of the development of a political function in ethnic organizations, it is necessary to identify the conditions under which a particular developmental process will occur.

Ethnicity as the Persistence of Cultural Tradition

Much of the urban anthropological literature dealing with ethnicity focuses on the retention of elements drawn from the culture of origin. Such items are especially important insofar as they lead to high rates of

[51] Nina Glick, "The Formation of a Haitian Ethnic Group" (Doctoral dissertation, Department of Anthropology, Columbia University, 1975).
[52] Kenneth Little, "The Role of Voluntary Associations in West African Urbanization," *American Anthropologist*, 59 (1957), 579-96 and *West African Urbanization: A Study of Voluntary Associations in Social Change* (Cambridge: Cambridge University Press, 1965).
[53] Paul Doughty, "Behind the Back of the City: Provincial Life in Lima, Peru," in W. Mangin (ed.), *Peasants in Cities* (Boston: Houghton Mifflin, 1970), pp. 30-46; and "Peruvian Migrant Identity in the Urban Milieu," in T. Weaver and D. White (eds.), *The Anthropology of Urban Environments*, Society for Applied Anthropology Monographs, 1972, pp. 39-50.

exclusive interaction and serve as symbols to maintain boundaries between groups. The persistence of a way of life derived from the culture
of origin will be apparent in the study of recent migrants. However, the
long-term intergenerational maintenance of such patterns is still an
issue. Such elements will probably not persist in the absence of continuing attempts to gain access or control over political and economic
resources.

In some studies of the success or lack of success of particular urban
ethnic groups, considerable attention is given to the cultural values of
the group to explain their condition. Cultural values are also used to
explain differences in group solidarity and cohesion. Group differences
are often attributed to different cultural aspirations, motivation, and
values about education. De Vos locates the reason for the differential
success of Japanese-Americans and Mexican-Americans in their respective cultures.[54] However, it is very difficult to demonstrate that values
are different. We are left with a tautological argument: rates of success
are different because values are different, and the proof of the latter lies
in the fact that rates of success differ!

Another example is a study by Weppner that attempts to explain
the lack of economic success of Navajos in Denver in terms of basic
values. He suggests that traditional Navajo time-orientation and fatalism
impede their potential success. On the other hand, he also notes that the
Navajo had a traditional work ethic, and he cannot explain why this does
not overcome the other "values." By wrenching Navajo "values" from
their traditional context and treating them as value generalities, he fails
to make a convincing case for values as the "cause" of success or
failure.[55]

Morrill attempts to explain the difference between the Ibos (immigrants) and Efik (local tribes) in Calabar, Nigeria in terms of their
economic absorption and cohesion.[56] He claims that the Ibo are more
successful because they have a more "generalized" culture, enabling
them to be flexible. The Efik culture is too specialized, too full of pro-
scriptions. His model of traditional Ibo culture is drawn from kinship,
political structure, and values.

Henderson refuted Morrill's argument in several ways.[57] First he

[54] George De Vos, "Ethnic Pluralism: Conflict and Accommodation," in George De
Vos and L. Romanucci (eds.), *Ethnic Identity* (Palo Alto, California: Mayfield Publishers, 1975), pp. 5-41.
[55] Robert S. Weppner, "Urban Economic Opportunities: The Example of Denver," in
J. D. Waddell and O. M. Watson, *The American Indian in Urban Society* (Boston:
Little, Brown, and Co., 1971), pp. 244-73.
[56] W. T. Morrill, "Immigrants and Associations: The Ibo in Twentieth Century
Calabar," *Comparative Studies in Society and History*, 5 (1963), 424-48.
[57] R. N. Henderson, "Generalized Cultures and Evolutionary Adaptability," *Ethnology*, 5 (1966), 365-69.

showed that an in-depth analysis of Ibo culture demonstrates that they are *not* "generalized," as Morrill describes, but very similar to the Efik in structure and culture. Moreover, he showed that in the city of Onisha, two groups of Ibo (one native and one in-migrant) who have the same cultural background vary in the same way as the Ibo and Efik in Calabar. The native group is relatively unsuccessful and unorganized, and the in-migrant group is relatively successful and cohesive. He links these characteristics to structural features in the city, rather than cultural values drawn from the area of origin. Moreover, he relates the respective role of each city in the national system to the discussion.

Certainly the previously mentioned comparative studies of Portuguese in two New England towns and the study of Malays in two Malasian cities point in the same direction. They show that structural variables are more significant for group success and cohesion than are values or organizational models drawn from the culture of origin. Parkin explicitly deals with this issue when he compares the structures of African tribal associations in the city. He looks at kin group systems in the rural tribal areas to see if these have an impact upon urban tribal organization. His conclusion is that demographic and class variables in the city are more significantly related to the nature of organizations than traditional tribal forms.[58] Schildkraut, in her discussion of ethnic groups in Kumasi, Ghana, is also emphatic about the irrelevance of culture for explaining the structure and organization of ethnic units.[59] It is obvious that if culture is to be used to explain group differences, we need better analyses of culture and less confusion between cultural and contextual factors.

Another comparative way of testing the issue is to compare two cultural groups in the same structural position to see if culture makes a difference. Gutkind, in his study of the long-term unemployed in Lagos and Nairobi, shows that members of different tribes in each city maintain different patterns of kinship obligations that are linked to tribal origin.[60] In this case, the economic position is held constant, so that tribe is clearly the variable. However, he also shows that, in the long run, economic positions lead to the same outcomes for all tribes. Similarly, Ashton shows that while the two lower class subgroups he studied (Afro-Americans and Mestizos) followed the same trend to re-

[58] D. J. Parkin, "Urban Voluntary Associations as Institutions of Adaptation," *Man*, 1 (1966), 90-94.
[59] Enid Schildkraut, "Ethnicity and Generational Differences Among Urban Immigrants in Ghana," in A. Cohen, *Urban Ethnicity*, pp. 187-222.
[60] Peter Gutkind, "The Energy of Despair: Social Organization of the Unemployed in Two African Cities: Lagos and Nairobi," *Civilisations*, 17 (1967), 186-211; and "The Poor in Urban Africa: A Prologue to Modernization, Conflict and the Unfinished Revolution," in W. Bloomberg and H. J. Schmandt (eds.), *Power, Poverty and Urban Policy, Urban Affairs Annual Review*, 2 (1970).

liance on networks for survival, there were differences. The first group stressed extended friendship ties, while Mestizos strengthened the domestic unit.[61]

The use of controlled comparisons in these studies can contribute to the problem of delineating those factors from the culture of origin that do influence adaptation of first generation migrants and their maintenance of traditional culture in the city. However, the control of socioeconomic variables is vital if valid conclusions are to be drawn.

Shack attempts to provide balance in his analysis of the Guraje of Addis Ababa.[62] He shows their position to be the result of interaction between basic values derived from the culture of origin and the structure of the city. Cultural beliefs about the economic role of women and the authority of the elders are perpetuated. Strong ties between urban Guraje and the rural tribe are maintained by fear of curses from tribal religious practitioners if obligations are not met.

Boundary Maintenance of Ethnic Groups

Although we have attempted to summarize some of the general literature dealing with urban ethnicity in somewhat neutral terms, it should be quite obvious by now that we would not *explain* the persistence of ethnic groups or their experience in adapting to the city in terms of the perpetuation of the culture of origin. Values and processes of intergenerational transmission are not sufficient to explain urban ethnicity. It is our contention that structural and contextual factors are more relevant.

However, elements of the culture of origin are significant as *symbols* in the maintenance of boundaries. Maintenance of the symbols also leads to activities and institutions which bring together and increase interaction between group members. Such symbols of group identity are emphasized for what they are: representations of a collective identity. Sometimes these cultural symbols may not even be derived from the culture of origin. They may be newly created; they may be radically modified but, as DeVos has suggested, they are usually believed to be derived from the heritage of the culture of origin.[63]

Symbols. There are a number of areas that are significant in the maintenance of ethnic group boundaries, that is, those aspects of life that separate insiders from outsiders, and that are used by individuals

[61] Guy Ashton, "The Differential Adaptation of Two Slum Subcultures to a Colombian Housing Project," *Urban Anthropology,* 1 (1972), 176-94
[62] Shack, "Urban Ethnicity."
[63] De Vos, "Ethnic Pluralism."

to *actively* identify with the group. Such symbols have shared meaning for the members of the group and frequently are recognized by out-siders as well as insiders.

Language is intimately linked to ethnicity. Since language is learned at a very early age, primarily within the context of the family, and is a major mechanism for the transmission of other aspects of culture, it is a fundamental source of ethnic identity. The use of native languages in certain mixed social contexts really serves to exclude outsiders and reinforce ties between insiders. In large urban institutions (schools, work places), small groups selectively use native languages in situations where they wish to exclude outsiders and reinforce solidarity with in-siders, even when they are perfectly capable of speaking the dominant language. Even if everyone speaks the same language, there is a ten-dency for groups to maintain differences in speaking styles. Kochman describes a complex system of styles appropriate for different contexts but unique to the Afro-American speech community.[64] Language re-mains important only as long as the ethnic group maintains a high frequency of interaction and boundary maintenance.

Greenberg has discussed language use in relation to tribal and ethnic identity in urban areas.[65] Citing the African urban literature, Greenberg suggests that there are many questions regarding urban lan-guage that have not received very much attention. The issue of *linguas franca* in polyglot urban areas of Africa is an intriguing one, since the maintenance of a native language that is not the dominant one used in a particular town or city is an obvious indication of the maintenance of ethnic identity. Greenberg notes that in older cities like Timbuctoo, which have drawn from a wide range of linguistic communities and have had a traditionally dominant language, particular linguistic com-munities may maintain a mother-tongue for very long periods of time.

In Ghana, migrants from the north who have a regional lingua franca, Hausa, do not adopt the Ghanaian language. Greenberg also cites material from Skinner and others indicating that the Mossi mi-grants in Ghana form a segregated linguistic community.

Citing Richards' material, he also notes that in some cases, mem-bers of a particular linguistic community who are subordinate economi-cally and politically, make an overt effort to acquire a dominant language in order to acquire higher status. In many parts of Africa that were under colonial domination, the most prestigious language was that of the colonial power. The native elite gained competence in this language.

---

[64] T. Kochman, " 'Rapping' in the Black Ghetto," *Trans-Action*, vol. 6, 1969.
[65] Joseph Greenberg, "Urbanism, Migration and Language," in Yehudi Cohen (ed.), *Man in Adaptation: The Biosocial Background* (Chicago: Aldine Publishing Company, 1968), pp. 259-66.

Obviously, there are many interesting questions about language persistence and language and power that can be pursued by the urban linguist and have relevance to questions about ethnic process.

Another area in which ethnic identity and boundaries are maintained is one that might be called *expressive* culture: body movement, dance, music, religion, folklore, and mythology. Styles of body communication—both *kinesics* (body movement) and *proxemics* (the use of space)—are used as ethnic markers. Many have shown how these aspects work for in-group identification. The use or nonuse of gestures is also an ethnic marker.

Folklore, mythology, dance, and literature are expressive arts, that affectively tie individuals to groups. Abrahams has demonstrated the maintenance of Afro-American expressive cultural forms and styles over time and their meaning and importance to the members of the group.[66] Keil, in his study of blues players, indicates the close relationship between the style of music characterized as blues and Afro-American ethnicity.[67] In Wolverhampton, England, Punjabi Indians have organized several music and dance groups, which performed for general audiences as well as Indian audiences. Many young people participated in these activities, and when performances were given for fellow-Indians, they drew large crowds.[68] Doughty indicates that a major function of weekly regional association meetings in Lima, Peru was to evoke the homeland through food, music, and dance.[69]

Differences in religious beliefs and practices are frequently a source of ethnic symbols. Beliefs in supernatural beings and magical practices are frequently used to separate insiders from outsiders. Similarly, cosmological beliefs are emphasized as distinctive cultural markers.

In some cases, core concepts are used to distinguish members of an ethnic group from outsiders. In the American urban context, one frequently hears that "soul" is a constellation of attributes unique to Afro-Americans. This fundamental characteristic is then related to many aspects of behavior and belief. It is the core from which particular styles of music, dance, language, interaction, and food are derived. Keil and Hannerz have both tried to deal with the soul concept, to describe its essence and its integrative function.[70]

---

[66] Roger Abrahams, *Deep Down in the Jungle* (Chicago: Aldine Publishing Company, 1970).

[67] Charles Keil, *Urban Blues* (Chicago: University of Chicago Press, 1966).

[68] Research on Punjabi migrants in Wolverhampton, England was conducted during 1969 and 1970 by Edwin Eames and Howard Robboy and was supported by a study leave from Temple University and N.I.M.H. Grant DHEW-IR03-01.

[69] Doughty, "Behind the Back of the City."

[70] Keil, *Urban Blues;* Ulf Hannerz, "What Negroes Mean By 'Soul,'" *Trans-Action,* 5 (1968), 57-61.

Another characteristic producing cohesion is the imputed reputation or stereotype of a given ethnic group. Sometimes the group internalizes the reputation imputed to it by outsiders and uses this as a symbol. In multi-ethnic urban situations, the various ethnic groups will be assigned characteristics considered to be peculiar or unique to them. To a very large extent, these reputational characteristics are contained within the stereotypes people use to explain the behavior of others. They are by no means always negative in content, and in many cases, the members of the ethnic group themselves may believe the characterizations to be valid.

In Suttles' description of the Italians in the multi-ethnic Addams area of Chicago, he notes that outsiders (Negroes, Puerto Ricans, and Mexicans) believe that the Italians have "connections"—that they are directly tied to the underworld and the local ward political leadership.[71] What is happening in this case is that identity and cohesion are magnified by the outsiders' belief in the potential power of the ethnic community. In addition, many Italians, although not having connections themselves, believe that others do, and operate on the assumption that the stereotype is true. Finally, some members recognize that their *reputation* to outsiders gives them greater power, and see the positive functions of the myth in spite of its questionable nature.

Dress and other cosmetic aspects of individual appearance could be the most visible ethnic markers. The wearing of saris by most Indian females is one example. Berreman notes that in Dehra Dun, India, regional dress styles are frequently maintained and are used as identity markers within the urban context.[72] However, in many instances, dress is the one item that has shown considerable homogenization on the world scene. Western style dress, at least for males in public places, has been diffused into most urban areas of the world. However, recent studies have shown that subtle distinctions in dress codes (differences in shoe brands, length of hair) still operate in some subcommunities. Often, however, these are not related to culture of origin, but to neighborhood or occupation and even to age.

Food Traditions. One symbol on which the authors of this text have done research and which lends insight into ethnic boundary maintenance is the use of food. We shall look at this phenomenon in some detail. A dietary pattern consists not only of the food items consumed, but also the style in which they are prepared, the order in which foods are served, and the types of foods served together. In addition, taboos or dislikes for certain foods are part of the pattern, as well as the time

[71] Suttles, *The Social Order of a Slum.*
[72] Berreman, "Social Categories."

of the day, week, or year (holidays) during which particular foods are consumed.

In many ways, food taboos can be seen as a part of dietary patterns that help maintain an ethnic group. Some well known examples of this phenomenon are the Muslim and Jewish prohibitions against the eating of pork and the Hindu prohibition against the eating of beef, as well as the Catholic former taboo on meat for Wednesday, Friday, and Lent. These taboos are not urban in origin, but when maintained in urban centers where various groups are in frequent contact, and often co-residential, they become designators of in-group and out-group membership.

For many groups, at least one meal a week (usually connected with the Sabbath) is a traditional ethnic meal for families maintaining a strong identity. On gala occasions (holidays, weddings), ethnic food is essential. A short-lived television comedy featuring Italian-Americans used the Sunday dinner, with the whole clan gathered, as its setting. The patriarch frequently used food behavior to designate the outsider status of his Episcopalian son-in-law. He called him "white bread eater" and asked if he wanted "mayonnaise" for his spaghetti—both items serving as negative symbols of bland American "WASP" food and a violation of the insider's pattern.

It should be noted that certain ethnic foods are adopted by other segments of the population and lose their importance as ethnic markers. It is interesting to note that the Italians of South Philadelphia consume a large amount of bagels. For them the bagel is not considered a Jewish food fixture and since it is not an ethnic food, there are no rules for eating bagels. Thus while Jews associate bagels with Sunday brunch and eat them with lox and cream cheese, Italians do not have any special associations or rules about bagel eating. While most Americans eat spaghetti and pizza, without special rules, the Italian-American dietary pattern contains many rules and expectations for what day and with what accompanying food pasta will be eaten.

Items that are part of a particular dietary pattern require the development of service institutions, which further reinforce the boundaries of a group. For example, in Philadelphia there are only three Greek food stores that prepare the phylo dough needed for many dishes. Greek households, which are dispersed throughout the city, must purchase dough at least once a week. Thus the storeowners become important nodes of communication for the community, and the stores important places for interaction. The Italian-American Food Study has shown that the specialized foods needs (Italian bread and pastries, imported cheese, homemade sausages for Christmas, spices, and other specialty items) have created a similar infrastructure of special Italian food stores and an open-air market for fresh produce.[73] In the same way, kosher butchers were essential for the Jewish population in the past and are still important for some segments today. One of the first commercial enterprises for Indians in England were specialty grocery stores, which provide necessary items for the cuisine. The Puerto Rican grocery store (*bodega*) provides many social services, in addition to purveying special food. In Philadelphia, many of them have pool rooms within them and serve as betting parlors. Baddeley discusses the importance of Greek and Turkish coffeehouses for immigrants in New Zealand.[74]

In many ways, food consumption patterns are a microcosm that can offer insight into the macrocosm of ethnic group identity and boundary maintenance in urban areas. In the urban area, an ethnic group brings with it particular dietary patterns. In the rural area, these patterns formed a highly integrated complex that was self-contained. Exposure to dietary items in the less bounded residential, work and leisure group units of the city leads to a degree of interchange between the groups. The new dietary pattern is a complex interweaving of original ethnic items and borrowed ones. However, original ethnic items are recognized as such, and rules about their use are maintained, thus serving to separate insiders from outsiders and maintain group boundaries.

Institutional Mechanisms. A variety of institutional mechanisms are used by ethnic groups to stimulate internal interaction and communication. The formal tribal and regional associations, native language newspapers, radio stations, and religious activities are based on cultures of origin. Specialty stores and restaurants such as those discussed above are necessary to purvey important symbolic items. Where strong rules of marriage within a group (*endogamy*) exist, there will be a tendency to heighten exclusive interaction. Much of the African literature emphasizes tribal endogamy as a basis of group maintenance in the city. Where intermediaries are necessary to arrange marriages, this further heightens group dependence. Shack notes the tendency for Guraje marriages to be arranged by intermediaries between townsmen and rural tribal girls.[75] However, he notes that Guraje women are considered quite desirable by other tribal groups in the city, and if a Guraje woman is divorced, there is a strong possibility that she will marry outside the

---

[73] Judith Goode, "The Philadelphia Food Project: A Study of Culture and Nutrition" (paper delivered at the Annual Meeting of the American Anthropological Association, 1974); "Modifying Ethnic Foodways: The Effects of Locality and Social Networks" (paper delivered at the Sixteenth Annual Meeting of the Northeastern Anthropological Association, 1976).

[74] J. Baddeley, "The Church and the Coffee House: The Social Organization of the Greek Community in Auckland, New Zealand" (Master's Research Essay, University of Auckland, 1973).

[75] Shack, "Urban Ethnicity."

tribe. Thus, while endogamy is a short-term response that reinforces cultural persistence, it is not perpetuated without external supporting circumstances.

In many African cities, the heterogeneous tribal mix frequently reflects differences in inheritance patterns. But where patrilineal and matrilineal groups come into contact, they often prohibit intermarriage because of conflicting demands that can be made upon rights to offspring or of offspring in case of death or divorce. Thus endogamy or selective intermarriage with groups who have similar descent systems may develop.

Little has concentrated much of his research activities during the last twenty years on describing and explaining the development and persistence of associations in West Africa.[76] Many other urban ethnographers have also focused their attention on such groups. Doughty and Mangin have both described the formation of regional associations in Lima, Peru and discussed their implications for both individual adjustment and city politics.[77] Fallers has edited a collection of descriptions of immigrant associations in a variety of historical and cross-cultural settings (nineteenth-century China, modern Africa).[78] In the succeeding discussion, we shall limit ourselves to those aspects of associations involving the use of ethnic symbols that bring people together for special events.

Frequently, *sports* are a central focus of associational activity. In some cases, native sports—such as *bocci* for Italian-Americans, *kabadi* (tag) for Indians in England—are played to promote ethnic solidarity. In other cases, ethnic groups are used for organizing urban sports; for example, the soccer leagues in Lima, Peru were organized along regional lines, and games fostered regional solidarity. The recreational activities of Indians in Wolverhampton, England, feature an annual round of tournaments using both soccer and native sports. For West Indians in Buffalo, New York, the cricket club was the only association that fostered West Indian identity.

An important device for maintaining ethnic boundaries in urban areas is the celebration of festivals derived from the culture of origin. The Chinese New Year as celebrated in urban America serves to reinforce ethnic ties. *Festas* for the patron saints of Italy are commonly found, as are the Puerto Rican celebrations of the Epiphany. Interestingly, the

[76] Little, *West African Urbanization;* "The Role of Voluntary Associations."
[77] Doughty, "Behind the Back of the City," "Peruvian Migrant Identity"; William Mangin, "The Role of Regional Associations in the Adaptation of Rural Populations in Peru," *Sociologus,* 9 (1959), 23-35.
[78] Lloyd Fallers (ed.), *Immigrants and Associations* (The Hague: Mouton Publishers, 1967).

particular holidays emphasized often vary from city to city, as does the content of the celebration.

In New York City in March 1976, two separate celebrations of the Hindu festival of *Holi* were held one week apart. One was held at Columbia University and presented drama and films. Another, sponsored by the Bihar Association, was held in a school auditorium in Queens and emphasized more traditional activities, such as the smearing of one another with dye. In both cases, identification through a Hindu festival was strong.[79]

In many American communities where large numbers of certain groups are found, overt recognition is given to the groups by the creation of new ethnic festivals. In the summer of 1975, Central Park became the arena for the celebration of Puerto Rican Day on one occasion, and the All-India Festival on another. Philadelphia designates a Puerto Rican Week; this celebration culminates in a parade, which is parallel to Columbus Day as an Italian recognition event and Saint Patrick's Day as an Irish recognition event.

In many discussions of ethnicity, the mechanisms discussed above are assumed to be directly derived from a "culture of origin" and are considered to be passed down immutably from generation to generation. However, on the basis of many of the studies we have previously cited, it becomes clear that these symbols and institutions are manipulated and change over time. Kinship and marriage systems, on the one hand, and religious institutions, on the other, are frequently changed to enable the group to manipulate economic and political situations. This is the central point in much of the literature on urban ethnicity in Africa, where much of the most sophisticated comparative study has been done.

Boundary Processes. The issue of maintenance of urban ethnic boundaries has two basic dimensions: one concerns an individual's relationship to the group; the other concerns the rigidity or expansiveness of the boundaries of the group over time.

The first issue is relatively simple to describe. Changes in individual identity over time do not have a great impact on the continuity or boundary maintenance of the group. Through intermarriage, change of name, religious conversion, and the like, individuals may shift their self-identification from one group to another. So long as this does not become a mass disaffiliation, the group is not threatened.

Plotnicov, in his study of migrant groups in Jos, Nigeria, indicates that one group is dominant demographically, economically, and politi-

[79] Observations were done by Bertha Hinden.

cally in the city.[80] Members of other groups will claim identity with the dominant group in order to maximize their access to political and economic resources; but they use their original identity in other situations in order to maximize their access to kin obligations and mutual aid.

The same phenomenon is observed by Shack when he attempts to explain the growth of the census-reported population of Amhara in Addis Ababa.[81] He suggests that many who claim such tribal membership are the offspring of mixed marriages who attempt to improve their position by identification with the dominant group.

In some cases, individuals deny membership in a denigrated group by changing names, speech, and behavior. This process is generally known as *passing*. Thus it would appear that ethnicity is not as much of an ascribed characteristic as is commonly assumed. However, the fact that individuals may move fully into and out of particular groups does not negate the fact that the groups as structures persist and maintain their boundaries.

There are a variety of factors that influence an individual's commitment to and interaction with a particular ethnic group. The concept of "situational ethnicity" refers to this phenomenon. For the individual, certain day-to-day situations develop that call forth actions that display or hide ethnic identity. In addition, at various points in the life cycle, a heightened or diminished sense of ethnicity occurs. Time may influence ethnicity in a cyclical manner as weekly, monthly, or annual celebrations call for ethnic identification or interaction. Finally, major political and economic crises affect the degree to which people identify with and interact within an ethnic group. The problem with many studies of urban ethnicity is that they do not take into account the contextual factors that influence this phenomenon.

One noteworthy development in the literature dealing with ethnic groups is the degree to which cultural differences and diversity that existed in the regions of origin have been discarded. Thus Gans and Hannerz both note for Italians in the United States, that regional differences that influenced language, dress, diet, and even created hostility between provinces in Italy were set aside in the United States in favor of an amalgamated Italian-American culture.[82] Regional subcultures that developed in Sicily, the Abruzzi, or Calabria that led to separate ethnic groups when peasants migrated to Rome were amalgamated in the United States. This amalgamation is the result of external categorization and stereotyping, as well as the existence of minimal cultural similarities

---

[80] Plotnicov, "Who Owns Jos?"
[81] Shack, "Urban Ethnicity."
[82] Gans, *Urban Villagers;* and Hannerz, "Ethnicity and Opportunity in Urban America."

in language and food. Amalgamation is also the result of demographic proportions and economic-political opportunity.

In the African literature, Southall has referred to this as "super-tribalism" while Cohen and Middletown have called it "incorporation." [83] Once again, minimal similarities in language, descent systems, and other aspects of culture interact with external stereotyping to produce a basis for the formation of an ethnic interest group.

In a study of American Indians in Los Angeles, Hirabayashi and associates note the development of pan-Indianism in the city.[84] This means the creation of identity as an American Indian through a political movement of groups coming from very diverse tribal backgrounds. Tribal differences, which include significant variation in language families and ways of life (nomadic hunters versus sedentary farmers), are minimized, although the authors note that different tribes participate differently in the movement. Some of the differences in participation seem related to demographic proportions.

In a more recent attempt to analyze the development of the American Indian movement, Price suggests that there is a process involved that ultimately results in a very high consciousness of kind and a heightened politicization of the group.[85] He notes differences between the process as it occurs in Los Angeles and Montreal. The process differs partly as a result of the proportion of Indians in relation to total society, and partly as a result of the different stereotypes of Indians held by dominant Canadians and Americans.

The process is reflected in the degree of control Indians have over institutions that service them. Initially, such institutions are established and dominated by the white population; subsequently, they are taken over by the Indians and recast in light of their own goals. Price notes the growth of publications developed by Indians and containing news of Indian life. This is one technique that solidifies both the urban segment and the dispersed rural segment.

Many anthropologists who have studied urban Indians examine their high rates of alcoholism and the choice of bars as major foci of recreational activities. Price notes that Indian activities have recently shifted from bars in the Los Angeles area. Since bars in the earlier phases brought together Indians from different tribal groups, they served as a

[83] Aidan Southall (ed.), *Social Change in Africa* (London: Oxford University Press, 1961); R. Cohen and J. Middleton (eds), *From Tribe to Nation in Africa* (Scanton: Chandler, 1970).

[84] J. Hirabayashi, W. Willard, and L. Kemnitzer, "Pan-Indianism in the Urban Setting," in T. Weaver and D. White (eds.), *The Anthropology of Urban Environments*, pp. 77-88.

[85] John Price, "The U.S. and Canadian Indian Urban Ethnic Institutions," *Urban Anthropology*, 4 (1975), 35-52.

source for developing cross-tribal linkages, which set the stage for a wider Indian identity. Bar activities led to cliques, which moved out of the bar and developed into formal institutions and pow-wow dancing circles to foster Indian political consciousness.

One of the most ambitious studies of the process of incorporation has been done by Paden. His study traces the historical development of all ethnic units in the city of Kano, Nigeria. He notes a process of large-scale incorporation into units that are not equivalent to original tribes. He sees the process as moving from interaction to group interdependency. The final step in this process is one in which formerly distinct units move toward similarity of values which becomes the reinforcing mechanism for the new solidarity group as it becomes segregated from others.[86]

Issues in the Ethnic Approach

One of the basic issues in contemporary urban anthropological research is the relationship between ethnicity and social class. The effects of these two phenomena upon one another and the interplay of these two factors in the city are among the central issues in urban social science.

Ethnic groups are bounded units and, as previously noted, develop these boundaries within an urban context so that they are, in fact, subcultural units. However, the question of the impact of cultural elements from a culture of origin on the lifestyle of these groups is still open to question. Where do the lifestyle differences come from? Why is conflict organized on this and not a class basis? Some of the recent literature has indicated that many ethnic characteristics that have in the past been attributed to culture of origin can, in fact, be more attributable to structural characteristics, particularly those that affect the economic condition of the group.

Gans, in his study of Italians in Boston, suggests that much of what has been designated as ` Italian ethnic behavior is, in fact, a result of socioeconomic position—namely, working class behavior.[87] Some of the content areas he uses to illustrate his point are family patterns, relationships between the sexes, the importance of male peer groups, attitudes and treatment of children—which he shows are not carry-overs from the culture of origin. LeMasters, in his study of bar life in a working class community, notes the similarity of behavior and values amongst a very diverse ethnic population.[88] Caine also demonstrates the same pattern

[86] J. N. Paden, "Urban Pluralism, Integration and Adaptation."
[87] Gans, Urban Villagers.
[88] E. E. LeMasters, Blue Collar Aristocrats (Madison: University of Wisconsin Press, 1975).

among Mexican-Americans.[89] Taking characteristics of family life, patterns of social interaction, and values, he shows that many characteristics that have been assumed to be Mexican in origin are the result of the conditions of economic deprivation rather than cultural carry-overs. Greaves has taken a similar position in relation to differences between Mestizos and Indians in Peru.[90] He suggests that what was formerly viewed as difference in learned tradition is in fact a response to class position.

It is worth noting that in many ethnographic studies of ethnic groups, there is a coalescence between ethnic group and occupation. Since we have been emphasizing the economic and political functions of ethnic groups, the degree to which ethnic groups develop particular economic niches for themselves is an indication of the close relationship of the two. Much of the African, Chinese, Southeast Asian, Latin American, and North American literature points in this direction. Thus these two bases for urban organization cannot be totally separate.

We have noted a tendency in some cases for an ethnic group to monopolize an economic niche and thus be roughly homogeneous in class. We have also noted the phenomenon of vertical integration, where class segments within an ethnic group remain interdependent. A third kind of relationship also exists. Much of the literature on African cities points out that the new bureaucratic elite tend to disassociate themselves from these ethnic groups, in contrast to their less mobile counterparts.

A major issue in urban ethnicity is the processes of ethnic group formation and boundary maintenance. The general model of this process is as follows: People from different hinterlands, regions, tribes, and even nation-states migrate to urban centers, where they initially maintain high degrees of social interaction based on common cultures of origin. Once they arrive in sufficient numbers, they become recognized as a separate group by others within the city. Because of the nature of the opportunity structure of the city and/or discrimination against the group, there are limits on available economic opportunities. The use of personal networks to get jobs or develop enterprises leads to a situation in which many members of the group establish themselves in the same economic niche. The similarity in socioeconomic position maintains and reinforces the patterns of interaction among them. The phenomenon of individual identification with ethnic groups through symbols and institutions is

[89] Terry Caine, "Class, Culture and Ethnicity in a Northern Mexican-American Community" (paper delivered at the 1971 meetings of the Society for Applied Anthropology).
[90] Thomas Greaves, "Pursuing Cultural Pluralism in the Andes" (unpublished mimeograph, April 1970).

related and follows the same trend. There are still many questions remaining about the way in which different urban contexts influence this process.

Being a member of an ethnic group and using ethnicity as an identity marker are not the same. *Feeling* ethnic identity and solidarity on occasion is one thing; being part of a bounded unit that is an important structural element of the city is another. The literature indicates that people's ethnic identities wax and wane over time. Events such as holidays or threats from outside forces may increase active ethnic identification. Individuals often use or hide ethnic identity in order to achieve their own particular goals. Yet the core of ethnic organization exists over time as an important political/economic structure in the total city.

GROUPS BASED ON THE DIVISION OF LABOR

For social scientists, groups based on the division of labor are of two kinds. The first are social classes—macro-structural, hierarchically ranked strata, defined in terms of their wealth, power, and prestige. The second are smaller units—different occupational groups defined by their specific role in the division of labor.

One of the difficulties in discussing the ethnography of groups based on the division of labor in the city is defining the concept of class. Unlike neighborhood or ethnic group, class is an analytic category and is not amenable to ethnographic research. It is not a geographically or historically bounded community, as are neighborhoods and ethnic groups. However, most definitions of class do incorporate occupation as a major component. An occupational group or related cluster of occupations may be used as the basis of ethnographic research.

Stub has suggested a concept labelled *the status community*, which is a pivotal concept bridging groups based on occupation and the notion of class.[91] A status community consists of a single occupation or a cluster of occupations whose members are regarded by both insiders and outsiders as equivalent in status and interest. Such status communities develop boundaries and are characterized by high frequencies of interaction, significant primary ties, and similarities in life styles. These subcultural boundaries are symptoms of the formation of significant interest groups or urban social components.

A good example of a status community based on a single occupation is the status community of musicians who, because of their recruitment, training, work settings, and reputation to outsiders, become a community

[91] Holger Stub, *Status Communities in Modern Society: An Alternative to Class Analysis* (Hinsdale, Illinois: Dryden Press, 1972).

of interests. This often leads to common residential patterns and a strong boundary maintenance reflected in lifestyles.

Work Places and Work Situations

Many studies concerned with occupation focus narrowly upon the work place and the work situation rather than occupational status communities as subcultures. Actual work activities, rules related to work, and social relationships with co-workers, superordinates, subordinates, and clientele are examined. Sometimes these insiders' work-related views of society and their evaluations of the world generated by work roles are described for their esoteric interest alone. Rarely are the implications for the social system of work-related views examined explicitly. Although limited in nature, such studies do provide insight into the way conditions of work produce, or fail to produce, solidarity; that is, what contributes to creating situations in which occupation becomes a primary identity and occupational groups become tightly bounded social components.

In a volume by Spradley and McCurdy called *The Cultural Experience,* a number of studies concerned the insider's view of his job, the spatial arena, temporal cycle, type of clients, as well as the way the job influences other aspects of life.[92] For example, the study of an airline stewardess shows the degree to which work time requirements and mobility influence leisure-time activities and interpersonal relationships. Airline stewardesses are very closely supervised and must conform to rules related to dress, makeup, and hairstyle. Competition for routes is high. Another occupation described in this volume is organized car theft. The group studied consisted of men who viewed this as a transitory occupation, used to build a stake for entering the business world or to pay for a college education. They developed set routines and set rules pertaining to the kinds of cars to be stolen, when to steal them, and how to dispose of them.

Brenda Mann's study of the cocktail waitress in a midwestern city focuses primarily upon the interaction between male bartenders and female cocktail waitresses.[93] Much of the interaction and communication is directed toward reinforcing the dominant position of the male in the work situation. She also notes different categories of customers who frequent the bar and their interaction with both bartender and waitresses.

[92] James Spradley and David McCurdy (eds.), *The Cultural Experience: Ethnography in Complex Society* (Chicago: Science Research Associates, 1972).
[93] Brenda Mann, "Bar Talk," in James Spradley and David McCurdy (eds.), *Conformity and Conflict* (Boston: Little, Brown and Co., 1974), pp. 101-11; James Spradley and Brenda Mann, *The Cocktail Waitress* (New York: John Wiley and Co., 1975).

Patch, in his studies of the central market in Lima, deals with a number of market-located occupations and provides insights into how individuals are recruited into and learn the rules of an occupation.[94] Thus a street vendor must learn from whom and how to obtain an inventory, where he can establish his venture (both official rules and the control of corners by other vendors), what techniques (hawking, the use of shills) are useful to attract customers, and how to strike bargains. Patch also notes the organization and division of labor among petty thieves and describes how one moves from one level to another. He indicates that elderly ex-convicts run "schools" for pickpockets and purse snatchers. They recruit "students" from the ranks of "fruit birds" (boys who steal fruit from stands).

Occupational Status Communities

Other studies emphasize a larger context than the actual work situation. They examine cultural institutions that unite members of an occupation outside the work situation and link the occupation to other aspects of life. They also investigate the importance of occupational status community membership on all life activities. While focusing on a limited segment of the status community as an ethnographic unit, they do provide insight into the formation of higher level urban components or interest groups based on occupational status. Some of the most interesting work done has been on stable working class groups.

For the Portland longshoremen described by Pilcher, individuals in this status community are recruited primarily from migrants from the Midwest who are sons of families in which the occupation of the father provided great work autonomy.[95] The longshoremen themselves say what they value most about their calling is its freedom and independence. They have little close supervision and can take off for days at a time to go hunting and enjoy outdoor life and still be assured of work when they return to the union hiring hall. Away from work, the longshoremen spend much time together in leisure-time activities and family visiting. Thus the group maintains social boundaries through high frequency of exclusive interaction. Values regarding women, child rearing, the outdoor life are also shared. The union as a core institution is a major integrative mechanism; the hiring hall is a spatial locus, and union politics are significant topics of concern and conversation. Union

[94] Richard Patch, "La Parada: Lima's Market," American Universities Field Staff Report, vol. 14, 1967.
[95] William Pilcher, The Portland Longshoremen (New York: Holt, Rinehart and Co., 1972).

meetings are well-attended and taken seriously as a force for discipline and social control.

A different sort of status community was studied by LeMasters and described in his book, *Blue Collar Aristocrats*.[96] This was a status community based on a cluster of similar occupations. The setting for this study was a tavern in a suburb of a Midwestern city. The clientele of the tavern was drawn primarily from the highest skill level crafts in the construction industry. In addition, some truck drivers and entrepreneurs in related areas (contractors and truck owners) were also part of the steady group. Concerning methodology, it should be noted that the status community being studied was not observed on the job or in the home, but exclusively in the tavern. However, the issues discussed were much larger. Like the longshoremen, this community too emphasized freedom and autonomy at work as a major value. They were proud of their skill levels and the products of their crafts. The buildings they helped to construct were viewed as permanent monuments to their skill. They also viewed their high level incomes as a source of self esteem.

The usual pattern of drinking was for the men to stop by at the "Oasis" on their way home and drink with fellow members of their work crew—demonstrating the importance of exclusive work interaction for the formation of tight-knit groups. They refer to this typical two-hour period of drinking as the "blue collar cocktail hour," thus poking fun at those white collar workers who spend less time and more money in social drinking. Friday night is couples night at the bar. Saturday during the day the men hang out together at the bar. There is a pool table and they often show off new hunting and fishing gear. Their common interest in hunting and fishing keeps them together in leisure activities outside the bar. On Sundays and holidays, whole families come to the bar. Thus the leisure-time activities of this group are centered on the bar. This tavern is one of a dozen taverns in the neighborhood that each serve different clientele. There is even one bar that serves the unemployed, injured, and retired. The lack of strong ethnic affiliation in this city means that work roles—rather than culture of origin—seem to be the basis for differentiation, solidarity, and out-group denigration.

The study provides some insight into the career patterns of the patrons of the bar. Some are proprietors who own trucking establishments or are building contractors. Obviously they used their skill base as blue collar workers to acquire the capital and knowledge used later in entrepreneurial activities. LeMasters notes that after a period of success, the entrepreneur sometimes changes his self-identity and moves away

[96] LeMasters, *Blue Collar Aristocrats*.

from the bar, but this is not always so. Many dabble in entrepreneurial activities, but do not like them or are unsuccessful, and go back to wage employment. This would indicate that the use of census data on self-employed (as opposed to blue collar categories) would not tell you as much about real bounded functional units as would ethnographic research, which points to stages in patterned career cycles.

Many patrons of the Oasis have been long-term residents of the suburb. Recently, white collar and professional middle class families have been moving into the suburbs in large numbers. Considerable resentment of this invasion by other status communities is shown by the men of the Oasis, and there is a continuing conflict between the new and old resident status communities over political control of the suburb.

We have noted the tendency to study slums and irregular settlements in our discussion of neighborhood ethnographies. In the literature on ethnicity, minority groups are studied more frequently than dominant groups. In relation to occupational status communities, there also is a tendency to study the lower segments, the marginally employed, and the unemployed.[97] Such a status community was the basis of Gutkind's study of the long-term unemployed in Lagos and Nairobi.[98] Gutkind notes that kinship and tribal ties are replaced by ties based on the common economic status of being unemployed. The Employment Exchanges in both cities serve as the spatial locus for "hanging out" activities. While tribal membership (ethnicity) is less important than unemployment in the creation of informal mutual aid groups, the creation of significant political movements based on the status of unemployment is hampered by tribal cleavages.

A similar status community in American society is that described by Liebow in *Tally's Corner*.[99] These men are employed intermittently or unemployed for a long period of time. When employed, their jobs are usually low paying, require high expenditures of energy or time, and are expected to be temporary. Much like several of the successful entrepreneurs in LeMaster's study, those in Liebow's study who obtain stable and relatively well-paying jobs move out of this status community into another. These men have close interaction, common leisure-time activities, and similar values about women and work. If the status community notion had been used, we would have found out how this unit relates to others in the urban center in terms of conflict and competition. The

[97] For a discussion of the implications of various marginal jobs for social capital and upward mobility, see Judith Goode, "Poverty and Urban Analysis," *Western Canadian Journal of Anthropology*, 3 (1972), 1-19.

[98] Gutkind, "Energy of Despair."

[99] Elliot Liebow, *Tally's Corner* (Boston: Little, Brown and Co., 1967).

degree to which this group might be amalgamated into a common status community of the marginally employed is not explored. The impression that one receives is that this clique is relatively isolated from other similar groups. Its locus of activity is a street corner. Ethnicity (Black) is basic to identities, but this group, because of its position in the division of labor, represents a specialized segment of the ethnic group.

Another marginal occupational category that tends to generate a bounded status community is pedi-cab driving. In parts of the Third World where mechanized public transportation facilities have not been highly developed, two- or three-wheeled bicycle- or human-propelled rickshaws provide a major means of intra-urban passenger movement. Gould and Textor have studied workers in this economic niche in Lucknow, India and Bangkok, Thailand respectively.[100] The nature of this occupation provides the opportunity for considerable social interaction between members of the group and thus tends to generate closed boundaries. Most of their day is spent in waiting for passengers in important central locations. Most drivers are employed by cab owners and develop common interests because of their relatively powerless position in relation to a "boss." They also develop common views of their clientele. In fact, Berreman, who was concerned with urban social categories in general, found these individuals to be a rich resource because of their ability to differentiate minutely between customers, and pick up cues that were frequently not noticed by others.[101] This particular occupation is of further interest to the urban anthropologist because the group knows more about specialized zones in the city than other groups. Because of their mobility, they frequently participate in ancillary errand-running and entrepreneurial activities throughout the city, often of an illicit nature. This also leads to tight social boundaries in order to protect covert information. In many ways, the taxi driver in the United States has a parallel role, although he is less marginal economically.

There are other marginal occupations that develop the same sort of closed corporate nature, but there are some activities that seem to preclude this kind of boundary formation because of the high degree of competition and isolation in work. As examples, we might cite scavengers or ragpickers, domestic servants, and street vendors. Even here, however, under certain conditions, cohesive bounded groups may develop. Thus, Taira notes for a group of ragpickers in Japan that they all had a parallel

[100] Harold Gould, "Lucknow Rickshawallas: The Social Organization of an Occupational Category," *International Journal of Comparative Sociology*, 6 (1965), 27-47; Robert Textor, *From Peasant to Pedicab Driver* (New Haven: Yale University Press, 1961).
[101] Berreman, "Social Categories."

patron-client relationship with a wholesale junk dealer whom they supplied.[102] He, in turn, provided housing for them, so they became a residential community. A common sect movement (religious conversion) further united the group and led to similarities in lifestyles and world views. By contrast, Carolina Maria de Jesus, a scavenger in Brazil, depicts the social isolation that can exist for those in this occupation.[103]

Recent literature on the female domestic servant has indicated that, despite isolated work conditions, this occupational status frequently develops occupationally based social solidarity. In many Third World areas, the regular scheduling of free days and afternoons has led to the generation of leisure-time arenas that bring members of the group together. However, the forces of isolation and frequent turnover generate strong pressures against long-term organization.

There are many descriptions in the literature of street vending activities. Patch's descriptions of the careers of several street vendors in Lima, Peru emphasizes the competition and difficulties in capital acquisition implied by this economic role.[104] Mayhew's early journalistic accounts of nineteenth-century London hawkers make many of the same points.[105]

McGee has intensively analyzed the socioeconomic position of the street hawker, focusing primarily on Hong Kong.[106] He sees these petty enterprises as parallel to peasant agrarian production systems. Whereas jobs in the formal labor market of the city are bureaucratically organized, highly capitalized, and feature regular hours and regular wages, these jobs have opposite characteristics. They tend to be family-organized, using the entire family as labor force. They are under-capitalized and feature irregular, long hours of work and unpredictable income. Jobs in the formal sector entail levels of supervision and "bosses," while street hawking is an autonomous enterprise—save for the dependency on creditors with whom one establishes informal ties of a patron-client nature. Although McGee does not discuss the implications of these activities for developing a status community, it would seem that the very structural implications that make it hard for peasants to establish solidarity also operate for this status community. Nevertheless, in many parts of the

[102] Koji Taira, "Ragpickers and Community Development: Ant's Villa in Tokyo," *Industrial and Labor Relations Review*, 22 (1968), 3-19.
[103] Carolina de Jesus, *Child of the Dark* (New York: The New American Library, 1962).
[104] Patch, "La Parada: Lima's Market."
[105] Henry Mayhew, *London Labour and the London Poor* (London: Frank Cass and Co., Ltd., 1967) (first published 1861-1862).
[106] T. C. McGee, "Peasants in the Cities: A Paradox, A Paradox, A Most Ingenious Paradox," *Human Organization*, 32 (1973), 135-42; and *Hawkers in Hong Kong* (Hong Kong: Center of Asian Studies, University of Hong Kong, 1973).

world, unions and syndicates of street vendors have developed under certain circumstances. These particular situations that permit the formation of a status community should be examined in greater detail.

Prostitution is another marginal occupational category studied by anthropologists. This activity tends to generate a high degree of cohesion as a bounded status community including prostitutes, pimps, and madams. The norm-violating nature of the activity, the need to develop protection against law enforcement, and the desire to decrease competition from amateurs leads to a high degree of organization. In this case (and others, like begging), social denigration by outsiders leads to strong in-group boundaries.[107]

An example of a traditional occupational status community that is now breaking down is the Jatavs of Agra, India. This group is a sub-caste whose traditional occupation of leather-working was considered impure and placed them at the lowest levels of the Indian caste hierarchy. In the city of Agra, they have remained a viable status community despite the occupational diversity of present day Jatavs. Although many remain employed as leather workers in factories, others have become successful entrepreneurs who themselves own factories, or have entered government service, politics, and academic life. There is a formal organization representing the entire Jatav community, and they have emerged as a powerful political factor within city and state governments. The group publishes a newspaper for its own members and maintains its own library and historical archives. The Jatavs are now more like an ethnic group than an occupational status community.[108]

Our discussion of status communities to this point has focused upon the working class and marginal segments of the occupational structure. Similar status communities exist among the middle and upper levels of this structure; however, they are rarely studied by anthropologists. Jacobson's study of higher echelon bureaucrats in East Africa notes the commonality of interests and closely knit patterns of interaction among this group.[109] Since these individuals are government employees and are frequently transferred from one urban center to another, their ties are primarily with others in the same position. Relationships between these bureaucrats are very close and involve emotional support, leisure-time activities, mutual aid (loans), and security. Jacobson emphasizes how

---

[107] J. James, "Sweet Cream Ladies," *Western Canadian Journal of Anthropology*, 3 (1972), 102-18; and Christine Milner and Richard Milner, *Black Players: The Secret World of Black Pimps* (Boston: Little, Brown and Co., 1972).

[108] Lynch, *The Politics of Untouchability*.

[109] David Jacobson, *Itinerant Townsmen* (Menlo Park, California: Cummings Publishing Co., 1973).

a common ideology of friendship and sentiment develops in the group. For this group, occupation is extremely significant, while residential neighborhood and ethnic allegiance lose almost all their significance for forming social ties. The boundaries of this status community are informal —not maintained through formal associations, newspapers, or any such technique. However, the community is strong, as measured by the degree of exclusive interaction and commitment. When its members move from city to city, they go armed with a list of former co-workers and friends of friends, so that they have a ready-made occupationally based network waiting in the new setting. The emergence of this community as a bounded interest group has significant implications for the cities and nation, as well as for individuals.

Not all occupational statuses develop an occupationally based community to protect their position. In a study of lawyers in Medellín, Colombia, Judith Goode found that, despite a high degree of friendship and informal interaction between small networks of lawyers (mostly former schoolmates), and in spite of serious economic threats to the profession, lawyers did not organize cohesively above the level of networks to protect their interests.[110] There were no successful formal organizations nor ramified informal ties for the profession as a whole. Some of the reasons for this were the geographic dispersion of professional activities, thus removing common spatial arenas for interaction, and the increasing specialization in work, leading to fragmentation and very great competition within each specialty. Finally, some strongly maintained traditional values mitigated against collective activity. These professionals, unlike most other professional groups in modern Colombia, eschewed membership in voluntary associations for recreation, charity, or any goal.

The difficulty in making generalizations about class behavior and/or occupational behavior is evident when lawyers in Colombia are compared to other professions (the same social class) in Colombia, or with lawyers in the United States. In Colombia, dentists and accountants are much more highly organized as status communities and are integrated into the larger social system, where they participate and protect their interests. In the United States, lawyers as a group are highly organized and participate readily in the full spectrum of voluntary associations. They are successful in protecting their interests. Oddly enough, in the United States dentists are singled out as a profession characterized by great social isolation.

[110] Judith Goode, "The Responses of a Traditional Elite to Modernization," *Human Organization*, 29 (1970), 70-80.

This kind of differential response makes it necessary to study the context of each particular status community in order to describe and explain differences that exist in relation to expected class and/or occupational behavior.

Class Studies

Some anthropologists working in cities have endeavored to study social classes, or segments that are larger than occupational status communities. The previous discussion should alert us to the problems inherent in looking at such aggregated concepts as "middle class," "upper middle class," "professionals" and the like.

We have previously noted the early influence of the work of Lloyd Warner on the development of urban anthropology. His early community studies in the United States served as a model for many later works. Part of the Warnerian approach emphasized the study of social classes within the community. Warner was interested in classes, not to examine their relation to the division of labor, but to describe them as separate, bounded lifestyle groups with some degree of exclusive interaction and consciousness of kind.[111]

Andrew Whiteford in Querétaro, Mexico and Popayán, Colombia and Ruben Reina in Paraná, Argentina have studied these respective cities using a social class perspective.[112] They point out that the various classes studied each have distinctive lifestyles, which include both consumption patterns and norms. Each class is recognized by those outside of the class as a distinct group and is labelled as such (reputation). Thus, the group is bounded both by inside solidarity and outside stereotypes. Paralleling what Warner found in the United States, the upper class in particular is the most distinctive group and is most concerned with maintaining its boundaries and excluding others. This kind of distinction is lacking in the more amorphous divisions of middle class, stable working class, and marginal groups. Here we find a more comprehensive view of status communities and their articulation within a single urban center. However, in all cases, including Warner's, the community studied is a relatively small provincial urban center, and the total view of the national elite and its activities or the relationship between local elites and

[111] W. Lloyd Warner and Paul S. Lunt, *The Status System of a Modern Community* (New Haven: Yale University Press, 1942).
[112] Andrew Whiteford, *Two Cities in Latin America* (Garden City: Doubleday & Co., 1964); Ruben Reina, *Paraná: Social Boundaries in an Argentine City* (Austin: University of Texas Press, 1973).

national elites is not made clear. This, in part, is a result of the limitations of the ethnographic approach.

Careers

One aspect of occupational analysis that holds many interesting possibilities for future urban ethnographic research focuses on the cycle of occupational sequences, or career patterns. Eames and Goode, looking at the lower segments of the industrial occupational structure cross-culturally, have suggested that there is a considerable amount of lateral (as opposed to vertical) mobility.[113] Individuals move from heavy day labor to petty entrepreneurship in a variety of sequences. Thus, there is frequently no upward mobility within the pool of marginal occupations. Where actual vertical mobility does occur, it is necessary to obtain detailed accounts to develop some notions of generalized patterns and the strategies used to facilitate upward mobility.

In the actual mobility process studied by many urban anthropologists, there is a tendency to utilize *social capital* as much or more than money. By this we mean the individual's ability to manipulate both effective (kin, friends, and mutual aid) and extended ties (access to information). Collective mobility is usually facilitated by ties to patrons (influentials or brokers) in the larger urban structure. A second alternative is the accumulation of *real capital* (private property). This may be the result of windfalls, savings, frugal lifestyles and/or the pooling of small amounts of cash. In many of the studies we have cited, these two forms of capital are frequently interwoven and are related to the successful mobility of either individuals or groups.

These two sources of capital can be used to enhance mobility in various ways. In many parts of the world, entrepreneurial activities are viewed as the major source of upward mobility. An alternative path is the acquisition of skills and/or education (formal credentials), which foster upward mobility in hierarchically organized production units in the formal labor market (factories, financial institutions, and government offices). Unskilled laborers can acquire skills that enable them to obtain better paying jobs. Education may lead to managerial and authoritative positions within such organizations. Thus, mobility strategies consist of investing various amounts of one's social and/or monetary capital in entrepreneurial and/or credential-seeking activities.

Social and monetary capital are not mutually exclusive. One can use social ties to generate money. On the other hand, kin and network ties may also deplete one's monetary resources. We have previously discussed

[113] Edwin Eames and Judith Goode, *Urban Poverty in a Cross-Cultural Context* (New York: The Free Press, 1973).

this issue in Chapter 4 and noted that many studies indicate that kin obligations can interfere with individual mobility.

In Watson's study of Chinese in London, he notes that the capitalization necessary to open a restaurant is usually beyond the reach of an individual, and the most frequent form of entrepreneurship is the partnership.[114] The capital invested is saved from wages in prior restaurant work. Partners are members of the same lineage-based village. Shack, as we previously noted, suggested that the large amount of capital necessary for import-export is beyond the capabilities of the Guraje.[115] However, they can generate enough capital to control local mercantile activities.

Peattie has noted for residents of LaLaja, that many individuals aspire to petty entrepreneurship and will use saved capital or windfall capital (lotteries, lump sum severance pay) to open small stores and bars.[116] Frequently these are undercapitalized, but more significantly, proprietors from the community who serve the community are expected to extend credit and perform free services. Overextension of credit and undercapitalization frequently lead to failure of small-scale enterprise.

This same form of explanation is used in the analysis of the success of Chinese grocery proprietors in small-town Mississippi described by Loewen.[117] He suggests that the Chinese were successful because they did not have personal ties with the Blacks whom they served. Although they did extend credit, the limits were clear. As opposed to this pattern, Loewen suggests that local Blacks could not have established successful enterprises because of kin and network pressures on them to extend credit.

The dual paths of entrepreneurship and credential acquisition are not mutually exclusive and may be combined in a variety of ways. Higher skill levels may generate higher monetary returns to be invested in entrepreneurial activities.

An example of this process can be seen in the career pattern of a Punjabi in Wolverhampton, England. Initially, he obtained employment in a tire factory as a janitor. He subsequently moved to on-the-line production and eventually moved into the highest skill level (tirebuilder). With the wages obtained, he accumulated enough capital to rent an abandoned movie house and began showing Indian movies. This was such a successful enterprise that he abandoned his factory job. He

[114] James L. Watson, "Restaurants and Remittances: Chinese Emigrant Workers in London," in G. Foster and R. Kemper, *Anthropologists in Cities* (Boston: Little, Brown and Co., 1974), pp. 201-22.
[115] Shack, "Urban Ethnicity."
[116] Peattie, *The View from the Barrio.*
[117] James W. Loewen, *The Mississippi Chinese: Between Black and White* (Cambridge: Harvard University Press, 1971).

then invested in two laundromats and eventually established his own clothing manufacturing enterprise.[118]

Not all attempts at converting skills to capital are successful. Eames and Goode summarize the life history of one of Peattie's informants as follows:

> Jorge was the son of an agricultural worker who himself began his career as a farm worker. He drifted into petty commerce until he arrived in La Laja [a squatter settlement in industrial Ciudad Guayana, Venezuela]. His arrival was fortuitously timed as the major industry, the Iron Mines Company, was just beginning to recruit ordinary laborers. His foreman became interested in him and he was given the opportunity to acquire electrician skills on the job. After seven years he was laid off by the company, a risk frequently present in blue-collar work but cushioned by severance pay. He found a job as an electrical repairman, but always dreamed of investing in his own business. Thus, he left his new job voluntarily to open a grocery store. When this business failed, he fell back on his skills and became an electrician at the steel plant where he rose steadily within the company to become a foreman. His many raises have enabled him to realize all his aspirations and he continues to work while also investing in a bar run by his kinsmen.[119]

Patch describes the plight of a street vendor/shoeshine boy who attempts to move upward by means of formal education and the acquisition of credentials. He describes how the prejudices of the private school system in Lima, Peru make this goal impossible. When the boy tries to keep his neighborhood (slum) and occupation a secret at school, he is unable to do so. The social pressures against his succeeding are very great.[120]

Interestingly enough, much of our information about career patterns comes from community studies, rather than from occupation studies. In most community studies, where diverse segments of the population are found, the variety of career patterns emerges clearly for the urban ethnographer. Diverse patterns of mobility sometimes seem to form separate bounded lifestyle groups. For example, Peattie notes a distinction between the upwardly mobile and those locked into cycles of underemployment and unemployment in the community she stud-

[118] Research on Punjabi migrants in Wolverhampton, England was conducted during 1969 and 1970. Researchers were Edwin Eames and Howard Robboy. Research was supported by a study leave from Temple University and N.I.M.H. Grant Number DHEW-IR03-MH18799-01.
[119] Eames and Goode, *Urban Poverty in a Crosscultural Context*, pp. 142-43.
[120] R. Patch, "Life in a Callejon," *American University Field Service Reports*, West Coast South America Series, vol. 8, 1961.

ied.[121] These include differences in consumption patterns, childbearing patterns, and behavioral norms between these segments.

Roberts, in his study of two communities, also focuses on the life career pattern as one attribute of individuals leading to the most significant social consequences.[122] He provides very important insights about the way in which urban economic development and the occupational opportunity structure affect the individual's life career.

According to Roberts, changes in the general nature of urban life and the economy in Guatemala City have led to changes in the labor market. Work now takes place in formal, large-scale bureaucracies, which require formal credentials; literacy is a fundamental requirement for jobs. In the older system, one's reputation or a personal reference (social capital) could lead to stable employment. Today there is greater competition for stable jobs as the migratory flow increases. Age has become a basis for employment as employers seek younger workers. Roberts states:

> Under these conditions, a successful occupational career is one in which a worker seeks out stable and well-paid employment, moving from one job to another as circumstances change. Those who are old and illiterate and cannot easily compete are thus likely to remain in, or soon enter, a marginal occupation where the income fluctuates with economic change or is so low as to make no difference. In contrast to those situations where the change occurs because large enterprises demand higher qualifications for their workers, individual characteristics become important to job recruitment in Guatemala City as a worker shifts from one small, ill-equipped workshop to another, as he sets up his own workshop with no more equipment than a sewing machine or a few rudimentary tools, or helps others to peddle merchandise around the city. This movement does include larger and more formally organized enterprises where literacy is more closely tied to job position; but, in general, the emerging significance of literacy and age occurs as workers move from job to job, seeking better employment or trying to avoid entering low-paid marginal employment.[123]

Roberts contrasts this situation to the opportunity structure in Monterrey, Mexico, a rapidly industrializing urban center studied by Balán and associates in which career patterns are quite different and relate mostly to large-scale industrial enterprises.[124] It would be inter-

---

[121] Peattie, *The View from the Barrio.*
[122] Roberts, *Organizing Strangers.*
[123] Ibid., p. 132.
[124] Jorge Balán, Harley Browning, and Elizabeth Jelin, *Men in a Developing Society: Geographic and Social Mobility in Monterrey, Mexico* (Austin: University of Texas Press, 1973).

esting to examine to what degree people with the same career directions form functioning social units (status communities), characterized by frequent interaction, common lifestyles, and recognition of common interests.

A very different view of working class careers comes out of the literature on urban Japan. In most industrial production units, the firm is based on the model of a large-scale kinship unit, and mobility is within the firm, not through movement from factory to factory. Thus, status communities are formed within a factory enterprise regardless of mobility patterns, and not between people in the same position in the occupational hierarchy or people with the same career direction.

Issues in the Occupational Approach

Despite some attempts to study social class ethnographically, the technique does not readily lend itself to such studies, particularly in larger urban centers. Studies of the actual work setting can be ethnographic, but they are frequently focused narrowly and exclude the implications of work for the total way of life of an individual. When a whole occupational status community is studied, it provides a view of a total way of life, and one can see how this structural unit relates to others in the city. Often such groups are too large and complex for ethnographic study and must be broken down into smaller components.

The career pattern is amenable to ethnographic techniques. Through intensive interviewing and life histories, the researcher can discern underlying patterns of career mobility. It is possible to link the patterns obtained from individuals to the generalized experience of occupational status communities. By delineating the various ways in which social and monetary capital are invested in either launching entrepreneurial activities or acquiring credentials, we can develop generalized patterns of career sequences, which may be the most meaningful interest groups based on the division of labor in the city.

There is also a need for more comparative studies dealing specifically with the effects of urban context. We have noted a tendency toward such studies for both the neighborhood and the ethnic group, but few such studies are found in the area of work.

OTHER CATEGORIES

Within those urban studies that are ethnographic in method and focus on small-scale units, many are directed at urban groups that either deviate from general societal norms in a way that is viewed as anti-social or are on the forefront of creating new normative patterns. Ethnographic studies of homosexuals, transvestites, skid row residents, prostitutes, and drug addicts are examples of the former category.[125] Ideological movements such as the antimaterialistic hippie and Hare Krishna movements, as well as other political and religious communal movements, would fit the latter category.[126] Unfortunately, most of these studies do not emphasize those urban conditions and aspects of structure that are significant for the incubation and development of the movement, nor do they explicitly describe the impact of these movements on the city. One exception is a study of the health food movement, which explicitly compares the movement in rural and urban settings.[127] Future studies of such groups and movements should be concerned more explicitly with the role of the city as a generator of change. These would be more central to the anthropology *of* cities rather than anthropology *in* cities.

SUMMARY

The three social units that have formed the core of this chapter are significant in urban anthropolgy because they are amenable to ethnographic research and are important in attempting to understand the structure of the city. Most of the studies referred to deal with only a small segment of a larger unit: neighborhood, ethnic group, or occupation/class. These small units are usually articulated into larger units, which are the major components of the city. Many neighborhood studies focus on blocks or single high-rise buildings. Suttles has labeled several levels of residential communities (face block, defended community, and community of limited liability).[128]

Most studies of ethnic groups focus on localized segments or associations and not the entire urban-based group. Even where large-scale ethnic voluntary associations are found and are the objects of study, rarely are they coincident with the total urban ethnic group. The expan-

---

[125] For example, Esther Newton, *Mother Camp: Female Impersonators in America* (Englewood Cliffs: Prentice-Hall, Inc., 1972); James Spradley, "You Owe Yourself a Drunk"; Jennifer James, "Sweet Cream Ladies"; R. S. Weppner, "An Anthropologist's View of the Street Addict's World," *Human Organization*, vol. 32, 1973.

[126] William L. Partridge, *The Hippie Ghetto* (New York: Holt, Rinehart and Winston, 1972); F. J. Daner, *The American Children of Krsna* (New York: Holt, Rinehart and Winston, 1976).

[127] Randy Kandel and Gretel Pelto, "Vegetarianism and Health Food Use Among Young Adults in Southern New England" (mimeo., n.d., 43 pp.).

[128] Gerald Suttles, *The Social Construction of Communities* (Chicago: The University of Chicago Press, 1972).

sion of boundaries and the movement toward supertribalism are other aspects of the large-scale integrative process.

In much the same way, small segments of occupational status communities (work place groups) that demonstrate high levels of interaction are studied. However, at some point these groups articulate with larger, more inclusive structures based on common work role. Pilcher's study of the longshoreman group in Portland [129] is perhaps the only one that attempts to deal with the entire status community on the highest level of inclusion.

In the preindustrial city, occupation, ethnicity, and neighborhood tend to be overlapping membership units with common boundaries. Individuals are born into occupational groups with territorial location and often common ethnic origin. The groups maintain strong boundaries through core institutions—economic guilds and separate ritual cycles focused on special gods or patron saints. They are endogamous and tend to emphasize occupational inheritance. In reality the system is not as static and clearcut as would appear; however, there is a tendency toward a social structure constructed of such stable bounded units.

In the urban industrial city or the city in developing nations, the three units show less overlap, and therefore barely share common boundaries. Where common boundaries are maintained, however, such as when an ethnic group monopolizes an occupational niche and tends to be co-residential, these units will be significant to the individuals in a sustained and continuous manner and will be extremely important as basic structural units in the city. There are obviously many questions that can be raised about these units, their relationship to one another, and their relationship to the larger context of the city, that require further research. We do not have enough information about the formation and development of these units—neighborhoods, ethnic groups, and occupation/class—in a sufficient *variety* of world regions to allow us to develop any empirically based generalizations.

Culture of origin and role in the division of labor can serve as a basis on which bounded interest groups are created. In the dynamic process of collectivization, one of these bases may be more important than the other, depending on urban context, and the relative significance of the two can change over time. Since the ethnographic method is based upon intensive interviewing and participant observation, it is possible for the urban anthropologist in the urban setting to obtain information about the shifting significance of these units over time in a variety of cultural settings. In the modern city, there is a high degree of occupational mobility, ethnic transference, and neighborhood transiency. The

[129] Pilcher, *The Portland Longshoremen.*

interaction between the individual life histories and the social unit (neighborhood, ethnic group, and occupational status community) can be studied cumulatively through fieldwork with large numbers of informants. Thus we can see the changing relationship of these three units even where they are not congruent. What conditions make ethnicity central or promote neighborhood cohesion? What can a description of shared patterns of life history careers contribute to understanding these conditions? How can the insider's view derived from intensive work with informants provide insights?

As occupational and residential units become more open in the modern city, the issue of recruitment into these units becomes a basic one that is amenable to ethnographic research. This process needs to be explored more fully in urban anthropology literature. With geographic and social mobility a distinct possibility (as opposed to ascription by birth as the only means for assigning membership), the process of initial selection and the cycle of changes within a life career must be understood.

We have noted some of the boundary maintenance techniques for these units: endogamy, segregated communication media, ritual segregation, need for special goods and services, language, and the general appeal to symbols. Although we have emphasized these characteristics under our discussion of ethnic groups, they can be relevant for developing cohesion in the other units as well.

All three of the major components—neighborhood, ethnic group, occupation/class—can be analyzed on three levels: the analyst can look at the degree of individual identity and allegiance to the unit, the degree of interaction within the unit, and the degree of boundary closure and segregation from other units.

An important approach that has great potential for the understanding of all three of these units looks at them in the larger context of the city and the even larger context of the city's historical and national setting. While urban anthropologists like Leeds, Roberts, Nagata, Bruner, Uzzell, M. E. Smith, Paden, Parkin, Cohen, Gutkind, Rollwagen, and others have begun to develop procedures for this contextual and comparative analysis, more needs to be done.

6

Units of Integration

In the previous two chapters, we looked at the ethnography of groups or quasi-groups that contain people who know each other, or at least recognize each other as belonging to the same relatively bounded social units. These tend to be primary units or localized segments (lower levels of inclusion) of social units based on residence, culture of origin, or work. Ethnographers are drawn to these groups because they are amenable to ethnographic techniques in that they resemble the small-scale social units of traditional ethnography.

However, a variety of other situations and structures draw various segments of the urban population together in meaningful interaction. These urban junctures will be the focus of this chapter. Such places, temporal events, and associations that serve as points of context for diverse urban elements are: markets, festivals, bars, schools, hospitals, political events, and courts.

William Hanna has alluded to the notion of "urban middleplaces" in an article concerned with urban integration.[1] To the notion of spatial node, he adds the concept of middlemen—those strategic brokers who serve as mediators to link diverse networks together. To these brokerage or linkage nodes, we would add the cycle of temporal events that bring people together and the voluntary associations that recruit from many components.

Much of the recent literature dealing with urban junctures emphasizes their basically integrative implications. In an older variety of urban research (some of which was done by anthropologists) there was considerable emphasis on group conflict rather than integration. Certainly many of the juncture points discussed in this chapter are nodes of conflict or reinforcement of negative stereotypes, rather than integration. Marketplaces and transportation depots can bring people together in conflicting as well as accommodating interaction.

Miner, in his study of Timbuctoo (1940), devotes a whole chapter to conflict between the Tuareg, Songhoi, and Arabs, the three major ethnic groups in the town.[2] Students of Indian urban life have noted the impact of public Hindu or Muslim festivals on violent Hindu-Muslim conflict. In studies of recent racial violence in the United States, public juncture sites have been important; the Philadelphia riots of 1944 heavily involved mass transit systems, and earlier incidents in Chicago occurred on the public beaches and led to flare-ups. However, the recent literature emphasizes the underlying integrating mechanisms in the city. Since cities are operating social systems, they must accommodate themselves to sporadic outbreaks of violent conflict.

SITUATIONAL URBAN JUNCTURES

The first type of urban juncture we shall look at can be subsumed under the notion of the situation. Situations can be spatially and temporally defined and can be studied ethnographically—through intensive interviewing and observation. We shall group them according to whether they are primarily defined by space or time: obviously, both elements are significant in all instances, but their relative importance will vary.

Urban situations serve to integrate in several ways: First, they constitute connecting points for increasing levels of inclusion of units based on single social attributes. Examples of this are cycles of temporal

[1] William Hanna, "The Integrative Role of Urban Africa's Middleplaces and Middlemen," *Civilisations*, 12 (1967), 12-29.
[2] Horace Miner, *The Primitive City of Timbuctoo*, Revised edition (Garden City: Doubleday & Company, 1965).

events that bring together localized branches of ethnic groups or occupational groups, as in folk festivals or conventions. Second, they constitute times and places where people from different components come together, as when ethnic groups mix or classes are in contact. Some situations potentially integrate a large number of segments, while others are more narrowly focused and bring together a limited set. A spatial node that is located between two neighborhoods and is used by both neighborhoods would serve a limited function as connecting point. However, central locations tend to draw from the entire spectrum of urban components and thus provide the potential for higher level junctures.

In the following discussion, a distinction should be made between contact points for *individual* interaction and contact points at the *group* level of organization. All the situations discussed fall somewhere on a continuum between bringing individuals together as isolates and bringing them together as representatives of particular urban components. A similar continuum can be envisioned between places and events that serve only sporadic linking functions and those that are so regularly integrative that they spin off permanent formal structures.

We are using the notion of situations to differentiate between them and more formal aspects of social structure. Such spatial or temporal foci are part of the permanent urban scene, but are less explicitly recognized as serving an integrative function than the formal associations that exist for this purpose. This is true even when we look at such institutions as schools, hospitals, or government agencies, for we are looking at these institutions as places that informally bring urban components together, rather than as objects of study themselves. We are not concerned—as are educational, medical, or legal anthropologists— with the internal organization of these institutions, their subcultures, their success or failure in achieving their goals, or their rules for patterned interaction. We are only concerned with them as settings within which diverse elements of the city are brought into close, regular contact. We are concerned with the effect of the urban on these institutions and their effect on urban integration in the informal, situational sense—not in the way they are supposed to be integrative (their formal reason for being), but in the way they accidentally bring people together.

Public Places

In any urban center, there are areas in which large numbers of individuals who are not known to one another are present. Actually, a simple division can be made between private space and public space. Private space would then be those areas in which domestic activities take place. Public space would consist of all other areas where access is not controlled. Vatuk, in her study of family life in Allahabad, notes the very clear distinction made between these two arenas of interaction.[3] Provencher also points out how density in the urban residential space in Malaysia has led to an accentuation of the difference between public and private space. Here, physical barriers to sight and sound are used as much as possible to separate the two arenas, but because of density, these are supplemented by formal rules of etiquette, which lead to conventions about ignoring or overlooking certain visual and aural events.[4] Sometimes even within household space, such distinctions are maintained. Based upon Chinese households in Hong Kong Singapore and George Town, Malaysia, Anderson suggests that the Chinese manage space and interpersonal relations in a way that minimizes the potentially negative effects of crowding. Space within the house, which is shared by several unrelated families, is carefully segregated into public and private areas. Members of families living in the same house are not required to interact with one another with a high degree of emotional intensity. Status is clearly defined, and role relationships are patterned and predictable. Children can be, and are, disciplined by any adult. Finally, individual privacy and isolation are not highly valued. These cultural responses to crowding do not completely eliminate conflict and stress, but do much to minimize them.[5]

In the domain of public space, there are certain distinctions that can be made. The public arena of the lanes in a neighborhood are different from the major thoroughfares, which serve as neighborhood boundaries. Suttles makes the same distinction in discussing the Addams area of Chicago. Some public spaces are not as open to free access as others. Some are socially bounded, that is, there are strict rules governing the interactions taking place, and people who do not know the rules are frequently ignored, ridiculed, or kept outside.[6] Several segments of the urban social structure may regularly interact in these places, as in ethnically heterogeneous neighborhoods or occupationally heterogeneous marketplaces, but the localized rules for such interactions are known only to regulars in these spatial areas.

Within the larger context of the city as a whole, there are recognized areas in which *strangers* interact, and the rules of behavior are more

[3] Sylvia Vatuk, *Kinship and Urbanization* (Berkeley: University of California Press, 1972).

[4] Ronald Provencher, "Comparisons of Social Interaction Styles: Urban and Rural Malay Culture," in T. Weaver and D. White (eds.), *The Anthropology of Urban Environments*, Society for Applied Anthropology Monographs, 1972.

[5] E. N. Anderson, Jr., "Some Chinese Methods of Dealing with Crowding," *Urban Anthropology*, 1 (1972), 141-50.

[6] G. Suttles, *The Social Order of the Slum* (Chicago: University of Chicago Press, 1968).

diffuse and generalized.[7] In all of these cases, urban ethnography is a potential source of information that has not been heavily emphasized by anthropologists. It is an area where several disciplines have done exemplary interdisciplinary work. Geographers, and social psychologists, and ethnomethodologists within sociology have been particularly active in this area, but they often miss the cross-cultural perspective or the perspective gained from long-term relationships with informants. Certainly the work of Goffman has been an extremely important component in the study of "stranger" interaction in public places.[8]

Mitchell was one of the first anthropologists to point out the uniqueness of public spaces in African urban centers. He says:

> There are, of course, many of these situations in the daily life of a large town, which is populated by people from many different tribes and where neighborhoods are always changing in composition. They may occur in urban crowds, in beer-halls, in markets and so on. Here town-dwellers tend to categorize people in terms of some visible characteristic and to organize their behavior accordingly.[9]

Berreman has developed a list of public places of interaction for an Indian city. The object of his research was to develop a comprehensive inventory of social categories that people use in identifying strangers. In order to develop such a list, it was essential for him to participate, observe, and interview others in situations that maximized the degree of strangeness and the fleeting or transitory nature of contact. The places observed were: teashops, retail stores, barber shops, wholesale markets, hospitals, recreation areas, political rallies, public transportation depots, and stalls of sidewalk vendors. He also included some of the quasi-public arenas discussed above with more controlled access, such as residental areas, crafts work places, and small factories. The teashop, which figured so significantly in this study, has as its analogue the bar, cafe, beerhall and other types of eating and drinking places found all over the world.

Berreman notes that a variety of cues are used in the attempt to categorize others that are primarily geared toward converting an anonymous stranger into an incumbent in a specific social category. Once this is done, the rules for social interaction are understood, and one is comfortable about knowing what behavior is appropriate. Berreman notes

[7] For a discussion of the "stranger" phenomenon and its implications for urban social structure, see David Jacobson, "Social Control and Urban Social Order," a paper delivered at the 72nd Annual Meetings of the American Anthropological Association, 1973.
[8] E. Goffman, *Behavior in Public Places* (New York: Free Press, 1966).
[9] J. Clyde Mitchell, "Theoretical Orientations in African Urban Studies," in M. Banton (ed.), *The Social Anthropology of Complex Societies* (London: Tavistock Publishers, 1966), p. 52.

that the specificity of categorization varies from one situation to another, depending on how transitory and fleeting the contact is. Specificity also depends on the status of the individual doing the categorizing; finer distinctions are drawn when the person doing the categorization is looking at someone perceived to be close in status. Although many designations are based upon traditional categories (caste, religion, place of origin), there are newer relevant categories like "officeworker-clerk" or "big man" (executive), which are based on urban occupations. Frequently, the cues used in the designation of others are derived from clothing styles, hair style, language, general posture, bearing, or movement style.[10]

In the categorization of others who are strangers, these cues may be accidentally misinterpreted or deliberately counterfeited. This uncertainty makes such interactions subject to an inherent wariness and mistrust. As Gomperz has pointed out, language is the most difficult of these symbolic codes to counterfeit or manipulate.[11]

Barnett mentions, in passing, a clear-cut example of the effect on behavior of the existence of public places where anonymity is anticipated. A relatively high caste association president wanted to see a popular movie. Since all the more expensive seats were sold, he had to buy a cheaper ticket. During the performance, he became aware of the fact that a low caste individual who performed menial services for him was sitting next to him. This compromised his ritual purity as a high caste member. As the servant became aware of the situation, he (the servant) got up and left. Such an event could only take place in the city. In the rural area, one knows how to avoid contact with lower caste individuals, but in the city, it seemed "safe" to buy a cheap ticket since anonymity was expected.[12]

Even in such public places as pornography stores, customers perceive the situation as less than anonymous and are still constrained by many social norms. They develop elaborate techniques to hide their identities, activities, and purchases.[13]

An even more tenuous kind of stranger interaction has been studied between people who pass each other in the streets or on transport

[10] G. Berreman, "Social Categories and Social Interaction in Urban India," *American Anthropologist*, 74 (1972), 567-87.

[11] Charles A. Ferguson and John Gomperz (eds.), *Linguistic Diversity in South Asia* (Bloomington, Indiana: Indiana University Research Center in Anthropology, Folklore and Linguistics, Publication No. 13, 1960).

[12] Steve Barnett, "Urban Is as Urban Does: Two Incidents on One Street in Madras City, South India," *Urban Anthropology*, 2 (1973), 120-60.

[13] David A. Karp, "Hiding in Pornographic Book Stores: A Reconsideration of the Nature of Urban Anonymity," *Urban Life and Culture*, 1 (1973), 427-51; Margaret R. Henderson, "Acquiring Privacy in Public," *Urban Life and Culture*, 3 (1975), 446-55.

vehicles; these include studies of walking patterns on crowded streets, and patterns of eye contact avoidance in subways. These contacts have almost no implication for social life and are of concern mainly to those interested in designing public space. Architects and design experts who wish to insure fast traffic flow or minimize levels of psychic discomfort may be interested in these studies, but they have little implication for understanding the social construction of cities. As an example, Milgram makes some general observations of New York City public behavior, in which strangers literally engage in combat for seats on trains and constantly bump each other on crowded sidewalks. As a general indication of the level of social interaction in densely populated cities, Milgram notes that an office-worker in the heart of Manhattan has potential contact with 220,000 others within a walking time of ten minutes.[14] These kinds of studies tend to lack the anthropologist's concern with the background and social context of the actors, which he would derive from long-term ethnographic contact.

Eating and Drinking Establishments

The preparation and sale of processed food and drink for large numbers is primarily an urban function. Such establishments may serve a limited segment of the urban population, like a neighborhood bar, or a bar near a work place that has a completely homogeneous clientele, or the Indian bars described by Price.[15] These establishments, although public, are in fact "closed" to outsiders in that a variety of social mechanisms are used to exclude outsiders. Others, while tending to be exclusive in their clientele, are more open to access by outsiders. Still others are located at juncture points, and thus tend to bring in a variety of urban components. Finally, there are those in centralized areas, which draw from the entire urban center.

Most of these establishments combine sociability with diverse items of food and drink. If they serve several classes, occupational status communities, ethnic groups, or neighborhood representatives, there may be a tendency for each segment to maintain social distance from the others and avoid interaction. However, the opportunity is provided to develop some contact or, at the very least, to observe from afar how members of other groups behave in quasi-private, personal interactions.

There is a literature within urban anthropology that deals with bars and taverns. The use of these facilities for leisure-time activities is

[14] S. Milgram, "The Experience of Living in Cities: A Psychological Analysis," in J. Helmer and Neil Eddington (eds.), *Urbanman* (New York: Free Press, 1973).
[15] J. Price, "U.S. and Canadian Indian Urban Ethnic Institutions," *Urban Anthropology*, 4 (1975), 35-52.

one of the characteristics of urban life in many parts of the world. Cara Richards has developed a typology for American drinking places describing the salient differences between taverns and middle class cocktail bars, local as opposed to downtown bars, and other important differences.[16]

Despite the fact that many bars develop a reputation for serving a particular clientele, the basis of the clientele selection may be such that diverse residential, ethnic, and occupational groups may be brought together. For example, a singles bar or a gay bar may attract a clientele drawn from a very diverse population. Since they exist to develop new links between people, they are obvious arenas for intergroup interaction, conflict, or avoidance.

Jacobson has noted that bars in the city center of Mbale are potential sources of intergroup contact. However, this potential is not realized, since the clientele is relatively homogeneous and represents only the new bureaucratic elite. In this case, financial and transportation constraints, even more than social pressure, act against the use of these facilities by non-elites.[17]

Many bars have a dual clientele. In her study of the cocktail waitress Mann notes that her bar serves a working class clientele until about 7 P.M. and then becomes a college student bar. Periodically working class people do come in after the change in clientele, but they do not remain long because they see themselves as outsiders.[18] Within the African beerhall studied by Wolcott, a variety of ethnic groups congregated; however, each group had its own location, and interaction was sustained within the group.[19]

In Epstein's discussion of Chanda's activities, there are some drinking situations that link him to others, while in other situations, social distance is maintained. Thus Chanda reestablishes prior contact with a woman who runs a beer hall and who did not even know that he had been living in the city for some time. On the other hand, a drinking party from a different tribal area had no interaction at all with Chanda and his drinking mates.[20]

[16] Cara Richards, "City Taverns," Human Organization, 22 (Winter, 1963-64), 260-68.
[17] David Jacobson, "Culture and Stratification among Urban Africans," Journal of Asian and African Studies, 5 (1970), 176-83.
[18] Brenda Mann, "Bar Talk," in J. Spradley and D. McCurdy (eds), Conformity and Conflict (Boston: Little Brown, 1974), pp. 101-111.
[19] Harry Wolcott, "The African Beer Gardens of Bulawayo: Integrated Drinking in a Segregated Society," Rutgers Center of Alcohol Studies Publication, Smithers Hall, Rutgers University, New Brunswick, New Jersey, 1974.
[20] A. L. Epstein, "The Network and Urban Social Organization," in J. C. Mitchell (ed.), Social Networks in Urban Situations (Manchester: Manchester University Press, 1969), pp. 77-116.

Gutkind has pointed out that in all of urban Africa, the beer hall is a strategic linkage point for various tribal groups. They were begun as African establishments, largely in response to exclusion from white establishments, and as such served the various ethnic components.[21] In his own fieldwork in a multi-ethnic parish (neighborhood) in Kampala, he describes the importance of the beer bar in linking the many tribal groups. He says, "Men and women of every tribe represented in the parish will sit together and jostle and joke with one another." Men pick up women, play cards, mock Europeans and Asians, and occasionally dance.[22]

In Berreman's study, teashops became significant public arenas for the observation of interaction between a wide variety of segments. There was some selectivity in clientele based upon regular patronage. In addition, in the public displays or advertisements for these establishments, some symbols were used to indicate the generalized identity of the proprietor (Hindu, Muslim, Punjabi).[23]

Denich notes that public restaurants used by the migrants she studied served as a source of recruitment of people into one's network. This was one place to make friends who were *not* ex-villagers or co-workers of the migrant.[24]

A study of East Indians (Punjabis) in England indicated that the pub was a vital institution for both British host and Punjabi migrant; however, the patterns of pub-related behavior varied for the two groups. The British population tended to select a neighborhood pub and spend the entire evening there. On the other hand, the Punjabis tended to "pub hop" and visit several during the course of the evening. Much of the movement was in small groups. Another significant difference between the two groups was that British men were sometimes accompanied by women to the pubs, while Punjabi men never brought their women.

Pub monopolization was a frequent complaint heard from the British, who saw many of their pubs being taken over by the Indians. On the other hand, many Indians complained of discriminatory behavior on the part of the pubkeeper. One complaint often heard was that the British pub tenders used different glasses to serve Indians. There was no dispute over short measure, but the symbolic meaning of the different

21 P. C. W. Gutkind, *Urban Anthropology: Perspectives on Third World Urbanization and Urbanism* (New York: Barnes and Noble Books, 1974).
22 P. C. W. Gutkind, "African Urbanism, Mobility and the Social Network," *International Journal of Comparative Sociology*, 6 (1965), 54.
23 Berreman, "Social Categories and Social Interaction in Urban India."
24 B. Denich, "Migration and Network Manipulation in Yugoslavia," in R. Spencer (ed.), *Migration and Anthropology* (Seattle: University of Washington Press, 1970), pp. 133-48.

pint glasses was considered important. Stereotypes about Indian behavior were frequently based upon observations made in pubs where the two groups co-existed. These were among the most significant contact points.[25]

A report of the conclusions derived from a study of bars in the San Diego area by forty anthropology students stated that ". . . it learned almost nothing about bars except that bargoers can't be stereotyped" and ". . . all types of persons go into bars at one time or another . . ." and that drinking was secondary to a wish to "meet with people and escape the daily routine." [26] It seems unfortunate that the emphasis was upon the study of bars as closed and isolated units, rather than upon the bar as a potential juncture between groups in San Diego. They were searching for "*The* Culture of Bar Life in San Diego"—as if there were such a culture. Obviously, there is no typical bargoer; whatever generalizations can be made have to be limited to particular types of bars or types of users. The differences in bars and the styles of use for various groups under particular circumstances are what is important in understanding bars as "middle places" in a city.

There are several reasons why bars can serve as feasible units of ethnographic research. They are public places where access is supposed to be relatively open. In many cases, the anthropologist is not an intrusive figure, at least initially. Furthermore, the bar often brings together diverse segments of the urban structure. Behavior in bars is informal and personal, making it possible to observe private behavior in a quasi-public setting. A wide range of activities and conversations about significant social topics are typical in this context for sociability.

Other Leisure-Time Places

In addition to bars, there are a number of other localized urban settings that serve as potential places for the mingling of diverse urban components. Most cities in the world set aside open space for parks. These areas attract various elements in the population and, like bars, are amenable to ethnographic research. As in the case of bars, some parks and open spaces are characterized by freer access than others. Some "belong" to the urban components discussed in Chapter 5 and thus are not junctures, since access is controlled and the area is defended. This is especially true if teen-age gangs control spatial areas. Suttles'

[25] Research on Punjabi migrants in Wolverhampton, England was conducted during 1969 and 1970. Researchers were Edwin Eames and Howard Robboy. Research was supported by a study leave from Temple University and N.I.M.H. Grant Number DHEW-IR03-MH 18799-01.
[26] "San Diego Barflies," *New York Post*, February 19, 1976, p. 3.

description of how various ethnic groups control different spaces in a single neighborhood is a case in point. Thus, it is the more centralized citywide facilities or the spatial areas located on the borders between groups that serve as junctures.

In an attempt to use parks to observe examples of national character, Wolfenstein observed families in parks in Paris, New York, and Vienna. She noted that in the Paris situation, families were self-contained units and children were not allowed to roam; thus the potential for interaction was minimized. In New York, on the other hand, children were encouraged to interact with other children. Although the goal of this research was not to study parks as an urban juncture, it has obvious implications for potential urban ethnographic research.[27]

Birdwhistell has compared public behavior in several zoos around the world, including San Diego, Mysore City (India), and London. Here again, he is examining cross-cultural issues of national character not related to the social construction of the city; but the zoo is amenable to examination of urban junctures as well. In such public places, groups observe each other and form stereotypes based on these observations.[28]

Marketplaces

In every urban center there are large market zones, stores, and street vending areas, which are non-local and serve the entire urban community or many segments of it. Frequently they attract large numbers of people and serve as points of interaction for people who are not usually in contact with one another. In contrast to leisure-time places, these centers contain much specialized commercial interaction. However, the sociability component of market area activities should not be ignored. Gossip and news are exchanged frequently, and anthropologists have long noted this function of marketplaces as communication media.

Students of market life have noted that commercial transactions are characterized by a different set of behavioral norms. These norms tend to be more formal and less personal and entail new styles of speech and interaction in haggling and striking a bargain. The aggressive and combative verbal interchanges that are frequent here are not found in other social contexts. This "bazaar behavior" has been noted in cities throughout the world. Similarly, interaction in department stores and other stores is different from other social interaction.

The control of market activities by different segments of the popula-

[27] Martha Wolfenstein, *Childhood in Contemporary Culture* (Chicago: University of Chicago Press, 1955).
[28] R. Birdwhistell has produced a film showing different behavioral patterns of visitors to urban zoos in a variety of nation-states.

tion is extremely important in understanding the relationships between ethnic groups. In certain parts of Africa, marketing activities have become the almost exclusive domain of women, who have gained considerable economic power. In other parts of the world, alien groups such as Arabs, Jews, Chinese, or East Indians control market activities, so that markets are important zones of constant interethnic contact.

In Middle East market activities, it is noted that rug merchants in the process of negotiating a sale will convert the stranger into a kinsman by using fictive forms of kin terms. Bargaining itself has a *social* goal in that both parties try to raise their social status in each other's eyes. Another element in the bargaining process is the attempt to change the situation from a strictly commercial activity into a social event by the serving of tea and other items.[29]

Geertz points out different aspects within the "pasar" or bazaar institution in Modjokuto, Java. He says this traditional market which dominates the town "is at once an economic institution and a way of life, a general mode of commercial activity reaching into all aspects of Modjokuto society, and a sociocultural world nearly complete in itself." [30] He characterizes the relationships between traders and customers as *not* affected by ties or social status. ". . . commercial ties are carefully insulated from general social ties. Friendship, neighborliness, even kinship are one thing, trade is another. . . . The market is the one institutionalized structure in Javanese society where the formalism, status consciousness, and introversion so characteristic of the culture generally are relatively weak. . . ." [31] Thus, the market is a mechanism that breaks down subcultural boundaries and links outsiders together, albeit in an impersonal way.

Oberschall, like Geertz, has studied the market in Lusaka, Zambia. He provides much information about the changing role of the market in the last decades, as well as the sociological characteristics of the vendors and the scale of their capital investment and economic activity. All this was obtained through questionnaire surveys. He is unable to tell us anything about observed market activity. In regard to the question of how customers choose among vendors, he says that besides differences in quantity and quality ". . . there exist personal relationships built up over time between some marketers and steady customers based on kinship, tribe, community of language, neighborliness, supported by favored treatment, credit, and a large *basela* (added weight). Only further research based on prolonged participant observation . . . could

---

[29] Fuad Khuri, "The Etiquette of Bargaining in the Middle East," *American Anthropologist,* 70 (1968), 698-706.
[30] C. Geertz, *Peddlers and Princes* (Chicago: University of Chicago Press, 1963).
[31] Ibid., p. 46.

provide the required information about the relative importance of various factors." [32]

In Patch's ethnographic work on Lima's central markets, his primary concern is with viewing the market as a self-contained unit. He describes ambulatory vendors, the hierarchy of theft activities, and special areas for secondhand and thieved goods.[33] There is little in it that relates to the relationship between market activities and city social structure. However, the implications for this kind of study are obvious: one could examine how different groups control different activities and how different urban components use the marketplace and relate to the groups therein.

In a recent study, a drugstore on the border of two neighborhoods in Philadelphia was the focus of long-term ethnography. The observer, by watching the activities in the drugstore and developing close relationships with many customers, began to see how this place served as the only safe and sanctioned meeting place between the elderly white population of one neighborhood and the young Black population of the other. The store was a hangout for the elderly white males, who were afraid of the streets. The Black population also used the drugstore, but mostly for commercial rather than social purposes. The two groups had their only face-to-face contact within the store, which became significant as an intercommunity spatial juncture.[34]

Service Institutions

There are a number of other spatially defined service institutions that may serve as juncture points between components of the urban population. Among these we would include schools, hospitals, and government agencies. Although there have been a large number of studies of these institutions, they have not viewed them as junctures. For the most part, they have been viewed as goal-oriented institutions and have been examined as *isolated* social systems to explore their modes of operation and the success or failure of their delivery of services. In this regard, the studies belong more to the fields of medical anthropology and educational anthropology. Many of the studies done by other social scientists who specialize in organization theory and bureaucracy do use participant observation techniques to examine the formal, goal-oriented operation of the institution as a closed system.

[32] R. Oberschall, "Lusaka Market Vendors: Then and Now," *Urban Anthropology*, 1 (1972), 107-23.

[33] Richard Patch, "La Parada: Lima's Market," American Universities Field Staff Report, vol. 14, 1967.

[34] Susan Silverman, "The Drugstore: Focal Point in a Changing Neighborhood" (unpublished student project, Temple University, 1973).

An example of a study that illuminates the potential integrative role of such institutions is Spicer's study of "The Patrons of the Poor." Spicer describes a situation in which three different types of patrons—one representing a missionary church, another representing the public schools, and the third representing the juvenile probation office—establish their own ego-centered network, with separate clienteles that cross-cut a low income neighborhood. This community in a southwestern American city was ethnically homogeneous, containing Mexican Americans who identified themselves as Indians. These three sets of patrons linked segments of the lower class community to certain institutions of the larger society. In the particular situation described by Spicer, however, these three types of patrons are viewed as disruptive, since they oppose community-wide organization based upon internal leadership. Another perspective would view them as important links to middle-class individuals and institutions.[35]

Since anthropologists are accustomed to developing long-term relationships with informants, and since they are more likely to wish to view the institution from the client's perspective, they might follow their informants into the institution and examine their perceptions and interactions with strangers and representatives of other groups. In effect, this is an extension of Gluckman's situational analysis, which focuses on describing in detail a situation that brings together diverse elements in a single spatial setting. In-depth knowledge gained about the *background* of the interacting elements is then used to explain the interaction and to derive implications for future interaction.[36]

A. L. Epstein has done considerable research on urban courts in the African Copperbelt. He notes that such courts are as concerned with moral and ethical issues as with legal ones. In Luanshya, the African courts handle most disputes involving Africans. Only when a European brings a complaint against an African does the African enter the formal European court. Since the African population is tribally heterogeneous, the courts are set up to reflect this diversity. Thus, each group selects its own representatives to act as judges in the tribal courts. Each case is heard by all the representatives of these groups, one of whom is selected as president. Epstein notes that much is made of customary differences among the tribes by tribal members themselves, but there is an overriding general agreement about what is considered to be proper or reasonable behavior. This generalized agreement allows the court to function in a diverse tribal setting. When a particular element

[35] Edward Spicer, "Patrons of the Poor," *Human Organization*, 29 (1970), 12-20.
[36] Max Gluckman, "Analysis of a Social Situation in Modern Zululand," *Bantu Studies*, vol. 14, 1940.

of tribal custom is involved, then the court representatives of that tribe intercede to explain the implications of the custom for the case. Epstein also notes that the courts cannot simply use tribal custom in the settling of urban disputes, since many of the cases involve urban phenomena, for which there are no tribal precedents. Thus the court, representing a diversity of tribal elements, must act as a mediating and socializing agency within the urban context.[37]

Lowy, in a study of conflict resolution and the use of courts in Koforidua, Ghana, notes a dichotomy in conflicts between those that focus on money and commerce and those that focus on prestige and honor. Disputes over money are brought to formal courts, whether they are between fellow tribesmen or not. For prestige and honor cases, a combination of courts and private mediators are used. Interestingly enough, Lowy finds no difference in court use based on migrant status, age, education, or occupation.[38]

The potential for the use of courts for study of urban junctures is indicated. Not only is participant observation possible, but court records and informant's memory of cases are available as data for analysis of the court as a setting in which urban components relate to each other.

Transportation

Transportation in urban centers serves as another spatial contact point between diverse elements of the population. Once again, the studies have centered upon the shallow, transitory interactions, rather than the full implications for the social actors. When more depth is added to the study, some interesting areas may be revealed. Thus, in a study of taxi cab drivers and riders in New York, Henslin notes that what is frequently viewed as an anonymous situation is, in reality, much less anonymous. For both riders and drivers, there is a tendency to develop techniques of "trackability." Thus, drivers responding to telephone requests note the place of pickup, while the riders frequently note the company and number of the cab. Potential trackability serves as a constraint on behavior and reinforces concern with appropriateness.[39]

One of the frequent assumptions about mass transit systems is that they bring together strangers in a situation of anonymity and desire for

[37] A. L. Epstein, *Politics in an Urban African Community* (Manchester: Manchester University Press for the Rhodes-Livingstone Institute, 1958).

[38] M. Lowy, "Me Ko Court: The Impact of Urbanization on Conflict Resolution in a Ghanaian Town," in G. Foster and R. Kemper (eds.), *Anthropologists in Cities* (Boston: Little, Brown & Co., Inc., 1974), pp. 153-74.

[39] James Henslin, "Trust and the Cab Driver," in M. Truzzi (ed.), *Sociology and Everyday Life* (Englewood Cliffs, New Jersey: Prentice-Hall, 1968), pp. 138-58.

avoidance. However, in many situations, this assumption is incorrect. Where people ride fixed-route vehicles, the cloak of anonymity frequently is discarded. The buses, trams, and trolleys themselves, as well as the depots where one waits for the vehicle, bring people together with regularity.

An article in the *New York Times* described a daily commuter train between Philadelphia and the New York metropolitan area.[40] Many of those riding the train have been doing so for years (in some cases twenty-five years or more). The conductors know most of the passengers by name, and the regulars know much about each other's personal and professional lives.

This view by a journalist provides an accurate description of the system, but an in-depth anthropological analysis, with greater knowledge of the social backgrounds and long-term interactions between passengers, could provide greater insights. Since one of the authors is a regular on the train, the following insights are examples of what could be added to the analysis:

1. There is a distinct division between those who live in Pennsylvania and those who live in New Jersey. The latter are regarded as interlopers.
2. Many contacts are made on the train between members of different occupational groups. Those in the textile and jewelry business provide their merchandise to fellow riders at advantageous prices.
3. Tuesday is called "ragpickers" day. Many of those from the Philadelphia textile industry go into New York to buy and sell. It is apparent that many of these people see each other only on the train and conduct business there.
4. The card players and drinkers form distinct groups, and these focal activity points draw together many disparate individuals.
5. The occupational and ethnic diversity of the ridership is marked. Included are bankers, stockbrokers, government employees, salesmen of all types, college professors, law students, wholesale brokers in meat and textiles, and manufacturers of toys, containers, and medical equipment.
6. Among the ethnic groups are two large blocks of Anglo-Saxon Protestants and Jews. In addition, there are small groups of white ethnics and several Blacks. There is much ethnic joking.

As public vehicles move through urban space, they pick up riders from different neighborhood areas, ethnic groups, and occupations who are together with great regularity for extensive periods of time. Examples

[40] *New York Times,* May 13, 1973, Section 10, pp. 1, 13.

can be found in commuter trains and stations, buses and bus depots, which are all amenable to long-term ethnography or in-depth study of the backgrounds and prior relationships of the participants.

Many of the public places mentioned above require waiting in lines. Since those who wait represent different segments of the population, the phenomenon of waiting in line can serve as an intersect situation. Thus, Leon Mann notes that those who wait in lines for any length of time tend to interact with one another, and norms about waiting in line are developed. Looking at the queuing phenomenon for football (soccer) tickets in Melbourne, Australia, he notes that rules are developed about how long one will watch a place for another and how places are reserved. Mann also notes that in New York City, people tend to wait in lines for opening day performances and that people talk a lot about how this line differs from others in their experience. One of the basic problems of line-waiters is the line-crasher, who is frequently discussed. Techniques are developed to handle crashers.[41]

It should be noted that Mann is a social psychologist primarily concerned with *individual* perception and behavior. Many of the studies of behavior in public places look at the individual's behavior and strategy totally apart from its social context. Once again, an anthropologist would be more interested in looking at the social statuses of the actors or the contact between members of bounded urban social components.

TEMPORAL EVENTS

There are many events that take place in urban settings that draw together segments of the population. Such events are amenable to urban ethnographic techniques although little has actually been done on them by anthropologists. In large-scale sporting events, diverse elements of the population are brought into close proximity and share common goals. However, we know little about the meaning of these events to people, the actual interaction, the effect of social diversity on interaction, and the consequences of such integrative events for other areas of life. For instance, we find a statement by Lever in her analysis of Brazilian soccer that representatives of various social classes travelled to England when Brazil played in the world cup matches. However, we find no data describing this high degree of integration created by a common focus.[42]

[41] Leon Mann, "Learning to Live with Lines," in Helmer and Eddington (eds.), *Urbanman*, pp. 42-61.
[42] J. Lever, "Soccer as a Brazilian Way of Life," in Gregory Stone (ed.), *Games, Sports and Power* (New Brunswick, New Jersey: Transaction Books, 1972), pp. 139-59.

Several sociological studies have been concerned with sports fans and the effect of particular urban contexts on fans. They have noted differences in the meaning of sports events, attendance, and behavior between old cities with sports traditions and new cities with no such traditions.[43]

Anthropologists have devoted more attention to urban festivals than to sports. These events are, after all, analogous to the ceremonial cycles in rural and tribal settings. Large-scale urban festivals (as opposed to festivals for particular neighborhood or ethnic groups) do bring together the various components of the city.

We noted previously (in the chapter on The Roles of Cities) that festivals play a significant integrating role for a city and its region. Such events were very important in the preindustrial city and have maintained some of their original significance in the modern city. Large-scale festivals frequently required the active participation of most of the diverse segments of the urban population. The large-scale processions and ritual events along the Street of the Dead in the ancient city of Teotihuacan are noteworthy examples. Visitors to the pyramids outside Mexico City remark that the thoroughfare and its many temple mounds and pyramid complexes seem designed for spectacular ceremonial events. A parallel event occurred in modern Mexico City that drew participants from a wide rural hinterland as well as diverse elements from the urban center. This was a procession to move the image and ritual paraphernalia of the Virgin of Guadelupe (national patron saint) from its traditional site in an earthquake-damaged basilica to a new location.

In the European medieval city, each guild of artisans or merchants had its respective role in ceremonial pageantry, which had to be coordinated to effect a unity symbolic of the whole city. Remnants of these ceremonial events still exist in many European centers. Not only does the need to coordinate groups lead to structural integration, but some urban festivals enhance integration by encouraging spontaneous interaction between groups that are usually non-interacting or whose contact is constrained by rigid rules. Festivals also permit role inversions and tension-release behavior. The "King-of-Fools" festival of the Middle Ages was supported by the aristocracy, who participated in the "fun and games" during which the class structure was temporarily inverted.

While we assume that urban festivals may serve these integrative functions, we cannot begin to classify types of festivals and their differences in integrative outcome until we have more actual descriptive data. Some data suggest that the coordination of specialized participation groups based on occupation, neighborhood, or ethnicity serve to forge structural links.

[43] Ray Didinger, "Philadelphia Fan: Boobird or Bluebird," *Philadelphia Bulletin,* February 15, 16, 17, 1976.

Leeds, dealing with the carnival in Rio, indicates that the formation of the various dance groups participating in the event is a source and reinforcement of cohesion for the neighborhood or occupational groups that are their base of organization. He also points out that monetary sponsorship of these groups is provided by wealthy entrepreneurs and high government officials of the city. Thus coalitions are created between fragments of the elite and fragments of the lower class, linking these two classes in patron-client relationships; the lower groups provide political support for the elites in return for favors.[44]

Buechler has described the complex group interrelationships formed in La Paz, Bolivia, in relation to the fiesta cycle. Each barrio has a saint and a fiesta to commemorate its saint. There is a cycle of barrio fiestas. Each fiesta has two types of sponsors: one concerned with the cost of church-related activities (mass, candles, food, alcohol), and one concerned with the cost of dance groups, musicians, and food and drink for dancers, musicians, and retainers. Barrio residents not only serve as sponsors and audiences for their own fiesta, but for neighboring barrios as well. Often dance groups based on place of origin or occupational union play a role in these local functions.

Markets and wholesale outlets for produce also have fiestas for their patron saints. Here, fiestas and dance groups are based on occupational lines and place of origin (since types of produce and produce specialists come from different highland regions). Buechler mentions that stevedores and vendors form dance groups according to the kind of produce they sell. Fiestas and dance groups are also associated with clubs of migrants from the same town. In these instances, unions of artisans and market sellers whose membership includes a high proportion of migrants from a particular town also may be affiliated with these clubs. Thus participation in club fiestas is frequently based on occupational differentiation.

La Paz is tied together by an annual cycle of neighborhood, market, and regional club fiestas. In each type of fiesta the organization of sponsors and dance groups may be based on neighborhood, occupation, or place of origin. General participation in the festivities draws from a still wider cross-section of components. Thus the fiesta cycle serves to knit together the structural components of the city.[45]

Events in urban America that perform the same integrative func-

[44] A. Leeds, "Housing-Settlement Types, Arrangements for Living, Proletarianization, and the Social Structure of the City," in W. Cornelius and F. Trueblood (eds.), *Latin American Urban Research*, 4 (1974), 67-100.

[45] Hans Buechler, "The Ritual Dimension of Rural-Urban Networks: The Fiesta System in the Northern Highlands," in W. Mangin (ed.), *Peasants in Cities* (Boston: Houghton Mifflin, 1970), pp. 62-71.

tion are Mardi Gras in New Orleans, the Rose Bowl Parade in Pasadena, and the Mummers Parade in Philadelphia. Each of these has many separate performance groups (dance or float organizations) based on neighborhood, ethnic group, or economic enterprise. Ethnographic analysis is needed to understand the linkages created by these festivals.

Gonzalez and Ossenberg point out that the integrative functions of urban festivals can be exaggerated. Gonzalez describes the activities of the pre-Lenten Carnival weeks in Santiago, Dominican Republic as institutions that reinforce class boundaries. For both upper and lower classes, activities involve elaborate costumes and related behavioral norms.

For the upper class, the activities take place within exclusive social clubs and do not lead to cross-class interaction. The activities do involve role reversal in that, while costumed, upper class women are permitted to behave in ways that would be considered scandalous at other times. Dance and skit groups perform, involving activities of many outside groups. Young boys often wear the garish costumes of the lower class festival street male, but only within the confines of the club.

Lower class activities take place in the street, where costumed, masked males (called "lechones") participate in unusual activities: pranks, foolishness, and stylized combat. A residue of the sixteenth-century urban festival exists, in which two sections of the city are considered to be rivals and engage in mock combat. However, the territorial units have not retained any real social integrity, and thus this stylized combat and its eventual resolution have only a very attentuated symbolic solidarity function.

The only point of contact between the two classes is the upper class' romanticization of the "lechon" as a folk hero. Upper class intellectuals collect and display the folklore of the lechon figure and sponsor a contest for mask-makers. Lechon masks have become collector's items. Leading mask-makers are patronized by the elite, who laud this form of folk art. This is the only formal, structured link between the two classes, who otherwise observe the festival in separate ways. However, the degree of participation is high for all classes.[46]

Ossenberg too has questioned the notion that urban festivals lead to cross-class interaction or even to a degree of common participation by different classes. He observed bar behavior during the Calgary Stampede in Canada to see if there was a similarity in participation by class and/or an increase in cross-class interaction. According to Ossenberg:

> The annual Calgary Stampede features a rodeo and related "cowboy" themes as central attractions. There is also the usual carnival

[46] N. Gonzalez, "The Social Functions of Carnival in a Dominican City," *Southwestern Journal of Anthropology*, 26 (1970), 328-42.

midway (larger than most), and street dancing is common. In addition, there is a general relaxation of formal social controls, with fewer arrests than usual of ambitious tipplers, "car-cowboys," women of ill repute, and the like.[47]

Ossenberg found that there was little cross-class interaction (at least in the bars), and that the middle class seemed to participate the most in the permissible norm-violating, role-reversing behavior, which occurs on the first ("green light day") and last ("last chance") nights. They most frequently wore the elaborate cowboy costumes and engaged in noisy, spontaneous, verbal and physical behavior emphasizing masculinity, aggression, and drinking. He suggests that such festivals may reflect social class structure but do not function to reinforce social solidarity of members of different social class status groups.

In one of Mitchell's earlier studies in urban central Africa, he focused on a ceremonial event, the Kalela Dance, and its functions in the city. The dance groups were organized on the basis of tribal identity. The basic organizing principle in the city was race. Africans and Europeans were regarded as basic groups. The opposition to Europeans mitigated against the division of the African into tribal or ethnic subunits. It is only during this ceremonial activity that tribal identities come to the fore.[48]

If one looks at the American urban scene, there is one major festival—Halloween—that could illuminate many of the ways in which the urban setting influences the particular activities involved in the festival and the way in which the festival brings together various groups of people.

The history of the festival of Halloween in the West is very complex, involving elements drawn from ancient Druid ceremonies and notions of witchcraft. The Catholic Church eventually converted these elements into a hallowed All Saints' Day. In early United States history, Halloween was apparently a time for displaying hostility toward deviant or unfriendly neighbors. It was thus a permissive context for social control mechanisms. In rural areas, where it was most pervasive, mischief included putting cows in the church belfry and dismantling fences to block roads.

Now an urban festival, the city has transformed the event and its functions. The use of costumes allows for a breakdown of social status and the possibility of role reversal. Males dress as females, elite in-

---

[47] R. Ossenberg, "Social Class and Bar Behavior During an Urban Festival," *Human Organization*, 28 (1969), 30.
[48] Clyde Mitchell, *The Kalela Dance: Aspects of Social Relationships Among Urban Africans in Northern Rhodesia* (Manchester: Manchester University Press, 1956).

dividuals become tramps, and lower income individuals wear costumes of royalty. In addition, people assume supernatural attire or become romantic folk heroes (pirates, gypsies, Batman, Superman).

The impact of an urban setting on the event has not yet been analyzed ethnographically. In many urban settings, the actual event involves younger children, who may be accompanied by their parents. There is a real incidence of stranger-stranger interaction at the boundary of the private domain. The right to privacy is abrogated for one night, and callers have their only visual access to the inside of the homes of their "stranger" neighbors. The existence of high-rise apartment residences has affected patterns of movement. A child accompanied by parents may roam a single building, which is perceived as safe and less unknown. Perceived dangers in the city discourage children from going out at night. These factors eliminate the romanticism but preserve the neighbor interaction. Even though the festival is foreign to migrants, many groups adopt it as an aspect of "American life." Thus, the Spanish language radio station in Philadelphia frequently talks about "El Trick y Treat."

Not only has the urban environment itself had an impact upon the festival, but the larger urban industrial society has totally changed Halloween through commercialization. Costume fads are created by the commercial costume industry. The candy and gum industry maintain and protect the festival. The festival has also taken on the symbols of a harvest festival, with the purchase of pumpkins, gourds, and Indian corn; the decoration of homes with a harvest motif; and the use of apples and apple cider, both natural autumn foods. Ethnographic analysis could draw out the full implications of the effect of city life on the festival and the functions of the festival for the city.[49]

Besides regular urban festivals, spontaneous events organized through the media frequently occur in the city. (For a description of such "happenings," see Chapter 3.) An example of an event shaped by the media was the celebration of a "birthday party" for a bridge linking Philadelphia with part of its surrounding metropolitan area in southern New Jersey. In this particular case, a radio personality suggested that it would be a nice idea for members of his listening audience to celebrate this event by congregating at the bridge at a particular time on the thirty-ninth birthday of the opening of the bridge. The fact that he was going to appear at this event and lead the participants in the singing of "Happy Birthday" drew a large audience. Observations during the event and a subsequent follow-up study (which included responses from one

[49] Much of this discussion is based upon a summary paper delivered by Eugene Cohen to the Department of Sociology and Anthropology, Bernard M. Baruch College, CUNY, 1975.

hundred participants and an interview with the event's originator) produced a number of interesting points.

This bridge had a particular image for many who used it or saw it as a basic landmark in their cognitive spatial map. Since the time of its opening, it had maintained a nickel toll, and on Christmas and New Year's Day, the toll was not collected. Many of those interviewed described the bridge as "friendly," "homey," like "small-time" people. They contrasted this bridge to two newer bridges that span the Delaware, viewing the others as "big-time," "unfriendly," and "imposing."

The analysis of the data collected suggests that for many participants the event itself was a form of protest against larger political and social institutions over which they had no control. Another immediate outcome was that people broke through barriers between strangers while participating in the event.[50]

STRUCTURAL FORMATION

Many *recurring* temporal events result in the crystallization of structures for the continuous integration of segments of the urban population. They thus become urban junctures in the *structural* as well as *situational* sense. This process can be seen in the area of political events. Elections and events such as boycotts and strikes lead to the emergence of structural elements that persist beyond the particular events involved. The effectiveness of the action is frequently a consequence of the degree of organization, and thus the structure is often more important than the event.

In Mayer's analysis of urban Indian politics, he observes that those running for electoral office mobilize *action sets,* or temporary coalitions centered around themselves. The action set attempts to recruit from all urban segments by using various events, issues, and symbols. Ethnicity, primarily defined in caste terms, is an important element, but no single group is strong enough to place its own members in office. Therefore, it is necessary to amalgamate various segments for support.[51] This contrasts with Lynch's work where one caste (the Jatavs in Agra) was a large enough group to elect representatives to the city council and the state legislature.[52]

[50] Edwin Eames and Howard Robboy, "Frustration and Indirect Aggression: Healthy Response in a Sick Society," *International Journal of Social Psychiatry,* 17 (1971), 217-24.
[51] A. Mayer, "The Significance of Quasi-Groups in the Study of Complex Societies," in Banton (ed.), *The Social Anthropology of Complex Societies,* pp. 97-122.
[52] O. Lynch, *The Politics of Untouchability* (New York: Columbia University Press, 1969).

In the election studied by Mayer in Dewas City, Madhya Pradesh, the relationship between the existing political structure, the Congress Party, and the particular action set (candidate-centered network) is a complex one. The party employs full-time workers, who recruit unpaid volunteer workers, and both sets work on the diverse caste segments of the population in order to elect their candidate. The candidate mobilizes his own personal contacts in addition to those developed for him by the party workers. Mayer sees the action set as a goal-oriented, bounded social unit that is focused upon a particular situation. One interesting example of the process was the attempt to gain the electoral support of a low caste group. A party worker of high caste was able to garner their support by validating their claim to higher status within the caste hierarchy. This was done through his willingness to dine with members of the group.

Barnett also provides an example of the potential of the political process for the integration of separate components. In this instance, the president of a relatively high caste interacted with and even dined with lower caste individuals as a necessary aspect of his political role. One of the members of his caste felt that he had broken caste norms and was impure, and he snubbed the president by not inviting him to a wedding dinner in his family. Other powerful members of the group applied pressure and an invitation was issued. The caste leaders recognized the fact that traditional notions of caste purity cannot survive in the urban system, where intergroup integration is necessary.[53]

This theme of urban integration through political organization is central to A. L. Epstein's analysis of urban life in Luanshya (in present-day Zambia). Epstein sees the creation of a local branch of the African National Congress as a real move toward urban integration that crosscuts tribal and occupational lines. A previous attempt at integration was the federation of tribal and urban welfare associations concerned with the betterment of African urban life. At the time of Epstein's study, the area was under the colonial domination of the British, and the development of both the Welfare Association and the African National Congress were attempts to gain collective power for the Africans. In the development of the African National Congress, there were obvious points of conflict between this organization and the existing trade unions, particularly the mine workers. The mine workers were forced to live in one African location, while all other Africans lived in another.

Epstein looked at the process of formation of a local branch of the party by analyzing a sequence of events. At its inception, the branch was established by an individual as a power base to challenge other urban

---

[53] Steve Barnett, "Urban Is As Urban Does."

"big men." Much of his original support was derived from street vendors, who saw the party as a vehicle to protect their own interests. They were discriminated against in favor of British and East Indian commercial interests.

Epstein shows how a series of political issues and their related events led to a rise and fall of certain political leaders and to changes in the political organization of the town. He also points out that the local processes affected national issues and how they were manifested and changed at the local level. His particular concern was with the events surrounding a national party-sponsored butcher boycott and how this was manipulated by local occupational groups and competing aspiring political leaders. The event solidified the local African National Congress branch.[54]

By the time Harries-Jones restudied the same community, the African National Congress had become the dominant party in the nation and its organization into localized sections was a dominant feature of local political life. Tremendous pressure was brought on residents to attend monthly meetings of the party. The section leader had acquired a great deal of power based upon his connections with various governmental agencies. Only one ethnic group was not integrated by the party. These were the Malawians, or people from the neighboring nation-state of Malawi, who were not part of the local party section and had their own political organization.[55]

Much of the current discussion of urban politics concerns the formation of interest groups and the coalition of these interest groups into higher order groups (parties). What we have been describing above for India and Africa pertains to such coalitions. Structures that are intergroup junctures—whether they derive from political events or from other events—can be regarded as interest coalitions when they are used to serve the common interests and goals of diverse segments of the population. The ways in which segments come to recognize common goals and maintain their coalitions are matters for urban ethnographic research. The ethnographer, with his concern for context, meaning, and primary network ties, is able to look at this process from a different perspective than the political scientist, who looks at formal government operations, formal party organizations, and their interactions.

One of the basic points in Leeds' analysis of Carnival is that this temporal event leads to structures (dance groups and sponsors) that link diverse class elements into coalitions that can ultimately be used in the political arena. Mutual advantages accrue to both the lower class

[54] Epstein, *Politics in an Urban African Community*, p. 19.
[55] P. Harries-Jones, " 'Home-Boy' Ties and Political Organization in a Copperbelt Township," in Mitchell (ed.), *Social Networks in Urban Situations*.

groups—who receive economic support—and the elites—who receive political support. The common focus for this coalescence is the desire of each group and its sponsor to win in the festival competition.[56]

An interesting example of the way in which sports can sometimes lead to structures that amalgamate urban populations is contained in Lever's analysis of soccer in Brazil. Lever notes that sports clubs have been developed in order to support soccer teams in Brazilian cities. In Rio, these clubs tend to be class-exclusive, while in the smaller city of Chatuli, these clubs recruit members from the entire class spectrum. In Rio, some sports clubs are socially exclusive, and individuals not only must have the economic resources for fees, but must also pass a rigorous screening for new members. Lever cites one individual member of an exclusive sports club who states that his favorite soccer team is sponsored by a middle class club and therefore not suitable for his status. There are other clubs in Rio that have completely open membership and are struggling for survival.

Soccer, when first introduced to Brazil by the British, was exclusively upper class. Over time, it was adopted by all segments of the population, and present-day professionals are almost exclusively recruited from poor segments of the rural and urban populations. The teams, however, are located in urban centers and professionals must live there. In Rio, social distance is maintained between the players and the elite members of the clubs. In the small city, there is much more interaction between the two.

Another level of integration can be seen in the recruitment of players. Wealthier clubs in the big cities recruit players from teams in smaller cities. This process of recruitment works to the mutual advantage of both clubs, since the smaller city clubs are well compensated for the loss of their players.

Some clubs have an ethnic base, such as the German club. Another basis for club formation is occupation. For instance, Lever notes that in the small city, the railway company started its own club to build morale among its workers. Players are offered part-time jobs in the rail system. Cross-class club membership exists, since management as well as workers belong.

In Brazil, the structure formed by sports activities is integrative in the smaller cities, but helps maintain class boundaries in Rio. Unlike the United States, with its diversified sports scene, in Brazil, soccer is the only major sport. The high degree of commitment to that sport serves a national integrative function, but the lack of single hometown teams or broad-based clubs precludes much integration at lower levels.[57]

[56] Leeds, "Housing Settlement Types."
[57] Lever, "Soccer as a Brazilian Way of Life."

Reina noted for Paraná, Argentina, that many of the older generation European migrants developed associations based on national origin.
However, the successful children of these migrants are now members of
multi-ethnic civic associations.[58]

Obviously, there are many other voluntary associations that focus
upon recreational or leisure-time pursuits that have the potential to
integrate segments of the population around a common hobby or skill.
Unfortunately, ethnographic studies are lacking of organizations of ama-
teur dog breeders, sky divers, motorcyclists—or practitioners of any
hobby that requires a high level of time, money, and commitment. We
do not know to what extent these activities are organized on an ethnic
or class basis or to what degree they bring together diverse groups.

Whiteford, in his data on church sodalities in two Latin American
cities, shows that such groups are often class exclusive, even when attached to the same church or saint. When not exclusive, they relegate
lower class members to menial roles and limit their interaction with
others.[59]

Wheeldon described a civic association oriented toward building,
maintaining, and allocating recreational facilities for the Coloured
(mixed racial) community in a South African city. While the association
was largely for the achievement of goals for Coloureds, Wheeldon shows
how white members were recruited and made leaders when resources,
influence, and patronage were needed, after which they were disengaged
from involvement. He also shows how the co-participation of whites and
Coloureds led to the exacerbation of negative stereotypes on the part of
whites about the Coloured community rather than adding to cohesion
and mutual understanding.[60]

NETWORKS AS LINKING MECHANISMS

One major concept that has emerged in recent theoretical literature
in urban anthropology and urban studies is that cities may ultimately be
viewed as *networks of networks*. This theme has been emphasized by
Mitchell, and the volume he edited, *Social Networks in Urban Situations*,[61] is an attempt to move in this direction. The personal centered

[58] Ruben Reina, *Paraná: Social Boundaries in an Argentine City* (Austin: University
of Texas Press, 1973).
[59] Andrew Whiteford, *Two Cities in Latin America* (Garden City: Doubleday &
Company, Inc., 1964).
[60] P. D. Wheeldon, "The Operation of Voluntary Associations and Personal Networks
in the Political Process of an Inter-Ethnic Community," in J. Clyde Mitchell (ed.),
Social Networks, pp. 128-80.
[61] Mitchell (ed.), *Social Networks in Urban Situations*.

social network of an individual is the lowest level of this scheme. At their outer, most extended ramifications, individual networks become meshed together. Brokers and strategic influentials, who are members of many networks, serve as linkage points.

Craven and Wellman, in their article "The Network City," make a similar point. Based on extensive network studies in Toronto, they show that working from lower level, individual networks, one can build successively wider nets of relationships using brokers as pivotal links. As the structure ramifies, groups and institutions become the nodes and linkage points in the diagramatic scheme. The ultimate model is one of articulated personal networks meshed together to form more formal groups and institutions and ultimately the entire urban structure.[62]

In our earlier discussion of networks (Chapter 4), we indicated that the study of brokers and influentials and their various network ties would be an important focus for ethnographic research, that could serve to illuminate the structure, functions, and types of social ties as basic integrative mechanisms. Detailed descriptions of their social ties and how they are manipulated to bridge gaps between groups and institutions would appear to be an important focus for future urban ethnographic research.

The City as a Whole

The ultimate description of the unit of integration in an urban center is the city as a whole. Many urban anthropologists take "holism" to mean the necessity of studying the whole city as an ethnographic target population. However, it is virtually impossible to study a whole city using the ethnographic method. The "team of anthropologists" approach, such as that used in Price's study of Reno, makes the goal more approachable, but the size of the team required for a metropolis is unrealistic.[63] As we pointed out in Chapter 3, the city as a whole as an object of study is not necessary to preserve the essence of holism. What is required is that any micro-unit be studied with the whole city systematically used as a context. Nevertheless, there have been several attempts at ethnographic studies of whole cities as more than the sum of their parts.

The classic early study of a city as a whole was Horace Miner's study of Timbuctoo. This description of a town of 6,000 was less a study

[62] P. Craven and B. Wellman, "The Network City," Sociological Inquiry, vol. 43, 1973.
[63] John A. Price, "Reno, Nevada: The City as a Unit of Study," Urban Anthropology, 1 (1972), 14-28.

of the urban center than it was an attempt to test aspects of Redfield's folk-urban continuum. This early study emphasized ethnography and intensive interviewing, and it was oriented to tribal groups as major components and the market as a juncture.[64]

In Gulick's study of Tripoli, Lebanon, he stated that he knew one ethnic enclave best since he was ethnographically familiar with it. He saw the rest of the city largely from the point of view of this group. He noted that the lack of available statistical data for the city forced him to collect much aggregate survey data himself, which was very time-consuming. Gulick did examine some of the economic and political relationships of this city to its larger context.[65]

Whiteford's work, which compares two cities in Latin America, does take the very different economic contexts of both cities into account as he compares their class structures. For Whiteford, class groups are the major components studied and are presented as having distinct lifestyles. The data was collected largely through ethnography. He deals with the interclass relationships of the city as well. Whiteford deliberately selected two relatively small cities and suggests the impossibility of this kind of analysis for large metropolitan centers.[66]

A number of studies that look at whole cities are concerned with the issue of change, primarily movement toward the Western model. Thus Geertz' comparison of two Indonesian towns is primarily concerned with the effect of differences in history, power relations, and cultural components on the rate and direction of change in the two towns. This is an extremely important book, emphasizing economic activities and economic institutions, and provides insight into how to use urban historical process as context.[67]

Another example of a study of Westernization is the study of "Caneville" by van den Berghe. Describing conditions in a small South African town, he discusses the relevant economic and political contexts at the national level. He uses ethnographic data primarily to describe the three racial/ethnic components (whites, Indians, and Africans) and the social classes. He also describes the economic and political institutions that bring them together. It must be noted that the population of this community is only 10,000, and the question is raised about the possibility of transposing this approach to larger metropolitan centers.[68]

[64] Miner, *The Primitive City of Timbuctoo.*
[65] John Gulick, *Tripoli: A City in Modern Africa* (Cambridge: Harvard University Press, 1967).
[66] Whiteford, *Two Cities in Latin America.*
[67] Geertz, *Peddlers and Princes.*
[68] Pierre van den Berghe, *Caneville: The Social Structure of a South African Town* (Middletown: Wesleyan University Press, 1964).

Banton's study of Freetown, Sierra Leone is based predominantly on surveys and describes the immigration of new tribal groups within a historical context. These newcomers had to adapt to a city controlled by Creoles (ex-Negro slaves), whose culture was greatly Anglicized. When he focuses on the migrants' adaptive modification of social institutions (tribal headman, tribal associations and households) he bases his conclusions on some intensive interviews.[69]

Reina's recent study of Paraná, Argentina, a city of 100,000, is the most ambitious attempt to study a whole city. The book contains both context and in-depth ethnography reflecting natives' viewpoints and meaning. Neighborhoods, voluntary associations, social classes, and life cycle stages are presented, with several intensively studied examples. We see how components are linked together to produce a unique city. This book is different from those previously mentioned because the size of the community is larger than most, and the range of types of components studied is broader than most.[70]

We must also mention here two strong advocates of the whole city approach—Fox and Price. Their studies of cities as wholes were discussed in Chapter 3. In these studies, the city is studied only in relation to its context and not through ethnography. Fox uses primarily historical, economic, and political data. Price's study of Reno included selected small-group ethnography, but his study of Tijuana and Tecate, Mexico was based primarily on survey data. Price directed a large team of students who did ethnographic research in selected neighborhoods and institutions, but the ethnographic data is not significant in the presentation. We learn much about the city as a product of dynamic interaction with its context, but little about its basic components and their interrelationships, as described in Chapters 4, 5, and 6.[71]

It should be noted that many of those who have created the mystique of studying the "city as a whole" must work within severe constraints. They must sacrifice ethnography or limit their choice of cities. The feasibility of the whole city as an ethnographic target population seems to depend on severe size limitations. Only a limited number of types of components can be studied. Within urban anthropology there is scope for both those who are concerned with the ethnography of

[69] M. Banton, *West African City: A Study of Tribal Life in Freetown* (London: Oxford University Press, 1957).

[70] R. Reina, *Paraná: Social Boundaries in an Argentine City.*

[71] R. Fox, "Rationale and Romance in Urban Anthropology," *Urban Anthropology,* 1 (1972), 205-33; and *Cities in Their Cultural Settings: The Anthropology of Urbanism* (Englewood Cliffs, New Jersey: Prentice-Hall, 1977); and J. Price, "Reno, Nevada: The City as a Unit of Study," *Urban Anthropology,* 1 (1972), 14-28.

internal micro-units, as well as those who are concerned with the whole city and its context as the system in which the micro-unit is embedded (that is, anthropology *in* cities as well as anthropology *of* cities).

RURAL-URBAN LINKAGES

In this chapter and in the two previous chapters dealing with urban ethnography, we selected social units in their urban setting. At this point, however, we would like to broaden our social field to include the rural as well as the urban setting. As before, we are concerned with those elements of the social field that are amenable to ethnographic research.

Rural and urban segments are obviously linked together in regional and national social, political, and economic institutions. However, these large-scale linkages are generally beyond the range of ethnography. What, in fact, becomes relevant is the linkage of rural and urban social fields through individuals (primarily migrants) and collectivities of migrants. Much of the literature emphasizes the degree to which rural ties are maintained by migrant populations.

The most commonly described relationships between rural and urban social fields emphasize continued social interaction between the two through patterns of visiting. Visiting may be for a specific purpose—such as participation in life cycle events, crisis events, or arrangement of marriages—or it may be tied to time and space variables. During vacation times, visits to the village of origin may be common; when the village of origin is nearby, casual visiting may be frequent. One of the most frequent reasons for planned visits is village calendrical ceremonies. In cases where male migration is the pattern, the men return to the rural areas for the selection of wives. In some cases, rural segments of a larger kinship unit send children to kin in the city for education or skill training and receive urban children for periods of time.

There are a number of ways in which the migrant has an impact on the economy of the village. One of the most frequent economic linkages is the pattern of monetary remittances sent back to the rural area. Frequently migrants retain property rights in the village or inherit property after they leave. Sometimes food produced in the village is collected periodically by urban visitors. Visiting frequently involves bringing gifts from the city, thus introducing urban items to the community. Collectivities of migrants in the city will frequently raise funds for rural development. Many urban entrepreneurs are migrants who use their home areas as sources of trade commodities, markets for their urban items, or labor for their enterprises.

There are a number of ways in which migrants enhance the political status or the community infrastructure of their homeland. Where they acquire political influence within the urban setting, either as individuals or collectivities, they use this power to establish their villages as regional capitals or parts of economic development schemes, or to acquire facilities like schools or roads for the area. In many cases, political activity is geared to developing the homeland rather than effecting changes in the urban setting.

Simic noted considerable rural-urban integration in Yugoslavia in his study of migrants in Belgrade. These individuals frequently visited their village of origin to participate in village-wide rituals and familial life cycle rituals. The central thesis of his work is that the rural and urban settings should not be looked at separately but as a single integrated social field.[72]

In the Central African urban literature, there are specific mechanisms noted for the maintenance of rural-urban ties. Both Harries-Jones and Epstein note that a number of tribal groups had official representatives of the tribe in the city who were designated by the rural tribal chief. These individuals were central mediating figures for members of the tribal group residing in the city. They were contacted whenever one went back to the homeland, so that goods and information flowed through this central person in the city.[73]

The Guraje in Shack's work in Addis Ababa maintain extremely strong ties with the homeland. Influential individuals from the rural areas visit tribal members in the city to collect money for schools and for economic development in the countryside. Many urban businessmen borrow capital from fellow kin-group members in the countryside. A common African pattern of the construction of retirement houses in the rural areas was characteristic of the Guraje. Urban-based marriage brokers arrange marriages between urban men and tribal women.[74]

In an early study of rural-urban migration in India, Eames noted the emphasis upon the maintenance of rural ties by urban migrants. Migrants were expected to send back a high proportion of their earnings to support the village family. The migrants were primarily males who left their wives and children to be cared for by members of the joint family. It is suggested that rural-urban migration helped maintain the continuity of large, joint families in the rural sector, and that when migrants returned to the village permanently, their joint families tended

[72] A. Simic, "The Best of Two Worlds: Serbian Peasants in the City," in Foster and Kemper (eds.), *Anthropologists in Cities*, pp. 179-200.
[73] Epstein, *Politics in an Urban African Community*, p. 19; and Harries-Jones, " 'Home-Boy' Ties and Political Organization."
[74] W. A. Shack, "Urban Ethnicity and the Cultural Process of Urbanization in Ethiopia," in A. Southall (ed.), *Urban Anthropology* (New York: Oxford University Press, 1973), pp. 251-86.

to be more stable than those of non-migrants. Some families in the village were able to become major land owners as a result of remittances. Those who migrated long distances to Bombay and Calcutta visited only once a year during the annual festival of Dashara. Males in Benares (Varanasi) (twenty-five miles away) came once a week, and those in cities several hundred miles away came home once a month. There was much circular migration, in which an individual spent several months in the city and several months in the village.[75] Singer noted that even successful large-scale entrepreneurs in urban India maintained village ties through patterns of visiting and economic aid.[76]

An interesting example of a rural community almost entirely dependent on remittances from migrants is the Hong Kong community studied by Watson. Young men who are employed in the restaurant industry in London send much of their earnings back to support families there. Even when individuals save to start their own business in London, the profits are funnelled off to the village. These migrants are committed to returning to the village and see their support as an investment in the future. Despite the distance between London and Hong Kong, visiting occurs on a regular and sometimes frequent basis.[77]

Doughty, in several well-known analyses of migrants' associations in Lima, Peru, has noted that these associations become very large and regional in scale, and have as their primary goal the support of the economic and political aspirations of the rural areas:

Lobbying in government offices and congress on behalf of the hometown is an important activity which is mentioned often. The amount of energy expended in this activity is incalculable. Congressmen and bureaucrats are wined and dined, invited to club fiestas, presented with awards, confronted with petitions, and invited to make pilgrimages to the remote provincial homeland. Many of these activities are coordinated by committees comprised not only of emigrants but also of the officials from the hometown itself, who make periodic trips to Lima to check upon the advances made by the club or to inform the club members about the progress in the terruño on some specific problem. Prominent here, particularly with the registered *Comunidades Campesinas,* are attempts to settle land disputes with haciendas, litigation in which emigrants often

[75] E. Eames, "Some Aspects of Rural Migration from a North Indian Village," *Eastern Anthropologist,* 7 (1953), 13-26.
[76] M. Singer, "The Indian Joint Family in Modern Industry," in Milton Singer and Bernard S. Cohen (eds.), *Structure and Change in Indian Society* (Chicago: Aldine Publishing Company, 1968).
[77] James Watson, "Restaurants and Remittances: Chinese Emigrant Workers in London," in G. Foster and R. Kemper (eds.), *Anthropologists in Cities,* pp. 201-22.

play major roles. Indeed, migrants and their organizations have played important if not key roles in achieving legal status and recognition for many of these communities. It is not surprising in light of this to discover that many clubs think of themselves as "defenders" of their homelands and often include this word in the name of the club.[78]

Buechler finds the same phenomenon in La Paz, Bolivia, suggesting wide Andean distribution. In this case, migrant associations lobby for schools and higher-level political status for home communities rather than regions. Buechler also notes the importance of the rural fiesta cycle for visiting, social interaction, and economic contributions to the village.[79]

For West African tribal groups, Little has noted the extensive development of urban-based voluntary associations that concern themselves with the enhancement of the rural area. Meetings are essentially fund-raising in nature and collect a great amount of money for schools and community projects.[80]

A similar function has been noted for urban-based caste associations by many students of Indian urban life. Barnett notes the building of a caste hostel in Madras that housed university students from all over the state (rural and urban) who attended college in the city. As a result of living in the hostel, recent leaders of the group form an age-based peer group and maintain a commonality of interest.[81] Srnivas and Gould have also analyzed this phenomenon.

Almost all the examples provided above deal with case studies of single areas. However, there are some explicitly comparative works that tend to temper the view that migrants always serve as links of integration for the rural and urban social fields.

Mayer, in his early classic work on migrants in a South African city, describes in detail the varied adaptations of different groups in the city. For one group, the maintenance of strong and continuous contact with their home villages led to the maintenance of a conservative enclave in the city. The relevant social field for these individuals was an inte-

---

[78] P. Doughty, "Behind the Back of the City: Provincial Life in Lima, Peru," in W. Mangin (ed.), *Peasants in Cities*, pp. 30-46; and "Peruvian Migrant Identity in the Urban Milieu," in Weaver and White (eds.), *The Anthropology of Urban Environments*, pp. 39-50.

[79] Hans Buechler, "The Ritual Dimension of Rural-Urban Networks"; and "The Reorganization of Counties in the Bolivian Highlands: An Analysis of Rural-Urban Networks and Hierarchies," in Eddy (ed.), *Urban Anthropology* (Athens: University of Georgia Press, 1968), pp. 48-57.

[80] Kenneth Little, *West African Urbanization: A Study of Voluntary Associations in Social Change* (Cambridge: Cambridge University Press, 1965).

[81] Steve Barnett, "Urban Is As Urban Does."

grated rural-urban field. For others, the homeland ceased to be relevant. Social status in the city was closely related to these different orientations.[82]

An even wider comparative perspective is found in Roberts' work in which he compares Guatemala and Peru. Roberts notes that in Peru urban migration is an extension of provincial economic and political strategies, and that economic interaction persists both in formal commerce and informal exchanges between migrants and the region. Similarly, the political goals and strategies of both migrants and provincials remain the same. Urban progress benefits the countryside. By contrast, in Guatemala out-migration is a last resort and leads to the severance of ties with the homeland. Roberts sees this difference as having significant social consequences for the city social systems themselves. In Guatemala City, migrants are cut off from an integrated rural-urban field and can develop only short-term, palliative coping responses. In Lima, the very structure of the city is affected by the formal and informal networks and associations, which reflect the integrated rural and urban social fields.[83]

Perhaps the most extreme position in relation to rural-urban ties is found in Plotnicov's study of migrants in Jos, Nigeria. He suggests that many of the migrants were effectively cut off from their tribal areas of origin. In the analysis, Plotnicov suggests that many in the rural areas believe the migrants do not support them to the extent they should. They suspect that migrants are using their incomes to enhance their own lifestyles in the cities. On the other hand, many migrants indicate that they are afraid to return to the rural areas, despite the fact that they have heavily invested in them.[84]

In addition to the issue of maintenance of rural-urban contacts through migrants, there is an issue related to the time depth of such ties. Many writers point out that long-term urban residents do not rupture ties. Doughty notes that regional associations in Lima have retained their commitment for thirty or forty years. Eames and Rowe note that migrants from a village in India have maintained their visiting patterns and commitment to the village over long periods of time.

The question is what will happen after several generations, since most studies look only at the first generation. In Stack's study of a rurally based kinship network, she does note the persistence of ties

[82] Philip Mayer, *Townsman or Tribesman: Conservativism and the Process of Urbanization in a South African City* (Capetown: Oxford University Press, 1961).
[83] Bryan Roberts, "The Interrelationships of City and Provinces in Peru and Guatemala," in Cornelius and Trueblood (eds.), *Latin American Urban Research*, pp. 207-36.
[84] L. Plotnicov, "Nigerians: The Dream is Unfulfilled," in W. Mangin (ed.), *Peasants in Cities*, pp. 170-74.

between urbanities and rural areas over several generations.[85] We need more studies that look at succeeding generations. However, even more important are studies that explain why ties persist in some circumstances but not in others.

There is another tactic that can be used in the study of rural-urban integration. We have thus far focused on the *migrant* as linkage. A major concern in the anthropology of complex societies focuses on *institutions* that serve to link regional and national systems particularly through economic and political activities. Thus markets, political parties, and ritual cycles, which cross-cut urban and rural components, are taken as units of analysis.

For example, the work of Bailey and his students in India focuses on political parties and their levels of integration. Beginning with village-level parties, they build to form state-level and national-level hierarchies, so that integration of a high order exists within one subsystem of the society—the political system—which contains both rural and urban components.[86]

Buechler has advocated that the best way to study Bolivia is by looking at political, ritual (fiesta cycle), and economic (markets) subsystems as they link rural and urban centers. He has studied all three subsystems, using ethnographic data from rural villages, towns, and La Paz itself to demonstrate the ways in which such subsystems unify the social fields.[87]

Another example of an institutional component that can be viewed as a subsystem of the total society is the judicial process. This point can be seen in Epstein's analysis of urban African courts. The judges in the urban court are representatives of tribal groups appointed by tribal chiefs in the rural area. Following Gluckman's analysis of judicial decisions, Epstein suggests that the urban courts have developed a general consensus of what constitutes a "reasonable man," and that the rural (tribal)-urban social systems are unified by this mechanism. Lowy found that the court system in Ghana was a unified and undifferentiated rural-urban social field. He expected differences between rural and urban courts, but did not find them.[88]

Studies of subsystems that unify rural and urban areas and lead to hierarchical integration into regional and national entities fall squarely

[85] C. Stack, "The Kindred of Viola Jackson," in N. Whitten and J. Szwed (eds.), *Afro-American Anthropology* (New York: Free Press, 1970), pp. 303-12.

[86] F. Bailey, *Politics and Social Change* (Berkeley: University of California Press, 1959).

[87] Buechler, "The Ritual Dimension of Rural-Urban Networks" and "The Reorganization of Counties in the Bolivian Highlands."

[88] Epstein, *Politics in an Urban African Community;* Lowy, "Me-Ko Court."

under the aegis of the anthropology of complex society. Many see this endeavor as the core of future anthropology and reject the notion of an "anthropology of cities." For them, the city is not unique, but merely a part of the system or subsystem which should be studied. We have already discussed this issue in Chapter 2. In Part III, our emphasis has been on the ethnographic studies that constitute "anthropology in cities" and "anthropology of cities." In the next chapter, we shall emphasize the importance of more emphasis on the latter.

It is our position that the city can, for analytic purposes, be viewed as a separate segment of the social system. Like every other segment of a system, the larger context that impinges on the segment must still be considered. While it is possible to isolate the segment for analysis, this is useful only if it is linked to its context. Those who focus upon institutional subsystems face the same reality. They may look at economic and political institutions, which crosscut both urban and rural areas, but they need to look at the total system context as well. Moreover, just as the student of city life can learn from the student of the political subsystem, the latter can learn from the former. The city is a system whose unique characteristics have a synergistic effect on the whole and the institutionalized subsystems. The reality, which all social scientists hope to grasp, is the *totality* of a sociocultural system. To attain this, several alternative approaches can be used; but none give the full view of social reality. If there were such an approach, we would all become converts.

SUMMARY

In addition to the bounded social units we have been discussing in Chapters 4 and 5, there are a number of social settings that serve to bring together various segments of the urban population. Some of these settings bring together individuals, while others bring together groups; some are transitory, while others are recurrent and develop permanent structures; some involve large numbers, while others involve a few individuals; and some involve people as spectators, while others involve them as participants. This aspect of urban ethnography has not been as heavily emphasized in the literature as those described in the preceding two chapters.

Social situations that act as urban junctures have been divided into two major categories: spatially localized (space) and temporally localized (time).

Among the spatially localized public places, we discussed bars and restaurants, markets, courts, service institutions, and transportation linkage points. Anthropologists have been particularly partial to bar studies, since such public places provide an easy entree for the anthropologist, as well as access to a wide range of information. However, not all bars (or their equivalents in other cultural settings) serve as points of contact between different segments of the urban population. Markets have also been selected by some urban ethnographers as the setting within which to do research, and several studies have tried to delineate urban "bazaar" or market behavior. However, not enough attention has been paid to the different styles of market behavior, which characterize different segments of the urban population. The emphasis upon service institutions (schools, hospitals) has not been characteristic of an urban ethnographic approach, at least from the perspective of seeing such institutions as nodal points of interaction between diverse groups or individuals. On the other hand, courts have been viewed in this way with some interesting results, particularly from Africa.

Two types of temporal events have been written about by urban ethnographers. The major one is urban festivals. These events have been described in many urban settings and their integrative role has previously been noted. The second type, sports events, have not received as much attention but potentially provide a basis for urban ethnographic research that may tell us a great deal about the way in which various elements of the urban population relate to each other.

Spatially localized social situations tend to be recurrent and develop permanent structures, as do many temporal events. Urban festivals tend to be cyclical and repetitive and require high degrees of organization for their success. Frequently diverse populations are needed as both participants and spectators in these events. Professional sports obviously require high degrees of structure for their maintenance and support, and such structures are characteristically found. Another set of events that require or lead to high degrees of structure are those that involve the political process. For the successful outcome of a political effort, formal or informal, structure is necessary to bring together the diverse elements of an urban population for common goals. This process works the other way as well; political events, such as strikes, may lead to the development of structure. One further element in the urban setting frequently related to structure is the existence of voluntary associations, which have a wide range of interest, constituents, and structures.

Some urban ethnographic literature attempts to develop a view of the entire city. Insights into the total integration of city systems have emerged from several of these studies. However, the difficulty of moving outward from an ethnographic base still plagues many of these efforts. In addition, they have usually been done in small urban centers. When urban anthropologists attempt to study entire cities, they are faced with

the necessity of taking into account the larger context of the entire social system. In many cases, they must look at large-scale (macroscopic)
historical, economic, political, and social forces, which impinge upon
the present condition of the target city.

Another form of integration links together the rural and urban
segments of the larger regional social system. Much of the urban
anthropological literature deals with migrants in the city, and as a result
the migrants and their organizations are viewed as linkages between
rural and urban sectors. Some analyses of rural-urban social fields have
been done.

Another variety of large-scale study has been pioneered by geographers who see cities as nested into a hierarchy of city and regional
networks. In this case, the network concept is used in a different way
from that used by the ethnographer of urban life. Such a notion has
been used by some anthropologists working in complex societies, particularly in the political sphere.

Part Four

WHAT TO DO AND
WHAT NOT TO DO

In the development of urban anthropology, there are a number of basic issues related to the process of doing research that will be dealt with in Chapters 7 and 8. Specifically, in Chapter 7, we shall deal with the development of explicit research designs that delineate independent and dependent variables; how to select a social unit to be studied and define it carefully; and how to recognize the difference between a social unit that is itself the object of study, as opposed to one that is the setting for studying another research problem.

An additional aspect of doing urban anthropological research that will be discussed in Chapter 7 is the transposition of ethnographic techniques from simple social systems to urban systems. Problems of locating oneself, contacting informants, establishing rapport, and the simple day-to-day problems of doing such research will be explored.

Still another aspect of doing urban anthropology concerns the issue of values and ethics. We shall include a discussion of reciprocity between anthropologists and informants, as well as the issues of the goals and potential misuses of research findings. A related subject to be discussed involves the protection of informants through concern over confidentiality and anonymity.

In Chapter 8, we shall look at an area of literature that is frequently treated as a core area of urban anthropology—the culture of poverty. Using material from earlier parts of this volume, particularly the discussion in Chapter 7, we shall attempt to show that this issue is not, in fact, central to urban anthropology and, in many ways, its overemphasis has misdirected urban anthropological research away from research foci that should be the core of the subfield.

7

Methods, Techniques, and Ethics

One of the basic issues in the emergence of urban anthropology is the degree to which methods based upon the study of small, tribal societies can be transposed to the study of large, complex urban social systems. By methodology we are not limiting ourselves to the simple techniques of data collection and analysis, but are including larger issues. There are four basic areas related to methodological issues that will form the core of this chapter. These are:

1. Precise definitions of research questions and tight research designs
2. Delineation of units to be studied
3. Logistics or the fieldwork enterprise in the city
4. Ethical and political implications of research.

RESEARCH DESIGN

In Chapter 2, we discussed the differences between anthropology *of* the city and anthropology *in* the city. Anthropology *of* the city consists of studies that explicitly take into account the urban context as either setting or problem. Anthropology *in* the city is the pursuit of traditional anthropological research in an urban setting, in which the impact of the urban is not an important factor. In the ensuing discussion of research design in urban anthropological studies, we shall confine ourselves to studies of anthropology *of* the city, since such studies form the core of urban anthropology.

We have previously distinguished conceptually the notions of *urban* and *urbanism*. In Chapter 3, we focused our attention on the urban in an attempt to discover the functional basis for the nature of cities as social institutions. As we have seen, most recent urban anthropological studies have been attempts to either delineate the nature of the urban or to examine urbanism (describing the effects of the city on smaller units in the city in terms of organization, values, and behavior).

A classic distinction is made in most scientific disciplines (in the formation of a hypothesis to be tested) between an *independent variable* and a *dependent variable*. The independent variable is the factor (or set of factors) that leads to a particular outcome—the dependent variable. The independent variable is the *affecting* component and the dependent variable is the *affected* component. This framework is extensively used in psychology and sociology. In many ways, this analytic device is artificial and oversimplifies a complex reality, in which feedback between both poles and the context in which the relationship takes place is ignored. For these reasons, many anthropologists avoid the development of designs that explicitly follow this format, since anthropology places so much emphasis on broader context, holism, and process. Anthropologists dislike the approach because it focuses on a narrow, specifically delineated variable. The ethnographic method is best for casting a wide net and seeing broad relationships, rather than narrowly defined variables. In spite of these inadequacies, however, we feel that the use of this analytical device can help us pinpoint and clarify some confusions in the literature and expedite more clearly focused future studies.

If we now turn back to the distinction between urban and urbanism, some general statements about ongoing research in urban anthropology can be made. Many studies, especially those discussed in Chapter 3, focus upon the urban (nature of the city) as the major dependent variable. Such studies attempt to obtain information about the form and function of the city by looking at the city as a product of either external forces or internal forces or a combination of the two. They ask such questions as: Under what external conditions do cities emerge? Does functional specialization produce urban similarities? What effect does changing function have on the city as an entity? How do the interactions between subunits in the city affect urban form and function? In all of these examples, the nature of the city is the dependent variable, and external or internal, historical or contemporary, political or economic processes form the independent variables. If we recall the work of Leeds and Fox cited in Chapter 3, we can see that the basic differences between Rio and São Paulo in terms of history and function are central independent variables affecting sexuality, carnival, and the nature of irregular communities. Fox uses the effect of the state on the city as the central independent variable affecting its form and organization.[1] Another research tactic is to use the city as independent variable and some subunit or area of behavior within the city as dependent variable. In effect, *urbanism* (or the consequence of urban form and function) is the dependent variable.

The basic problem is the lack of clear-cut distinctions between two types of studies. Some assume universal attributes of the urban, and then study the effects of these universal attributes. Others look at the particular set of attributes in a given urban context and try to determine their effects. Thus, a hypothetical article entitled "Tanzanian Migrant Adaptation in Wichita" could fall into either one of the two categories suggested. If the anthropologist were to focus upon the particular attributes of Wichita that led to Tanzanian migration and/or had a direct impact on adaptive strategies of the migrants, that would be using the attributes of a particular urban center or type of urban center. If, on the other hand, the article were to deal exclusively with Tanzanians and assume a generalized urban milieu or set of urban characteristics affecting the migration flow or adaptive strategies, that would be using "urban" as a universally defined independent variable. Most anthropologists would find studies of the universal type less significant in view of its overemphasis on the Western city as the standard for definition of the urban. As Rollwagen points out, most urban studies incorrectly assume that cities are sufficiently known and are sufficiently alike to serve as background for particular studies.[2]

Recent anthropological efforts have shifted away from general discussions of the nature of cities (The City) to specific discussions of particular cities. This shift can be seen in Redfield's own work. Following

[1] Anthony Leeds, "The Anthropology of Ctiies: Some Methodological Considerations," in Elizabeth Eddy (ed.), *Urban Anthropology* (Athens: University of Georgia Press, 1968), pp. 31-47; Richard Fox, "Rationale and Romance in Urban Anthropology," *Urban Anthropology*, 1 (1972), 205-33.
[2] Jack Rollwagen, "A Comparative Framework for the Investigation of the City-As-Context: A Discussion of the Mexican Case," *Urban Anthropology*, 1 (1972), 68-86.

Wirth in his earlier discussion of the folk-urban continuum, Redfield emphasized the general traits that distinguish the folk from the urban. In Redfield and Singer's later work on the cultural role of cities, they emphasized a typology of cities that can be illustrated by particular cities. Finally, in Singer's own work in Madras, he emphasized the uniqueness of the particular urban context and the changes this particular setting produced in religious life.

Between the extremes of a generalized model of urban social structure (a model which would include absolute or relative levels of such characteristics as size, density, heterogeneity, and specialization of spatial form and/or function) and the set of particular attributes of particular urban places, there exists a middle ground, which in many ways is more useful than the other two. This is the creation of a typology of cities. An attempt to develop such a typology of the varieties of urban form and function would involve focusing on the city as the dependent variable, to develop categories based upon similar external forces and internal components and their interactions. When we can derive an adequate typology, we will then be able to use urban *types* as the independent variables in the study of the effects of city type on organization and ways of life.

Tightening Research Design

The uneasiness with which many anthropologists treat research design is related to the early development of the ethnographic method. Most early ethnography had as its goal an open-ended description of the way of life of a particular group of people. There was little concern with specific hypotheses concerning the relationship between explicitly delineated variables. Margaret Mead, in her volume *Coming of Age in Samoa,* provides an example of the shift toward research problem centered ethnography.[3] The major thrust of her volume is to disprove the hypothesis that the onset of biological puberty resulted in adolescent role confusion and revolt. Before Mead's work, most social scientists assumed this hypothesis to be true. In her study of Samoan adolescent females, Mead demonstrated the invalidity of this assumption. The independent variable, biological puberty, did not produce role confusion and revolt (dependent variable).

In many ways, Mead's effort is part of a tradition in anthropology that might be called "myth debunking." There are many assumptions made by western social scientists about human nature that anthropologists refuted through comparative fieldwork.

[3] Margaret Mead, *Coming of Age in Samoa: A Psychological Study of Primitive Youth for Western Cilivization,* Revised edition (New York: William Morrow and Company, 1930).

A further methodological development is the explicit use of controlled comparisons. As we noted in Chapter 1, the notion of comparison has been part of an anthropological approach from its inception; however, until recently, the group being studied was implicitly compared with the culture of the anthropologist. In Mead's study of Samoa, this comparison was made an explicit part of the myth debunking process.

Subsequently, the explicit comparison of tribal societies with one another began to emerge. Once again we can illustrate this shift by looking at another study by Mead. In *Sex and Temperament,* she attempted to describe the variation in sex roles within three different tribes in New Guinea. In this study, three different patterns of male-female role relationships are described and each pattern is linked to the contextual pattern of the tribe.[4]

As a research design, explicit controlled comparisons are more sophisticated and lead more directly to an understanding of patterns of variation within the human species than does the case study approach or implicit Western comparison. However, single ethnographers trying to do controlled comparisons would be greatly hampered by time and money limitations. Thus, the case study in a single tribe or peasant village remains the mode.

The use of controlled comparisons, where rural and urban communities are used, can throw some light upon an issue raised earlier—the degree to which there is discontinuity between urban and rural lifestyles (or urbanism versus ruralism). There can be no argument that urban centers in any given system are different phenomena from rural communities, at least in form and function. However, there is considerable variance in views of whether these differences affect behavior. By using controlled comparisons between urban and rural communities within a single system, we can begin to answer this question. Any common aspect of sociocultural life could be selected in both rural and urban settings to see whether differences are found. Provencher, Mangin, and Hammell have all explicitly adopted this methodological strategy in order to compare interaction styles, community organization, and family structure respectively in rural and urban settings.[5] What are frequently considered to be unique urban or rural characteristics may prove not to be so.

[4] Margaret Mead, *Sex and Temperament in Three Primitive Societies* (New York: William Morrow and Company, 1935).
[5] R. Provencher, "Comparisons of Social Interaction Styles: Urban and Rural Malay Culture," in T. Weaver and D. White (eds.), *The Anthropology of Urban Environments,* Society for Applied Anthropology Monographs, 1972; W. Mangin, "Similarities and Differences Between Two Types of Peruvian Communities," in W. Mangin (ed.), *Peasants in Cities* (Boston: Houghton Mifflin Co., 1970), pp. 20-29; E. A. Hammel, "The Family Cycle in a Coastal Peruvian Slum and Village," *American Anthropologist,* 63 (1961), 346-54.

Since urban anthropology is a relatively recent development, one might expect it to reflect more sophisticated research designs. This, in fact, is rarely so. The urban anthropologist is primarily concerned with myth debunking. He or she attempts to test universal assumptions about urban life, using cross-cultural data to refute myths and stereotypes about the city. Referring back to Mead's work, we can say that studies are more like *Coming of Age in Samoa* than *Sex and Temperament*. Thus, in most studies of migrant adaptation, we find descriptions of ways in which the migrants have adapted to urban residence while still maintaining many aspects of traditional behavior—thus refuting the notion that the city is a disorganizing force. In studies of squatter settlements (see Chapter 5), we find descriptions that indicate that these communities are often highly organized and cohesive—thus refuting the notion that these are slums or cancerous growths. Finally, studies of family and kinship in urban settings (see Chapter 4) have shown us that these principles of social organization remain significant, despite assumptions that they break down in the city.

It seems apparent that the time has come for an emergent urban anthropology to go beyond such gross generalizations, important as they were in the past, and begin to delineate conditions that would lead to the kind of change or behavior being described. In some of the most recent literature, these issues are in fact being confronted, and controlled comparison is being explicitly utilized. This process must be continued and expanded. If we look at migrant studies as an example, controlled comparisons can be achieved by comparing two groups in one city, the same group in two cities, or by maintaining continuous longitudinal studies of rural and urban components of the same group.

To summarize the previous discussion, we would suggest that an emergent urban anthropology begin to delineate specific problems to be studied beyond general descriptive ethnographies or general myth refutation. Such design statements must be precise, and the city must be explicitly defined as either independent or dependent variable. Narrowly defined variables with overly precise measures however, are not essential. They lead to a loss of context, interrelationship, and process. Such emphasis on holism and context has been a strength of anthropology and ethnography. Finally, most research questions can be answered most adequately by developing research strategies that encompass an explicit comparative framework.

UNITS OF ANALYSIS

In any ethnographic research design, a major consideration is the selection of a basic unit, or ethnographic target population, in which the fieldwork is to be done. In some cases, the population unit is chosen as a result of considerations of convenience or feasibility, without being very significant to the variables in the research design. Such a unit is a setting within which research is to be conducted. In other cases, the social unit is central to the research design, as either the unit being studied (dependent variable) or the independent variable. When the target population unit is merely a setting for research, we rarely find analytic definition and detailed description of the basic social unit. When the unit is the focus or object of study, careful explication of the unit is essential.

The former type of study is very evident in the genre of studies dealing with migrant adaptation to urban life. A wide variety of target social units have been selected. Neighborhoods (squatter settlements, slums and housing projects) and occupations (Bangkok pedicab drivers) have frequently been ethnographic target groups in which to study migrants. The neighborhood or occupation is not being studied to understand its nature.

Specific examples of these distinctions can be seen in the well-known works of Elliot Liebow and Ulf Hannerz. Liebow's volume *Tally's Corner* might be described as a study of poor Blacks who congregate on a certain corner in a neighborhood in Washington, D. C. However, the study, while seeming to have a spatial focus, says nothing about the neighborhood. On the other hand, it contributes to our understanding of family, kinship, and networks, as well as a particular socioeconomic segment of a particular ethnic group.[6] In Hannerz's book *Soulside* the data source unit is a block (once again located in Washington, D. C.). However, the primary research focus is on delineating the variety of lifestyles of an ethnic group, which is represented by the block residents. This is essentially an ethnic group study, as opposed to a neighborhood study. Hannerz is more interested in ethnicity and its processes than neighborhood cohesion or process.[7] In both these cases, the researcher has bounded his unit in terms of space, but the geographic unit is a setting within which to pursue other particular research problems. They have frequently been misclassified as neighborhood or community studies when, in fact, they tell us little about the nature of the neighborhood.

In the following section we shall discuss the units of analysis most frequently selected in urban anthropological research. Each unit will be discussed in terms of why it has been selected frequently, what problems are involved in identifying and sampling from the total universe of such units, and how boundaries are drawn around the selected unit.

The boundary issue becomes very important in urban anthropology.

[6] Elliot Liebow, *Tally's Corner* (Boston: Little, Brown and Co., 1967).
[7] Ulf Hannerz, *Soulside* (New York: Columbia University Press, 1970).

In traditional anthropology, the unit studied seemed to be a "natural system" with obvious boundaries in time and space. Tribal groups or agricultural villages in agrarian societies had the advantages of being small, bounded, and readily recognized units. However, most of these characteristics are not found in groups in an urban setting. This lack of readily discernible and functionally separate social units presents a significant problem in urban anthropology.

Units Based upon Common Residence

A large number of studies labeled urban anthropology or urban ethnography have used as their basic unit a neighborhood or cluster of blocks in a city. These spatially bounded residential units are considered analagous to those traditionally used by cultural anthropologists. Just as an anthropologist would "move into" a band or village, so he/she can "move into" a neighborhood. For example, urban anthropology in Latin America emphasized squatter settlements or spatially designated residential areas. In the United States, there has been a similar emphasis on ghetto communities as bounded geographic units.

Underlying this preponderant selection of spatial units is the assumption that a residential unit in the city has many of the same characteristics as similar units in peasant and tribal societies. It is assumed to contain most of the roles, activities, and institutions of the society. It is assumed to be a microcosm of the city, or even the society. It is assumed to be characterized by face-to-face interaction and by a sense of community. However, the nature of urban life—with so many activities taking place outside the residential community and with the availability of other intimate social interaction and other public and private arenas—makes these assumptions questionable. The testing of these assumptions, in fact, is an interesting research problem, but the assumption that they are true or that the neighborhood is a "natural" unit (making it the best ethnographic target population for all research problems) is questionable.

One could view the neighborhood as either a dependent variable or an independent variable vis-à-vis the city. If the neighborhood is the object of study (the dependent variable), then one must explicitly delineate the independent variables that influence the nature of the neighborhood. Such independent variables could be at the external contextual level, such as national or municipal government policy related to zoning. On the other hand, the independent variable could also be the internal neighborhood properties related to the dynamics of the internal units.

Jones illustrates how a neighborhood attempt at organization was frustrated by external municipal authorities affecting internal cohesion and solidarity. Suttles focuses on the effect of internal heterogeneity on the formation of social order, and Uzzell uses both external and internal independent variables when he analyzes the effect of geographic and historical forces and residents' life cycles as factors that account for neighborhood variation.[8]

Many studies dealing with the assessment of neighborhood cohesion are unclear about the relationship between external and internal variables and solidarity. On the other hand, many social network studies use neighborhood as an independent variable affecting networks. In Bott's study, highly connected networks are characteristic of those who live in stable neighborhoods.[9]

As we have previously noted, social units may either be explicit variables in a research problem or merely the setting in which fieldwork is done. For both Liebow and Hannerz the latter is the case. In the area of kinship studies, Vatuk and Young and Wilmott start with neighborhood samples and move on from these.[10]

In most studies that use the neighborhood as either dependent or independent variable or setting, there is little discussion of the procedure used for selecting the particular neighborhood. The issue of identifying the total range of neighborhoods and selecting logically from them is too frequently ignored.

Delineation. There are several ways in which neighborhood can be defined or delineated. These are: official designations, and physical, social, and cognitive definitions.

In urban situations, local authorities subdivide the city into component units for a variety of administrative purposes, such as census divisions, electoral wards, and school districts. For most anthropologists, these units are too large so they frequently select subunits. One advantage of using official units is that statistical data are available for these units. Unfortunately, these units are often defined differently by separate agencies and therefore boundaries do not coincide. This dilutes the potential advantage.

The major disadvantage for the anthropologist, however, is that the residents do not view these official boundaries as significant. Where

[8] Delmos Jones, "Incipient Organization and Organizational Failures in an Urban Ghetto," *Urban Anthropology*, 1 (1972), 51-67; Gerald Suttles, *The Social Order of the Slum* (Chicago: University of Chicago Press, 1968); J. Douglass Uzzell, "The Interaction of Population and Locality in the Development of Squatter Settlements in Lima," in W. Cornelius and F. Trueblood (eds.), *Latin American Urban Research*, 4 (Beverley Hills: Sage Publications, 1974), 113-34.

[9] Elizabeth Bott, *Family and Social Network*, 2nd ed. (New York: The Free Press, 1971).

[10] Liebow, *Tally's Corner;* Hannerz, *Soulside;* S. Vatuk, *Kinship and Urbanization* (Berkeley: University of California Press, 1972); and M. Young and P. Wilmott, *Family and Class in a London Suburb* (Baltimore: Penguin Books, 1957).

the neighborhood is merely a target population for studying other variables, this does not matter. When the neighborhood is an independent variable, such units are convenient for controlled comparisons. However, when the neighborhood is the object of study (the dependent variable) such official units are not very useful if they have no social or cognitive meaning.

Another way of defining the community is to use clear-cut physical elements. Unlike a village, which may be surrounded by wild, natural buffer zones, a geographic settlement within the city usually does not have a clear-cut buffer unless it has a natural boundary (formed by a river or hill) or a man-made buffer (formed by a commercial street, transportation lines, factory zones, or walls). One of the reasons that Latin American squatter communities were so frequently studied was that they were usually isolated and bounded by such features. The Puerto Rican shantytown in Lewis' *Backgrounds to La Vida*, the barrio in Peattie's *View from the Barrio* were distinct both from other residential areas and from the central city proper.[11]

When the neighborhood is merely a setting for a study, physical boundaries are quite appropriate. Where the neighborhood is either an independent or dependent variable, it is more essential to determine the degree to which physical boundaries are significant for the residents' activities and their definition of the neighborhood.

This issue is an important research question itself. We have previously noted the important influence of the Chicago School on urban studies (Chapter 2). The ecological approach of Park and Burgess suggested that certain spatial zones of the city were "natural" areas, which would maintain their boundaries, activities, and integrity over time—despite changing populations. This assumption of the continuity of such natural areas has led to a strong belief in the effect of spatial location and physical boundaries on neighborhood integrity over time. Thus, an investigation of whether such units are meaningful can be a significant issue to be investigated ethnographically. In this case, the degree of physical boundedness would be the independent variable.

In many of the earlier discussions of urban neighborhoods, the issue was raised about the degree to which such units based on common residence are *communities*—in terms of the frequency and intensity of social relationships—rather than *localities*—characterized merely by physical propinquity. As a result, many of the cohesion studies start with the neighborhood as geographically defined and investigate the degree of "communityness." It is impossible to delineate a "social" neighborhood

---

[11] Oscar Lewis, *Backgrounds to La Vida* (New York: Random House, 1968); Lisa Peattie, *The View from the Barrio* (Ann Arbor: University of Michigan Press, 1968).

a priori, since such meaningful interaction units can only be outcomes of research. It would therefore seem necessary to initially define the unit loosely, but to bound the unit more precisely as the study develops, rather than stick to predetermined delineations.

Many social scientists are beginning to emphasize the neighborhood as a mental construct, the insider's view. The cognitive approach directly taps residents' views of their environments. The degree to which physical boundaries, official designations, and frequency of social interaction affect cognitive notions of the neighborhood is itself an important issue. It has also been suggested that because of differences in activity spheres, sex and age affect the cognition of neighborhood. Thus, non-working women and children's definitions differ from those of adolescents, whose roaming range is broader. In turn, working adults have further differences in perception.

Where the neighborhood is a dependent variable (the object of study) a modified cognitive definition, which incorporates the natives' notions of a meaningful unit, is the best. In all cities, certain neighborhoods are relatively easy to delineate; they are named, physically demarcated, and seem to have a shared cognitive view of their boundaries. However, in all cities, there are other areas that are more ambiguous. In these cases, perfect a priori delineation is of course impossible, but at least the problems of delineation must be explicitly recognized.

The Valentines have developed an approach that does attempt to do this by working outward from a micro-unit, the block, in which intensive fieldwork is done, to larger units, such as clusters of blocks using the same stores and services, and finally to the district as a whole, which shares institutions and common problems. Beyond the block, the Valentines would thus sample situations of interaction within other larger units.[12]

This scheme parallels Suttles' three-fold analytic scheme, which moves outward from the "face block" to the "defended community," to the "community of limited liability." The face block is one where most people tend to know one another personally and interact with some frequency. The defended community is larger in scale and includes certain common arenas of interaction (stores and service areas) and a high degree of visual recognition, so that strangers can be distinguished and can be defended against. The community of limited liability is imposed more from the outside, through the proliferation of administrative units. It is recognized from the outside as the viable community and

[12] Charles Valentine and Betty Lou Valentine, "Making the Scene, Digging the Action, and Telling It Like It Is: Anthropologists at Work in a Dark Ghetto," in N. Whitten and J. Szwed (eds.), *Afro-American Anthropology* (New York: The Free Press, 1970).

dealt with in policy planning. It is the unit that is the basis for assigning institutions such as schools, health facilities, and law enforcement.

If this three-tiered community approach is accepted, then urban ethnographers should pursue their studies at all three levels, especially to examine the junctures between all three. Since the first two are defined and created by insiders and smaller in scale, they are obviously more amenable to ethnography. However, the very important brokerage function of the third level must also be studied.[13]

Another problem with the geographically bounded residential community is its lack of population stability over time. One of the characteristics of urban life is a high rate of geographic mobility. However, such mobility is not equally characteristic of all residential areas in the city. For some, transiency is a major characteristic. Such instability affects the composition and nature of the unit. If a research problem that does not involve the neighborhood, but for which the neighborhood is the setting, is selected, then the effects of mobility could have significant consequences for the research problem. However, if the research problem is directly related to the nature of neighborhoods, or the interaction between neighborhoods and the city, then high transiency as a neighborhood characteristic can itself be useful to the understanding of community formation and change. Interesting examples of this developed out of the Chicago school's studies of the continuity and maintenance of ecological zones in the city, despite high transiency. Suttles' more recent ethnographic work is a further exploration of the problem of the nature and process of neighborhood boundary coherence.[14]

The issue of sampling has always been a thorny one in anthropology. How does one select a *typical* village? How does one select informants to reflect the *total* range of social activities? Chilungu, a Nigerian anthropologist trained in Europe and the United States, raises the issue of sampling and representativeness in relation to many large African tribal groups. Citing specific examples, he notes that in some instances a handful of informants have been used as the data source to obtain information about the lifeways of a tribal group numbering more than 100,000. Thus, the question of representativeness is not one that confronts the urban anthropologist exclusively.[15]

In urban anthropology, the issue is of great significance. How does one select a typical neighborhood and how does one select informants within it to represent the total collectivity? The intensive nature of the

[13] Gerald Suttles, *The Social Construction of Communities* (Chicago: University of Chicago Press, 1972).
[14] Gerald Suttles, *The Social Order of a Slum.*
[15] S. Chilungu, "Issues in the Ethics of Research Method: An Interpretation of the Anglo-American Perspective," *Current Anthropology,* 17 (1976), 457-82.

ethnographic method precludes the use of a random scientific sampling procedure. However, some holistic awareness of the geography of the city, its activity zones, and the characteristics of its residential zones should be used to select a neighborhood (or more than one, if controlled comparison is a goal), rather than merely selecting on the basis of convenience. Moreover, some awareness of the range of internal heterogeneity must be used in selecting informants.

Unfortunately, many anthropologists are so committed to paralleling traditional fieldwork by "moving in" with their informants, they select a residential unit when such a unit is either unnecessary or even hampering. When such a unit provides a setting in which long-range participant observation can be pursued—where the anthropologist is interested in studying the neighborhood as a product of external or internal forces or to determine how the neighborhood affects the urban whole—then such a unit is necessary. If the activity or group being studied is largely in a delineated territory, such a unit makes sense. However, if the research focus has nothing to do with delineated territorial space, then this unit might be inappropriate.

Groups Based on Common Culture of Origin

Another "natural" unit of urban anthropological research because of its analogous nature to traditional anthropological studies is the delineation of ethnic (and/or minority) groups in the city. Here, the boundaries of the group are based upon presumed common cultures of origin or learned traditions, rather than common residential niches.

There has been a tendency in urban anthropological literature to confuse the two units of migrants and ethnic groups. In fact, anthropologists working in the Western industrial world and those in the Third World can be differentiated on the basis of which of these two units they emphasize. Ethnic or "minority" groups are important units selected as settings or research foci in American cities. In contrast, migrants are frequently the unit selected in the developing world. Migrants are those who left the rural hinterland and moved to the city during their lifetime. Ethnic groups are those who share a common cultural heritage but include long-term and cityborn urban residents as well.

Since cultural heterogeneity is one characteristic of the urban community, we would expect to find diverse ethnic groups represented in all cities. In some cases, these groups may be alien to the nation-state (foreign immigrants) or to the smaller regional context of the particular city. Thus, there are groups from other nations as well as from other regional areas within the nation itself. Even in nation-states viewed as ethnically homogeneous by outsiders, such as Norway, there are significant enough regional differences to be recognized. Thus in Oslo, in addition to alien groups, one finds ethnic distinctions between people from different regional backgrounds. The existence of different ethnic origins, however, doesn't mean that ethnicity is a significant aspect of Oslo urban organization or life. The *importance* of ethnicity is itself a research question and cannot be assumed.

The existence of ethnic/migrant groups is a universal characteristic of cities, the anthropologist's desire to study a "cultural" unit has meant that much urban anthropology has focused upon such units. Since different tribal or regional areas are often defined by linguistic or religious differences, aliens from other regions have frequently been the basis for urban anthropological research.

Just as in studies of residentially localized units (neighborhoods), studies of ethnic migrant groups can either utilize the groups as the setting within which certain research questions are asked or as the focus of the research effort. As we saw in Chapter 5, the formation of ethnic groups and their maintaining or changing boundaries are frequently responses to the urban setting, the stereotypes held by the dominant groups, and competition with other groups. If this kind of process of ethnic group formation and maintenance is the research *focus* of the anthropologist, then the selection of this unit follows directly from the research problem. Thus, if one wants to study the development of group solidarity among Blacks or Puerto Ricans in New York City as an urban process, then the selection of the unit is indicated. However, if the research focus is not on Blacks or Puerto Ricans or on any other ethnic group, but on questions of the effects of economic marginality, then the selection of Blacks or Puerto Ricans (or any minority group) would not be as strongly indicated, even though they have a high frequency of economic problems. However, the assumption is made very often in anthropology that you have to study a group with a common learned tradition.

Perhaps the urban anthropologist has been too zealous in the attempt to recapitulate the discipline's traditional culturally bounded unit in the urban area. He or she assumes that this group is "natural" and therefore more amenable to participant observation. The anthropologist has given primacy to the concept of culture or groups based on separate learned traditions and has assumed that the impact of such traditions dominates an individual's life. This assumption is problematic and should be researched rather than assumed.

Where ethnic group membership is the basis of social and economic relationships, it is obviously a basic unit in the social fabric. However, where such internal solidarity does not exist, the impact of ethnic group membership on the individual's lifeways may be relatively minor, and focusing on such a unit of study may be somewhat misguided.

Since residential groups lend themselves to "moving in," they are often merely the setting for research and not themselves the focus of the research problem. However, in most cases where ethnic groups are selected, they are usually the research focus as well as ethnographic target population; that is, they are either the dependent variables or independent variables.

When the ethnic group is viewed as dependent variable, the general characteristics of the city and historic, geographic, and economic contextual variables are usually the independent variables. Thus when M. Estellie Smith describes the different positions of the Portuguese in two New England towns she sees these as the result of the time of migration, the initial opportunity structures, the subsequent history, and the stereotypes held by the dominant groups. The processes of ethnic group formation, boundary maintenance and assimilation are thus tied to contextual variables. In a similar way, Nagata describes the position of Malays in two Malaysian towns.[16]

Studies that use urban ethnic groups as independent variables also exist. Many African urban studies look at ethnic group membership as the independent variable. The work of Southall, Gutkind, and others focuses on ethnic differences in the retention of kinship obligations.[17]

Many studies are concerned with the economic position of urbanites. Ethnicity is often treated as the independent variable, affecting economic success either in the sense of ethnic "values" or control over economic niches. The work of Cohen and Shack exemplify this approach.[18]

Delineation. When anthropologists select an ethnic/migrant population as either the setting or focus of the research, they have a difficult time identifying their total universe. This is not true if the group is very small or is completely represented in the formal organizations or religious institutions of the group. Thus, in several cases, a small group defined

[16] M. Estellie Smith, "A Tale of Two Cities: The Reality of Historical Differences," *Urban Anthropology,* 4 (1975), 61-72; Judith Nagata, "A Tale of Two Cities: Life in Two Malaysian Towns," *Urban Anthropology,* 3 (1974), 1-26.
[17] Aidan Southall, "Urban Migration and the Residence of Children in Kampala," in W. Mangin (ed.), *Peasants in Cities* (Boston: Houghton Mifflin, 1970), pp. 150-59; Peter Gutkind, "The Energy of Despair: Social Organization of the Unemployed in Two African Cities: Lagos and Nairobi," *Civilisations,* 17 (1967), 186-211.
[18] Abner Cohen, *Custom and Politics in Urban Africa* (London: Routledge and Kegan Paul, 1969); W. A. Shack, "Urban Ethnicity and the Cultural Process of Urbanization," in Aidan Southall (ed.), *Urban Anthropology* (New York: Oxford University Press, 1973), pp. 251-86.

by a common village of origin has been traced in its entirety in a particular city.[19] Ablon was able to trace most of the geographically dispersed Samoans in a city in California by working through several churches.[20] If the ethnic or migrant group shares a common residential locus, the problem is less difficult. However, residential enclaves often contain only a minority of ethnic group members in the city. Delineating the total population set is thus difficult, because of geographic dispersion and invisibility in public record sources. Key individuals sometimes exist who can identify all the ethnic residents, but this is rare. The anthropologist must often resort to a method analogous to cluster sampling: he makes some contacts, is referred to new people, and thus pushes out from a core of informants. However, he can never be too sure about the significance of the segment of the group he has reached. An additional problem of delineation exists when continued migration is taking place.

If a migrant or ethnic group has a common geographic residence pattern, then the "moving in" type of fieldwork or participant observation is feasible as a basic technique. However, where the group is dispersed, this becomes much more difficult. One may select seemingly typical domestic units to focus upon, but this bypasses the nature of the ethnic group as an entity. Where ethnically based associations exist, their activities may be used for fieldwork, but the totality of ethnically generated activities cannot be observed.

Where the goal of the urban anthropologist is to determine the very nature of the way in which the group maintains its identity and keeps itself separate from others, the delineation of the unit becomes one of the research outcomes, rather than a matter of predefinition. Rigid early delineation in such cases could cloud meaningful results. A willingness to change delineation and unit boundaries as work continues would seem to be necessary.

Groups Based on Emergent Belief Systems

In the city, in addition to groups based on common pasts, groups based on a commitment to future-oriented belief systems (both religious and political) proliferate. Since such groups are continually emerging,

---

[19] R. Kemper, "Tzintzuntzeños in Mexico City: The Anthropologist Among Peasant Migrants," in George Foster and R. Kemper (eds.), *Anthropologists in Cities* (Boston: Little, Brown and Co., Inc., 1974), pp. 63-72; Bernard Gallin and Rita Gallin, "The Rural-to-Urban Migration of an Anthropologist in Taiwan," in Foster and Kemper (eds.), *Anthropologists in Cities*, pp. 223-48.

[20] Joan Ablon, "The Social Organization of an Urban Samoan Community," *Southwestern Journal of Anthropology*, 27 (1971), 75-96.

many of them are no more than a generation old. During this first generation many of them recruit through conversion. Because of the totality and intensity of commitment, many of these groups share common residence, and thus ethnography is relatively easy. Some examples of these groups in American society are the Hari Krishna movement, converts to Sikhism, radical political communes, and therapeutic communities. What distinguishes these groups from relegious sects discussed earlier under ethnic groups is that they are products of the urban setting itself and are not based on national or regional cultures of origin.

One reason such groups are heavily represented in the urban anthropology literature is that they are easy to demarcate (as opposed to other groups) and the impact of membership is great. They often are residential, affecting all aspects of life for their members. The frequency of interaction is great. Thus, they are the closest analogues to the self-contained sociocultural systems anthropologists have studied and present no problems for the traditional anthropological methodology.

When the urban is the dependent variable, the significance of these groups for urban social structure and urban life is not easy to see. Where these groups are not actively anti-social, their significance to the city is not great. Such studies are interesting esoterically as anthropology *in* cities. They are concerned with illuminating an "exotic way of life." On the other hand, there are real possibilities for illuminating the nature of the urban as a generator of change if the city is seen as an independent variable. What is it about city life that enables a vast array of such groups to incubate and grow into movements that lead to social change? Do different types of cities tend to be the setting for different types of ideologically based groups? Are some cities more fertile ground for movements than others? Here again, a comparative framework, which would look at different groups in one center or similar groups in different centers, would be a useful research strategy to enable us to understand the relationship between urban social structure and change. Studies comparing the same movement in rural and urban settings would also fit this need.

Groups Based on Common Work

Since one basic characteristic of the urban social system is specialization of occupational function, it would seem appropriate that urban anthropologists study specialized occupational groups. However, this has not often been the case. While cultural and residential units have been overrepresented in urban anthropology, this type of unit is underrepresented. Although sociologists have recognized the significance of occupation as a variable in understanding modern society, for a considerable period of time, urban anthropologists have not moved in this direction. Perhaps this oversight is a result of the sort of studies anthropologists have traditionally done. In tribal societies, work was such an integral part of life and daily activity that it was treated as a functionally integrated segment of the cultural system. In village studies of peasant societies, in spite of the greater division of labor, peasant farming was treated as work had been in simple societies—as an integral aspect of life and the sociocultural system.

The city contains the full range of occupational specialization of the social system. The effects of the division of labor on social differentiation within the city means that the study of occupational groups helps us understand the city. The impact of urban forces on occupational niches may be studied, as well as the effects of occupational groups as independent variables influencing the nature of the city.

If we begin with the notion of the city as independent variable, then at any given moment, there is an extant job market in the city that is the result of its function and accumulated history. This job market is a vital element in sorting people who enter the system and who must acquire sources of income. However, the newcomers also influence the job market over time as they move through occupational careers. In this sense, occupational experiences may be viewed as independent variables, influencing both the job market and stratification systems in the city. People may enter a factory with the goal of becoming independent entrepreneurs and, if successful, may reshape the nature of the job market.

The process of such sorting and the effects of work in socializing incumbents is a vital research area. Occupational groups may, like all of the other units, be used either as ethnographic target populations (settings in which to study other research questions) or as the research focus itself.

Delineation. One of the difficulties social scientists face when dealing with work is finding meaningful categories of occupations. Job titles are often misleading and not indicative of the type of daily activity on the job, or the lifestyle generated by the occupational status community. For instance, the category of manager is such an amorphous one that the researcher must go beyond this to identify those who really perform the same occupational role or share the same status position from the point of view of the system. Alternative categories preferable to job titles include definitions of occupational groups that emphasize common work experiences, consciousness of kind, and common views of clients or the outside world. It becomes incumbent upon any social scientist studying occupations to specify the occupational group he or she is at-tempting to analyze. Once again, this is a problem of modifying the boundaries of the group as the research develops, rather than using a priori assumptions. Here again, ethnographic methodology puts the an-thropologist in a better position to illuminate the real conceptual and functional boundaries of experiential worlds, and perhaps this is his leading contribution.

Paralleling some of the problems of identifying the population uni-verse for ethnic groups are similar concerns for occupation. Obtaining a total list of all the scavengers in Sao Paulo or all the working engineers in New York City is an impossible task. This is why some of the most interesting information we have about occupations comes indirectly from studies of migrants or neighborhoods. For some occupational groups, (rickshaw pullers in Lucknow, India, who are all licensed; longeshore-men in Portland, Oregon, who belong to a single union) a complete roster of the total population is available. Job turnover presents the same kind of problems to the researcher as transiency in neighborhood groups and continuous in-and-out migration in ethnic groups.

An obvious solution to some of these problems of delineation is to focus on ethnography in the work situation. The researcher assumes that the unit being studied in depth is representative of the total universe.

Since work in most urban situations is removed from the home and is time-bounded, the use of participant observation in the study of groups based on the division of labor is somewhat limited. If the anthro-pologist is concerned not only with the work situation, but with its effects upon other areas of life, he or she must also use participant observation in these other situations. Once again, the sheer magnitude of the pop-ulation being studied and the complexities of their interaction present problems.

The very nature of the work situation may also present problems to the participant observer. Where members of an occupational category work in a central location, such as a factory, office, bank, or store, they form an interacting social system. However, where practitioners are dis-persed, participant observation is not as simple. Taxi drivers, traveling salesmen, street vendors, and professionals in private practice are exam-ples of such dispersed occupations. However, even for those in such isolated work situations, there are spatial points of intersection. For the taxi driver, it might be the garage or coffee shops near the garage; for the traveling salesman and the street vendor, it might be the place where inventory is acquired; for the professional, it might be the hospital or court area of the city. In all these cases, it is also possible that formal professional organizations or labor unions provide an arena for common interaction.

Units Based upon Primary Relationships

Among the major social units anthropologists have long studied are those based upon primary social ties, such as domestic units, kinship units, and social networks. A major urban research focus of many of these studies is the attempt to determine the *effect* of the urban on such units. As previously mentioned, earlier theoretical writings about urban life suggested a decline in the significance of such primary relations. Much of the subsequent research has attempted to show their continuing significance and is thus at the myth-refuting stage. In most of these studies, the focus of the research has been upon studying the nature of the units.

Since these basic social units form the context for socialization and meaningful interaction, they function as important integrative structures, bridging the structural units described above. The study of such egocentric units in conjunction with sociocentric units (neighborhood, occupation, and ethnic group) can enhance the understanding of the interrelatioships between them.

Delineation. An issue in primary social unit studies is how to determine the extensiveness of the unit to be studied ethnographically. In social network analysis, one begins with an individual or ego and traces his ties. How far should one go? Determining the limits is a difficult problem and really depends on the research question. One could determine limits based on time, space, or intensity of contact.

A slightly different problem occurs if a domestic unit is used. One could define the unit in terms of common residence in a household, but recent research has shown that urban domestic units are greatly constrained by the urban housing market and physical structure, and it is therefore useful to look at relationships outside the scope of the household.

Many of the same problems of identifying the total universe apply here as well. If the goal of the study is to determine how domestic units, kin units, or networks are affected by the urban, then problems of universe delineation and sampling occur. On the other hand, a particular network of an important individual can be viewed as an independent variable affecting urban organization, and thus the problem of sampling is not as critical. The ideal number of units to be studied and the way they are selected are determined by the nature of the research question.

SITUATIONAL ANALYSIS

A very different kind of unit that can serve as the focus of urban anthropological research is the *situation*. By this, we mean an event that takes place in delimited time and space and either brings together segments of urban structure and organization (thus pointing out their inter-relationships) and/or is directly influenced by urban conditions. Within this category, we would include studies of the effects of density in public places (waiting in line, riding the subway), the effects of residential density, and architectural variation in housing. These are studies of the effects of density conditions, using situations rather than social units as data sources. Another type of situational study focuses upon the interaction of heterogeneous units of the urban population by looking at a situational context that is the nexus (juncture) between them. Any public arena—open marketplaces, stores, bars, sports events, festivals— can be used in situational analysis. It is possible to select situations that are so strategically placed that they will illuminate the issues of urban social structure. Examples are studies of bars and stores that are shared or used for different purposes by different populations.

The arena of public performances in urban social situations (the transitory interaction between strangers) is another important aspect of study for which techniques of urban ethnography are quite adequate. The situation studied may vary from non-recurrent interactions to those of high regularity (but still between strangers). Some of the situations studied occur within institutionalized contexts with a high degree of rules; others focus upon mass events, such as sports victory celebrations, political rallies, and music festivals. Public disputes and conflict situations are another type of situational unit that can illuminate aspects of urban life.

What differentiates these units of analysis from those we have previously been discussing is that participants in the situations are not members of groups and there is no degree of group boundedness or continuity over time. These are the very aspects of the urban situation that make it different from non-urban life. Analysis of such performances and interactions is thus a vital element in urban anthropology. Here, the move-in resident ethnographic approach is not possible, but the skills of observing and translating observations into rules and patterns are key techniques translated from traditional anthropology. Placing such events in a larger social system context is another fundamental aspect of the anthropological approach.

FORMAL INSTITUTIONS

The prototype of a bounded unit in the city is the formal institution —school, hospital, court. Specialists in how these institutions deliver their services are educational anthropologists, medical anthropologists, and legal anthropologists. However, the urban anthropologist might also be interested in these formal institutions in two ways. First, they can be the situation within which other questions are asked. They are particularly useful as junctures between different components of the city. Secondly, the institutions can be viewed as a dependent variable, influenced by either the universal attributes of the urban or a particular urban context.

THE CITY AS A WHOLE

In all of the units described above (whether they are ethnographic target populations for research concerning other variables *or* the focus of research design as dependent or independent variables), the larger context of the city, region, nation, or other relevant context must be explicitly recognized in the research. Much of the criticism of urban anthropology has been based on the tendency *not* to do this, but to look at micro-units as self-contained. We have previously noted (in Chapter 3) that there is a growing emphasis in urban anthropology on context. A related trend is the tendency to study entire urban centers or the "city as a whole." In some cases, the anthropologist concerned with the city as a whole has given up ethnographic emphasis. In other cases, however, the anthropologist still uses the smaller social unit, but relates that unit to other small units and to the larger urban setting. The combination of in-depth knowledge about a micro-unit within the larger system gained from ethnographic research and other sources of data can perhaps be the most effective contribution of urban anthropology.

THE FIELDWORK ENTERPRISE IN THE CITY

Wayne Cornelius, a political scientist, comments on some urban anthropological research in Latin America by saying, "It demonstrates that intensive microethnology in an urban setting can ultimately provide a basis for macro-level explanation and conceptualization which leads to important insights into the dynamics of urban life." [21]

We have previously discussed the major shift in cultural anthropology in the early part of the twentieth century as one that took anthropologists out of the library and into the field. They no longer relied on descriptions of the behavior of people by others, but collected their own descriptive material. They used both the verbal statements of informants and direct observation and participation in the lifeways of other social groups. The effectiveness of these techniques of doing an ethnography has been demonstrated in the voluminous anthropological literature.

[21] Wayne A. Cornelius, "Introduction" in Wayne A. Cornelius and Felicity M. Trueblood (eds.), *Latin American Urban Research*, vol. 4 (Beverley Hills: Sage Publications, 1974), p. 14.

In studying urban populations, this same basic approach has a great deal to offer those who are concerned with the understanding of urban reality in terms of what it *means* to different people—how events and activities are perceived and valued. In addition, ethnography can be used as the basic technique for describing those informal relationships and structures missed by formal techniques. Furthermore, the cycles of activity and process are also revealed. There is far from unanimous agreement among urban anthropologists as to whether ethnography *is* the essential element in an urban anthropology. However, it seems to us that without the ethnographic perspective, urban anthropology would be a redundant and sterile endeavor.

Even for those concerned with the relation of cities to the national system or the development of typologies of urban centers, some ethnography would seem to be essential to get at those areas of reality that are missed by more formal measurements. In addition, an ethnographic data base can help avoid some of the difficulties encountered when one initially imposes culture-bound categories and analytic frameworks.

The difficulty of selecting research problems or units has previously been discussed. Whatever is selected, the key elements of ethnography, firsthand contact, direct observation, intensiveness of contact, and relation of all data to context must be involved. How the city may create difficulties for the fieldwork enterprise will be discussed below.

When anthropologists did their studies of ongoing tribal or village groups, they could simultaneously live with their subjects for an extended period of time and cut themselves off from their traditional cultural elements and social linkages. They "moved in" with the people they were studying. Their analysis was based upon direct and continuous observation. Such intensive contact is much more difficult in the urban setting, but must still be maintained as an ideal. Thus continuity of contact, intensiveness, and intimacy are still essential and possible.

One of the basic characteristics of an urban existence is that one's relationships are single-stranded rather than multiplex; that is, all role relationships are not overlapping or played by a small number of individuals. Roles, activities, and space are specialized and segmented. This has implications for the way the anthropologist works and how he or she relates to informants.

One of the classic stipulations for doing fieldwork—suggested by Malinowski more than half a century ago—is the necessity of severing all ties with one's culture of origin, including one's prior statuses, social linkages, duties, and obligations.[22] For the urban anthropologist, par-

---

[22] Bronislaw Malinowski, *Argonauts of the Western Pacific* (New York: E. P. Dutton and Co., 1922), Introduction.

ticularly the American anthropologist in an American city, such isolation is impossible and no longer seems necessary.

The disassociation of anthropologists from their own culture was a concomitant of doing fieldwork in a foreign setting. It was supposed to immerse them totally in the field situation and enable them to observe and analyze what they observed "in a more objective way." At this time, most anthropologists realize that objectivity is an ideal rather than a reality, and this ideal can be maintained and strived for even if the anthropologists do not sever their ties with prior social relationships and totally immerse themselves in the field situation. The informants themselves have multifaceted lives and many kinds of relationships. Therefore, they understand such conflict and outside pressures.

One of the unresolvable questions is the degree to which it is essential for an anthropologist—even an American anthropologist specializing in American groups—to be exposed to some sort of experience in an alien setting as part of his training. Although this kind of cross-cultural field research may be considered essential in the training of anthropologists, to sensitize them to being "outsiders," it is not essential in every research project. Thus, an anthropologist who has learned to decipher the codes of behavior followed in a different system and has learned how to play the role of an outsider should be able to transpose these skills and orientation to the study of urban phenomena in his or her own system. Since, in some cases, anthropologists have been socialized in the very system they are studying, they must constantly be aware of the potential problems resulting from being an insider—the problem of sensitizing oneself to one's internalized assumptions and biases.

If studying one's own social system is a problem, it also is an advantage. If we imagine a foreign anthropologist coming to the United States and pursuing ethnographic fieldwork in New York City, we can see how learning to operate in the city, with its social complexity, would be extremely difficult. Having to cope with a new culture would present even more difficulty. The anthropologist as "outsider" would not only be faced with the usual problems of "culture shock," but also with the need to become familiar with an extremely large spatial area and differentiated social structure. The urban anthropologist studying in his or her own social system is faced with social complexity, but the problems of culture shock are minimized. In some ways this is unfortunate, since culture shock does contribute to the sensitization of the "outsider."

For those anthropologists who see the block, neighborhood, or local community as the basic unit for participant observation and for urban ethnography, the more traditional fieldwork tactics are possible and essential. Valentine made this point when he studied Blackton (pseudonym). He cut himself off from his network, told no one where he was except his university, which forwarded his mail.[23] He tried to reconstruct Malinowski's field isolation and to depend entirely on the resources and services available in the neighborhood he studied. Stack also "moved in" and tried to reconstruct traditional anthropological field-work conditions.[24] If the study is focused primarily on the domestic unit, nature of the neighborhood, community interaction, solidarity, and street life, then full time fieldwork seems essential, and living in the community is useful. However, if social units that are not residential and territorial in nature are being studied, then moving in would be impossible, irrelevant, or even disadvantageous. Occupations and dispersed ethnic groups, networks, and situations do not, in fact, lend themselves to "move in" participant observation.

An illustration of what is being suggested might be useful at this point. If the social unit selected for study is an urban sect or storefront church, the need for residential propinquity depends on the research question. If one wanted to do anthropology *in* the city and describe the church organization and activities, one might want to live near the church. However, if one wanted to study the recruitment process to see how the church articulated different social elements, one would have to follow active recruiters as they go through their daily activities. Thus, one would want to live near them, rather than the church headquarters, or near good transportation for movement around the city.

This issue is treated in some detail in most of the essays in the volume *Anthropologists in Cities*.[25] In one of the articles, the anthropologist specifically notes that establishing residence based upon initial research design assumptions led to the need for relocation. Thus Gonzalez shifted her residence as she shifted her research focus in her study of Santiago, Dominican Republic. Initially she wanted to study migrants and felt that an outlying neighborhood would be well-suited to gaining access to migrants. However, she discovered that the migrant population was not geographically localized and that she could neither "move in" with them nor locate a best place of access on the urban periphery. Recognizing that she was too far from the city center, which might be considered a point of equal access she relocated her residence there. As the research developed, she recognized that residence in the central

23 Valentine and Valentine, "Making the Scene."
24 Carol Stack, *All Our Kin* (New York: Harper and Row, 1974).
25 George Foster and R. Kemper (eds.), *Anthropologists in Cities* (Boston: Little, Brown and Co., Inc., 1974).

area gave her a better view of urban process. As she observed the process, she recognized a need to shift from a focus on migrants to one on elites.[26]

In Watson's study of Chinese restaurant workers in the London metropolitan area, he found that the nature of their occupation dispersed the community he was studying, since the men worked in suburban restaurants throughout the fringe. The men, all migrants from a single community in the Hong Kong New Territories, had no common meeting places, churches, or club, which could have served as a spatial focus. Watson and his wife actually lived in a rooming house twenty minutes out of the city center and commuted to informants.

Kemper, dealing with migrants from Tzintzuntzan, notes that his informants were scattered in forty-nine neighborhoods and had no common spatially focused institutions. Pilcher could not live among his residentially dispersed longshoremen, since no longshoreman neighborhood or suburb existed.[27]

In other cases, living in the neighborhood is unfeasible, even when the informants are neighborhood-based. Thus Elliot Liebow notes that he did not live in the neighborhood where he carried out his fieldwork because of the nature of race relations. He did, however, spend as much time as possible "hanging out" with the men of Tally's Corner. The same was true for Hannerz on Winston Street. Byrne, in her study of a retirement community, could not live in the community because of the age requirement for residence. When Niehoff studied factory workers in Kampur, India, he could not live with the workers, since housing was scarce and most workers lived in restrictive settlements built and subsidized by the factory organization for their workers. Ogbu notes that he was unable to move into the school district that was the center of his research because of the lack of available housing. In all these cases, good ethnographic data was collected without full-time co-residence.[28]

---

[26] Nancy Gonzalez, "The City of Gentlemen: Santiago de los Caballeros," in Foster and Kemper (eds.), *Anthropologists in Cities*, pp. 19-40.
[27] James Watson, "Restaurants and Remittances: Chinese Emigrant Workers in London," in Foster and Kemper (eds.), *Anthropologists in Cities*, pp. 201-22; Kemper, "Tzintzuntzeños in Mexico City"; William Pilcher, *The Portland Longshoremen* (New York: Holt, Rinehart and Co., 1972).
[28] Liebow, *Tally's Corner;* Hannerz, *Soulside;* Susan Byrne, "Arden, an Adult Community," in Foster and Kemper (eds.), *Anthropologists in Cities*, pp. 123-52; John Ogbu, "Learning in Burgherside: The Ethnography of Education," in Foster and Kemper (eds.), *Anthropologists in Cities*, pp. 93-121; Jeanne Guillemin, *Urban Renegades: The Cultural Strategy of American Indians* (New York: Columbia University Press, 1975); Arthur Niehoff, *Factory Workers in India* (Milwaukee: Public Museum Publications, 1959).

An interesting contrast between rural and urban research is provided by Guillemin. In working with the Micmac Indians on a Canadian reservation, she lived with one family. In working with the same group in Boston, she was not intimately tied to a household. She lived away from the group in her own household and used her car as transportation, but often spent two or three nights in one of the homes of her five or six closest informants.

The alternative to "moving in" is to commute to one's informants. It is still possible to spend long, continuous time in their midst during day and evening hours without living there. If one does a "commuting" kind of fieldwork, there are problems of time allocation. For Liebow, Hannerz, and Byrne, the time spent in commuting was not that significant, because they went to the same location each day and spent long periods of time there. For Watson and Kemper, on the other hand, the major segment of their research time in the field was spent in trying to reach people—commuting rather than data collecting. Watson estimated that he spent three to four hours in transit for every hour with informants, and he also noted a futile two-day search for one individual whom he never found. Obviously, when one has to move around the whole city, access to transportation systems becomes a paramount issue in location.

An interesting example of the impact of location of housing on the pursuit of research is illustrated by the work of the Gallins in Taipei, Taiwan. In their first urban effort, which focused upon migrants from a village in which they had done prior fieldwork, they were housed in facilities at a university compound, which effectively cut them off from intimate contact with their target population. They were distant from public transportation and food sources, which minimized their contacts and their ability to entertain their informants. In their second urban research experience, they located themselves in an accessible, middle class community near public transportation and easy shopping. They still did not live with the migrants, but were able to maximize their personal contacts.[29]

One intriguing circumstance requires mobility, regardless of location; if one wants to follow one's informants through their daily round, as in traditional ethnography, one has to move around the city. This provides a view of the full range of contextual and spatial relationships that impinge on one's informants' lives. Even when anthropologists "move in" and see much of the localized activities of the target popula-

---

[29] Gallin and Gallin, "The Rural-to-Urban Migration of an Anthropologist in Taiwan."

tion, they must *not* remain so locked into the locality as to lose the relationship with the larger city context.

Entry and Rapport

The necessity of direct contact, intensive relationships, and continuity require participant observation of daily activities and special events on the one hand, and intensive interviewing and verbal questioning on the other. The anthropologist's ability to gather such data is based upon being accepted by those being studied. This is what is meant by *entry* and *rapport.*

It is only through such acceptance that anthropologists will be allowed to interact with the people and ask the kinds of questions they think are necessary. If we think in role performance terms, then anthropologists want information on *front-stage* or *public performance*. The performance they wish to observe is not that constructed for their benefit, but rather that which is typical of normal everyday life. But they also wish to see *backstage* performance as well—the private, enclosed, domestic scene. This requires a delicate personal relationship. Both Stack and Guillemin have described with great sensitivity the development of their relationships with their informants.[30]

An additional characteristic of urban life that poses difficulties for the ethnographer is the emphasis on privacy. This results from the possibilities for privacy that come from technology (houses with ventilation that are soundproof and visually protective), as well as the tendency to develop closed boundaries that results from urban density. One could suggest that this has been a problem in traditional ethnography too, since certain rites and events are classified as private or secret. However, domestic privacy has not been heavily emphasized in many traditional anthropological studies. In the city, the whole domestic arena is closed, and gaining access is often a difficult process.

An example of research that recognized the problem of domestic privacy is that done by LeMasters. One of the central foci of his research was male-female interaction patterns in the occupational status community he studied. However, he recognized the difficulties of gaining access to private domestic life and obtained his information through observations in a quasi-public arena, a bar.[31] Here he observed husbands and wives, joined in conversations about domestic life, and probed relatively private areas.

[30] Carol Stack, *All Our Kin;* and Guillemin, *Urban Renegades.*
[31] E. E. LeMasters, *Blue Collar Aristocrats* (Madison: University of Wisconsin Press, 1975).

In other cases, urban domestic life is not as private as we have indicated. Because of the nature of slum housing, there is less opportunity for privacy. Lewis, in his work in shantytowns and tenements in San Juan and Mexico City, was able to directly observe the domestic arena.[32] In such housing areas, the small, poorly lighted, poorly ventilated housing with common courtyard space for laundry, plumbing facilities and cooking led to a deemphasis on private domesticity. However, even in such cases, there may be socially created rules for maintaining privacy under difficult conditions. Provencher and Anderson describe the etiquette developed by urban Malays and Chinese to make up for a lack of physical barriers to visual and sound contact between households.[33]

The problems of entry and rapport can sometimes be solved through the anthropologist's manipulation of status and connections. There are several techniques that can be used in this attempt: 1) use of professional ties or status; 2) use of personal ties; 3) joining formal associations; or 4) "hanging out" or "moving in."

There are many ways in which anthropologists can use professional status as scientist, professor, or anthropologist to gain access to agencies that will help them meet those they wish to study or to gain access to informants themselves. Even in traditional anthropological research, it was not unusual for an anthropologist to gain entry to a particular group through the sponsorship of missionaries, colonial officials, government officers, or influential local leaders contacted on the basis of professional status. For the urban anthropologist, parallel forms of sponsorship are often used.

In Kemper's study of Tzintzuntzan migrants to Mexico City, he used Foster, his own advisor who had previously worked in the village, as his basic entry contact. Gonzalez used government contacts gained through her funding agency and her status as professor to gain direct access to the elites she wanted to study in the Dominican Republic. Goode used her university connections to gain access to law school graduates in Colombia.[34]

In conducting research with Punjabi-speaking Indians living in the city of Wolverhampton, England, the initial step was to gain entry

[32] Oscar Lewis, *Five Families: Mexican Studies in the Culture of Poverty* (New York: Basic Books, Inc., 1959); *Children of Sanchez* (New York: Random House, Inc., 1961); *La Vida: A Puerto Rican Family in the Culture of Poverty* (New York: Random House, Inc., 1965).
[33] Provencher, "Comparisons of Social Interaction Styles"; E. N. Anderson, Jr., "Some Chinese Methods of Dealing with Crowding," *Urban Anthropology*, 1 (1972), 141-50.
[34] Kemper, "Tzintzuntzeños in Mexico City"; Gonzalez, "The City of Gentlemen"; Judith Goode, "The Response of a Traditional Elite to Modernization," *Human Organization*, vol. 29, 1970.

through a government agency concerned with problems of intergroup relations in the city. The executive officer of the Community Relations Council was contacted, and he provided Eames with a list of Indians who belonged to organizations loosely affiliated with his agency. The executive officer's name was obtained initially through social science researchers at the Institute of Race Relations in London, who accepted the researcher as a colleague based upon his credentials.[35]

The status of professor at an academic institution provides access to students who may be potential informants, that is, members of the target population. Many urban anthropologists have used university students as research assistants. Often these students themselves become informants, as in the case of Epstein's work.[36] Goode and her colleagues used Italian-American students at Temple University as informants in their study of food as a symbol in ethnic boundary maintenance.[37]

In many ways, the problems of the urban anthropologist are again analogous to those of the traditional anthropologist. One wants to select "good" entry contacts—individuals who will provide a wide range of informants, or whose information will be valid if they are themselves informants. Thus, it is important to develop contacts with "influentials." Such influentials may be insiders or "gate-keepers" who control the access of outsiders to their group. They might be outsiders who are strategic brokers or who are important enough to the group so that their sponsorship is not ignored.

A problem confronting the urban anthropologist is gaining access to a variety of segments of the target group. Thus, Kemper notes that his initial contacts were with middle class migrants, and this influenced his total perception of migrant adaptation until he fortuitously tapped a less successful group.[38]

In many studies of migrants that follow them from their rural to urban locations, anthropologists have already established ties with informants, which gives them ready access to the migrant population. This is one of the most typical modes of entry.

A case in which this did not prove to be as successful is in Watson's

[35] Edwin Eames and Howard Robboy (Research was supported by a study leave from Temple University and N.I.H.M. Grant Number DHEW-IRO3-MH 18799-01).
[36] A. L. Epstein, "The Network and Urban Social Organization," in C. J. Mitchell (ed.), *Social Networks in Urban Situations* (Manchester University Press, 1969), pp. 77-116.
[37] Judith Goode, "The Philadelphia Food Project: A Study of Culture and Nutrition" (paper delivered at the Annual Meeting of the American Anthropological Association, Mexico City, 1974); "Modifying Ethnic Foodways: The Effects of Locality and Social Networks (paper delivered at the Sixteenth Annual Meeting of the Northeast Anthropological Association, Middletown, Conn., 1976).
[38] Kemper, "Tzintzuntzeños in Mexico City."

study of Chinese restaurant workers in London. When he used his knowledge of the village setting, local dialects, and kinsmen of the London group, the migrants became very suspicious of his presence. Even when he met individuals whom he had previously known in the village, he was unable to establish immediate and warm relationships. The change in context had affected their views of the past.[39]

Besides professional ties, personal ties based on kinship or friendship can be activated to gain access to informants. When anthropologists are working in a city where they have lived for some time, they can usually mobilize their own egocentric network. Thus an anthropologist working in the Philadelphia Italian-American food project was able to use several childhood and adolescent friends as well as relatives of her stepfather as informants and entry facilitators.

Laura Nader's ability to gain entry to a Washington, D.C. law firm was based upon her sibling relationship to Ralph Nader. Pilcher's work with longshoremen was facilitated by contacts he had made by having previously worked as a longshoreman.[40]

The use of personal ties can also occur in research in foreign cities. In research done by Goode among a professional group in Colombia, one personal tie proved very successful in locating three gatekeepers, who then introduced the researcher to an unlimited number of informants. The personal tie was a member of the professional community who had done postgraduate work at an American university and had a close relationship with the ex-neighbors of the researcher. Since the researcher only communicated with the ex-neighbors at Christmas time, the contact was almost accidental. Through this person, the researcher was sponsored by the local university professional schools and professional associations. She probably could have made the contacts on her own eventually (using formal letters of introduction from her university provost and her role as professor at the local university), but the personal tie proved most useful.[41]

Frequently, anthropologists use both professional and personal ties, if they have them. Professional ties are used to gain initial entry and quickly lead to personal referrals; informants whom you meet begin to introduce you to their personal networks, and you expand the world of informants through personal referrals. In the previously mentioned Italian food project, both professional and personal ties were used simultaneously. Parish priests introduced the researchers to key officers

[39] Watson, "Restaurants and Remittances."
[40] Laura Nader, "Up the Anthropologist—Perspectives Gained from Studying Up," in Dell Hymes (ed.), *Reinventing Anthropology* (New York: Random House, 1974), pp. 284-311 (originally published in 1969); Pilcher, *The Portland Longshoremen.*
[41] Goode, "The Response of a Traditional Elite to Modernization."

in the parish women's clubs, who in turn referred the researchers to the members. Parallel to this, the anthropologist's childhood and adolescent friends were contacted for referrals to their kin and friends. In this case, the rapport established with informants met through the personal chain was greater and longer lasting than the relationships established through more formal channels.

Sometimes there is no easy way to discern points of entry. In this situation, urban anthropologists frequently enter their target populations by participating in formal organizations, by "hanging out" in the semi-public arenas (bars, stores, corners), or by "moving into" the group. By mere frequency of spatial prescence, they hope to gain acceptance and establish ties. In order to study Sikhs in Los Angeles, Fleuret joined their organization. Eames, in his study of Punjabis in Wolverhampton, visited their two temples frequently and visited local pubs with his informants, who introduced him to new contacts. Rainwater and his associates used the stores and service areas of the Pruitt Igoe housing project to make the acquaintance of potential informants. They then followed informants into more private arenas, such as their homes. Pilcher used the union hall in a similar fashion for his study of Portland longshoremen.[42]

Stack provides one of the best descriptions of the strategy of entry and rapport. While her initial entry into the community was through a former student who introduced her to several friendly families, she "moved into" the community as well. Her best and most strategically placed informant was met, however, through a casual encounter and self-introduction at the laundromat. This parallels Liebow's entry through "hanging out" at a take-out shop.[43]

Obviously, these various means of gaining access to informants are not mutually exclusive. The anthropologist will mobilize whatever routes are available to him or her: professional ties, personal ties, informal organizations, gatekeepers, brokers.

Another characteristic related to the multiplicity of routes of access is the possibility of pursuing research despite several false starts or ruptured relationships. As an example of the latter, when one of the authors of this text returned to resume research after a one-year absence, he arrived on the eve of the marriage of the daughter of one of his best informants. Since he had had no contact with him during the preceding year, he did not know this event was occurring. When the father of the

[42] Anne Fleuret, "Incorporation into Networks Among Sikhs in Los Angeles," *Urban Anthropology*, 3 (1974), 27-33; Eames and Robboy research study; Lee Rainwater, *Behind Ghetto Walls: Black Families in a Federal Slum* (Chicago: Aldine Publishing Co., 1970); Pilcher, *The Portland Longshoremen*.
[43] Carol Stack, *All Our Kin;* Liebow, *Tally's Corner.*

bride discovered that the anthropologist was in the city but had not attended the ceremony, he was extremely annoyed and eventually dropped out of the pool of informants. In a traditional closed community (tribe, village), this might have meant the expulsion of the researcher and the termination of research. In this case, however, because of the size and diversity of networks in the target population and the urban community, the anthropologist was able to pursue his research without significant disruption.

Explaining the Mission

Explaining the mission or goal of the anthropologist has always been a problem. Traditionally, anthropologists could explain to an isolated, non-literate group that their people were interested in the way of life of those being studied. Such an explanation is obviously inadequate in the modern urban world, and even more so when one is studying a city in one's own system. An "explanation" that works better with a literate population is that *research* is being done. Scientific knowledge has enough acceptance as a positive value that this alone leads to acceptance without many additional details.

On the other hand, knowledge of social science research has, to some degree, fostered suspicion of the anthropologist, who may be seen as a potential threat. Some past social science research has had negative political effects for those being studied, and many potential informants are aware of this. As one example, a research group might be sent into a neighborhood where urban renewal is being contemplated. Based upon their findings, policy decisions may be made that will disrupt the lives of the residents. When the researcher approaches groups who have learned of the potential threat of the research, they may be quite distrustful.

Unlike a tribal or village situation, where the mission, however explained or accepted, need only be established at the beginning, in urban research, when one is dealing with a dispersed and unintegrated population, the mission may have to be explained many times when new contacts are being made. Watson notes this problem in his work with Chinese in London.[44]

Obviously, no universal explanation for doing a particular ethnographic study can be suggested that will be acceptable to all groups. Each ethnographer must decide upon the type of explanation that will adequately and honestly describe the nature of the research in a way that will be understood by his or her informants.

[44] Watson, "Restaurants and Remittances."

VALUES AND ETHICS

Thus far we have been discussing some general methodological and logistical problems of gaining access to the unit of study. Another issue, which must be discussed in the context of methodology and research design, is that of the *values* underlying urban anthropology and the ethical issues involved.

In general terms, the issue of a value-free anthropology (or social science or any science) has generated considerable discussion in the recent literature. Many take the position that no such possibility exists. The acts of selecting a group or a problem, seeking funds for research, and selecting the techniques to be used to collect and analyze data are all choices exercised within a context of values and priorities. For some, the solution is to make their own values and biases as explicit and overt as possible, and then pursue their research within this framework. Those who strive to make their research as value-free as possible recognize the difficulties of such an attempt.

Stated in its simplest terms, when earlier work was done on isolated tribes, anthropologists could take the position that they were being objective and that their values were kept out of observation and analysis. Today, even when anthropologists study isolated tribes, they are aware of their own biases and attempt to deal with them consciously and explicitly.

The fact that urban life is characterized by multifaceted, intertwined institutional complexes that impinge on the life of all citizens, and the fact that structured inequality of access to resources exists, make the results of the study of urban lifestyles more open to manipulation by the politically dominant.

The Issues of Reciprocal Obligations

When urban anthropologists do research with a particular group of people, there are certain obligations to them which they must recognize. This would not be as true of situational research or research that focuses on the city as a whole. Where, however, anthropologists are in continuous contact with a segment of the population and establish close and personal relationships with them, they must recognize that they "owe" them something.

First, they owe an honest explanation of their mission. The kind of explanation used in traditional societies—"We want to learn about your way of life"—often had no meaning for a population. It is certainly not adequate for anthropologists in most urban settings today. It would seem ethically essential for anthropologists to tell their informants about the purpose of the study, although they might try to represent it in a way that is non-threatening, meaningful, and interesting to those being studied. It seems unethical for an urban anthropologist to completely disguise the fact that he or she is *studying* a group, which is sometimes done.

Although anthropologists frequently collect information that benefits their careers, they fail to recognize the exploitive nature of the relationship. Spicer, in his catalogue of patrons of the poor in an American city, includes the social scientist (and particularly the anthropologist) and notes that several theses and publications have been based on studies of this community, with a minimal amount of reciprocity on the part of the anthropologist.[45] Guillemin also recognizes the potential role of the anthropologist as a patron of the poor. However, she notes that when anthropologists are aware of this potential, they may break away from the dominant/subordinate relationship and establish more egalitarian bonds with their informants.[46]

It is interesting to note that when American anthropology was in its infancy, it was not unusual for anthropologists to pay informants for their time. This practice was looked on with disfavor by later anthropologists, who felt that the anthropologist should elicit information by developing a relationship, and not through direct payment. However, they might offer other kinds of rewards or services. At the present time, it would seem that some anthropologists are moving back to the notion of direct payment to informants, especially in urban situations where "time is money." There are other ways in which the urban anthropologist can reciprocate for time and information. Some feel that occasional gifts or services (running errands, providing transportation, translating, or serving as an intermediary with a public agency) are more personal.

One way in which this can be done is through "advocacy" anthropology. When anthropologists talk about advocacy anthropology, they regard themselves as individuals who can and should help their informants understand their social position and gain greater access to some of the scarce resources in the social system. In contacts with outside institutions (police, courts, hospitals, schools), they attempt to work on behalf of their informants and, in many cases, educate them (and the institutions) to become more effective actors in relation to each other. One example of this is Peattie's intervention in the "sewer controversy" described in Chapter 5.

Another set of reciprocal obligations exist in addition to "com-

[45] E. Spicer, "Patrons of the Poor," *Human Organization*, 29 (1970), 12-20.
[46] Guillemin, *Urban Renegades*.

pensating" for time and information. These involve the anthropologist's attempts to influence the use of data, to avoid misuse, and to protect informants' anonymity. It has now become fashionable to use the term "client" instead of "informant" by many of those in the advocacy role. In the past, the "client" of the anthropologist could be viewed as the government that supported the anthropologist's research, either directly or indirectly, and reaped policy or action benefits from the data. The newer form of clientage sees those being studied as the ones to benefit primarily from the knowledge, and many anthropologists would therefore prefer funding that is not "tainted." In fact, they would prefer working for the clients themselves. However, the limited resources of potential clients and their reluctance to allocate these to anthropological research should be apparent.

The *advocacy* approach should not be confused with *applied* research. In applied research, the client is not necessarily the informant group itself, but can be a public or private policy-oriented agency. The anthropologists in this case must always be explicitly concerned with protecting the rights and interests of their informants. They must always be aware of unbalanced power relationships and structured inequality.

Any anthropologist—whether advocate, applied, generating "pure" or "basic" research—must still be concerned with who has access to data and the potential misuse of such information. In the past, the academically oriented anthropologist has been interested in knowledge alone. Thus, anthropologists might take the position that, as students of human behavior, whatever insight they gain is part of the general scientific pursuit of knowledge, and their data are in the public domain. Misuses are therefore beyond their control and should not concern them. However, this position has come under attack and is increasingly recognized as untenable.

This same issue is relevant in genetics today. In a recent issue of *Science News*, it was reported that a group of genetic biologists decided not to pursue further sudies of the breaking of the genetic code (the basic source of the origin of life) because of the potential misuse of such research.[47]

While physical anthropology might have repercussions for the total course of human life, cultural anthropology presents no such species-wide threat. But a particular study of a particular group could lead to massive implications for control or change of a lifeway.

It is now recognized that literate elites or policy-oriented specialists have greater access to data in specialized journals than does the informant group. In the case of research in the Third World, the English-

[47] "Rules for Gene Research," *Science News*, 110 (July 3, 1976), 3.

speaking elite have greater access to data that are not reported in the language of informants. One must make an effort to insure that *first* access to information goes to informants. An additional benefit of such initial access is that it provides a source for checking the anthropologist's intuition and hypotheses against the views of the informants themselves.

In some cases, data may be collected that the anthropologist recognizes as potentially harmful to the informants. In such cases, the information should probably not be published at all.

A related issue is that of protecting the confidentiality of sources of information. In the past, anthropologists tried to insure confidentiality by using pseudonyms for the communities they studied and by disguising the individuals who were their major sources of information. In urban anthropological research, the anthropologists generally have given up the attempt to disguise the city in which they work, although Valentine and Stack do carry on this tradition. The difficulties of hiding the city's identity should be apparent. Even if one uses a pseudonym to describe an Eastern seaboard city of eight million, anyone could identify the city. Leaving out specific geographic and demographic descriptions would render the study useless for comparative purposes. However, it is still customary to disguise the identity of geographically based local units such as neighborhoods or blocks.

Although location might be impossible to hide, individual informants are still protected. Frequently, anthropologists obtain information about illegal or illicit activities and are faced with legal problems of revealing sources, privileged communication, and so forth. The information, if made available publicly, could also be used by outside agencies in investigations and eventual punitive action.

As one example of this problem, we can cite the work of one of the authors of this text who, while studying Indians in England, uncovered much information about illegal immigration. Although the British government was quite aware of these activities, the publication of such data would have informed the authorities of the particular techniques and modes of illegal entry developed by the community and would have posed a threat to their continuance. As a consequence, the data were never published.

In a recently published volume, *Migration and Anthropology,* one article deals with illicit alcohol consumption among workers in South African factories. Since any anthropologist working in South Africa must be approved by the government, it is quite possible that this information could be used against the workers who, in effect, trusted the researcher.[48]

[48] H. A. Alverson, "Labor Migrants in South African Industry," in Robert Spencer (ed.), *Migration and Anthropology* (Seattle: University of Washington Press, 1970), pp. 49-60.

When one studies groups like drug pushers, the Black Mafia, or prostitutes, this question of hiding identity is really central to the study and usually is discussed at length.

In other cases, the researcher may feel that attempting to disguise sources of information and preserve anonymity, may diminish the impact on policy formation. Thus, a recent article published by one of the authors described the case of an Indian who attempted to visit relatives in England. In this instance, the case had become a *cause célèbre* and full details—including the name of the individual involved, the names of government officials, official correspondence, and newspaper accounts—were used. Since one goal of the article was to change British Home Office policy in relation to Indian visitors, it was felt that full disclosure was essential.[49]

Another specific ethical problem relates to the use of mechanical equipment (tape recorders and cameras) without the explicit permission of informants. We would hope that the days in which microphones were hidden and cameras concealed are past. Obviously, making explicit the purposes of the study and obtaining permission to use mechanical devices may make the research more difficult. However, it would appear to be easier to live with these difficulties than with the ethical implications of not informing one's informants.

Third World Issues

What are the special problems faced by American and Western European anthropologists working in a Third World nation-state? It should first be noted that such nation-states have had a colonial past, and in many cases the new elites view the foreign anthropologist as a neo-colonial force. Although direct political domination has ended, many of these countries are still economically dependent on, and exploited by, the West. Today, many nations in the Third World are barring or curtailing the research activities of foreign-born researchers, particularly Americans.

Urban ethnographers must be aware that they are viewed as at least exploiters (if not spies), taking information out of the country and providing nothing in return. One response by many anthropologists has been to publish their research materials and analyses in the language of the country and in journals or monographs easily accessible there. Another approach has been to deposit data and materials in libraries in that country. Western anthropologists can also help in the training of local

---

[49] Edwin Eames and Howard Robboy, "Not Welcome: The Punjabi Visitor and British Immigration Officials," *International Journal of Contemporary Sociology*, 9 (1972), 44-55.

social scientists by imparting their knowledge and tools as a social scientist. This is frequently done by involving local students in research projects as assistants—providing economic resources as well. Schwab has described the techniques he used in the training and employment of native researchers in the study of urban Africa.[50]

The above procedures involve a risk. If you provide access to information to the local elites (political and intellectual), you create the possibility of their using it against the less powerful—your own informants or target population. The problem of protecting informants is similar in the anthropologist's own society when doing research among the powerless. However, as a foreigner requiring visas and political clearance for research, the anthropologist has obligations to both the state and the informants and must be very careful to protect individual informants and groups in terms of confidentiality and non-release of potentially harmful information.

Another problem the anthropologist faces in the publication of materials collected in Third World nations is that of nationalism and national pride. The anthropologist is still viewed by some as the student of the strange and exotic. Educated elites who hold this view of anthropology fear that the portrayal of aspects of their lives or the lifestyles of subgroups in their social system will show them in a negative light and damage their international image. Here again there is no solution, other than the sensitivity of the anthropologist to these feelings and the avoidance of ethnocentric descriptions of lifeways.

BEYOND GROUP ETHNOGRAPHY

Thus far we have discussed some basic methodological issues in urban anthropology which primarily focus upon ethnographic research in a target population. Research design, selection of units, strategies of entry, and ethical concerns have been discussed. At this point we will shift our attention to some other methodological issues, including the use of non-ethnographic sources of data and the study of the larger context in which the target population is embedded.

The nature of ethnographic fieldwork requires the development of a relationship between anthropologist and informant that must be based upon trusting, close, continuous, and intimate contact. Such a technique works against a scientifically based sampling procedure, which would enable the ethnographer to make general statements about the entire

[50] William B. Schwab, "An Experiment in Methodology in a West African Urban Community," *Human Organization*, 13 (1954), 13-19; "Looking Backward: An Appraisal of Two Field Trips, *Human Organization*, 24 (1965), 372-80.

community. When anthropologists fall into the trap of not recognizing this, they open themselves and their findings to serious scientific criticism. Despite this lack of sampling procedures, however, the efforts of the urban anthropologists are more than descriptive journalism and do fall within the range of scientific disciplines that attempt to probe the realities of urban life.

Surveys and Questionnaires

The urban anthropologist will probably want to supplement intensive ethnographic research with extensive information derived from surveys. From intense, firsthand observations and interviews about everyday life, he or she may develop a questionnaire that can be used with a much larger and more carefully sampled population. It can also be administered by less well-trained personnel. J. Clyde Mitchell was one of the first British social anthropologists to discuss what he perceived to be the necessity for the use of surveys in urban areas.[51] The use of the survey has become commonplace in African research. In the United States, Ellis and Newman tested their images of different lifestyles in a Black ghetto in Chicago by using questionnaires based upon their earlier ethnography.[52]

Uzzell and Provencher also emphasize the importance of ethnography in the development of questionnaires and survey instruments.[53] Leeds goes further than this by insisting that no adequate questionnaire can be developed without prior *extensive* and *intensive* participant observation. Such ethnography helps to elicit relevant categories. Some words may mean different things in different contexts for the *same* people. Others mean different things to different class or regional subgroups. For example, Leeds notes that in Brazil, *malandro* means "delinquent" and "hood" to some, while it means "cool guy" or "clever fellow" to others.[54]

On the other hand, Plotnicov illustrates the difficulties of premature surveys conducted before achieving ethnographic understanding. He

[51] J. Clyde Mitchell, "Theoretical Orientations in African Urban Studies," in Michael Banton (ed.), *The Social Anthropology of Complex Societies* (London: Tavistock Publishers, 1966).
[52] H. C. Ellis and S. M. Newman, " 'Gowster,' 'Ivy Leaguer,' 'Hustler,' 'Conservative,' 'Mackman,' and 'Continental': A Functional Analysis of Six Ghetto Roles," in E. B. Leacock (ed.), *Culture of Poverty* (New York: Simon & Schuster, Inc., 1971), pp. 299-315.
[53] Douglas Uzzell and R. Provencher, *Urban Anthropology* (Dubuque, Iowa: William C. Brown, Inc., 1976).
[54] Anthony Leeds, "Brazil and the Myth of Urban Rurality," in Arthur Field (ed.), *City and Country in the Third World* (Cambridge: Schenkman Publishing Co., Inc., 1970).

collected survey data early in one of his studies and noted, to his dismay, that responses initially obtained were contradicted by his informants when he developed a close and intimate relationship with them.[55] The Gallins, in their first urban research in Taipei, depended heavily on surveys, using a team of assistants. They note that analysis of the data after returning from the field had little meaning for them. In their subsequent field trip, they went back to ethnographic techniques.[56]

Plotnicov warns the urban anthropologist about the seductive nature of survey material and the use of the computer for analysis. He suggests that when the anthropologist moves too far in this direction, he or she may lose the humanistic element so vital to the anthropological perspective.[57]

Although the survey technique offers certain advantages to the anthropologist, particularly when the questionnaires used are based upon prior ethnography, this technique has certain basic weaknesses. Frequently a questionnaire obtains verbal responses about hypothetical behavior rather than actual behavior; the respondent answers the way he thinks the researcher wants him to respond. In addition, questionnaries are usually time-bounded.

The ulitmate goal of urban ethnography is not simply to build better surveys. The questionnaire is an additional technique the urban anthropologist can use in obtaining more extensive data, but it must be recognized for what it is: a technique that has limitations and can only complement, but not replace, ethnography.

Larger Contexts

Since anthropologists doing research in the city on a particular social unit recognize that their slice of the system is part of an integrated whole (the city and its context), they must obtain a great deal of information about these other segments of the system. In some cases, this may involve the collection of ethnographic data on these related units. Thus, anthropologists working with a community group may be interested in the relationship between members of the community and courts, hospitals, and schools. In addition to studying specific situations in which informants are involved (interface between the two), they might also find it useful to have some ethnographic data about their operations on a day-to-day basis. They might wish to observe how the co-workers in the agency interact, how staff meetings are conducted, how decisions are

[55] Leonard Plotnicov, "Anthropological Field Work in Modern and Local Urban Contexts," *Urban Anthropology*, 2 (1973), 248-64.
[56] Gallin and Gallin, "The Rural-to-Urban Migration of an Anthropologist."
[57] Plotnicov, "Anthropological Field Work."

made, etc. The staff's views of their role, their different daily activities, and their clients might be very illuminating. Valentine illustrates how such insights about a community hospital proved useful to his understanding of the community's relationships.[58]

In the study of ethnic groups, stereotypes of the group held by others would be an important variable to explore. This could be done ethnographically. For example, M. Estellie Smith indicates how in two New England towns in close geographic proximity, the populations have very different images of the Portuguese.[59] Ogbu also looks ethnographically at the stereotypes held by administrators and teachers about their local clientele of Mexicans and Blacks.[60] An ethnographic understanding of these views obviously contributes to understanding the nature of ethnic adjustment. Not enough systematic ethnography of external population units has been done or reported on in the literature.

For the urban anthropologist interested in the anthropology of the larger context, a variety of informational documents exists. These include documents collected by government agencies, private corporations, and other researchers, which can add a vital element to his study. Historians have been collecting and publishing material dealing with the development of urban centers in many parts of the world. Public archives exist where secondary analyses have not yet been made. Many small groups have their own historians. Thus, Lynch studying Jatavs in Agra was able to use documents contained in archives maintained by the group itself.[61]

Urban space is well documented by geographers, and maps are one of the most useful sources of information. Much urban geography deals with the social and cultural characteristics of different zones. Rowe, in comparing migrant populations in Bombay and Bangalore, uses maps to note the greater degree of residential segregation by caste in Bangalore.[62]

Many formal bureaucratic urban institutions (courts, schools, hospitals) maintain their own documents. Where these are available to the anthropologist, they can be valuable supplementary sources. With the widespread literacy found in the city, newspapers can become a useful source of information, both for news content and for social analysis of feature articles. Several studies of the desirable characteristics of mates in urban India have been done through content analysis of matrimonial

[58] Valentine and Valentine, "Making the Scene."
[59] Smith, "A Tale of Two Cities."
[60] Ogbu, "Learning in Burgherside."
[61] Owen Lynch, *The Politics of Untouchability* (New York: Columbia University Press, 1969).
[62] William Rowe, "Caste, Kinship and Association in Urban India," in A. Southall (ed.), *Urban Anthropology* (London: Oxford University Press, 1973), pp. 211-50.

advertisements carried by newspapers.[63] Trends and changes over time can also be useful gauged through systematic content analysis.

Most contemporary nation-states collect vast amounts of demographic data in periodic censuses. These censuses contain the social contours of the city: sex, age, occupation, literacy, income, housing, place of birth, and so on. In most field situations, whether in modern urban or rural areas, anthropologists working with any target population will usually attempt to do their own census, which will serve as background or context for most research questions. The census technique has also been characteristically used in peasant village studies. In the course of these micro-unit studies, certain criticisms of the large-scale aggregate data collected by governments have emerged.

Statistics are only as good as the categories used to collect them. These categories may not reflect reality. Categories used to measure unemployment and labor force participation have been criticized as not meaningful. Further, statistical categories are imposed by collectors, frequently members of government agencies, who sometimes manipulate them to control the public's view of a situation. They may also be manipulated to increase the political power of particular groups. As Guyot has shown, the definition of the ethnic category of "Spanish speaking" in the United States census changes as it is manipulated by government agencies to prove that their policies are working.[64] Unemployment figures have also been manipulated by changing definitions.

We have previously criticized social surveys because they frequently lack shared meaning between the researcher and those being interviewed in regard to the questions asked. The same criticism can be directed at the misuse of census data by social scientists. For instance, a census usually lists individuals who live together in a domestic unit. To use these data as the basis for the analysis of trends in family life may be extremely misleading. Although in American middle class culture the co-residential unit and the family are the same, this is not true for many other groups in American society. For instance, no amount of census analysis would reveal the nature of cooperating domestic units of the Black poor in America, although Moynihan uses such statistics to make statements about the Negro family.[65] The variety of domestic groups found by Stack could never be obtained from census documents.[66]

[63] Paul D. Wiebe and G. N. Ramu, "Marriage in India: A Content Analysis of Matrimonial Advertisements," *Man in India*, vol. 51, 1971.
[64] J. F. Guyot, "Who Counts Depends on How You Count: The Political Consequences of Census Counting for Ethnic Minorities," mimeo., 1973.
[65] Daniel Moynihan, *The Negro Family*, Washington, D.C., Department of Labor, 1965.
[66] Carol Stack, *All Our Kin*.

The same can be said about the meaning of employment data contained in the census. Those who are employed in illicit occupations or irregular activities like street vending, begging, or domestic work will appear as unemployed, whereas they may be working full-time as measured by time and money. Thus, unemployment may be overestimated for some groups. Anthropologists interested in the impact of the labor market on a group must move beyond collected statistics. They may have to collect their own demographic data from their target population.

A fundamental criticism of some statistics available for analysis of urban life is that they measure a phenomenon at a single moment in time. This approach obviously limits the analyst's ability to follow fundamental processes. For example, students of Indian life have emphasized the significance of the joint family in that country. The census of 1971, like all previous censuses, showed that only a small minority of the total population lives in a domestic unit that could be characterized as a joint family. The percentage has shown no significant change in the last two decades. However, what the census does not show is that in the intervening years between censuses, some families that were joint have broken into nuclear units, while others that were nuclear in the first census have become joint. Thus, there is a high probability that a given individual, particularly in an upper caste, has lived in a joint family at some time in his life, even though the total proportion of such families is small at a given point in time. Indian families go through cycles of structural phases, of which the joint family is a common one. The same is true for the female-centered family found in the Afro-American population. This seems to be a phase in a complex cycle which includes matrilocality, nuclear units, and cooperative units (see Chapter 8).

Another example of the weakness of many statistical sources can be seen in relation to rural-urban migration. In Colombia, comparisons between two censuses showed that the city of Medellín has increased in population at a rapid rate, while rural regions were being depopulated. The assumption was made that people were coming into Medellín from these rural regions. Political violence, which had increased in the country, was assumed to be driving people away from the countryside. However, as more case studies were done, it was found that most of the new migrants in Medellín were second-generation urbanites from smaller cities, who had been displaced by the real movement of the refugee peasants into these smaller cities. These cities were experiencing both incoming and outgoing movement, but statistically showed no change. If the focus of research interest had been the smaller cities and the censuses had been used, there would have appeared to have been little change in population, when in fact two-way mobility was great. Aggregate statistics are very important data, but they have to be used with an awareness of their limitations. Once again, it is possible to see a potential for basic ethnographic research itself in the improvement of categories used to collect such statistics.

Critical Indicators

In most ethnographies dealing with tribal people there is general agreement about what information should be collected as background or context for the actual study. One can predict what will be included in the "background" or "setting" section. Almost every account begins with a description of the geographic area, including the extant flora and fauna as well as the history. If the purpose of the fieldwork is the description of a people's way of life, then the natural setting within which the culture exists and to which it adapts is an essential aspect. In addition, if the ethnographer is concerned with the major historical events of the past, such as contacts between groups, this aids in understanding the culture. However, in urban anthropology, no equivalent format has been established, because no consensus has been reached on the critical indicators that best describe the city and its external setting.

With the city as the basic setting within which the research is being conducted, it should be possible to develop a set of standard characteristics that would serve as an analogue to those described in most standard ethnographies. These would include basic demographic characteristics such as size, sex, and age distribution of the population; a description of the occupational structure, which is an index of the dominant function of the city; and aspects of the labor market and housing market. Patterns of land use (the distribution of types of residential and non-residential usage) as well as public transportation routes would clearly indicate the spatial aspects of the urban container. Geographers have developed models of land use and techniques for measuring the functional specialization of cities; these techniques could be used. Historic features—such as function at origin, rate of growth through time, major historical events, successive political dominations, changes in recruitment of migratory streams—could be described. Recent government (national or local) policy affecting housing, labor markets, and urban planning should also be included. Administrative units could also be delineated (feeder areas for hospitals and schools, political and religious subunits). An attempt to map the distribution of ethnic groups, if in fact they have a spatial component, can be made. The time depth of different ethnic groups can be measured in terms of generations. Relative demographic ratios of ethnic groups can be developed.

Some techniques for measuring these characteristics are being and have been developed in urban studies and could be adapted as a standard format. It is obvious that data of this type can be obtained only through the efforts of other researchers, and not through the anthropologist's own data generation.

Since the goal of urban anthropology is to develop generalizations about urban life, and since the basic technique that will allow us to develop these is comparison, it is essential to develop some set of agreed-upon procedures for describing the critical context variables that will become essential to all urban ethnography. The difficulty has been the variety of procedures in the research done to date, which is context-oriented. This work has not used a common set of indices or criteria. Some emphasize history, others demography. Some focus on the relationship between external political units and the city, others on economic relationships. Among those who favor history, different procedures are used and different aspects are emphasized or ignored. When we, as urban anthropologists, can agree upon common indices and procedures, then each case study would be potentially comparative, and generalizations could be made.

In many ways urban anthropology is a universal pilot study. Once the real meaning of patterned behavior is described, then more meaningful and extensive techniques can be used to determine the extent to which these patterns hold true.

Throughout the foregoing discussion we have encouraged controlled comparisons and tighter research designs. On the other hand, there is a long tradition in anthropology of being humanistic. Advocates of this emphasis still suggest that anthropologists, urban or otherwise, should not narrowly define their focus, but cast their nets widely to grasp the most they can about meaning and context. They should be concerned about illuminating the particular situation being studied, rather than searching for comparative data. The two approaches are very different, in that one is rigorous and controlled, and the other loose and unfocused. While urban anthropology seems to call for tighter research designs, it must still accommodate the humanistic search for meaning.

SUMMARY

A number of methodological issues have been raised, some of which are unique to urban anthropology, while others are common to all anthropological efforts. Much of early urban ethnography, paralleling earlier studies of tribal groups, attempted to disprove certain commonly assumed characteristics or universal propositions about human life. More recently there has been a shift toward comparative studies with more sophisticated research designs.

Selection of the unit of study in an urban setting is a problem faced by the urban ethnographer that the tribal ethnographer did not face. The most commonly selected units are based upon common residence (neighborhoods), common culture of origin (ethnic and migrant groups), common beliefs (movements), and common work (occupations). For all of these units, delineating boundaries is a common problem. Sometimes the unit selected is the focus of study; at other times, a research problem is selected and the unit becomes the setting within which the problem is studied. One popular research problem in urban ethnography focuses upon the way in which various units maintain and change their boundaries.

Some particular difficulties face the ethnographer doing fieldwork in urban areas. The ethnographer frequently studies a geographically dispersed population, which creates logistical problems. Much time is consumed in "getting to" informants. The close and intimate relationship between anthropologist and informants is frequently absent, or at least more difficult to achieve in an urban setting. Some of the frequently used techniques to gain access to a target population are the use of professional ties, the use of personal ties, joining associations, "hanging out," and "moving in." Some of these are used to gain initial entry, while others are used throughout the study. A further problem faced by urban ethnographers is explaining the purpose of the research to those being studied.

Urban ethnographers have an advantage of being able to tap sources of data not available to ethnographers of tribal life. Historical data, census data, and data collected by urban agencies and institutions can be incorporated into the study. Frequently, social surveys and census data are used to supplement direct observation of behavior, but a number of critics have cautioned their colleagues about too heavy reliance upon information collected by using questionnaires or aggregate statistics.

Urban ethnographers must recognize the issues of ethics and values. The belief in a "value-free" cultural anthropology has been discarded, and anthropologists who work in urban areas must recognize their own values and biases. Reciprocal obligations to informants are now generally recognized. Frequently, the data they collect can be used by formal agencies for controlling the population being studied by the ethnographer. Some urban ethnographers see themselves as working for those being studied and become advocates of their target population in the urban political and economic system.

Those working in Third World cities face particular ethical problems. Frequently their research must be approved by government agencies. Attempts are made to incorporate local scholars in the research efforts and to avoid portrayal of local lifeways in negative tones.

8

The Culture of Poverty:

A Misapplication of Anthropology

to Contemporary Issues

In almost every volume that has appeared in the rather loosely con-
federated field of urban anthropology, there is a section devoted to the
"Culture of Poverty" concept.[1] Therefore, we would assume that this
topic is also included in most urban anthropology courses. The issue of
the culture of poverty, the development of the concept, its potential as
an explanatory device, and its policy implications, particularly in American society, have all received considerable critical attention in the recent
literature.

[1] For example, the introduction to W. Mangin (ed.), *Peasants in Cities* (Boston:
Houghton Mifflin Company, 1970) deals primarily with the culture of poverty; a
whole section of the reader edited by John Friedl and Noel Chrisman, *City Ways: A
Selective Reader in Urban Anthropology* (New York: Thomas Y. Crowell Co., 1975),
is devoted to poverty; and R. Fox, *Cities in Their Cultural Settings* (Englewood
Cliffs, New Jersey: Prentice-Hall, 1977) refers to one of the three major areas of
urban anthropology as "the anthropology of poverty."

We feel that a discussion of this concept will serve as a classic illustration of what *not* to do in an emerging urban anthropology. In addition, problems of ethics, methodology, units of analysis, and application of traditional anthropological concepts to complex society can be clarified and illustrated in this discussion. In the ensuing discussion, we shall use as a structural outline the various issues discussed in Chapters 1, 2, and 7.

The development of the culture of poverty concept is intimately linked to the work of Oscar Lewis. We have already noted the work of Lewis in Mexico City as one of the early examples of urban field research. Lewis was one of the earliest anthropologists to shift his attention from peasant village studies to studies of the adaptive techniques employed by villagers who migrate to the city. His article, "Urbanization without Breakdown" is a classic rebuttal of the notion that the city destroys the individual, the family, and the social order. Thus Lewis was one of the early "myth breakers" (see Chapter 7).

The criticisms we make of the culture of poverty concept deal with only one aspect of Lewis' work. His total life's work included many significant contributions, including peasant village studies using innovative data-collecting techniques and further innovations in his studies of slum residents. He was a pioneer in the development of the intensive focus on the family unit in the city, and his development of the method of portraying the "typical day" and the life cycles of individuals did much to accentuate the humanistic emphasis of anthropology. His informants were portrayed as real people, and Lewis has received kudos for his incisive biographical portrayals. However, the repercussions of his culture of poverty concept often seem to overshadow the positive contributions of his career.

We can see that Lewis began his career by attacking Redfield's folk society and folk-urban dichotomy; he continued by doing ethnographic studies in Mexico City, which initially emphasized strong persistence of organization (family, *compadrazgo*, religion), only later to shift to an almost exclusive concern with the Mexican and Puerto Rican underclasses, which culminated in the development of the culture of poverty concept, in which he described the families he studied in terms of their disorganization and pathologies.

Lewis thus became the target of attack in much the same way that Redfield was earlier, when Lewis led the attack. Beginning his career by attacking overgeneralized and weakly documented concepts, Lewis ends his career being attacked for the same reasons. Beginning his work with a direct assault upon the concepts of social disorder and disorganization, he ends his career creating similar models of disorganization for the culture of poverty.

A further peculiarity in the development of Lewis' work is that, in his earlier criticisms of Redfield's folk society concept, he used a variety of scientific and empirically based arguments, which were quite effective. But in the development of his own concept, he made the very same errors of overgeneralization and non-empiricism that he discovered in Redfield's work.

The first mention of the culture of poverty concept appears in a volume, *Five Families*, dealing with Mexico City residents. Subsequently mentioned in *Children of Sanchez*, the fully developed statement appears in the Introduction to *La Vida* and in an article in *Scientific American* in 1965. These two discussions have been reproduced in a number of subsequent publications.[2]

THE CULTURE OF POVERTY CONCEPT

Lewis suggests that the culture of poverty is an integrated set of values, norms, and behaviors characteristic of some of those who live in poverty conditions. It is found in an industrial/capitalist society characterized by a cash economy, production for profit, social mobility, and high rates of underemployment and unemployment. It should be noted that Lewis himself sees the culture of poverty as a response to *industrial capitalism* and *not* to the *urban*. Lewis does not imply that the nature of the city influences the development of the culture of poverty, but many others assume that since his work is done in urban areas, he is implying that poverty and the culture of poverty are *urban* phenomena.

Lewis claims that there are some seventy traits that are diagnostic of those in the culture of poverty. These are subdivided into four subcategories: the nature of integration with the larger society, the nature of the slum community, the nature of the family, and the nature of the individual personality.

Under the category labelled relationship to the larger society, Lewis notes the general lack of participation in the institutions of the larger society (political parties, labor unions, health, education, financial, and cultural institutions). Prisons, courts, and welfare systems, however, are institutions where the poor are overrepresented. He notes that distrust and hostility toward these institutions is also extended toward the church.

2 Oscar Lewis, *Five Families: Mexican Studies in the Culture of Poverty* (New York: Basic Books, Inc., Publishers, 1959); *Children of Sanchez* (New York: Random House, Inc., 1961); *La Vida: A Puerto Rican Family in the Culture of Poverty* (New York: Random House, Inc., 1965); and "The Culture of Poverty," *Scientific American*, vol. 215, 1966.

Regarding the nature of the community, Lewis notes a lack of organization beyond the family level, but offers little in the way of a description of the community level.

The family is described as a "partial" structure, with high rates of consensual (or informal) unions, desertion, and separation, as well as female-based households. Some of the characteristics of the household units were overcrowding and lack of privacy.

At the individual level, those in the culture of poverty are seen as present-time oriented and fatalistic. They have "weak ego structures" and ambiguity about sex roles, despite an emphasis on masculinity. These latter attributes are allegedly related to maternal deprivation. Certain individual characteristics are related to the nature of the life cycle: an early initiation into sex and a relatively short period of childhood (the period during which the child is protected and dependent).

Lewis includes in his description a number of economic characteristics unrelated to the four-fold classification. These would include high rates of underemployment and unemployment, low wages when employed, frequent purchases of small quantities of goods, lack of saving, usurious borrowing, small-scale informal credit mechanisms, pawning, and the use of secondhand goods.

It should be apparent that lack of organization or evidence of disorganization is found at all four levels in the culture of poverty. Lewis suggests that the culture of poverty, once it comes into existence, tends to be perpetuated through time, *regardless of changes in the circumstances of the people*. He views it as a subculture that is transmitted intergenerationally. He indicates that by the time a child is six or seven, he or she has been irreversibly molded into the culture of poverty. Thus, an individual raised in the culture of poverty is viewed as unable to take advantage of changing circumstances.

The Use of Anthropological Concepts

In the first chapter of this volume, we discussed four continuing themes in anthropology that should be carried over into urban anthropology: ethnography, holism, comparison, and relativism. The culture concept was discussed as central to anthropology, but problematic in its usage in complex society.

In Lewis' research in Mexico City, the basic techniques of ethnography were used. He obviously was intimately concerned with his informants, and provided us with detailed descriptions of everyday activities and life histories. The research in San Juan is not as clearly ethnographic. Leeds has raised questions about the actual data collection process.[3] Lewis did not live in the community, nor were his contacts with informants as continuous and long-term as those in Mexico City.

Concerning holism, Lewis' work appears to fit the general model in some ways. His emphasis upon the multiplicity of relationships between the culture of poverty and the larger external system that generates it is quite explicit. However, he frequently confuses the two; that is, he includes as part of the culture of the poor aspects of life that are characteristic of the external system, not responses to it. For example, he talks of unemployment as a trait of the culture, when it is the generator of poverty itself. Unfortunately, Lewis develops a trait list rather than a systemic view of the relationships between aspects of the culture. Therefore, what is finally derived as the culture of poverty is a series of characteristics, not carefully linked to one another or to the nature of the larger society.

While Lewis was comparative, in that he compared Mexico City to San Juan, he did not clearly depict the similarities and differences in the nature of both places, as would be required in a controlled comparison. Moreover, the fact that he did not study any non-Hispanic cultural system, and still generalized to all of the Third World on the one hand and the United States on the other, belies the kind of careful comparison called for in Chapter 7.

A major difficulty with the use of the culture concept in conjunction with poverty (or with any question relating to complex societies), is that the concept of culture has varied and changed over time. Although accepted as basic, the concept has never been successfully defined in a universally accepted way by anthropologists.

In Lewis' use of the culture concept when dealing with poverty, he emphasized the self-perpetuation of the culture of poverty—the notion that children are doomed to the culture of poverty by age six. The use of early childhood socialization as the explanatory device for the transmission of culture has been characteristic of anthropology since its beginning and is even reflected in Tylor's influential definition. More recent studies have focused upon this process as a central research problem in order to determine when early socialization is important and when it is not. Lewis, on the other hand, simply accepts early childhood cultural transmission as the only significant enculturation process, without recognizing the issues involved.

In recent times, one sees two emergent views of culture. In one view, culture is a system of cognitive categories or cognitive maps,

[3] Anthony Leeds, "The Concept of the 'Culture of Poverty': Conceptual, Logical and Empirical Problems with Perspectives from Brazil and Peru," in E. Leacock (ed.), *Culture of Poverty: A Critique* (New York: Simon and Schuster, Inc., 1971), pp. 226-84.

THE CULTURE OF POVERTY 309

which individuals carry around in their heads and transmit through symbolic codes. The *sum* of the overlapping elements of individual cognitive maps is *culture*. The other point of view sees culture as a set of adaptive strategies for survival, usually linked to a particular setting of available resources and external constraints. This is an ecological approach to culture.

Lewis does not recognize these two trends and uses a traditional definition of culture as a "way of life." Thus, the ecological approach—the generation of culture and continued culture change resulting from interaction with the ecosystem—is not found in Lewis' formulation. Lewis views the culture of poverty more as a shared set of cognitive maps. He presents a view of the carbon copy recapitulation of a way of life, generation after generation, without any notion of the interaction of this way of life with changing external systems.

For both the cognitive and ecological approaches, the issue of *change* is fundamental. It is generally recognized that modern society is characterized by rapid rates of change, particularly in the technological and economic spheres. Thus, modern culture concepts must be able to deal with change. In Lewis' definition of the culture of poverty, however, the issue is dealt with by suggesting that those in the culture of poverty are relatively immune from changes in the external system. Thus we have a view of cultural traditions which are self-perpetuating and closed to outside influences.

To some degree, the concept of culture can be useful in the study of urban poor. For one thing, it focuses our attention on shared behavioral patterns, rather than on behavior as individually derived. The culture concept can thus be used productively in showing variability of patterned behavioral responses which differ because of the socioeconomic position of a group in the system to which they are responding. Thus, class subcultures or subcultures of occupational status communities can be fruitfully studied.

It might be suggested that we modify the cultural concept for use in modern life. There seem to be many temporal levels involved. As a situation changes, many shared (socially transmitted) responses can be developed. Some of these may be short-term coping responses, in the sense that they tend to disappear, while still others may become part of permanent adaptive strategies and persist over generations. Thus, in Chapters 4 and 5, we have noted changes that have occurred in the manipulation of kinship and ethnic linkages in urban settings. The issue of the persistence or duration of these changing patterns through time is a research problem which most anthropologists have not yet studied.

The aspect of the culture concept that seems least appropriate in the study of urban poverty groups is that which focuses on intergenerational transmission of basic values and belief systems, which serve as the basis of behavioral responses. We would agree that social learning remains as the major process for the transmission of values and beliefs. However, the learning may be intragenerational in peer groups, rather than intergenerational, leading to persistence for over four hundred years as Lewis suggests. Attributing behavioral responses solely to early parent-child socialization seems unwarranted on the basis of empirical data. We need a modified definition of culture that takes into account different temporal durations and intragenerational modes of social transmission in order to understand modern society.

Another major difficulty with the culture concept that emerges from Lewis' work is that it cannot handle well the phenomenon of social and geographic mobility. In a general way, the culture concept used by anthropologists does not lend itself well to the study of mobile societies. Since individual mobility is so significant in modern industrial societies, this problem is very serious. In any group of poor people, there are going to be segments moving out of poverty and manifesting behavioral response patterns quite different from those suggested by Lewis. Moreover, the elderly have usually been downwardly mobile and thus have had very different life experiences from the long-term poor. They too manifest a very different set of behavioral responses. Lewis says that some poor people are not in "the culture of poverty" but he does not explain why. If the traditional culture concept is maintained, then one would have to look for differences in childhood socialization or social transmission to explain the difference in behavior of those who manifest upward or downward mobility. If, however, a definition of culture is used that recognizes the life cycle as containing many situations that lead to resocialization following changes in social status, then mobility can be seen as a response to situational changes leading to new social learning.

One of the characteristics of members of complex societies is that they not only change status paths, but they also occupy a variety of statuses simultaneously. In addition to the universal statuses of age, sex, and kinship, other statuses relate to work or lack of work, location of residence, leisure-time preferences, ethnic group, and class. The culture of poverty notion is based solely upon class and thus disregards many of the other statuses that are significant for any poor individual. Each of these statuses generates a patterned set of shared rules appropriate to the incumbents of the status. The total cultural system is an articulated combination of these subcultural rules. Lewis himself recognizes this by suggesting that the culture of poverty might be understood as a subculture, not a full culture. However, Lewis sees his individual informants and their nuclear families as members of only one subculture—the subculture of poverty—and he relies upon very few individual cases to derive the shared patterned rules for their "worldwide" subculture.

We previously noted that the concept of culture was derived from the traditional study of small, isolated, homogeneous tribal groups. On the basis of an analysis of a particular society with a particular culture, the description of culture as a way of life became the vehicle for explaining differences in behavior in various parts of the world.

However, the transposition of the concept to the study of whole complex societies presents many difficulties. Any attempt to describe the total culture of large, industrial nation-states—such as Great Britain or Germany—is bound to fail, since there is no easy way of summing up the totality of the way of life in such large-scale, complex societies.

Walter B. Miller, recognizing this, attempted to develop a mapping scheme to delineate all logical possibilities for subcultures in American society. Each status (sex, kinship, class, and geographic location) generates a subculture. From the logically possible combinations of statuses, we can empirically select those that actually exist. We could then describe an individual actor in terms of the multiple status subcultures in which he or she has been socialized. We could then examine such questions as which subcultures are important in which situations, and how do aspects of different subcultures reinforce each other in combination. Moreover, we could delineate groups of people with similar combinations of status-based subcultures to see how these units operate in society. Finally, after looking at all regional, class, age, and sex subcultures we might be able to develop (at a very high level of abstraction) the common themes of American culture.[4]

Even this approach has its difficulties, because when we look at individual behavior, we introduce a *static* notion to a dynamic process in which the individual moves from status to status, changing his behavior. The attempt to artificially delineate actual subcultural systems stagnates this processual flow, but does focus attention on the interaction betwen age-grade rules, sex rules, regional rules, and ethnic rules, thus showing how they can sometimes reinforce each other and sometimes negate each other.

Another view of multiple roles in an urban setting is found in Southall's article on the density of role relationships.[5] In it he attempts, as Miller does, to map the role system of the urban setting, although he does not probe the cultural rules generated by each role and their

---

[4] Walter B. Miller, "Subculture, Social Reform and the 'Culture of Poverty,'" *Human Organization*, 30 (1971), 111-25.

[5] A. Southall, "The Density of Role Relationships as a Universal Index of Urbanization," in A. Southall (ed.), *Urban Anthropology* (New York: Oxford University Press, 1973), pp. 71-106.

implications for behavior. He is interested more in mapping role relationships and predicting their structural outcomes than in examining their behavioral implications, but his system can be used as a starting point for the generation of subcultural behavioral rules. Both Miller and Southall are analytically breaking down the complexity that Lewis treats in an overgeneral manner.

Relativism and Ethnocentrism

Lewis' concept lacks the perspective of cultural relativism, a conceptual tool which we have previously discussed as one of the *strengths* of anthropology. His ethnocentrism shows in his description of the culture of poverty as a *thin* culture and his equation of the culture of poverty with a "poverty of culture." The latter may indeed be a catchy phrase and a neat linguistic aphorism, but it demonstrates an attitude toward a particular segment of society that is pejorative. This attitude carries over into the discussion of traits, many of which Lewis describes as "lack of _____" rather than describing what is present. It is obvious that Lewis is working from a framework of middle class notions of what *should* exist.

Lewis suggests that those in the culture of poverty lack organization, but he subsequently notes their ability to develop informal credit groups and mutual aid mechanisms. He obviously views organization from a middle class vantage point, which assumes that only formal structures with specific goals are "organized." We have previously mentioned that one strength of urban anthropology is its ability to uncover informal structures and networks that have no labels and titles. It is obvious from Lewis' own data that much informal organization does exist, without the formal characteristics of names, officers, and archives.

This ethnocentric view is particularly apparent in Lewis' description of family patterns and personality types. Disregarding diminishing marital stability throughout the entire class spectrum, Lewis focuses on marital instability for this group alone. In characterizing the female-based household as a partial version of the "normal" family, he is neglecting anthropological literature on domestic cycles and domestic variations that tend to occur under certain conditions. In addition, his description of individuals as having weak ego structures, as being fatalistic and present-time oriented, or as having confused sex identities is obviously based upon class-biased psychological models of what constitutes adequate egos, time orientations, and sex identities.

Also he is comparing the middle class *ideals* of planning for the future and deferred gratification with the actual *behavior* of the poor. This is not the same as comparing middle class *behavior* with poverty *behavior,* since recent middle class consumption patterns indicate a lack of concern for the future. Lewis notes that many of those in the culture of poverty hold middle class ideals about the desirability of a stable nuclear family but do not follow their ideals. This same discrepancy between *ideal* and *real* behavior exists for the middle class as well.[6]

In all fairness to Lewis, his informants are portrayed in their own words as sympathetic human beings. However, the culture of poverty concept denigrated their behavior and their beliefs.

WHAT IS URBAN ABOUT THE CULTURE OF POVERTY?

In Chapter 2, we discussed problems in defining the concept of urban. The culture of poverty literature contains many examples of these confusions.

The emphasis upon poverty groups in urban areas in modern and developing societies is primarily the result of an erroneous association of the term *urban anthropology* with the so-called urban crisis, which leads to an interest in the poor, the marginal, and the disenfranchised. Fox has divided urban anthropology into three categories, the largest of which is "the anthropology of poverty."[7] He includes in this category most of the urban ethnographic literature that does not deal with migration or with the city as a whole. As we noted in Chapter 1, one of the trends in early urban anthropology was a concern with social problems and the search for solutions. However, we would maintain that continued overemphasis of this one area will distort the subfield.

Poverty is not an exclusively urban phenomenon, nor is it generated by the nature of cities. Gulick has noted for American society that poverty, racism, and sexism are fundamental characteristics of the larger social system and not merely aspects of urban localities.[8]

Lewis himself explicitly recognizes that the development of the culture of poverty is a consequence of modern industrial capitalist society—with its labor market, its materialism, and its profit orientation— rather than the urban setting. He suggests that, as traditional agrarian societies follow a capitalist industrial model, a culture of poverty will

---

[6] For an important discussion of the tendency to confuse ideal behavior with real behavior in comparing class subcultures, see S. M. Miller, F. Reissman and A. Seagull, "Poverty and Self-Indulgence: A Critique of the Non-Deferred Gratification Pattern," in L. Ferman et al. (eds.), *Poverty in America* (Ann Arbor: University of Michigan Press, 1965), pp. 416-32.

[7] Fox, *Cities in Their Cultural Settings.*

[8] J. Gulick, "The Outlook, Research Strategies and Relevance of Urban Anthropology," in E. Eddy (ed.), *Urban Anthropology* (Athens, Georgia: University of Georgia Press, 1968), pp. 93-98.

emerge. However, his poverty research has been carried out exclusively in urban areas; his selection of the slum community as the geographic locus in which the culture of poverty will be found does give the concept an urban appearance.

The culture of poverty issue falls more neatly under the rubric of anthropology of *urban industrial society*, rather than anthropology *in* or *of* the city. If one were tempted to convert this issue to the anthropology *of* cities, then it would be essential to study the effects of the urban setting on the poverty population. As we will subsequently see in our discussion of methodology, this is difficult but can be done. The lack of clearly defined urban poverty research can only lead to a continuing confusion between urbanism, modernism, and industrialism.

METHODOLOGY

In concept formation, there are two mutually interacting processes involved: induction and deduction. The *inductive process* is one in which a concept or model is derived from prior empirical research. The *deductive process* is one in which the theorist starts with a series of assumptions, develops a model in a logical manner, and then tests the concepts or model by doing empirical research. Most philosophers of science distinguish these two modes, but in reality they are often joined in a process of formulating and testing.

Lewis' concept was derived from his original fieldwork in Mexico City and was thus inductively derived. Lewis contends that in his later study of Puerto Rican slum life, he was testing the validity of the concept in a different cultural setting. It must be noted that the thrust of Lewis' work was the development of a cross-cultural, generalizable model of the values and behavior of a poverty segment of the population. However, it does not appear from the work in San Juan that the model developed earlier was actually tested in the field situation. What seems to have happened is that Lewis undertook the study in San Juan with a preconceived notion of what he would find, and then selected from the available research material those segments that substantiated his original formulation. This point is apparent in the *La Vida* volume, where we note a significant discontinuity between the introduction to the volume, where the concept is outlined, and the rest of the volume, where the data are presented. Rarely do we find in this volume an interplay between theoretical formulation and empirically derived data, which could serve to sharpen the theoretical focus and aid in the interpretation of empirical data.

This disassociation between formulation and data is the basis of

Valentine's critique of Lewis. By selecting from the mass of data presented in the body of the *La Vida* volume, Valentine is able to demonstrate repeatedly areas in which the behavior of members of the Rios family completely contradict the culture of poverty trait list.[9] These obvious contradictions remain unexplored and unexplained by Lewis and thus become a basic issue related to the validity of the concept.

In terms of research design, Lewis' initial work in Mexico City was a traditional anthropological study without a problem focus. Lewis felt that he had discovered an unexplored constituency for anthropological fieldwork—the urban slum dweller. He was studying the "way of life" of this group in traditional fashion. In his long-range study of this constituency, he developed the culture of poverty notion as a by-product.

When Lewis shifted his research focus to Puerto Rico, he had more clearly formulated a problem—the testing of the culture of poverty model. In this latter formulation, one could say that the culture of poverty is a dependent variable, or the outcome of a set of society-wide conditions, which are independent variables. However, by not explicitly following this kind of logical procedure, he was trapped into the position of viewing the culture of poverty as a self-perpetuating subcultural system.

In the translation of a conceptual formulation into a research design, an important element is the development of ways to define the variables. When we look at the multiplicity of variables that comprise the culture of poverty, we are given no clues as to how most of them are defined.

Another methodological source of confusion in Lewis' work is the lack of any clear-cut separation of those aspects of the larger social system related to the position of the poor in the social system from those aspects that form the culture (or adaptive response to the position). Thus, when Lewis includes within the *traits* of the culture such items as high rates of unemployment, lack of cash reserves, and other situational constraints, he is adding attributes to the dependent variable that really comprise the independent variables.

Problem of Selecting a Unit of Study

In our discussion of social units in Chapter 7, we suggested that either a particular unit may be selected to study its characteristics, or a problem may be selected to study within the context of the unit as an ethnographic target population. Lewis' tactic is to take the latter ap-

[9] C. Valentine, *Culture and Poverty: A Critique and Counterproposals* (Chicago: University of Chicago Press, 1968).

proach. However, the research problem—the description of the culture of poverty—cannot be readily disassociated from the social unit. Lewis assumes that the slum is the geographic or spatial unit within which one can study the culture of poverty. He notes that not all slum residents can be characterized in this way. They cannot even all be characterized as poor. But he never selects a pool of poor defined in material terms as the ethnographic target population. He also notes that not all the characteristics of the culture of poverty can be found in any slum group.

Eventually, he narrows the lens through which one sees the culture of poverty to a single family. Once he turns from the slum community to the family as the unit of analysis, the question of whether the family is an appropriate unit for the study of a culture or subculture is immediately raised. If one were to accept Lewis' notion (which we do not) that there is little organization above the family level, then perhaps one could derive a culture or subculture from family studies. However, it would then be incumbent upon Lewis to describe the similarity in values and behavior *among* the families who share the common tradition of the culture of poverty and indicate the means of social transmission, namely, networks and informal social structures. In Lewis' *La Vida* he relies on only one family, and one which he himself states is atypical. He states that the Rios family is characterized by the most "unbridled id" that he has ever observed. Prostitution is also not typical of other families. Thus we have no indication of the extent to which the Rios family represents a shared pattern that could be called a subculture of poverty.

Going beyond Lewis' work in the culture of poverty, it can be suggested that the study of "the poor" as an urban anthropological research problem brings to the fore many basic issues in the selection of units of study. Selecting an inner-city slum, or an irregular community (squatter settlement), or a minority ethnic group as the unit in which to study the behavior of the poor is a basic error. Even communities and ethnic groups that have a high proportion of poor people within them will still contain large numbers of non-poor or temporarily poor, which make such units inappropriate.

Some examples of the inappropriate use of the ethnic minority group as the unit within which to study poverty can be seen in the work of Valentine and Parker and Kleiner.[10] In both cases, the work was used in relation to the culture of poverty concept. Valentine cites the literature on Black Americans in a discussion of the culture of poverty and he seems to make the assumption that Blacks are equivalent to "the

[10] Valentine, *Culture and Poverty;* and S. Parker and R. Kleiner, "The Culture of Poverty: An Adjustive Dimension," *American Anthropologist,* 72 (1970), 516-28.

poor." Parker and Kleiner use data collected in a previous project on Blacks and mental illness to discuss whether these Blacks have culture of poverty beliefs. This particular work presents two problems. It assumes that being Black is being poor. It also confuses the relationship between racial minority status and poverty status. If the research in a Black population does indicate feelings of hopelessness and fatalism, are these related to being poor or to being in an oppressed underclass?

The problem of selecting an appropriate social unit is also demonstrated in a number of community studies used to refute Lewis, where it is assumed that the neighborhoods selected are equivalent to "the poor." Mangin uses his experiences with *barriadas* (squatter settlements) in Lima, Leeds, his data on *favelas* in Rio, and Safa her data on a shantytown in San Juan to disprove the culture of poverty notion. They do not explicitly point out that their communities were, in fact, not equivalent to *the poor,* but contained people of different occupational levels, career directions, and income.[11]

Poverty must be defined in economic terms, since it is basically an economic condition. The consequence of economic deprivation for behavior is the area that must be studied. However, a population defined merely by income characteristics tends to be a social aggregate of unrelated, non-interacting people. Such an aggregate is not a useful ethnographic unit. A search for a common culture among this aggregate is inappropriate.

Probably the very best unit to use in the ethnographic study of poverty and its consequences would be an occupational status community. In every complex society, there are certain low-paying occupations. Those pursuing such occupations would therefore represent a group who live in conditions of poverty, characterized by instability or intermittency of employment. These jobs are frequently time-consuming, and/or require heavy physical effort. They are considered menial, dirty, and unpleasant and are frequently viewed by other members of society as defiling to those who pursue them.

In urban areas, specific occupations that would fall into the poverty level category are: non-mechanized construction labor, dockwork, pedicab drivers, porters (carriers of heavy items), domestics, janitors, scavengers, street vendors, and watchmen. In some of these occupations, the individual is self-employed and has relative autonomy over his time

11 Mangin, *Peasants in Cities* and "Poverty and Politics in the Latin American City," in L. Bloomberg and H. Schmandt (eds.), *Power, Poverty and Urban Policy,* Urban Affairs Annual Review, vol. 2, 1970; Leeds, "The Concept of the 'Culture of Poverty' "; and Helen Safa, "The Social Isolation of the Urban Poor: Life in a Puerto Rican Shanty Town," in I. Deutscher and E. Thompson (eds.), *Among the People: Encounters with the Poor* (New York: Basic Books, Inc., Publishers, 1968), pp. 335-51.

and effort. However, the monetary rewards are minimal, unpredictable, and often lead to depending on creditors for survival. In other cases, the individual works for others, often on a day labor basis, so that he or she has no job security and has little control over the work situation. The common thread in all of these jobs is that returns are small, insecure, and sporadic, so that those who do this kind of work live in conditions of material deprivation and insecurity.

Most of the occupations catalogued above abound in cities in societies that are not fully industrialized. Mechanization frequently leads to the elimination of such work. Another way in which some of these occupations are transformed is through unionization and bureaucratization. For example, construction workers and longshoremen, through union organizations, developed the bargaining power to assure them a secure income above the poverty level. Bureaucratic organization of work has eliminated such jobs as the small-scale watchman, replacing him with private and public security organizations, which are hierarchically organized and guarantee employment security and better pay. In the transformation from a preindustrial to a postindustrial society, many occupations formerly characterized by poverty level income and insecurity are eliminated or transformed.

Despite technology and the organization of work, there are still some analogues to these marginal occupations in the industrialized world. These include menial workers in restaurants and hospitals, janitors, domestics, and vestiges of premechanized construction work and commerce. Even when attempts have been made to unionize or bureaucratize day laborers on some of these jobs, they have not been able to prevent high turnover, mass lay-offs, and the poor working conditions that encourage turnover. Furthermore, some powerful unions seek to exploit the organized low-level worker.

Economists recognize that there is a *secondary* labor market in the United States in which jobs are characterized by short-term employment, low wages, and no fringe benefits. In fact, this labor market recruits from a pool of labor characterized by low income, sporadic employment, and job sequences characterized by horizontal movement rather than vertical career progression. The secondary labor market consists of dead-end jobs.

The phenomenon of poverty in contemporary American society is clearly related to an economic system that, under normal economic conditions, assumes an unemployment rate of approximately six percent. A certain segment of this "normal" population of unemployed consists of those who are long-term unemployed (out of work one year or more). Despite a social welfare system that provides some compensation, the amount of income while unemployed is well below the poverty line.

Based upon this discussion, we would contend that the most ap-

propriate social unit within which the urban anthropologist might study
the impact of poverty is one based upon occupation or participation in
the secondary labor market, rather than a unit based on space or minority status. Interacting units of people in marginal career cycles or
long-term unemployed can be studied.[12] The particular effects to be
studied could be selected by the particular researcher, but the independent variable—material deprivation—could be clearly defined and measured. Gutkind is one of the few urban anthropologists to use such a unit.
He selected the long-term unemployed as an ethnographic target unit in
some of his African urban research. His dependent variables were kinship and network ties.[13]

ETHICS AND POLICY IMPLICATIONS

In an earlier discussion of ethics in urban anthropology (see Chapter 7), we noted that anthropologists working with an urban population
have a commitment to the group with whom they work. Part of this commitment is to avoid generating data and/or analyses that can be used
against informants. They should be aware at all times of the consequences
of public use of their data and generalizations.

This criterion pertains as well to the culture of poverty concept.
Many of those who have attacked the Lewis formulation have done so
on the basis of its implications for the development of programs dealing
with poverty. It should be noted that at the time Lewis was writing
about the concept, a major thrust of American domestic policy was the
eradication of poverty. The various programs that were developed in
the 1960s to deal with this problem were subsumed under the notion of
the "War on Poverty." For those involved in determining what programs
could be established to eliminate poverty conditions, there were two
major alternatives: either attack the economic system, which created unemployment and underemployment *or* attack the values and behavior
of the poor, which were assumed to be intergenerationally transmitted
and which *by themselves* perpetuated poverty by interfering with upward mobility. Although Lewis did accept the larger social system as
generating poverty, his emphasis on the self-perpetuation of the culture
of poverty was the point of departure for elaboration by those developing specific anti-poverty programs. Thus, many programs of the War on

[12] For a discussion of this issue, see E. Eames and J. Goode, *Urban Poverty in a Cross-
cultural Context* (New York: Free Press, 1973), Chapter 4; J. Goode, "Poverty and
Urban Analysis," *Western Canadian Journal of Anthropology*, 3 (1972), 1-19.
[13] P. C. W. Gutkind, "The Energy of Despair: Social Organization of the Unemployed
in Two African Cities: Lagos and Nairobi," *Civilisations*, 17 (1967), 186-211.

Poverty were designed to change the behavior and values of the poor. These included compensatory education programs, manpower training programs, and community action programs. Since Lewis himself maintains that the only way of changing the culture of poverty in the United States is through a psychiatric or social work approach, his "scientific credentials" reinforced such government programs.

Another reason for the attractiveness of Lewis' formulation to policy makers was that it explained failures in education, health care, and job training programs. If programs failed, the inappropriate values of their clients could be blamed, instead of the ill-conceived or misapplied nature of the program itself. Finally, the concept was broadly accepted because it bolstered the popular view that had developed since the Industrial Revolution that the poor were responsible for their own condition. Lewis, by providing a "scientific" explanation based on notions of intergenerational transmission and early childhood socialization, was reinforcing already existing beliefs.

Another ethical issue mentioned in Chapter 7 is that of national pride. In his later work in Mexico City and San Juan, Lewis' descriptions of the life of the poor offended many Mexicans and Puerto Ricans. They felt his presentation of life in these countries was unbalanced and pejorative. When one reads some of the anti-Lewis statements, and when one is exposed to Puerto Rican students who have read *La Vida*, this national dismay is quite apparent. Since Lewis' work is so widely read by non-professionals, many Puerto Ricans feel it has simply reinforced the negative stereotypes of Puerto Ricans held by the American public. As a result of such strong feelings, Lewis became *persona non grata* in both Mexico and Puerto Rico, making further research in these sites impossible for him.

When he popularly disseminated an untested hypothesis, which was then generalized to the total capitalist-industrial world, Lewis acted contrary to the standards for concern about the uses and possible misuses of anthropological studies.

Once again, we must temper this criticism by looking at Lewis' work in the context of its time. The issue of the social responsibility of the anthropologist was not explicitly raised until the latter part of the 1960s.[14] Lewis' work on the urban poor considerably antedated this. In his day, anthropologists sought "knowledge for its own sake." The belief that one owed one's informants something in return, or that one must protect them from the potential misuse of data had not become widespread. It is too easy to castigate with hindsight. And Lewis was by

[14] G. Berreman, G. Gjessing and K. Gough, "Social Responsibilities Symposium," *Current Anthropology*, 9 (1968), 391-435; Diane Lewis, "Anthropology and Colonialism," *Current Anthropology*, 14 (1973), 581-602.

no means the only one responsible for developing notions of cultural deprivation and poverty culture. Many other social scientists also developed similar concepts to explain the non-success of the poor.

The Overemphasis on Poverty

In the larger arena of urban anthropology, the body of literature dealing with poverty segments or underclass segments in the city is the most voluminous.

As Gulick pointed out, the overemphasis on poverty studies has given a particular bias to urban anthropology, which should be recognized and guarded against. Gulick suggests that if we continue this emphasis, we might very well find that such segments of the population will become suspicious of the motives of the anthropologist and will exclude him.[15]

Of even greater concern is the fundamental social science issue of relating poverty to an understanding of the nature of urban centers and urban processes. We have looked at Lewis' work in some detail and noted that in many ways the fundamental issue of the relationship between the urban and poverty is unexplored.

The poverty literature in urban anthropology has been a dead-end literature. One reason for this is that only the lower segments of society were studied. To understand poverty in urban industrial systems or to study the nature of urban centers, one must also understand the middle and dominant groups in the system, and how they relate to each other. The forces in the larger system must also be examined as to their interaction with all social segments (or ethnographic target populations). Throughout this entire volume, we have been emphasizing *context* and *interactive process*. No social unit—from the level of the microscopic to the macroscopic—is autonomous or independent. To study poverty by focusing entirely upon the poor is to disregard the larger context and the continuous interactive process.

Certainly if one wishes to study the nature of urban life, concentration upon the poor is even more misplaced. As we have seen in Chapters 4, 5 and 6, an overemphasis on lower social segments is both illogical and misleading.

Unfortunately, the publication of Lewis' work and the controversy generated by the culture of poverty concept directed the attention of a disproportionately large number of urban anthropologists to the study of poverty groups. In many cases, these studies were explicitly designed

---

[15] Gulick predicted this in 1968 ("The Outlook, Research Strategies and Relevance of Urban Anthropology") and it is now a reality.

to test and/or refute Lewis' contentions. Another reason for this concentration on the lower segments was because they seemed easy to define and were relatively accessible. As we noted earlier, the rich can avoid the anthropologist, while the poor do not have the resources to do this. Many of the more radical contemporary anthropologists view the poor and/or minorities in the United States as neocolonial populations or internal colonies. It is interesting to note that these populations have been the most "exploited"—in the research sense—by these same anthropologists. However, these anthropologists do consciously provide something in return, whether it be aid or political advocacy.

Another factor that has led to an overemphasis on lower social segments is the concern with rural-urban migration. In fact, migration literature and poverty literature have become inextricably intertwined in many instances. As an example of this, Mangin, as the editor of a volume specifically concerned with migration, devotes most of his introduction to the culture of poverty concept.[16] Not all migrant groups enter the urban arena at the bottom, but few anthropological studies (especially in America) have focused upon any but the lowest segments.

Poverty studies can be seen as one phase in the development of urban anthropology. At the conceptual level they are extremely peripheral to the field and fraught with error. When poverty is clearly connected with urban process in terms of both research design and methodology, then it becomes more relevant. In Chapters 4, 5 and 6 we have seen the results of urban ethnographic studies geared to issues other than poverty. If we continue to pursue the research questions suggested in those chapters, we can perhaps redirect our energies to the more central issues of urban anthropology.

SUMMARY

We have frequently noted the tendency of urban ethnographers to concentrate upon the poorer segments of the urban population. This bias can be seen in the controversy over the culture of poverty concept.

Oscar Lewis' work has been central to this controversy. A pioneering figure in the development of urban anthropology, he focused toward the end of his career almost exclusively upon the study of poverty. From such studies he developed the notion of a common subculture that characterizes segments of the poor population in many areas of the world.

The poverty subculture concept has many theoretical limitations. Many contemporary anthropologists avoid the use of the culture concept,

[16] Mangin (ed.), *Peasants in Cities*.

particularly when dealing with complex societies. Most of the core characteristics of the poverty subculture concept have been questioned by other anthropologists as representing a list of traits, many of which are contradictory, not testable, and negative in tone.

Poverty is obviously not an exclusively urban problem, and a culture of poverty—to the extent to which it might exist—is not a particularly urban problem. The inclusion of the literature dealing with this issue under urban anthropology is an error. It does not fall into the category of anthropology *of* the city, or anthropology *in* the city, but rather the anthropology of complex society.

Although many ethnographic studies have been concerned with refuting or testing the Lewis formulation, the selection and delineation of a social unit within which to study poverty subculture remains problematic. Many issues of methodology and ethics raised in Chapter 7 become critical issues in the study of the poor. The overemphasis on poverty in urban anthropology has misdirected much energy. In many cases, urban ethnographers are now shifting their attention to other segments of the urban population.

Selected Bibliography

Because of limitations of space, we have selected only recent collections of articles, ethnographic monographs, and classic articles for inclusion in this list.

BANTON, M. (ed.), *The Social Anthropology of Complex Societies*. London: Tavistock Publishers Ltd., 1966.

BOTT, ELIZABETH, *Family and Social Network* (2nd ed.). New York: The Free Press, 1971.

CHILDE, V. GORDON, "The Urban Revolution," *Town Planning Review*, 21 (1950), pp. 3-17.

COHEN, ABNER, *Custom and Politics in Urban Africa*. London: Routledge and Kegan Paul, 1969.

COHEN, ABNER (ed.), *Urban Ethnicity*. London: Tavistock Publications, 1974.

CORNELIUS, W. and F. TRUEBLOOD (eds.), *Latin American Urban Research*, Vol. 4. Beverley Hills: Sage Publications, 1974.

EAMES, EDWIN and JUDITH GOODE, *Urban Poverty in a Cross-Cultural Context*. New York: The Free Press, 1973.

EDDY, E. (ed.), *Urban Anthropology*. Athens: University of Georgia Press, 1968.

EPSTEIN, A. L., *Politics in an Urban African Community*. Manchester: Manchester University Press, 1958.

FALLERS, L. (ed.), *Immigrants and Associations*. The Hague: Mouton Publishers, 1967.

FOSTER, G. and R. KEMPER (eds.), *Anthropologists in Cities*. Boston: Little, Brown and Company, 1974.

FOX, RICHARD, *Urban Anthropology: Cities in Their Cultural Settings*. Englewood Cliffs: Prentice-Hall Inc., 1977.

FRIEDL, J. and N. CHRISMAN (eds.), *City Ways*. New York: Thomas Y. Crowell Co., 1975.

GANS, HERBERT, *The Urban Villagers*. New York: The Free Press, 1962.

GEERTZ, C., *Peddlers and Princes*. Chicago: University of Chicago Press, 1963.

GRAVES, NANCY and THEODORE GRAVES, "Adaptive Strategies in Urban Migration," in B. J. Siegel (ed.), *Annual Review of Anthropology*, 1974, pp. 117-151.

GUILLEMIN, JEANNE, *Urban Renegades: The Cultural Strategy of American Indians*. New York: Columbia University Press, 1975.

GULICK, JOHN, *Tripoli*. Cambridge: Harvard University Press, 1967.

GUTKIND, PETER, *Urban Anthropology*. New York: Barnes and Noble Books, 1974.

HANNERZ, ULF, *Soulside*. New York: Columbia University Press, 1970.

JACOBSON, DAVID, *Itinerant Townsmen*. Menlo Park: Cummings Publishing Co., 1973.

LEMASTERS, E. *Blue Collar Aristocrats*. Madison: University of Wisconsin Press, 1975.

LEWIS, OSCAR, "Urbanization Without Breakdown: A Case Study," *The Scientific Monthly*, Vol. 75, 1952.

LIEBOW, ELLIOT, *Tally's Corner*. Boston: Little, Brown and Co., 1967.

LITTLE, KENNETH, *West African Urbanization: A Study of Voluntary Associations in Social Change*. Cambridge: Cambridge University Press, 1965.

LYNCH, OWEN, *The Politics of Untouchability*. New York: Columbia University Press, 1969.

MANGIN, W. (ed.), *Peasants in Cities*. Boston: Houghton Mifflin, 1970.

MARRIS, PETER, *Family and Social Change in an African City*. London: Routledge and Kegan Paul, 1961.

MAYER, PHILIP, *Townsman or Tribesman: Conservatism and the Process of Urbanization in a South African City*. Capetown: Oxford University Press, 1961.

MINER, HORACE, *The Primitive City of Timbuctoo*. Garden City: Doubleday & Company, 1965 (Revised Edition).

MINER, HORACE (ed.), *The City in Modern Africa*. New York: Frederick A. Praeger, Publishers, 1967.

MITCHELL, J. C. (ed.), *Social Networks in Urban Situations*. Manchester: Manchester University Press, 1969.

PATCH, RICHARD, "La Parada: Lima's Market." American Universities Field Staff Report, Vol. 14, 1967.

PEATTIE, LISA, *The View from the Barrio*. Ann Arbor: University of Michigan Press, 1968.

PILCHER, WILLIAM, *The Portland Longshoremen*. New York: Holt, Rinehart and Co., 1972.

PLOTNICOV, LEONARD, *Strangers in the City*. Pittsburgh: University of Pittsburgh Press, 1967.

PRICE, JOHN, *Tijuana: Urbanization in a Border Culture*. Notre Dame: University of Notre Dame Press, 1973.

REDFIELD, ROBERT, *The Folk Culture of Yucatan*. Chicago: University of Chicago Press, 1930.

REDFIELD, ROBERT, "The Folk Society," *American Journal of Sociology*, 41 (1947), 293-308.

REDFIELD, ROBERT, *Peasant Society and Culture*. Chicago: University of Chicago Press, 1956.

REDFIELD, ROBERT and MILTON SINGER, "The Cultural Role of Cities," *Economic Development and Culture Change*, 3 (1954), pp. 53-73.

REINA, RUBEN, *Paraná: Social Boundaries in an Argentine City*. Austin: University of Texas Press, 1973.

ROBERTS, BRYAN, *Organizing Strangers*. Austin: University of Texas Press, 1973.

ROLLWAGEN, J. (ed.), "The City as Context: A Symposium," *Urban Anthropology*, Vol. 4, 1975.

SIMIC, ANDREI, *The Peasant Urbanites*. New York: Seminar Press, 1973.

SJOBERG, GIDEON, *The Preindustrial City*. New York: The Free Press, 1960.

SOUTHALL, A. (ed.), *Urban Anthropology*. New York: Oxford University Press, 1973.

SPENCER, R. (ed.), *Migration and Anthropology*. Seattle: University of Washington Press, 1970.

SPOEHR, A. (ed.), *Pacific Port Towns and Cities*. Honolulu: Bishop Museum Press, 1963.

SPRADLEY, JAMES, *You Owe Yourself a Drunk*. Boston: Little, Brown and Co., 1970.

SPRADLEY, JAMES and BRENDA MANN, *The Cocktail Waitress*. New York: John Wiley and Co., 1975.

SPRADLEY, JAMES and DAVID MCCURDY (eds.), *The Cultural Experience: Ethnography in Complex Society*. Chicago: Science Research Associates, 1972.

STACK, CAROL, *All Our Kin*. New York: Harper and Row, 1974.

SUTTLES, GERALD, *The Social Order of the Slum*. Chicago: University of Chicago Press, 1968.

SUTTLES, GERALD, *The Social Construction of Communities*. Chicago: University of Chicago Press, 1972.

UCKO, P. J., R. TRINGHAM, and G. DIMBLEY (eds.), *Man, Settlement and Urbanism*. London: Duckworth, 1972.

UZZELL, DOUGLAS and R. PROVENCHER, *Urban Anthropology*. Dubuque: William C. Brown Inc., 1976.

VAN DEN BERGHE, PIERRE, *Caneville: The Social Structure of a South African Town*. Middletown: Wesleyan University Press, 1964.

VATUK, SYLVIA, *Kinship and Urbanization*. Berkeley: University of California Press, 1972.

WEAVER, T. and D. WHITE (eds.), *The Anthropology of Urban Environments*. Society for Applied Anthropology Monographs, 1972.

WHITEFORD, ANDREW, *Two Cities in Latin America*. Garden City: Doubleday & Co., 1964.

WIEBE, PAUL, *Social Life in an Indian Slum*. Durham: Carolina Academia Press, 1975.

WIRTH, LOUIS, "Urbanism as a Way of Life," *American Journal of Sociology*, 44 (1938), 1-24.

YOUNG, M. and P. WILMOTT, *Family and Class in a London Suburb*. Baltimore: Penguin Books, 1957.

Index

328

SUBJECT INDEX

Accommodation, in pre-urban societies, 41
Action sets, in political events, 238-39
Addis Ababa (Ethiopia):
  ethnic groups, 178, 180, 186, 191-92, 194
  rural-urban ties, 247
Administrative cities, 95, 106, 107-8
Advocacy anthropology, 291-92
Africa:
  British colonialism, 7
  British urban migration studies, 16-17
African cities:
  beer halls, 223-24
  bureaucracies, 197, 205-6
  courts, 229-30, 251
  dance groups, 236
  fictive kinship, 145
  gossip networks, 128
  kinship networks, 142, 144, 147, 149, 150
  linguistic communities, 187-88
  marketplaces, 227-28
  neighborhood studies, 161
  political organization, 239-40
  public spaces, 220
  social networks, 121-22, 124-25, 133, 138
  rural-urban ties, 247
  tribalism, 175-76, 182, 183, 191-92
Afro-Americans, 185-86, 188
  culture of poverty, 316-17
  female-centered families, 300
  language styles, 187
  "soul" concept, 188
  symbols of identity, 173
Agra (India), 84
Agrarian societies, 41-42

Agriculture, and the origin of cities, 74, 76-77, 111
Akhetaton (Egypt), 85
Alienation, 49, 117
Allahabad (India), 89, 152, 219
American Anthropological Association, 9
American Indians, 10
  political movements, 195-96
  social control mechanisms, 129
  urban publications, 94
  U.S. government domination, 7
Andaman Islands, 7
Anomie, 117
Anthropology, history of, 3-13, 28-29
  "armchair" anthropologists, 5
  colonialism, 4, 6-7, 28
  comparative approach, 4-6, 28
  complex societies, 9-13
  generalization problems, 6
  government direction of, 7-8
  relativistic bias, 6
  World War II, 7-8, 9, 28-29
Anthropology *of* vs. *in* the city, 30-35, 68, 71, 252, 258
Anti-urban bias, 11, 24, 53, 54-57, 62
Applied anthropology, 8, 21-22
Arab cities, 85
Archeology, 13, 15
  origins of cities, 74
  urban definitions, 39-40, 46
Architecture, specialization of, 39
Artisans, 81, 82-83
Ascriptive kinship, 115, 118
Assur, city of, 85
Athens, 105

Babylon, 84
Baghdad, 85